Psychoanalysis International

Psychoanalysis International

A Guide to Psychoanalysis throughout the World

Edited by Peter Kutter

Volume 2
America, Asia, Australia
Further European Countries

frommann-holzboog

Printed with kind support of the Sigmund Freud Stiftung, Frankfurt.

Articles *Brasilia* (partly), *China, Mexico, Peru, Russia* (2nd part), *Psychoanalysis against the grain, Foreword* translated by
Rod Koeltgen, Germany
Articles *Chile, France, Romania, Uruguay* translated by
Paul Ferguson, Channel Islands

Die Deutsche Bibliothek – CIP-Einheitsaufnahme

Psychoanalysis international :
a guide to psychoanalysis throughout the world /
ed. by Peter Kutter.
– Stuttgart-Bad Cannstatt : Frommann-Holzboog.
NE: Kutter, Peter [Hrsg.]

Vol. 2. America, Asia, Australia, Further European Countries. – 1995
ISBN 3-7728-1510-3

Printed and bound in Germany.

Contents

Foreword

by Peter Kutter

Political changes leave fissures and rifts on the landscape of nations and inevitably affect the development of the sciences. This became clear for psychoanalyis particularly during the tyrannical regime of the national socialists, which was to make lasting changes on the landscape of psychoanalysis: with the expulsion of Jewish psychoanalysts from Germany all over the world, with the phases of conformity to the prevailing circumstances (especially in Germany) but also with committed resistance or work underground (e.g. in Hungary, former Czechoslovakia, former Yugoslavia). Later the dictatorships in Argentina and Chile had a tragic effect on psychoanalysis.

As a cultural theory and social criticism psychoanalysis can help to understand such political processes better; by exposing warded-off mourning and shame, as Alexander and Margarete Mitscherlich did for Germany. It can expose latent prejudices and concepts of an enemy and even change them for the better; by, for instance, helping to recognize projections of parts of oneself in concepts of an enemy, and by helping cope with newly established political situations which no longer contain the stabilizing concepts of an enemy, such as between East and West, after the unification of the two German states in 1990. In this way more and more inter-national exchange processes towards a multicultural society can come into being.

The vast expanse which the world once represented to us has become smaller and easier to grasp. On television news about distant countries reaches us just as quickly as about events from close by, such as the cautious rapprochement of Israel and Palestine, China's economic consolidation, the political difficulties of the former Soviet Union, the re-emergence of radical right-wing forces in Germany, the uprising of the Indios in Chiapa (Mexico), the civil war that recently broke out in Yemen or the first free elections in South Africa.

Whereas individual nations used to go their own way, today their relationships with each other are on a permanent reciprocal basis. As the theory of systems shows, no single action of one country leaves the other countries unaffected. There are no longer causal processes of cause and effect, but overlapping processes which affect every country in the political system if only one country changes.

In international politics it is Nato, UNO and the World Security Council which permanently discuss and observe local conflicts such as that in former Yugoslavia. UNO-troops are now stationed in a number of countries, monitoring, more or less effectively, local political disputes.

Scientific and scholarly associations are also no longer nationally but multiculturally or, in the truest sense of the word, inter-nationally orientated. One scientific association, namely the psychoanalytical association, has from the very beginning resisted any national orientation in favour of an international opening. Having originated in Vienna, it was soon to spread beyond the limits of that city as well as the borders of Austria, first of all because people interested in psychoanalysis went to Vienna, later to Berlin and later still to New York, the centres of the new psychoanalytical movement; and also because those who had got to know psychoanalysis in the old centres enthusiastically spread it to all the countries in the world. Edith Kurzweil has described this graphically in her beautiful book "Freud and the Freudians". What was supposed to be annihilated between 1933 and 1945 with the forced emigration of many German-speaking analysts to distant countries started to thrive all the more, particularly in the USA, but also in Latin American countries and Israel, with undreamt-of effects on all areas of culture and civilization, especially literature and art.

In its turn the development of psychoanalytical associations also caused fissures and rifts. Hardly a country managed to avoid splits/schisms in the history of psychoanalysis (theme of the 5th Conference of the "Association internationale d'histoire de la psychoanalyse" 1994); problems which started already with C.G. Jung and Alfred Adler in Vienna, then the Anna Freud/Melanie Klein controversies in London, and continued with Lacan in France and "progressive" social critics and "politicians" in Germany (such as Alexander Mitscherlich and Horst-Eberhard Richter) and unpolitical or "conservative" clinicians in Germany.

The first aim of this compendium of Psychoanalysis International is a historiographic one. Volume 1 of the work recapitulates the historical development insofar as Europe as Western culture provided the fertile ground in which psychoanalysis, seen historically, could grow well: Vienna in Austria, Berlin in Germany, London in England.

Exploring the history of psychoanalysis in the individual countries right down to the last sources is no more the aim of this second volume than it was of the first. (Historical research of this kind is carried out by special organizations such as the "Archives and History of Psychoanalysis Committee" of the IPA, the "Association Internationale d'Histoire de Psychanalyse" with its headquarters in Paris or the "Archiv zur Geschichte der Psychoanalyse in Deutschland e.V." with its headquarters in Berlin). The editor and publisher are concerned solely with providing as graphic an overview of the respective historical development in the individual countries as possible.

The second aim of Psychoanalysis International is to provide a kind of "map of psychoanalysis": in this respect the choice of contributions is in fact based on geographical criteria. A critical reader may wonder why Israel is included in Volume 1 on Europe, and the reason for this is that although Israel is situated geographically outside of Europe it is culturally very closely connected to Europe. And if European countries like Norway and Portugal are not included in Volume 1 on Europe but appear instead alongside other European countries in Volume 2 on America, Asia and Australia, this has simple organizational reasons: the contributions were not ready by the deadline for Vol. 1. Furthermore, some of these countries were in the process of such rapid political change that a historical examination with the necessary objectivity was not yet possible. This applies just as much to the former countries belonging to the Eastern bloc, Bulgaria, Romania, Croatia, Serbia and Slovenia as to the former Soviet Union with today`s Russia including the so called "Commonwealth of Independent States".

Today psychoanalysis has spread over almost the whole world. Let's take a look at a map of the world: in the old world psychoanalysis is represented in every country. Only Ireland, Iceland, Greenland and the European part of Turkey are missing. On the other hand, some new countries have now come on the scene following the fall of the Iron Curtain. They deserve the full support of the West. It is astounding to witness what is being created there out of a passionate love for psychoanalysis, for the most part autodidactically and based on the specific history of each of the countries concerned and against the background of the subtly diversified special culture of each country.

In the new world the strong influence of the USA and Canada on modern psychoanalysis is undisputed, but the Latin American countries too are being recognized more and more. With Horacio Etchegoyen, the IPA has its first Latin American president. Of the larger Latin American countries only Ecuador, Bolivia and Paraguay are missing.

Conspicuous is the absence of psychoanalysis in Africa and the Arab countries. Although represented in South Africa by psychoanalysts such as Joseph and Annemarie Sandler for periods of time, with its apartheid policy the country did not seem to provide a favourable setting for psychoanalysis. In the Arab countries and in Iran fundamentalist Islam and progressive psychoanalysis seem to be mutually exclusive. Thus Africa and the Arab world are absent from the map of psychoanalysis.

The contributions on Japan and Korea show not only the high standard of psychoanalyis (from a traditionally European perspective) in these Eastern countries but also the quite specific cultural features of Eastern philosophy. The same applies to India. R. T. Martin's contribution on Australia, on the other hand, shows that the fifth continent, despite its great distance from Europe and America, is culturally closely connected to its origins (New Zealand and the economically important region around the centres Singapore, Bangkok and Djakarta still seem to be developing countries for psychoanalysis.) The editor owes China`s inclusion to a committed psychoanalyst who has travelled in this country many times out of psychoanalytical and socio-critical interest, Alf Gerlach, and to his acquaintanceship with the former director of the Psychiatric Hospital in Guangzhou, Kan-Ming Mo.

There will be protests about Erika Danneberg's contribution, which, under the title "Psychoanalysis against the grain", describes how in Argentina, Chile, Cuba and Nicaragua a committed attempt, inspired by Marxist political action, was made to establish a new society with greater justice with the help of psychoanalysis as a cultural theory and therapeutic practice.

The third aim of this book, besides giving an overview of the history of psychoanalysis and of the geographical distribution of psychoanalysis throughout the world, *is to describe the current situation of psychoanalysis.* The editor has certainly not always been successful in doing this. Regarding the former countries of the Eastern bloc, the aim of appropriately catching the exciting atmosphere of new beginnings in psychoanalysis in these countries was for the most part achieved, thanks to the enthusiastic collaboration of the authors concerned. The latest news on the tragic as well as exciting situation with respect to the war in former Yugoslavia was sent to us by Eduard Klain from Zagreb just as we were going to press. Since the contribution on France in Volume 1 only went up to 1965, a special supplement dealing with the current situation there has been added.

Moreover, the second volume, just like the first, is supposed to bring out the various schools and directions and not to suppress differences and controversies. In this way it becomes clear that the traditional groupings in various societies are more likely to come to an agreement with the prevailing circumstances and to negotiate arrangements for daily practice with the ruling institutions there, such as with the National Health Service in Great Britain and the medical authorities and the health insurance companies in Germany. Other groupings want nothing to do with them because the freedom of psychoanalysis seems to them to be more important. Indeed, psychoanalysis in different countries has the chance to gain access to undreamt-of sinecures in medical and psychological practice. But this also involves a great danger of being controlled by regulations from outside.

Finally, the book is intended to serve as a reference book so that the reader can obtain information about the institutes of the IPA, look up addresses, telephone and telefax numbers and get an idea of the relevant periodicals in the countries concerned.

The editor would like to explain why most of the contributions, in the second volume, too, focus with few exceptions on the development of psychoanalysis within the IPA: the simple reason is that this association, from a historical viewpoint, was the first one to organize psychoanalysis on an international level, with professional standards, with legal by-laws and with the aim of spreading and organizing psychoanalysis internationally. Of course, it would have been interesting to follow up how psychoanalysis has unfolded outside the IPA; in Germany, for example, within the German Psychoanalytical *Society*. It would also have been interesting to examine the influence of C. G. Jung or Alfred Adler in an international context. In the USA Theodor Reik helped to form a "National Psychological Association for Psychoanalysis". In England W. R. Bion and S. H. Foulkes applied psychoanalysis to groups and institutions through the organization of the London Group Society, with branches in many countries.

All of this would have been interesting, but would have been beyond the scope of the two volumes as well as exceeding the authority of the editor. Thus any mention of the further development of psychoanalysis towards an analytical psychotherapy that is easier to teach and learn, let alone any mention of so-called "new" forms of therapy such as client-centred therapy (Carl C. Rogers), Gestalt therapy (Fritz Perls), bioenergetics (Alexander Lowen), or primal scream therapy (Arthur Janov) has been omitted. The contribution on Austria in the first volume contains a supplement regarding further very lively associations and working circles which feel committed to psychoanalysis, even though they may have distanced themselves from positions of Freud and modern psychoanalysis with their for many perhaps orthodox emphasis on transference, countertransference and resistance analysis. In this respect the second volume contains even more perspectives and insights, such as the possible role of psychoanalysis in the revolutions in Argentina, Chile and Nicaragua, such as China, and particularly the situation in the countries of the former Eastern bloc.

A portrayal of historically later developments in psychoanalysis, within groupings outside the International Psychoanalytical Association, also in the fields of group psychotherapy or analytical psychotherapy, must be reserved for the future and other editors and authors!

In conclusion, the editor would like to thank all the authors for their excellent cooperation, particularly for the generous patience of those who had submitted their contributions very early and have had to wait a long time for this volume to appear. Those who finished their contributions only later under great time pressure deserve the same thanks for their readiness to put other important obligations temporarily aside for the sake of the project.

The editor has had personal contact with most of the authors, having met many during the conferences of the IPA in Rome in 1989, Buenos Aires in 1991 and Amsterdam in 1993. Others he knows from academic collaboration at the university, such as Edith Kurzweil and Raúl Páramo-Ortega.

Regarding the valuable contributions on formerly Eastern bloc countries, the editor deems himself lucky that contacts made at the congress in Amsterdam in 1993 have led not only to the contributions of friends in Hungary, Poland, Lithuania and former Czechoslovakia contained in Vol. 1, but also these of Vera Şandor for Romania (with the kind support of the Sigmund Freud Romanian Translation and Publication Center in New York) and Matjaž Lunaček for Slovenia in this volume. Personal visits to still communist Bulgaria not only made the contribution on Bulgaria possible but also an official cooperation between the universities of Sofia and Frankfurt. The contact to Peter Klein (Serbia) came about at the Congress of the European Psychoanalytical Federation in Stockholm in 1991. Eduard Klain (Croatia) has been familiar to the editor for a long time through earlier international group-therapy congresses in Opatjia in 1985 and Zagreb in 1986. During the international conference of the Association d'Histoire de la Psychanalyse in Brussels in 1993 the editor had the good fortune to meet Alexander Etkind and Alexandre Mikhalevitch as well as the charming Michelle Moreau-Ricaud.

Some authors have had to accept painful abridgements for unavoidable reasons of cost. They either saw to this themselves or allowed the editor to do it.

Finally the editor would like to thank the publisher and his staff for their extremely good and pleasant cooperation.

Argentina

by Leonardo Wender, Delia Torres and Inés Vidal

The history of psychoanalysis in Argentina is a complex and at times a fascinating saga. This young Latin American country with barely 34 million inhabitants after 177 years of independence from Spanish rule has 80,000 medical doctors, 20,000 psychologists, more than 1000 analysts who are members of the IPA and at least an additional 1000 independent analysts. A scenario such as the one described cannot but arouse the curiosity of those interested.

All pioneering movements are formed by small groups which actually reflect the spirit of larger socio-political currents and the same can be said of the dawn of psychoanalysis in Argentina.

For purposes of this paper 1942 shall mark the beginning of Psychoanalysis in the social history of Argentina, when the Argentine Psychoanalytic Association (APA), the foundation stone for local psychoanalysis, was first established.

Argentina – 1942: Historic Background of the APA Foundation

During World War II Argentina held a privileged position. As a politically conservative nation it still maintained a neutral position at an international level. Rich and full of perspectives, it had a large, hard working middle class striving for social progress. For Argentine workers it was a dream come true. They felt assured that future generations were going to attain higher standards of living than those of their parents. However, both urban and rural life reflected poverty and social injustice that demanded improvement.

Since 1930, the country had been governed by a conservative political regime mainly through electoral fraud. And although individual rights were formally respected, the democratic system was in fact degraded.

The war exposed the vulnerability of the entire system. It proved that Argentina could become completely paralyzed, not only due to a lack of basic products, such as fuel, but also because the country's economy was exclusively based upon cattle raising and farming, the exportation of raw materials, and was totally dependent upon maritime trade.

The war added to a scarcity of products which were mainly imported, giving rise to a new phenomenon. Industries sprouted in the area surrounding the Federal Capital, attracting thousands of people from all over the country seeking a job. These people left their roots and political loyalties behind.

This rural migration to the city demonstrated the political frustration as well as the economic hardships which prevailed under the conservative regime. This situation was ripe for a political movement of a nationalistic and popular character – Peronism – that would dominate the political scenario of the country for many years to come.

Meanwhile, wartime foodstuffs exports earned hard currency for the nation and its society's intellectual and bourgeois circles expanded both economically and scientifically.

In the Argentina of those days, forever curious and eager about intellectual movements, there was a certain knowledge about Sigmund Freud and his works resulting from publications of several literary and journalistic reports during the decade of the 30s. Freud's "Complete Works" published in Spain in 1923 provided early access to such thinking to Spanish speaking readers. Travelling physicians who occasionally contacted European and North American centers for academic purposes also helped to share such thoughts.

During the early stages of development psychosomatic medicine became a link between official school medicine (university and hospitals) and Freudian theories. Access to the medically-focused American psychoanalytic culture, as concerning both psychiatry and new psychosomatic concepts, allowed pioneering medical doctors to absorb Freudian psychological concepts. They returned with new ideas which began to appear quite unobtrusively in asylums and hospital wards, as well as in several offices of dilettante practitioners.

But these forebearers did not consider psychoanalysis their main point of interest and did not become part of the group of people who would later found the Argentine Psychoanalytic Association (APA).

The foundation of the APA clearly distinguished between those who studied at the Association and those who did not. From then on, distrust, rivalry and antagonism towards the Establishment became reciprocal: the classical psychiatrists were regarded as oligarchs, while the leftists of those times became Pavlovians and took an anti-analysis stand. Thus, a limit was defined. A scientific barrier arose together with ideological, political and even sociological characteristics.

For good or for evil, the fact is that psychoanalysis in Argentina developed within the cultured bourgeoisie. Institutional psychoanalysis was normally conducted by people from this social class: young individuals willing to add to the challenge of their own future the passion for a new discipline they felt identified with. Thus, personal and scientific history became intertwined.

Arnaldo Raskovsky and Enrique Pichon-Rivière, to mention two, came from the provinces and moved to the capital in search of intellectual and professional progress. Other European immigrants fled from fascist regimes in Spain and Germany. Such was the case with Angel Garma, Heinrich Racker and Marie Langer. Celes Cárcamo later joined them. Cárcamo was an upper class medical doctor, who specialized in psychoanalysis in Europe, the scientific mecca of those days.

The common objective of this pioneering group was to secure this new science in an "exotic" and attractive institution, which could be a continuous source of reference and individual identity.

Foundation of the Argentine Psychoanalytic Association (APA)

After several years of preparation, on December 15th 1942, the Argentine Pyschoanalytic Association was finally established. At first there were only six members: Angel Garma, Guillermo Ferrari Hardoy, Enrique Pichon-Rivière, Arnaldo Rascovsky, Celes Cárcamo and Marie Langer. All were medical doctors and were, at the beginning, adherent members. With the exception of Ferrari Hardoy, who moved to the United States in 1945, the others prepared a scientific paper during the first year that promoted them to Full Members to act as training analysts in this field.

After its foundation, the APA acquired the approval as Provisional Society of the IPA during the XXVI International Congress in Zurich (1949) through a presentation made by Dr. Ernest Jones, the approval was ratified and the APA became a Component Society of the IPA.

Angel Garma was elected as the first president and conducted the first seminar sponsored by the Institute. The by-laws adapted from the London Institute foresaw the training of future analysts through three basic fundamentals: training analysis, supervisions, courses and seminars.

At first, the APA did not demand that members be medical doctors. The candidates had to have certain qualifications for scientfic research and an interest in applied psychoanalysis within their own discipline. From 1951 to 1987 candidates who were not medical doctors were excluded.

From the beginning Argentine psychoanalysis was and has continued to be independent of university medical training. Such an attitude, which was advocated by Freud for such new movements, proved to be particularly suitable for a country subjected to military coups and unstable university campuses. Therefore, for many years, psychoanalysis was developed outside hospitals and university classrooms with the exception of a few individual or group cases that had earned some presence in or contact with generally acknowledged scientific groups.

This actual and ideological separation was encouraged by both state institutions and the APA due to a variety of reasons. At first, in response to the need to consolidate and strengthen the psychoanalytic institution and train its members. Later, to maintain an illusory standard of psychoanalytic purity as well as to preserve its hegemonic role as the sole psychoanalytic institution. Such a restrictive policy generated harsh judgement concerning the participation of its members in the *outside* scientific community.

In fact, this approach was helpful in that it allowed the APA to continue functioning without getting involved in the political upheavals the country was undergoing. Later on, the situation changed abruptly and several of its members had a different fate: some suffered persecution, were imprisoned, disappeared or were forced into exile.

Due to the nature and scope of the hardships and resulting dispersion of so many members or ex-members of the international psychoanalytic community, this specific subject would merit a special study because of its scope and meaning.

Pioneers and Their Ideas

From the onset, these pioneers were interested in four main areas that covered almost all the fundamental psychoanalytic categories: neurosis, psychosis, psychosomatic disorders and children. This was the result of the different individual backgrounds involved.

Angel Garma was born in Bilbao in 1904 and died in Buenos Aires in 1993. He graduated as a medical doctor in 1927 and went to Berlin in order to pursue psychoanalytic training. Upon returning to Spain, the Civil War forced him to move to Buenos Aires. In a hommage to Garma after his death, Horacio Etchegoyen referred to a conversation he had had with Garma in which he had asked him when he had stopped supporting Kleinian ideas. Garma had replied that this had occured when Melanie Klein introduced the concept of "depressive position". He considered this a concept that favoured masochist submission of the ego to the sadistic super-ego. He was always keen on this subject and a great deal of his contributions were based on such notions. He suggested that masochist submission to external aggressions was the origin of psychosomatic illnesses. His interest was always close to these pathologies and he wrote many important papers about migraines and gastroduodenal ulcers. He also developed a thesis according to which dreams are hallucinations of disguised traumatic situations.

Arnaldo Rascovsky (1907), a pediatrician and an endocrinologist, became interested in psychoanalysis in 1935. His work as a professor started at the "Hospital de Niños" (Children's Hospital). In 1958 he started to develop his theory on fetal psychism and described bi-dimensional dreams as belonging to this psychic stage. His work on filicide led him to create an institution, "Filium", devoted to children's rights and related issues.

Celes Cárcamo (1903). Cárcamo was born in the province of Buenos Aires and died in 1990. He was trained in Paris were he did analysis under Paul Schiff. He became a member of the Psychoanalytic Association of Paris in 1939.

Enrique Pichon-Rivière was born in Geneva in 1907 and died in 1977. He was always interested in psychosis. The ideas of Pichon-Rivière were original and independent of the theories of his times. Despite the fact that he did not leave much written material he had a remarkable influence on both theory and Argentine pschoanalytic techniques. Pichon-Rivière was not a writer: he loved to convey his ideas verbally. He was always surrounded by people who were interested in following his teachings, which many considered unsurpassable. For that reason his beliefs are more present in those who were his disciples (José Bleger, David Liberman, Edgardo Rolla, for example) than in the papers he wrote. His ideas about analysis as a "spiral process" in conjunction with the "hic et nunc et mecum" continue to be used today to understand the psychoanalytic process. He proposed that resistance to change was based on a basic fear: fear of a loss or fear of attack. The analytic process starts out from a "fantasy of illness" and is directed towards a "fantasy of cure". Pichon-Rivière takes into account the history of the patient in a dialectic form, thus avoiding the obstacles of unidirectional genetism and of the non-historic "here and now".

Pichon-Rivière created the concept of oligotimy which he differentiated from oligophrenia and from Kanner's early autism. He devoted most of his intellectual work to the concepts of social psychology.

Arminda Aberastury: Teoria y Técnica del Psicoanálisis de Niños ("Theory and Techniques of Child Psychology") is the title of a major work by Aberastury which for many decades has been an essential reference book for most Argentine and Latin American child psychologists. Aside from her contributions to the techniques of child analysis, she also suggested the existence of a genital period previous to the anal period during the first year of life. She also studied how children walk and the language children use as activities related to the separation from objects and the magical reparation of them.

Elizabeth Goode de Garma collaborated with A. Aberastury in the translation of Melanie Klein's *The Psychoanalysis of Children.* She travelled to London where she presented the case of a 21 month-old baby, and immediately attracted the interest of many professionals, since at that time no analysis was conducted for such young children.

Maria Glas de Langer (1910) came from Vienna. She started analysis with Richard Sterba while she attended seminars. One year later, because of her leftist ideas the political situation became unbearable and so she went to Spain with her husband and worked as a medical doctor with the International Brigades during the Spanish Civil War. In 1942 Maria Glas de Langer and her husband came to Buenos Aires. She had a pioneering spirit and a gift for foundations. Her book *Maternity and Sex* is still considered a classic within the scope of female sexuality. Maria Langer was one of the analysts who resigned from the APA with the Plataforma Group in 1971. She later became President of the Argentine Association of Psychiatrists. During the military Process she went into exile in Mexico where she continued to work for many years. She was 77 years old when she died in Buenos Aires in 1987.

Heinrich Racker was born in Poland in 1910 and died in Buenos Aires in 1960. In 1914, as was the fate of many Jews, he had to emigrate to Vienna where he received a solid humanistic education and a Ph. D. in Philosophy. Racker presented his first paper on countertransference in 1948. In this paper he pointed out that countertransference reactions can give the analyst the evidence of what occurs to the analysand. Racker and Paula Heimann reached the same conclusions despite the fact that they never met each other.

Luisa Alvarez de Toledo: In her book *El Análisis del Asociar, del Interpretar y de las Palabras* ("Analysis of Association, Interpretation and Words"), published in 1954, Luisa Alvarez de Toledo suggested that it is possible to analyse the meaning of speech and of each word independently of their content. Words are not lived in their symbolic meaning but rather as objects of reward or aggression. As a result, the concept of the voice as drive object appears. This study, which was quite original for its time, also marked Argentine psychoanalytic thought. This was therefore left open to the theory of psychoanalytic language that David Liberman would develop, and perhaps to Lacanian theories as well.

Women Analysts in Argentina

The participation of women in psychoanalysis was greatly facilitated by a renewed emphasis on children within the Freudian concept of the psyche, and later by both Kleinian developments of early psychology and Winnicott's contributions.

The first meetings at Melanie Klein's school in England were attended by two remarkable women, Arminda Aberastury and Elizabeth Goode. Later on Arnaldo Rascovsky's theories on foetal psyche created the framework within which Argentine women, who then were growing professionally and culturally, directed their intelligence and sublimated maternal nature towards the analytic vocation. In fact, a large number of the analytic population is made up of women.

Women's initial role may have been the result of this contact with the Kleinian School, whose approach might have seemed to them closer and wider than Anna Freud's.

Although such an easy acceptance of women in psychoanalysis is not only true of Argentine culture, we believe that certain local characteristics brought about multiple effects, both in the development of local psychoanalysis and its epistemological approach. As Argentine psychoanalysis has had a great impact on analytic training and teaching in Latin America and later in Europe (mainly in Spain), we believe that the understanding of its origins might contribute to the clarification of later developments.

Therefore, it might be worth considering also the male analysts and their family constitution.

During the 1940s in Argentina traditional customs of Spanish culture still prevailed together with a certain Victorian flair due to the European background of the emerging middle class.

Women had already started participating in science, art and even politics; but they were still separated from the professional and scientific interests of their husbands. Couples did not normally work in the same profession. This was not the case among analysts. Wives joined the analytic group both intellectually and politically from the very beginning. One of the reasons for this was that the meetings attended by the spouses to study and debate Freud's ideas were held at the houses of prospective analysts. There were, in fact, several "pioneering families", such as Pichon-Rivière and Arminda Aberastury, Angel Garma and Elizabeth Goode, and Arnaldo Rascovsky and Matilde Wencelblatt.

This pattern of "analytic spouses" continues at present, and marriages between analysts are frequent. This early tendency to "cohabitation" may have been the source of certain tolerance and acceptance of scientific and political differences in the local environment.

In turn this special form of phylogeny gave rise to a particular endogamical and sociological feature of the analytic population. At present, such a feature tends to appear also in the intellectual middle class, where whole families do analysis or receive some other kind of therapy.

On the other hand, this widespread endogamical trend entails the transference of ambivalences and pregenital struggles over masculine and feminine identities within the professional field. It is worth noting that this situation may have led, at least, to two significant events: frequent neurosis among analytic spouses as well as a strong endogenous incentive for the psychoanalytic study of marital and familial conflicts.

Both psychoanalysis and the APA were very active and expanded during the fifties and the sixties. We shall outline the major institutional movements from which psychoanalysis has expanded to hospitals, universities, the provinces, etc.

Psychoanalysis and Hospital Practice

The development of psychoanalysis in hospitals is linked to a pioneering experiment done by Dr. Mauricio Goldenberg, a famous psychiatry professor. His work deeply influenced the history of mental health in Argentina.

In 1956 he was appointed Head of the Psychopathological Service in a general hospital:"Policlinico Gregorio Araoz Alfaro" which was situated in the working class suburban area of Lanús. From there, working together with interdisciplinary teams, he started to develop a plan that would integrate contibutions of dynamic psychiatry, social psychology and psychoanalysis.

Confronted with the classical system in asylums for the insane, he created a psychopathological service that became a part of the services of the general hospital as well as of the community. At that time it was the only place in the country where free psychoanalytic therapies were provided.

This became immediately sucessful. The idea was born and then adopted by many other hospitals throughout the country as well as abroad.

Goldenberg's teachings also reached many university students. Amongst the several young doctors who accompanied him, some were already candidates for the APA , while others would apply later on stimulated by their professor, who had a good relationship with the Association.

This project, as many others, was interrupted by the 1976 *coup d'état.*

The return of democracy encouraged the continuation of hospital services. In 1984, Dr. Mauricio Goldenberg together with Dr. Horacio Etchegoyen, who had also been a Psychiatry professor in Mendoza, finally managed to include Medical Psychology at the school of Medicine of the University of Buenos Aires.

Today, the presence of psychoanalytic groups of a Lacanian orientation is quite strong in both hospital services and Schools of Psychology.

Psychology as a University Career

Psychology as a university degree had started to be taught in three cities in 1956: Buenos Aires, Rosario and La Plata. Many renowned psychoanalysts and other professionals taught in these institutions. This was the golden era of integration: Psychoanalysis-University. Kleinian theories were then hegemonic.

The university with its characteristic autonomy always fostered politization and therefore it soon became the privileged target of authoritarian power.

A good part of the first stages of its development were interrupted by a *coup d'état* in 1966. This event was also a hard blow to all campus activities. In July 1966 a new law dissolved the autonomy of all universities, a measure that was immediately rejected by deans and rectors. More than half of the professors at the University of Buenos Aires submitted their Letters of Resignation. The military government violently invaded university campuses.

The terrible acts committed by the police upon taking over the School of Exact Sciences of the University of Buenos Aires became widely known as the "Noche de los Bastones Largos" or the "Night of the Long Sticks".

Psychology students affected by mass resignations in protest at such events and all related activities were from then on considered as suspicious by the military regime.

At the beginning of 1967 a 1954 resolution was ratified subordinating the work of psychologists to the supervision of medical doctors. Only in 1985 was this law repealed.

On the other hand, Schools of Psychology marginated from official, "authentic" and respectable psychoanalysis, and received Lacanian theories as a contestatory knowledge and an agglutinant element of pertinence and identity.

In due time, these new theories dialectically enriched official analysis[1] and increased extra-institutional psychoanalysis.

The repression period was the moment of greatest antagonistic polarization between official psychoanalysis represented by the APA and psychologists. The former were protected within their corporative institution – which the military regime never persecuted. On the contrary, combative, politicized university psychologists were deprived of their institutions and of their outstanding and well loved professors. This difference, which arose from the most incredible complex causes and which exceeds the limits of this chapter, has been and still is, the source of deep envy and antagonism.

If, to the general political situation we add the contradiction between the APA psychoanalysts who taught psychoanalysis beyond its framework and, at the same time, the longstanding impediment to psychologists to enter the institution, one can clearly understand the magnitude of the resulting implications.

We can declare that psychoanalysis overflowed the diverse IPA branch institutions as a presence not only in Buenos Aires but also in other major cities throughout Argentina.

Psychoanalysis as a theory of the psyche and as a psychopathological theory and initiator of a wide range of therapies continues to be hegemonic regardless of the fact that its present dissemination is anarchical and of an irregular level as concerns excellence.

We shall now leave aside such chronological details to continue describing the facts of the 70s that were crucial for Argentina and therefore for our history. We hope that the facts narrated hereafter shall help to understand and revalue the different movements which we shall refer to once we have provided the overview.

The Decade of the 70s. State Violence and Psychoanalysis

During the decade of the 70s Argentina was shaken by violence from both the extreme right and left.

1 When we refer to official psychoanalysis or official institutions, we refer to those psychoanalytic associations that belong to the IPA.

However, 1973 seemed to be the beginning of a new phase full of hope as the military withdrew from public power after the military coup of 1966. During this return to democracy Peronism became triumphant, a movement inscribed in national and popular history, as pointed out before, and which had been banned for 18 years.

Civil illusions soon faded, basically due to acute contradictions between sectors within Peronism. Violence sprouted once again. The Peronism of those times was a movement which gathered varied and radical ideas.

A new military coup in 1976 installed a regime of state terrorism until the year 1983. This was not unknown to the country before; however, the magnitude of the unleashed repression was unexpected.

The State called this type of terrorism "a Process of National Reorganization" and applied the well known "Doctrine of National Security", dividing the world into two halves, one occidental and Christian and the other communist.

A general of the Process declared "First we kill off the subversives, then their collaborators, then [...] their sympathizers [...] then those who are indifferent and lastly we'll kill off the doubtful".[2] The outcome of this confrontation left a toll of thirty thousand missing persons.

Psychoanalysis was dangerously confused with power, Marxism and totalitarian subversion. The time had come to withdraw into private practice. Analysts gathered more than before in their Association and in private study groups seeking refuge from time and place.

During this decade the life of psychoanalysts in official societies was also affected due to the deep transformation and crisis which finally led to a schism of the then sole official association: the APA.

In 1977, during the XXX International Psychoanalytic Congress in Jerusalem, a new group, the Psychoanalytic Association of Buenos Aires (APdeBA) was acknowledged as a Provisional Association.

However, we cannot speak of a birth of this new group without considering the critical institutional moments in its wake as well as the national context in which all these episodes took place.

2 General I. Saint Jean, *International Herald Tribune,* Paris 26-5-1977. Reproduced in *La Crisis Mundial* ("World Crisis"), Frank A. G. Bruguera, 308.

Crisis and Expansion of Official Entities during the Decade of the Seventies

In 1969 in Rome, simultaneous to the International Congress, a Congress of candidates met to carry out a critical review of the standard training imposed by the IPA in its institutes throughout the world. The Argentine Platform was born from this International Platform.

Restrictions arising from the extended waiting period prior to admittance to psychoanalytic training as well as the recently imposed extention of the seminars to four years brought about institutional malaise.

In 1971 the first institutional schism occurred. Thirty members and twenty candidates belonging to two internal groups "Plataforma" and "Documento" left the APA.

On the one hand, *Plataforma* and *Documento* sought to politically include the APA in the mainstream and socio-political changes of the country in view of the eventual return of Peron to Argentina. Several youth and intellectual sectors considered that in such event the former leader would propitiate a social restructuring.

On the other hand, they also struggled to liberalize teaching and to secure the political conduction of the APA administration at its Training Institute. Many of these ideas had their immediate source in the unionized positions which were typical of the Peronist resurgency.

Resignations launched a review process within the APA that led to "the proposal for institutional reorganization" submitted in 1974 by some leading members. This political program won the elections and became the ideological axis of the APA. According to its authors, this axis intended to provide a realistic frame of reference leading towards a merge of such contradictions. However, in practice it actually was a clashing point between incompatible criteria concerning admission and the promotion of members as well as the teaching of psychoanalysis and relationships with the community. The most extreme antagonism was sustained by the "Ateneo" group which later on would break away to establish a new institution.

The national situation torn apart by such struggles was worsened by internal confrontations. Finally the APA, which until then had been the sole official center, split into two autonomous associations.

During the International Congress of Jerusalem the formal separation was agreed upon in peacemaking terms and without previous APA interventions. It was a painful separation for everybody because it involved the dispersion of close friendships, transferences and scientific ties. Even today it is still difficult to evaluate its scope due to the proximity of the facts and to the institutional implications.

There are no differences in concept or ideology in the regulations or ethical codes of both institutions, nor are there any true differences concerning their scientific organization or manner of administration.

However, certain differences of criteria do exist between both institutions concerning the training of their candidates, the academic curriculae and responsibility of the institution. The Psychoanalytic Association of Buenos Aires (APdeBA), which is the most recent, has a set study plan in pre-established stages. In the APA, the curriculum has set mandatory parts, while other study subjects are optional and chosen by each candidate. The APA is more confident in the self-regulation of its members while the APdeBA considers that the Institution must be more responsible for the training, promotion and professional performance of its members.

After overcoming the initial distances, and with the passage of time, a series of scientific links between both institutions became apparent. After Argentina officially acknowledged the right of psychoanalysts to exercise psychotherapy, both institutions started admitting psychologists to be trained in analysis. This decision coincided with the re-institutionalization of democratic freedom, a turning point after the military Process and the return to free elections (1982). This change of circumstances must also be revaluated in view of the current economic crisis and the resulting difficulties in employment throughout the country.

Both institutions tend to become different in the measure in which each expresses the true interests of its members. Each competes maturely for different degrees of power and influence within the community and to earn a growing respect for independence. Lately both institutions have shared in the sponsorship of foreign analysts, local Psychoanalytic Congresses and the organization of the 1991 International Psychoanalytic Congress in Buenos Aires.

Evolution of Psychoanalysis After the Institutional Schism and The Return to Democracy

Eighteen years have elapsed since the APA and APdeBA schism occurred. Both institutions have become strengthened and currently there are two more bringing the number up to four: APA, APdeBA, and two psychoanalytic associations in the interior of the country, IPA branches: the Psychoanalytic Association of Mendoza and that of Córdoba, besides a series of study groups fully acknowledged or in formation.

During the dictatorship and in the years thereafter, for personal as well as professional reasons, many Argentine psychoanalysts have confronted the task of psychoanalytically understanding and interpreting the traumatic effects of social violence. They hoped they would be able to transform the inexplicable horror suffered by so many into a "thinking" which would symbolize these acts, thereby rescuing the individual and also holding a deadly message for future generations.

Despite the fact that leading psychoanalysts resigned due to political and ideological differences, paradoxically, serious studies were submitted by members of both official institutions expressing theories that were published on a national and international level containing genuine psychoanalytical contributions on socio-political problems and violent dictatorships.

A whole corpus of theory has developed around psycholanalysis and the state of violence. In summary, these ideas, which shook the basis of classical psychoanalysis, were presented by Janine Puget at the Congress of Montreal (1987) as well as in other papers.

These efforts, as well as those of many other authors, led to the writing of papers that were often published abroad since Argentina did not ensure the safety and respect for individuals' rights and memories of terror still lingered in the minds of citizens.

Under these circumstances controversies on the theoretical, practical and ethical principles of psycholanalysis were made evident. Specific characteristics of psychic trauma generated under these conditions including their "generational transposition" were studied. Emotions such as horror as a negative impact on the psyche required further study and explanation. As a result, studies were conducted on the specific techniques of how to deal with these traumatic levels within a psychoanalytic framework.

It was revealed that when real violence appears in an analytical situation, listening acquires a factor of distortion. And since the analyst is dealing with a shared traumatic experience, he/she lacks the necessary psychic distance to maintain an adequate instrumentation.

Work undertaken with relatives of survivors was the study basis of the specific experiences of the mourning of the "disappearance" of a loved one. The relatives had no information about the whereabouts or fate of those missing. Under this psychotising induction of what was not made known, the natural process of mourning was hampered. Psychoanalysis of these relatives revealed that in order to allow an individual to duly process the mourning, a collective acknowlegment of death was needed.

The lack of representations of the loss ruptures the psychic functions and generates a void in the transmission of family and social history. The unfathomable horror in the psyche of the parents is inscribed in the bodies and minds of the following generations.

The numerous orphans resulting from the "Proceso de Reorganización Nacional" also gave way to specific developments concerning the elaboration of mourning in infancy. This socio-political circumstance experienced by Argentina is related to the difficulty presented by many adolescents in planning their future and the prolonged dependence that this brings about. These adolescents also have a tendency to choose the easy way out and have a strong sense of confusion due to the difficulty of sharing values with their elders who try to help them find their own. Within poorer social segments there is a marked difficulty to think. This was most probably due to the attack on thinking maintained by State terrorism.

With the return to Democracy in 1983, several analysts started working with Human Rights Commissions studying how social events are inscribed in the apparatus. Is there some form of direct register that does not pass through the way classically pointed out by theory? How does the transfer from one generation to the other take place? How do disavowed historical situations articulate with individual history?

The APA held an important congress in 1986. It focused on the subject "Uneasiness in Our Culture".

Other Psychoanalytic Institutions

For over three decades, the Argentine psychoanalytic movements were centered around the APA. At present there is a wider variety of training opportunities.

These new options have been the result of a series of pressures on medical and psychology students in particular.

First, State repression that ravaged both university faculties and students resulting in the immediate dispersal of students, leading them towards marginal professions and those obviously more radical within psychology and psychiatry.

The second, of a quite different nature, was the impotence of the APA. This institution, limited by a shortage of training analysts, could not meet the demand for training analysis from a large number of candidates. An additional factor was the necessary and possibly complacent compliance with the legal regulations that forbade the training of clinical psychologists. This impediment, which was in fact repressive, also had an atomizing effect which in the long run also became a multiplying effect for the dissemination of psychoanalysis.

A third factor of diversification has been and continues to be a growing demand for other therapeutic modalities such as short therapies (the most frequent case), which official institutions are not prepared or willing to encourage in their training institutes.

Now there are over fifty independent institutions in Buenos Aires that provide systematic psychoanalytic training. Some of their study programs are identical to those of the seminars held at official institutions. Such is the case of the Escuela de Psicoterapia para Graduados (Psychotherapy School for Graduates), founded in 1964, in which most of its faculty members come from the APA or the APdeBA. The difference lies in the fact that training analysis is not mandatory.

The Asociación de Psicología y Psicoterapia de Grupo (Association of Group Psychology and Psychotherapy) is one of the oldest, and is also the closest to official institutions. It was founded in 1954 by a group of analysts, mostly from the APA.

The Propagation of Lacan's Ideas in Buenos Aires

The resignation of Jacques Lacan and his colleagues from the IPA in 1953 and their harsh criticism of the institution were the reasons why Lacan's work was not included in seminars until after his death. However, his ideas drew considerable interest and had a wide dissemination in Argentina since the fifties.

Oscar Massota is considered to be the first person to introduce and teach Lacan's work. Massota had studied philosophy and never belonged to the APA.

Psychologists were not able to join the APA until 1987. In view of this restriction, they viewed the extra-academic groups coordinated by Massota and other remarkable dissidents as a particularly attractive training opportunity. Such groups provided fascinating psychoanalytic ideas and a physical space to revile the APA on the basis of the ideas of Lacan, Massota and others who had not been able or did not want to join the psychoanalytic establishment.

Other psychoanalysts who were also medical doctors became aware of the fact that their clinical practice differed from Freud's. Therefore a concept of "a return to Freud from Lacan" – which at least in Buenos Aires implied disdaining Melanie Klein – had a powerful influence.

In 1972, Maude and Octave Mannoni visited Buenos Aires. It was the first time that Lacanian analysts presented their ideas and discussed clinical cases. Their visit undoubtedly made a strong impact.

The *Cuadernos Sigmund Freud* ("Sigmund Freud Bulletins") and the *Revista de la Escuela Freudiana* ("Freudian School Magazine"), both Lacanian publications, were then being published.

At present, Lacan's ideas and the development of his theories are included in different ways in seminars and post-graduate courses at practically all the official psychoanalytic institutions of Argentina.

During the late sixties and the early seventies, French psychoanalytic thinking drew a great deal of attention through the works of S. Leclaire, J. Laplanche, J.B. Pontalis, P. Aulagnier, D. Anzieu, A. Green and others.

Psychoanalysis of the Family and The Couple

In 1987 both psychoanalytical Associations (APA and APdeBA) together with the "Asociación Argentina de Psicología y Psicoterapia de Grupos" ("Argentine Association of Group Psychology and Psychotherapy") and the Escuela Argentina de Psicoterapia para Graduados" ("Argentine Psychotherapy School for Graduates") organized the First Argentine Congress on Psychoanalysis of the Family and the Couple. It was a remarkable scientific and political event, as it was the first Congress held by both Associations after the schism. The Congress began with a conference on "Family Group, Psyche's Matrix". The subjects dealt with at the conference articulated the concepts of state terrorism and the family, the status of the unconscious in marital and family psychoanalysis, transference and countertransference, techniques, psychopathology and human rights in family and marital psychoanalysis.

It would be possible to say that in Argentina there are three approaches to family and marriage: systemic, structural and psychoanalytic. The latter was the main approach of this Congress.

The analytic approach basically articulates Freudian findings so as to describe relationships among psychic mechanisms of family members or spouses. According to this concept, both the couple and the family may be understood as an effect of a process whereby individuals become articulated in terms of certain laws put forth by Freud to account for the relationships between psychic mechanisms. Within the different psychoanalytic currents, there is a group of authors who considers it necessary to build a theoretical object – the couple's unconscious formation (I. Berenstein and J. Puget) – in order to reflect on the problems existing in this field. Other psychoanalysts do not agree on this point. They assume the hypothesis of a matrix structure of which each couple or family would be a transformation. They are not concerned about how basic family structures are created.

Another approach considers that it is not necessary to work with new theoretical tools and examines the problems of these areas in the light of concepts such as Oedipus, transference, and the paternal role within an exclusively clinical framework. According to this approach, the couple and the family is a complicated network resulting from a wide range of transactions of desires, judgements and defences, all encouraged by drives and desires and limited by each member's restrictions.[3]

Child Psychoanalysis

During the first generations of child analysts, the pioneering contributions of Anna Freud and Melanie Klein on an international level, as well as the ideas of Arminda Aberastury in Argentina, were the subject of fruitful debates. We could say that child psychoanalysis found its principles and its implementation, as was mentioned before, in the Kleinian theory. The initial triumph of Kleinian theory was later re-enhanced with contributions made by E. Bick, W. Bion and D. Meltzer who rekindled the former Argentine interest of child psychoanalysts in the analysis of very small children and children with serious pathologies.

Melanie Klein's pioneering and, at one time, unique way of thinking provided rich conceptual tools and a model that allowed to capture in depth children's fantasies and mental processes. Nevertheless, with the passing of time, the restraints and blind spots of this theory were exposed.

Several child analysts suggested that the Kleinian model did not give importance to other factors that influenced the determination of children's symptoms. Some of these were concrete traumatic situations or particular pathological family situations. They considered that the symptoms could not only be attributed to the intolerance of frustration or to excessive amounts of the death instinct, as had been considered at first.

At the beginning they expected child analysis to bring about the necessary changes in the entire family. Later the field opened to new technical modalities such as a greater contact of parents to parental treatment or extended to all the family.

Winnicott's contributions, which opened a totally new dimension, allowed a more complex, rich and less schematic study of the problems.

Also here, Lacan and other French psychoanalysts, such as Dolto and Mannoni, deeply influenced the approach to problems.

3 David Maldavsky, *Minutes of the Congress* Vol. 3, 144, 1987.

Nonetheless, conceptual restraints also arose. And from that point of view child analysis was looked down upon and the correct question as to who was the subject of analysis led to a restriction of the child's own space in exchange for the listening of the parents. In summary, at the beginning when the child's pathology was considered as autonomous and his symptoms were thought of as mere expressions of intrapsychic pulsional conflict, he was made to depend entirely upon his parent's desires.

At present, psychoanalytic thought revolves around questions such as: What is the specific element of infantile psychoanalysis? What is the subject of study: the child, his parents? Are the symptoms determined by the parents or do these specifically pertain to the infantile psyche? What techniques should be favored: games, words, individual analysis, family or specific aspects of familial relationships?

So, over the years, heated debates have reflected extreme positions concerning genetism and structuralism; the prevalence of the internal or external world; and, the constitution of the pulsion by endogenous or exogenous methods.

When we summarize these thoughts about the development and evolution of the ideas involving children, we inevitably refer to everything that has passed through Argentine psychoanalytic thinking during these last years.

The criteria for indication of analysis has also varied. At first, the indications were extremely extensive. Then, when Lacanian ideas started to circulate, the subject of the demand for analysis became a central issue that decreased the indications. At present, the indication is thought of within a wider conceptual framework, discouraging indications that most certainly at the beginning came up from an excessive idealization.

First International Congress in Latin America
Horacio Etchegoyen – First Latin American President

In July 1991, the XXXVII. International Congress of the IPA took place in Buenos Aires. It was the first congress to be held in the Southern Hemisphere, in Latin America, and the one attracting a large audience. The hosts were the Asociación Psicoanalítica Argentina, the Asociación Psicoanalítica de Buenos Aires, the Sociedad Psicoanalítica de Mendoza – a component society since 1981 – and a study group from Cordoba that was acknowledged as a Provisional Society during the Congress.

The Congress was attended by 3,300 participants, 1,000 more than had been present at the previous Congress in Rome. Buenos Aires considered this event as one of the most outstanding of its intellectual life. Major newspapers publicized the event since psychoanalysis is connected to the teaching of psychology, psychiatry and other related professions, as well as general culture.

During the Congress, Horacio Etchegoyen, a distinguished Argentine psychoanalyst, was elected as IPA President. This was an international acknowledgement of the efforts and importance awarded to psychoanalysis in Argentina. He was the first Latin American person to occupy this position and with his election Latin America became formally incorporated as the 3rd largest IPA area on the same level as Europe and the United States.

Horacio Etchegoyen was born in 1919 and he underwent analysis with H. Racker. In 1966 he won a scholarship and went to London to study in the Tavistock Clinic where he did analysis with D. Meltzer. He is the author of more than 60 psychoanalytic works that have been published as well as some books such as: *Estudios de Clínica Psicoanalítica sobre la Sexualidad* ("Studies of Psychoanalytic Clinical Medical Practice on Sexuality") and *Los Fundamentos de la Técnica Psicoanalítica* ("The Fundamentals of Psychoanalytic Technique"), an important reference book for many analysts and Psychoanalytic Institutions. He was Vice-President of the IPA during two periods. In 1957, he set down the principles of the future association in Mendoza where he lived and analyzed many of the present day members of that institution. He was the first President of the APdeBA, and was twice elected as its Scientific Secretary.

Final Reflection

Prior to concluding this chapter we wish to refer to two key issues that, surely, the reader has in mind: first, to try to understand how and why there was such an important development in psychoanalysis in these latitudes and second, to try and foretell the future of this same phenomenon.

But it seems easier to describe the expansion of psychoanalysis in Argentina than to understand it. We will situate ourselves within the historical context we have developed, aware of the fact that this is only one possible vertex of a greater knowledge.

We have seen how a new and curious country adopted psychoanalysis. A knowledge that was fascinating and that was immediately recognized as something useful and applicable. Proof of this is the immediate and uninterrupted response of the population that, with a growing demand for psychoanalysis, fed back necessary circuit for its dissemination and permanence. Psychoanalysis in Argentina was not a boom, it was a success.

This local response allowed and stimulated at the same time an early insertion in the scientific world and intellectual power of the Northern Hemisphere, a part of the world which has always been a fountain of inspiration and competitiveness. It should be remembered that as soon as 1942 the APA petitioned its incorporation as a study group of the IPA. In 1943, its Psychoanalytic Magazine appeared for the first time, a real landmark for the local bibliography. In 1945, trips were being made in the opposite direction: Arnaldo Raskovsky, as President of the Association, was invited and travelled to Rio de Janeiro and Sao Paulo to give conferences. After, other Latin American countries followed.

In 1949, Argentina presented papers at the International Congress in Zurich and was recognized as a component member.

What could have been better for a society rich in sensibility and intelligence than to accede to a scientific discipline in its creation and which required no major infrastructure nor academic tradition? A new science that only asked for thinkers, books to discuss, and as a subject of study and observation the same individuals that brought it about and acted it out? … These "tools" existed in great quantities in Argentina – simple resources that would prove to produce great effects as different facts have confirmed. The Argentines, who are traditionally fast and ubiquitous, knew how to capture this opportunity. In this manner they went forth guided by Freud, an ideologist who at first alone, and then with a small group of followers, managed to question the scientific world of the establishment of those times. Perhaps the Argentine intelligentsia, in a great moment of ductility, found itself identified, not only with his theories, but also with the idealized biography of its great teacher.

Psychoanalytic Argentina was also distant and marginal and sufficiently Jewish so as to, in an approriate conjunction of humility and megalomania, invent its own historic opportunity.

What Can Be Said About the Future of Psychoanalysis in Argentina?

In Argentina, as in the rest of the world, demand has diminished lately as a result of the economic crisis and the competitive dispersion of numerous alternative psychotherapies that have sprung up. But no interpretation can be lineal in this protean and contradictory country, much less so a forecast.

There are multiple variables to be taken into consideration. For example, the fact the expansion and standards of psychoanalysis were never diminished by former economic or military crises. This had been true for four uninterrupted decades. Now, Argentina has just suffered its most terrible dictatorship and an economic crisis that reached more than 2,000% annual inflation.

Just ten years have elapsed since the Argentinian people recuperated their elemental civil rights and liberties, lived through a few years of economic stability and progressed through a transition towards Democracy.

The effects that all these factors will have upon the different social classes is yet to be seen.

One positive thing to be taken into account which should be pointed out is that even before going back to the State of Law, Argentine society most quickly recuperated its "return to culture". The arts and sciences once again became part of everyday life.

The intellectuals, one of the most valuable groups of a nation, are also one of the cheapest, as they create themselves without any help (even in spite of the media), they are brave and idealistic by nature, they persist and come back. They return to continue inventing and reinventing. Psychoanalysis understands them, respects them and can and will help them to resist the worst moments. Culture and psychoanalysis in Argentina are intimately related.

But the urgent and easily gratified desire for immediate things, so stimulated by the universal culture, the media and even the present technology of the instantaneous, conspire directly and indirectly against a slow and meticulous process whose most profound and valuable aim is to make possible the individual's appetite for the search of Truth.

The greatest question lies not in evaluating if the population will keep its daily habits, its ideals, and above all its ethical parameters, after suffering the double trauma of punishment by the dictatorship and the instability of hyperinflation.

Until what point has the population transformed its demands of culture and health? ... And as to psychoanalysis, will those who have been soliciting it so conspicuously continue to do so?

These questions have been left open. It will be seen then, for the first time, if the supply and demand for psychoanalysis will decrease and never return, or if, psychoanalysis will locally adapt new concepts and answers to an atavistic claim of man: to understand himself and be understood by others.

Finally, for those who are interested in making a final reflection, we include some references about the state and production of psychoanalysis in Argentina for the first half of 1993.

Professionals dedicated to mental health in Argentina (psychoanalysts, psychiatrists, psychopedagogues, social assistants, occupational, psychomotor and music therapists	more than 30,000
Psychologists (about 1,000 university students graduate each year)	more than 17,000
Institutions	
– Asociación Psicoanalítica Argentina (APA)	1,200 members
– Asociación Psicoanalítica de Buenos Aires (DPdeBA)	400 members
– Asociación de Psicólogos de Buenos Aires	11,500 members
– Psychopathological and Mental Health Services of the Municipality of the City of Buenos Aires	33 services in general hospitals with about 1,700 professionals
– Private institutions dedicated to Mental Health (clinical assistance, courses, conferences. Many have their own publications)	about 400
Publications	
New publications each year (1993)	152
Number of editions per publication	1,500 to 3,000
Editorials exclusively dedicated to psychoanalytic works	11
Specialized magazines	There is a very important production. The two most sold print 2,000 issues of each edition. *Revista de Psicoanálisis* and *Psicoanálisis*

References

ABERASTURY, A. / F. CESIO / M. ABERASTURY (1987): Historia, enseñanza y ejercicio legal del psicoanálisis, Buenos Aires: OMEBA.

APA. Departmento de Historia del Psicoanálisis (1982): Associación Psicoanalítica Argentina 1942–1982, Buenos Aires.

– (1986): El malestar en nuestra cultura, XV Congreso interno y XXV Symposium.

BALAN, J. (1991): Cuéntame tu vida, Buenos Aires: Planeta.

– (1987): 1er Congreso Argentino de Psicoanálisis de Familia y Pareja, Buenos Aires, Vol. 1.

DEL MAZZO, GABRIEL (1957): La reforma universitaria y la universidad latinoamericana, Argentina: Universidad Nacional del Nordeste.

ETCHEGOYEN, R. HORACIO (1992): On the beginning of psychoanalysis in Latin America. [Not published].

FENDRIK, SILVIA INÉS (1989): Psicoanálisis para niños. Ficción de sus orígenes, Buenos Aires: Ariel.

– (1993): Desventuras del psicoanálisis, Buenos Aires: Ariel.

GARCÍA, GERMAN (1978): La entrada del psicoanálisis en la Argentina, Buenos Aires: Altazor.

GOLDENBERG, MAURICIO et al. (1986): La psiquiatría en el hospital general: Historia y estructura del Servicio de Psicopatología y Neurología del Policlínico Profesor Dr. Gregorio Araoz Alfaro, *La Semana Médica,* 47–54.

GRINBERG, LEON et al. (1961): Historia y evaluación de la psicología y psicoterapia de grupo en la Argentina. *Revista de Psicología y Psicoterapia de Grupo,* I. 1.

JACCARD, ROLAND (1982): Histoire de la psychanalyse: La psychanalyse en Argentine – Antonio Corel, Haydee Faimberg et Leonardo Wender, Paris: Hachette.

LANGER, MARIA (comp.) (1971): Cuestionamos, Buenos Aires: Granica.

– (1981): Memoria, historia y diálogo analítico, Buenos Aires: Folios.

LUNA, FELIX (1971): El 45, Buenos Aires: Sudamericana.

– (1986): Ortiz – Reportaje de la Argentina opulenta, Buenos Aires: Sudamericana.

MALDAVSKY, DAVID (1987): Actas del XXI Congreso Argentino de Psicoanálisis de Familia y Pareja, Buenos Aires, Vol. 3, 144.

PELENTO, MARIA LUCIA (1991): Duelo y trastornos psicosomáticos. La niña de la pregunta sobre los UFO. "Cuerpo, historia, interpretación". Piera Aulagnier et al., Buenos Aires: Paidos.

PUGET, JANINE (1987): En la búsqueda de una hipótesis. El contexto social. *Revista Ref. de Psicoanálisis* 44, 4.

PUGET, JANINE / LEONARDO WENDER (1986): Aux limites de l'analyzabilite: Tyrannie corporelle et sociale. *Revue Francaise de Psychanalyse,* 1987, 3.

PUGET, JANINE / RENE KAES (1991): Violencia de estado y psicoanálisis, Buenos Aires: Centro Editor de America Latina.

SAIDON, GABRIELA: La increible cultura del psicoanálisis en la Argentina, *Diario Clarin* 16-9-93.

VERA OCAMPO, R. (1977): Conversaciones con Mauricio Abadi, Buenos Aires: Timerman.
VEZZETTI, HUGO (1985): La locura en la Argentina, Buenos Aires: Paidos.
ZITO LIMA, VICENTE (1976): Conversaciones con Enrique Pichon-Rivière, Buenos Aires: Timerman.

Journals

Revista de Psicoanálisis
since 1943; Ed.: Asociación Psicoanalítica Argentina
Dr. Andres Rascovsky

Psicoanálisis
Revista de la Asociación Psicoanalítica de Buenos Aires
since 1979; Ed.: Asociación Psicoanalítica de Buenos Aires
Dr. Julio Najamkis

Imago
since 1974; Ed.: Letra Viva
Coronel Diaz 1837, Buenos Aires

Eos
Revista Argentina de Arte y Psicoanálisis
since 1991; Ed.: Fundación Banco Credito Argentino
11 de Septiembre 1990, 1428 Buenos Aires

Institutions

Asociación Psicoanalítica Argentina
(Argentine Psychoanalytic Association)
Rodríguez Peña 1674, 1021 Buenos Aires
Tel.: 54-1-812 3518; Fax: 54-1-814 0079

Asociación Psicoanalítica de Buenos Aires
(Buenos Aires Psychoanalytic Association)
Maure 1850, 1426 Buenos Aires
Tel.: 54-1-775 7867; Fax: 54-1-775 7985

Asociación Psicoanalítica de Córdoba
(Córdoba Psychoanalytic (Provisional) Study Group)
Jujuy 48 1° - Oficina 4, 5000 Córdoba
Tel./Fax: 54-51-229293

Sociedad Psicoanalítica de Mendoza
(Mendoza Psychoanalytic Society)
Lisandro de la Torre 355, 5500 Mendoza
Tel./Fax: 54-61-340029

Asociación de Psicoanálisis de Rosario
Rosario Psychoanalytic Study Group
Santa Fé 1785, 2° B, 2000 Rosario
Tel./Fax: 54-41-25 7355

Dr. Leonardo Wender, Av. Santa Fé 1785/8°, 1060 Buenos Aires
Dra. Delia Torres, Julián Alvarez 1049, 1414 Buenos Aires
Dra. María Inés Raitzin de Vidal, Jorge Newbery 2943, 1426 Buenos Aires

Australia

by Reginald T. Martin

Although psychoanalytic practice in Australia did not commence until the early thirties, the effects of the new and controversial discoveries of Freud were being felt here twenty years earlier. In his Biography of Freud, Ernest Jones reports a number of events that accord Australia a significant place in the early history of Psychoanalysis. In 1909 Freud reported having received a letter from Sydney telling him there was a group eagerly studying his work. A Dr. Donald Cameron had established a little group and had lectured many times before various Societies on Psychoanalysis. Before acquiring a medical qualification in 1907, he had been a minister of the Presbyterian Church but had had to resign his position on account of his "Freudian Views". Jones notes this as "the first instance, but far from being the last, of this kind of victimization".

Two years lager, at the request of Dr. Andrew Davidson, who was the Secretary of the Neurological Section of the Australian Branch of the British Medical Association, Freud, Jung and Havelock Ellis were invited to read papers on Psychoanalysis before the Australian Medical Congress in Sydney in 1911. Freud's paper "On Psychoanalysis" was read before that Congress and was printed, for the first time, in the October 1989 issue of The Scientific Proceedings of the Australian Psychoanalytic Society.

Dr. Roy Winn was the first analyst to practice in Australia. Returning to Australia after the First World War and after having some analysis in London, he worked as an analyst in private practice in Sydney for a period of some thirty years, in isolation, until 1960 when he retired.

As early as 1930 Winn, who was Honorary Assistant Physician at Sydney Hospital, published a paper entitled "Psychology in Relation to Medical Pracitice" in the *Medical Journal of Australia.* This was followed in February 1936, when he was an Associate Member of the British Psychoanalytical Society, by an article in the same journal entitled "Psychoanalysis and General Practice". This paper provoked the most critical and scathing attacks on analysis, one from a Professor of Medicine and another from a leading psychiatrist who was later to become the New South Wales Government Psychiatrist. In these attacks psychoanalysis was described as the work of 'quacks', and among other scurrilous remarks it was claimed that [...] the theory of Infantile Sexuality is the greatest libel that has ever been published about the human race". One of the writers asserted that "[...] a scientific journal is hardly the place for such balderdash".

These remarks are expressive of the prevailing attitude of the medical establishment of the time and of the alien environment Winn worked in during the early years. It might be added however that there was a minority interested and favourably disposed to psychoanalysis, for in the same Journal referred to, two other prominent psychiatrists wrote to the Editor supporting Winn and psychoanalysis. Despite opposition, Winn continued to speak up for Analysis, and in March 1936 published in the *Australian Medical Journal* "Contributions of Psychoanalysis to General Medicine", and in 1940 "Psychoanalysis and Allied Forms of Psychotherapy".

In 1939 Dr. Siegfried Fink, an Associate Member of the Swiss Society, migrated to Sydney. After spending some time working in State hospitals in order to have his medical qualifications accepted, Fink practised as an analyst in Sydney until he died in the early sixties.

In the period before World War II, keen interest was shown in psychoanalysis, not only in Psychiatry but in the wider intellectual community. Educationalists, churchmen, the judiciary, philosophers and psychologists had all been intrigued by the promise and the challenge the new 'depth Psychology' offered. In Melbourne an enthusiastic group of supporters, including an Anglican Bishop and a number of psychiatrists, together with the support of Roy Winn from Sydney, actively worked to support the efforts being made at the time by Ernest Jones to enable psychoanalysts to migrate to Australia. As early as 1938, Jones had raised the possibility of six analysts from Europe migrating to Australia and New Zealand. Despite the support given by a number of influential people both in Australia and in Europe, considerable difficulty was encountered in obtaining Government support and approval for displaced European analysts to enter the country.

As events transpired, none moved to New Zealand and it was only possible for one of the six to come to Australia. That was Dr. Clara Lazar-Geroe from Budapest. With the strong support of Dr. Paul Dane, a psychiatrist, and the generous financial bequest made by Miss Lorna Traill, the Melbourne Institute was established in 1940. Dr. Geroe commenced work the following year. As the first, and for many years the only analyst in Melbourne, Dr. Geroe was faced with a difficult and lonely task, for although there were a number of keen and loyal supporters, establishing psychoanalysis and especially psychoanalytic training without the support of other analysts was a lonely pioneering task. The Board of Directors of the Melbourne Institute from the beginning was comprised of interested psychiatrists with Roy Winn as the only analyst. This arrangement whereby non-psychoanalysts were members of the Institute Board continued until 1964 when Dr. Reynolds retired as Chairman.

Dr. Geroe, from the outset, saw her major task as that of presenting psychoanalysis to a large and diverse audience with an interest in mental health. She addressed herself with vigour to this task and for many years a great many seminars were conducted for psychiatrists as well as for educationalists and parents. Very early on she established a Child Guidance Clinic in which she was assisted by a number of lay people interested in the psychoanalytic approach. This clinic, which provided psychoanalytic services for those who were unable to pay, continued to function up to the early sixties, although its viability was reduced by the existence of a Commonwealth Health Insurance Scheme which provided cover for psychoanalytic treatment. The Clinic was finally closed in 1968 when it was decided that analysts in training should take responsibility for the selection and management of their own cases.

Acting as a Training Analyst and being solely responsible for the development of training to the standard of Associate Member was, however, a most difficult task to demand of any analyst working in isolation, and for many years Dr. Geroe filled this role despite the serious limitation of resources.

One of the arrangements made by those (notably Ernest Jones) encouraging Dr. Geroe's migration, was that she was made a Training Analyst of the British Society. Another, which was, in time, to create many difficulties, was an agreement that Melbourne was to function as a branch of the British Society. This arrangement was made so that whoever was trained in Australia would, subject to certain conditions, become an Associate member of that Society. This arrangement was agreed to by the British Society and was regularly reported in that Society's Annual Report. It continued until it was challenged by the IPA in 1965. The conditions laid down by the British Society were that those candidates trained by Dr. Geroe would, on her recommendation, and subject to their submitting a written clinical-theoretical paper on one of their analysed cases, be admitted to Associate Membership of the Society. This meant that for those analysts trained in Australia until the arrangement was rescinded in 1968, the one analyst, Dr. C. Geroe, was responsible for their selection, analysis, teaching, supervision, assessment and, finally, for recommending them for election to Associate Membership. Such an arrangement would not, of course, be acceptable today in any component Society of the IPA. However, it should be remembered that it was the only possible arrangement if training was to proceed in Australia. It should also be remembered that analytic training fifty years ago was far less sophisticated than it is today and that coming from Hungary, where the tradition of the personal analyst also being the supervisor was standard practice, meant that this mixture of roles was not as alien to Geroe's way of working as it would be to contemporary analysts. The continuation of these arrangements which became the acceptable mode of training in Australia was, in time, to prove a great difficulty for Geroe and a source of considerable conflict in the Australian Society.

In the twenty years from 1941 when she first commenced training, Dr. Geroe analysed many people, including a number of analytic trainees, but by 1961 however, only three had qualified as Associate Members. They were Drs. Graham in 1952, Southwood in 1953 and Rothfield in 1956. Many others who had been in analysis with her for lengthy periods had to wait longer before they were approved by her for qualification. Dr. Graham, who had initially been in analysis with Winn in Sydney and later moved to Melbourne, and Southwood, who had moved to Adelaide and commuted to Melbourne for part of his training, had both become Members, and in the late fifties were both involved in the training scheme.

In 1957 Vera Roboz, who had trained in Budapest, moved to Melbourne. Her acceptance as an Associate Member of the British Society was delayed for 5 years until 1962, although she was active in analytic practice and the affairs of the Melbourne Institute all that time. Six years later she was admitted to full membership. She continued to make important contributions to the practice and teaching of analysis in this country until the time of her death in 1989. In 1949 Dr. Andrew Peto, also a Hungarian who was a Member of the British Society, moved to Sydney. Although Peto was a respected Training Analyst his medical qualifications were not accepted in New South Wales and despite representations from many quarters he could not gain acceptance. This was, ultimately, the reason for his departure from Australia in 1955 to take up an appointment to the Albert Einstein University in New York where he continued to practise until his death in 1986.

When Peto arrived, the Sydney Institute was established by a generous bequest by Roy Winn. The management of this Institute, unlike the one in Melbourne, was solely in the hands of psychoanalysts. The intention was to enable training to take place in Sydney, as the problem of distance between the capital cities was then, as is now, a serious handicap to training. Distances of 600 miles or more make it very difficult for the regular or frequent contact between analysts which is so important if the work of each other is to be understood and appreciated. It also creates serious difficulties for regular supervision. Peto's departure resulted in a lengthy delay before training on any scale could be undertaken in Sydney. During his stay Peto did analyze a number of psychiatrists and medical practitioners but only one of these, Dr. Maida Hall, proceeded to full training as an analyst. Dr. Hall, who subsequent to her training in Sydney spent some time in London where she gained her membership of that Society, was the first Australian analyst to practice Kleinian-oriented analysis. She unfortunately died in 1962.

In 1952 the analysts in Melbourne, Sydney und Adelaide who together totalled four, established themselves as a group which they named "The Australian Society of Psychoanalysts" (a name that was retained until 1968), and which they described as a sub-branch of the British Psychoanalytical Society. This organization of course had no validity either with the British Society or the IPA. Its members were simply Associate Members and Members of the British Society living in Australia without any corporate existence. That Society acted as the body of psychoanalysts in Australia and served as the organization for conferences and scientific meetings, which from the early forties to 1967 were attended by analysts, students and interested psychiatrists. From 1965 until 1968 this Society of Australian Psychoanalysts was actively involved in working for the establishment of the Australian Study Group.

From the time Peto left Australia 1955 to the early sixties there was little development in analysis, though regular meetings of the Australian Society of Psychoanalysts were held at which both analysts and students-in-training presented papers. After what had been hoped would be the start of psychoanalytic growth in Australia, Melbourne once again became the centre, as there alone was training available.

In Sydney, Institute meetings continued to be held which a group of interested psychiatrists attended. Janet Nield, who had been involved as a trainee for a long period, initially in Melbourne, and whose qualification as an Associate Member was not accorded her until 1962, played an important role representing analysis through her teaching and supervision of psychiatrists and other therapists at the Children's Hospital in Sydney.

From 1963 onwards there was a progressive increase in the number of analysts. Prof. Martin had returned from London, Dr. Brookes, who had gained his Associate membership of the British Society, commenced practice in Sydney and there was an increase in the number of candidates qualifying from Melbourne. Prior to this happening, there were in Australia but 8 analysts, five in Melbourne, two in Sydney and one in Adelaide. As the numbers increased from 1973 onwards, ferment developed concerning the nature and hegemony of training that centred about Melbourne. There was a growing interest in broadening the base of training. This was linked with the growing awareness in London that the authority that had earlier been accorded Dr. Geroe to train in the name of the British Society was no longer defensible. In 1965 Southwood, who was at that time the President of the Australian Society of Psychoanalysts, had discussions with the British Society on the matter. This was the beginning of the British Society's move to disentangle itself and to involve the IPA in the problem of training in Australia.

While there existed a considerable amount of friction in Australia about the role of a number of individuals and their involvement in the various discussions, the British Society arranged with the IPA to assume responsibility for training in Australia. This it did at the Copenhagen Congress in 1967, when it appointed a Sponsoring Committee to organize and establish the Australian Study Group. The members of this Committee were Dr. F. Wride, Chairman, Dr. A. Limentani, Secretary, and Drs. Montessori, M. Mitscherlich-Nielsen, L. Munro, L. Rangell and Ilse Hellman.

In August 1968, Drs. Limentani (London) and L. Rangell (Los Angeles), representing the Sponsoring Committee, visited Australia. Agreement was reached between them and the members of the Australian group about future development towards Provisional Society status, about broadening the training arrangements, the formation of a Curriculum Committee, and about the need for a new constitution. The Sponsoring Committee revoked the earlier training arrangement and appointed a new body, The Training Committee in Australia (TCIA), which became responsible for training in Australia and answerable to the IPA through the Sponsoring Committee. The members appointed to that Committee were Drs. Geroe, Southwood, Graham and Rothfield, Vera Roboz and Professor R. Martin. Some months later Dr. Brookes was invited by the Committee to become a member. The two representatives of the Sponsoring Committee not only appointed four new Training Analysts, Dr. Rothfield, Vera Roboz, Janet Neild and Professor Martin, but they also heard presentations from a number of the Australian analysts, two seeking Associate Membership and four Membership. It should be noted that prior to this time it was necessary for an Associate Member wishing to gain full Membership to present himself, in person, before the Membership Committee of the British Society in London.

In 1970 Dr. L. Munro, another member of the Sponsoring Committee, visited all three States and gave valuable assistance to the newly formed Study Group. In that same year Dr. Southwood resigned as President of the Australian Society of Psychoanalysts and was replaced by Professor Martin, who continued the organizational work required in preparation for the Australian Study Group's acceptance as a Provisional Society at the 1971 Congress in Vienna. He went on to serve as the Foundation President of the newly created Australian Psychoanalytical Society.

In the early years of the new Society's life, a great deal of time and effort was devoted to the task of reforming the Society's training procedures. There was still a great deal of opposition to the reforms that were being urged by the newer group. Much of the difficulty was, of course, linked with personal differences of outlook and theoretical orientation, with the difficulties of communication that long distances between centres heightened, and to the beliefs that the entrenched authority of the earlier group was being threatened and that there was a deliberate attempt to prevent training taking place other than in Melbourne and Sydney.

The organization of the new Society and the important role that training was to occupy meant that for a long time almost all of the attention and time of the Society was devoted to the issues of training and the establishment of standards. This, combined with the relatively few analysts available, meant that a great deal of authority was given to the Education Committee, which now took over, on behalf of the Society, the functions that had hitherto been carried out by the TCIA on behalf of the Sponsoring Committee. This Committee, which was elected by the Society, was responsible for all aspects of training. It thus had the difficult task of replacing the older methods with new ones, for designing and monitoring programmes in all three centres, for selecting candidates and for authorising their progression to Associate Membership. It also had the responsibility for assessing and recommending Associate Members who sought to become Members and finally, for assessing and recommending for or against members wishing to undertake the analysis and supervision of candidates.

The work of the Education Committee was first of all to replace the previous system that had worked well enough in the past, but which lent itself to the charge of nepotism and which was so widely at variance with contemporary psychoanalytic training, with more democratic procedures. Its other task was to ensure that the standards of the Australian Psychoanalytic Society were firmly established and accepted. This inevitably resulted in some conflict of interest, for the understandable desire to increase numbers did, in one centre, pose the threat that expediency would influence the standard of training in that centre. The Education Committee's action in asserting its right, on behalf of the Society, to decide on the competence of those who could train and on the viability of a centre's resources was strongly contested and led to a long standing controversy concerning the autonomy of individual centres.

The Education Committee was faced with the invidious task of having to dismantle the earlier system, where the analyst had almost exclusive say in determining the candidate's future, and of replacing it with a more appropriate one. In addition it also had to struggle to preserve the right of the

Society, rather than the separate centres, to determine training standards. Inevitably there arose many difficulties and very often feelings of discrimination when its decisions were unfavourable to the hopes of some individuals or groups. Some of these difficulties continued, and in later years resulted in one centre (Adelaide) in desperation seeking direct intervention by the IPA. This eventually appointed a Site Visiting Committee to investigate the problem. The work of this SVC and a second one which made its final visit in 1987 resulted in the restructuring of the Australian Society which is described below.

The first Site Visiting Committee, comprising Drs. E. Joseph, J. McLaughlan and Prof. R. Moses, was in 1983. Theirs was a difficult task for none of them was familiar with the history and culture in which the Australian Society had developed, the distances between the cities were considerable and the Society itself was divided. There were very few members at that time who did not hold very intense feelings about the nature and the origin of the problem that had led to the visit of the SVC. Despite their very serious efforts to reconcile the differences, the Committee's efforts were not very effective. The majority of members of the Society were left with the feeling that the SVC had too readily reached its conclusion that the plaintiff centre had been badly treated, and that the Committee had failed to appreciate the efforts that had been made by the majority of the Society to find solutions to the problems. In the face of continued pressure the Committee was unable to consistently maintain a point of view acceptable to the majority of members of the Australian Society. The problem, especially as it revolved around training and the claim for autonomy by one of the centres, continued, and in 1986 the IPA appointed a second Site Visiting Committee to further investigate the problem.

The Australian Society expressed its dissatisfaction with the composition of the first SVC, and insisted that as the Australian Society had a long and continuous association with the British Society, the new visiting committee should include at least one representative from that Society. The IPA agreed with this demand and the second committee comprised Prof. J. Sandler (Britain) and Dr. A. Cooper (USA).

The task of the new committee was, in many ways, easier than that of their predecessor. The membership of the Society was larger and a substantial number of new graduates and recent arrivals were unfamiliar with the past history; and consequently they felt less interested and involved in the issue. Over the intervening years the older members had grown weary of the persistent divisiveness and conflicts in the Society and were eager for a solution to be found.

The new Site Visiting Committeee approached the problem from a rather different standpoint from the previous one. They were intent on widening the issues from the initial problems of standards and the role of Adelaide in the Australian Society. They were concerned with a formula for power sharing, of increasing the membership and also the number of training analysts and of developing the scientific life of the Society. After lengthy discussions about the implementation of these proposals the membership accepted the Site Visiting Committee's new style of organisation and proceeded to adopt a new constitution. A number of decisions which the SVC believed would resolve the immediate problem were taken. Analysts over the age of seventy were excluded from all standing committees of the Society and from training rights. A number of new training analysts were appointed and greater autonomy was accorded to local centres.

Under the new constitution which emerged from the work of the second SVC the Australian Society today operates largely as a federation of three branches to which responsibility for training has been devolved by the Society. Each branch has a considerable degree of autonomy although they are required to work within the training guidelines laid down by the Society and to coordinate their activities through a committee of the Society in which they have equal representation. In each of the three centres there is an Institute which is free to undertake any psychoanalytic activities it chooses other than training, provided these do not contravene the constitution of the IPA and that they do not conflict with the work of the Australian Society. This arrangement has meant that a great deal of psychoanalytic work other than training is now taking place in each city. This includes lectures, workshops, seminars and the provision of services such as supervision and clinical discussions for members of associated professions. Psychoanalysis today is well regarded by the psychiatric and psychotherapeutic communities. It is also increasingly being appreciated by the Universities. Much of this interest has been due to the work of the local Institutions, which, over the past few years, have introduced important public relations programmes.

The Society, which is governed by an elected executive, alone has authority to train and to qualify analysts. It is responsible for all national decisions concerning analysis, for regular Scientific meetings of the Society and for the publication of the Scientific Proceedings. Currently the existing organisation functions satisfactorily. Whether, in time, and with the inevitable growth in the membership, there will be a demand for the Branches to become separate Societies remains to be seen. Certainly in a continent as large as Australia where the distances between cities are comparable with the distances between London, Rome and Copenhagen, the presence of a large number of analysts in any one city would create a demand for a separate Society that would be hard to argue against. At present, however, the degree of autonomy allowed each branch and the relatively small membership has temporarily quelled separatist feelings. Although psychoanalysis in Australia has a long history, the growth of the Society was for many years slow. A combination of circumstances may be invoked to explain this but it is certainly the case that isolation has been a very important one. The attraction for established analysts to migrate or for students to seek training is severely reduced if there is no established community of analysts present. There is now a large enough number of analysts in each of the three cities to attract new members.

Australia has one important feature that distinguishes it from most other countries and which is playing an important role in the growth and use of psychoanalysis. That is the existence of a generous Commonwealth Health Insurance Scheme. This scheme, unlike that in most other countries, covers the cost of analysis for the patients of medically qualified analysts except those who are in training, regardless of the frequency or duration of their treatment. Thus apart form a nominal annual sum a patient with a medical analyst charging the scheduled fee is able to have an analysis of five times weekly over a period of years and have it covered by the scheme. This has undoubtedly made it possible for many patients who might not have been able to afford analysis to have one and has in an important way facilitated the growth of the Society.

The provision of Health Insurance cover for patients in analysis has not, however, been an unmixed blessing. A number of other difficulties have inevitably arisen. The most obvious one being the complications that develop in the relation between the analyst and the patient when a third party is involved. This is one that creates some difficulties for every medical analyst but in general has not been insuperable.

The fee charged by medical analysts, which is linked with that of other medical specialists, has however created a somewhat different problem for the non-medical analysts who make up 30% of the membership. These analysts, particularly junior ones and non-medical trainees, sometimes experience difficulty in obtaining patients who can afford to pay a fee that approximates the medical fee. The scheduled fee charged by medical analysts for a five times a week analysis amounts to a sum that is approximately the average adult weekly wage, hence few patients are able or willing to pay that amount for an analysis with a non-medical analyst. Most non-medical analysts therefore negotiate a lower fee for their analytic patients and supplement their practices by providing briefer analytically oriented psychotherapy, where necessary.

There is, however, another side to this problem. Because medical analysts are able to treat a range of patients who, without insurance benefits could not afford analysis, they rarely have vacancies for new patients. As a result of this the patients who are able to afford to pay for their own treatments are the very ones who seek analysis with non-medical analysts. In recent times there has been a marked increase in the number of non-medical persons, particularly women, applying for analytic training. If this trend continues and the proportion of non-medical analysts in the Society continues to increase it will be interesting to discover whether the number of patients who can afford treatment in their own right will be large enough for the present situation to continue. If it does not that could result in a change in the nature of non-medical analysts' practices which could, in turn, change the nature of the Society.

As early as 1971 the Society was involved in a variety of discussions both internally and with psychiatric organisations and with Government instrumentalities about the issue of medical benefits. Initially there was considerable conflict between members concerning the proposal that the Government should be approached with the request that benefits for analysis should be paid to patients of all analysts, medical or not. Some anxiety was expressed at the time that such an application would not simply not succeed but would draw attention to the fact that psychoanalytic treatment is not exclusively a treatment provided by medical practitioners. There has been, however, in recent years an acceptance by the Society that benefits under a Medical Insurance Scheme will not be paid to non medical practitioners and that it would de fruitless to pursue that matter further. While this view has been accepted by the membership there is still some underlying resentment felt by some of the more junior non medical analysts and some students who, while doing precisely the same work as their medical colleagues, feel they are disadvantaged financially because their patients are not eligible for health insurance benefits. However, this feeling is, in general, mitigated by the knowledge that a government subsidised scheme does enable a range of patients from a wide socio-economic background to be analysed and that this greatly strengthens the demand for and the future of analysis in Australia.

Psychoanalysis in Australia today is now well established. Although the origins of analysis were very much in a particular Hungarian tradition, that orientation is now nowhere to be encountered. While there is no one clear style or theory of analysis being practised in the country, the influence of the British Society is clearly evident. Most of the analysts in the Society have either been analysed and trained by Members of the British Society resident in Australia or have themselves been trained in London. Just as in the British Society there is no single theoretical orientation so, too, is that the case in the Australian Society. Most of the members subscribe to a theoretical position based on object relations and are influenced in their clinical work by such British writers as Balint, Fairbairn and Winnicott while a smaller number are Kleinian in their orientation.

Psychoanalytic training which is available to medical graduates and to others with appropriate University degrees and relevant clinical experience is spread over a period, on average, of five years. Candidates are required to analyse a minimum of two patients, five times weekly, and to receive supervision on each case from an approved senior analyst other than their personal analyst. On the recommendation of their local branch they are elected as Associate Members by the Australian Society. Training in child analysis, which has recently been introduced, is available to those who have already satisfied the requirements for Associate membership of the Australian Society.

Members and Associate Members of the Australian Psychoanalytical Society have equal rights within the Society except that Associate Members are not eligible for election to the governing body of the Society (the Executive Committee) nor to be training analysts. Membership of the Society may be attained two years after qualification as an Associate Member and after providing satisfactory evidence to a small committee of senior analysts representing the Society of one's competence and that one is engaged to a substantial degree in genuine analytic work. Approximately seventy percent of the membership of the Society are full members. To be appointed as a training analyst one has to be an experienced Member and to demonstrate one's analytic competence to an ad hoc committee of training analysts, whose findings are the basis on which the Training Appointments Committee recommends to the Executive of the Society, which makes the final decision.

The total membership of the Australian Society at the time of writing is 62. Of these, 26 belong to the Melbourne Branch, 26 to the Sydney Branch and 9 to the Adelaide Branch. The remainder reside outside the cities where there are branches of the Society.

Journals

The Australian Psychoanalytical Society has published since March 1982 a journal for limited readership entitled *Scientific Proceedings.* It is intended in the near future that this will appear as *The Journal of the Australian Psychoanalytical Society* and that the restricted readership condition will be abandoned. There is also the Journal of the Australian Psychotherapy Association entitled *Australian Journal of Psychotherapy.* It is published by that Association and has appeared twice annually since it first appeared in 1982.

Institutions*

Australian Psychoanalytic Society
14 Havilah Street, Chatswood, NSW 2067
Tel.: 61-2-411 58 59; Fax: 61-2-331 26 39

Melbourne Institute of Psychoanalysis
400 Tooronga Rd., East Hawthorn. Vic. 3127

Adelaide Institute of Psychoanalysis
1 Frederick St., Frewville S.A. 50 63

Sydney Institute of Psychoanalysis
5 Penshurst St., Willoughby NSW 2068

Professor Reginald T. Martin, 26 Viret Street, Hunters Hill 2110, NSW

* There exists also an "Australian & New Zealand Association of Psychotherapy" (ANZAP) and a Psychotherapy Section of the "Royal Australian & New Zealand College of Psychiatry" (RANZCP). Courtesy Eng-Kong Tan. The editor.

Brazil

by Germano Vollmer Filho

In this chapter, which deals with psychoanalysis in Brazil, I intend initially to describe, through a historical summary, the hard work of the pioneers who introduced and spread the word of psychoanalysis in Brazil. It is also my intention to briefly report on theoretical approaches that have influenced Brazilian psychoanalytic thought during recent years.

History

Nowadays there are, in Brazil, four Psychoanalytical Societies and two study groups. The oldest is the Brazilian Psychoanalytical Society of São Paulo, and next the Psychoanalytical Society of Rio de Janeiro and the Psychoanalytical Society of Porto Alegre. There is a study group in Recife and a more recent one in Pelotas, also in Rio Grande do Sul. The Brazilian Association of Psychoanalysis encompasses the four societies and the two study groups.

The history of the psychoanalytic movement in Brazil can be divided into two periods. The first starts in the middle of 1919 with the publication of Freud's first papers and the foundation of the first groups interested in psychoanalysis, and goes up to 1937 with Dr. Adelheid Lucy Koch's arrival in Brazil to begin the training of psychoanalysts in São Paulo. The second period of the psychoanalytic movement in Brazil goes from 1937 to the present.

We should point out that during these early stages it was in São Paulo and in Rio de Janeiro that the first groups to study Freud's work were formed. This is well described in the works of Professor Virginia Bicudo, Dr. Luiz de Almeida Prado Galvão and of Dr. Marialzira Perestrello. These authors emphasize the pioneer role of the Professor of Psychiatry, Franco da Rocha, from the School of Medicine of São Paulo and the outstanding work of Durval Marcondes as showing the way for the beginning and spreading of psychoanalytical training in Brazil

In 1919 Professor Franco da Rocha gave a lecture at the School of Medicine entitled "About Delirium in General" in which he pointed out the possibility of understanding delirium, dreams and literary creation, having as a basis Freud's discoveries about the Unconscious. The lecture, published in the well-known paper, "O Estado de São Paulo", captured the interest of the medical student Durval Marcondes who, concluding his course in 1924, started to use, based on his sensitivity and intuition, the psychoanalytical concepts which he read about in books and in the International Journal of Psychoanalysis, to which he had subscribed since 1919.

In 1926, Durval Marcondes presented, as a thesis to become a Professor of Literature at the Ginasio do Estado, the paper – "Aesthetic Symbolism in Literature" – an essay in literary criticism based on what he had learned from psychoanalysis. The thesis, with a preface by Franco da Rocha, received a letter of praise from Freud on November 18, 1926.

One year later, Durval Marcondes organized a group to study and spread psychoanalysis; on October 24, 1927 the Brazilian Psychoanalytical Society was founded. Franco da Rocha was elected president and Durval Marcondes was elected secretary. The formation of the society was communicated to Freud who, in a letter to Ferenczi on January 4, 1928, expressed his satisfaction about the event.

The new society decided to spread the word of psychoanalysis to other states and to found a national society. Durval Marcondes, as representative of the São Paulo Society, organized a meeting in Rio de Janeiro, then capital of Brazil, of a group of people interested in the study of psychoanalysis.

The meeting was held at the National Psychopathological Hospital on June 17, 1928. Dr. Juliano Moreira was elected president of the Rio de Janeiro Branch of the Brazilian Psychoanalytical Society and Dr. Porto Carneiro was elected secretary.

The new society was recognized by the executive committee of the International Psychoanalytic Association at the 2nd International Congress of Psychoanalysis held in Oxford on July 30, 1929. The Brazilian Society lasted only a few years but during its existence it was responsible for several scientific activities which were the decisive factors for the distribution of psychoanalysis in the country in a stable and lasting way. Among the activities there were courses, conferences, publications, etc. Luiz Almeida Prado Galvão, in his paper about the history of psychoanalysis in São Paulo, states that Durval Marcondes wanted to make psychoanalysis known to medical doctors so that its usefulness would spread to medicine in general. In an interview given to the newspaper *Folha de Noite* on August 19, 1929, Marcondes says: "It is not only for specialists in nervous disorders that psychoanalytic knowledge is useful; it is also helpful in the General Clinic, too, where therapeutics is closely linked with the patient's emotional situation. The doctor's personal influence, so relevant in certain cases, finds support in the patient's emotional disposition which is something the general practitioner has to recognize."

All the effort Durval Marcondes dedicated to the distribution of psychoanalysis had the purpose of the foundation of a Psychoanalytical Institute in Brazil modelled on the International Psychoanalytical Association. However, a training analyst had to come to Brazil for the Psychoanalytical Institute to become viable.

In 1932, there was a first attempt to bring Rene Spitz, a foreign analyst, to Brazil, who was frustrated due to political problems in the country.

There was another frustrated attempt in 1934. In that year the University of São Paulo was being organized. Durval Marcondes, who thought it very important to link psycholanalytical training to the university, received a letter from A. A. Brill, then president of the Psychoanalytic Society of New York, asking him to organize opportunities for work for European psychoanalysts who wanted to move to South America.

Durval Marcondes attempt to get the analysts accepted by the university was also unsuccessful. In spite of these initial difficulties to create a Psychoanalytical Institute in São Paulo, Durval Marcondes went on with his project, which finally, in 1937, succeeded, with the arrival of a training analyst in Brazil.

In October 1936, Dr. Adelheid Lucy Koch started a trip to Brazil with her family, arriving in São Paulo in November. The preliminary arrangements for Dr. Koch's emigration were made during the International Congress in Marienbad in 1936. At this congress, knowing that Dr. Koch intended to emigrate to Brazil, Ernest Jones, then the IPA's president, gave Dr. Koch Durval Marcondes's name telling her he was interested in bringing a training analyst to Brazil.

The official meeting between Dr. Koch and Durval Marcondes took place in July 1937 in the latter's consulting room. According to Luiz Almeido Prado Galvão, "this date marks the beginning of the training of analysts in Latin America".

Dr. Koch, who had graduated in Medicine at Berlin University in 1924, held, for several years, the roles of analyst, teacher and supervisor of the initial group of candidates in São Paulo.

In 1929, she started her psychoanalytical training as a candidate at the Institute of the Berlin Society; she did her training analysis with Dr. Otto Fenichel for four and a half years. Besides the theoretical course she took in Berlin, Dr. Koch worked under the supervision of Dr. Salomé Kempner and Theresa Benedek. In November 1935 she was elected as a member of the Psychoanalytical Society of Berlin, after presenting a paper entitled "Analysis of Resistance in a Narcissistic Neurosis".

The initial group, which became the embryo of the future society of São Paulo had, as its headquarters, Durval Marcondes' consulting room and as first students, Durval Marcondes, Virginia Bicudo, Flávio Dias and Darcy Mendonça Uchôa, joined, a little later, by Frank Philips, Ligia Amaral, Henrique Mendes and others.

In 1944 the IPA recognized the initial group as an affiliated society and in 1951, at the International Psychoanalytical Congress in Amsterdam, it was given full status as the Brazilian Psychoanalytic Society.

We should point out that the spread of the psychoanalytic movement in São Paulo was not limited to the increase in the number of analysts and to the growing of the Society. Even before the recognition of the Society by the IPA, Durval Marcondes founded, in 1938, the Department of Mental Hygiene at the Health Service of São Paulo. In this department, as Galvão notes, psychoanalytic knowledge was used to benefit the community in general and, more specifically, to solve psychological problems of the students in state schools. Several members of the Brazilian Psychoanalytic Society of São Paulo contributed with their voluntary work to this department, such as Virginia Bicudo, Ligia Amaral and Henrique Mendes.

In 1940, in the Sociology and Politics School, linked with the University of São Paulo, the first course of psychoanalysis at university level in the country was founded. Durval Marcondes was the first Professor, followed by Professor Virginia Bicudo.

In 1954 Durval Marcondes, together with members of the Psychoanalytical Society, founded the course of clinical psychology at the University of São Paulo.

The gradual and stable influence of psychoanalytic teaching spread to all branches of human knowledge. Psychiatry, more specifically, and general medicine benefitted scientifically from psychoanalysis. The discipline of psychiatry of the School of Medicine at the University of São Paulo had as its professor Darcy Mendonça Uchôa, a member of the 1937 pioneer group.

The history of the psychoanalytic movement in Rio de Janeiro is described in detail and accurately, in the book *The History of the Brazilian Psychoanalytic Society of Rio de Janeiro*, compiled by Dr. Marialzira Perestrello. The book does not only describe the birth and growing of psychoanalysis in Rio de Janeiro, but also in other regions of Brazil, such as Bahia, Recife, São Paulo and Porto Alegre.

Dr. Marialzira divides the history of the psychoanalytic movement in Brazil into two periods, separated by the recognition of the São Paulo Society by the International Psychoanalytical Association. Another point to mark this division was the beginning of the psychoanalytic training of Drs. Danilo and Marialzira Perestrello, and Dr. Walderedo Ismael Oliveira, at the Argentinian Psychoanalytical Association, in Buenos Aires, in November 1946. The three doctors from Rio de Janeiro met, in Buenos Aires, Mário Martins and his wife Zaira, from Porto Alegre, who at that time were already finishing their psychoanalytical training. A little later Dr. José Jaime Lemmertz, also from Porto Alegre, arrived in Buenos Aires (Marialzira p. 38).

Yet another event which might be considered as a milestone dividing the two periods was the arrival of Dr. Mark Burke in Rio de Janeiro in February 1948. Dr. Burke, a medical doctor recommended by Ernest Jones, was a member of the British Psycho-Analytical Society and had undergone analysis with James Strachey.

Another predecessor of the psychoanalytic movement in Brazil was Antonio Austragésilo, a doctor at the National Mental Hospital who was renowned among Brazilian medical doctors. Since 1916 he had been writing about some of Freud's ideas (Marialzira, p. 16). However, it was José Joaquim de Campos da Costa Medeiros de Albuquerque who, for the first time in Rio de Janeiro, exposed systematically Freud's ideas. He was not a doctor, but a politician, journalist, a member and eventually president of the Brazilian Academy of Literature. On November 19, 1919 Medeiros de Albuquerque gave a lecture entitled "The Psychology of a Neurologist – Freud and his Sexual Theories", which can be considered as one of the first theoretical landmarks of psychoanalysis in Brazil.

Another important predecessor was Mauricio Campos de Medeiros, Professor of the National School of Medicine. He was a member of the National Academy of Medicine and of the Brazilian Academy of the Fine Arts, politician and Minister of Health, who became a Professor of Psychiatry. It was due to his initiative that the psychiatry programmes started to have psychoanalytical teaching elements. Mauricio de Medeiros was also the founder of the Childhood Orientation Clinic at the Institute of Psychiatry having invited as collaborators, two psychoanalysts, Marialzira Perestrello (1953) and Décio de Souza (1955), who gave the clinic a psychoanalytical orientation. However, it was Julio Pires Porto Carrero (1887–1937), a medical doctor born in Olinda, Professor of Forensic Medicine at the University of Rio de Janeiro, who was the most important person for the spreading of psychoanalysis in the then capital of Brazil. According to Marialzira Perestrello, the importance of Porto Carrero's work is based on its seriousness and scientific element.

Porto Carrero started his prolific scientific production in 1924, writing firstly a paper on hysteric monoplegia, cured using Freud's theories. In the same year he presented to the Society of Neurology "A Case of Sinistrosis Treated by Psychoanalysis". For approx. 10 years Porto Carrero published his lectures and articles. His scientific studies between the years of 1925 and

1929 appeared in his book *Psychoanalytic Essays,* published in 1929. This book was a tribute to Freud, who wrote a letter to the author saying that chance could sometimes affect feelings because the 'beautiful essays' were received exactly on May 5 and had been a most treasured birthday present. Freud also said that Dr. Eitingon, from Berlin, was in his house visiting and he had shown him Porto Carrero's letter. They were both pleased with the good news of the Brazilian colleagues and were surprised to see how many themes Porto Carrero had analysed in his book. It is important to point out that Porto Carrero studied German to be able to read Freud in the original.

In his essays, Porto Carrero studied the clinical and theoretical aspects of psychoanalysis as well as their application to education and sociology. Thus, one can find in his book essays entitled "Clinical Aspects of Psychoanalysis", "Variations on Narcissism", "Curing Alcoholism through Psychoanalysis", "Education and Psychoanalysis", "The Student's Character According to Psychoanalysis" and "Application of Psychoanalysis to the Child's Moral Formation".

Besides the essays and a series of lectures, Porto Carrero published three other books: *Depth Psychology or Psychoanalysis,* in 1932 and, in the following year, *Sex and Culture* and in 1934, *Greatness and Misery of Sex.*

Other predecessors of the psychoanalytical movement in Rio de Janeiro besides Proto Carrero, were, according to Marialzira Perestrello, Drs. Deodato de Moraes, Carneiro Airosa, Murilo de Campos, Inaldo de Lyra Neves Manta and Aloysio de Paula. The name of Arthur Ramos de Araujo Pereira (1903–1949) is also of great importance among them. Arthur Ramos, who was from the state of Alagoas, graduated in Medicine in Bahia and was soon influenced by psychoanalytical concepts. He was a psychiatrist and forensic doctor and when he moved to Rio de Janeiro he became Professor of Anthropology and Ethnography. He left extensive scientific contributions based on psychoanalytic knowledge, beginning with his Ph.D. dissertation in Medicine, *Primitivism and Madness* in 1925.

Among other titles written by Arthur Ramos there are *Augusto dos Anjos, under the Light of Psychoanalysis* (1926), *Study of Psychoanalysis* (1931), *Freud, Adler and Jung* (1933), and *Psychiatry and Psychoanalysis* (1933).

In 1934, Artur Ramos moved to Rio de Janeiro where he started writing about Social Psychology and Anthropology and, due to his great interest in African culture, he became an internationally recognized specialist in this field. He was working at UNESCO in Paris when he died suddenly.

Psychoanalytical training started properly in Rio de Janeiro, with two, mostly medical, groups. The first, formed by psychiatrists from the Mental Illnesses National Service, founded, in 1944, the Juliano Moreira Study

Centre. The founders were Drs. Danilo Perestrello, Walderedo Ismael de Oliveira, José Afonso Netto and Julio Peternostro. The new Study Centre wanted, after some time, to bring a training analyst to Brazil to make analytical training possible according to the standards of the International Psychoanalytical Association.

Due to several unsuccessful attempts at doing this, in 1945 some members of the Study Centre had the idea of doing their analytical training abroad. In 1946 Danilo and Marialzira Perestrello went to Buenos Aires to start their training. In March of the following year it was Walderedo I. de Oliveira's turn. It should be added that in 1945 Alcyon B. Bahia, a psychiatrist from Rio de Janeiro, was already undergoing psychoanalytical training in Buenos Aires.

While this group studied in Buenos Aires, another group founded, in Rio de Janeira, the Brazilian Institute of Psychoanalysis and elected its first executive council in December 1947, with Drs. Domicio de Arruda Câmara, José Mariz de Moraes, João José Barbosa Quental and João Cortes de Barros.

The new institution, immediately established contact with Dr. Ernest Jones , the IPA's president, and asked for his help to bring a training analyst to Brazil. After some initial difficulties, Dr. Mark Burke, associate member of the British Psycho-Analytical Society, who had undergone analysis with James Strachery, arrived in Rio de Janeiro on February 2, 1948. In the same month the candidates Drs. José Mariz de Moraes, Januário S. Bittencourt, Sebastião Fontes Lorenço, João José Barbosa Quental, Domicio Arruda Câmara, Manoel T. Moreira Lyra, João Cortes de Barros, Luiz de Lacerda Werneck and the professors Edgard Guimarães de Almeida and Pedro Figueiredo started their analysis. A little later, Dr. Mário Pacheco de Almeida Prado joined this group and said to Dr. Marialzira Perestrello: "During 1948 the Brazilian Institute of Psychoanalysis experienced moments of total integration, not only internally but also externally". Scientific exchange trips to São Paulo, Buenos Aires, Santiago and London were undertaken by the members of the new Institute. They were still attempting to bring another training analyst to Rio; that was finally accomplished in 1948 with the arrival, in Brazil, of a German psychoanalyst, Dr. Werner Kemper. In the following year, Drs. Erika de Almeida, Inês Besouchet, Zenaira Aranha, João Marafelli Filho, Gerson Borsoi, Fábio Leite Lobo, Souza Viana, Inaura Carneiro Leão and Celestino Prunes, the latter from Porto Alegre, started their analyses with Dr. Kemper. When Dr. Prunes went back to Porto Alegre he was one of the founders of the Psychoanalytical Society there. Also a member of this first group was Dr. Luiz Guimarães Dahlheim, who later would be the IPA's vice-president.

The two groups were on good terms until 1951 when the Institute suffered a crisis caused by the fact that Dr. Kemper appointed his wife to the position of training analyst without her having any title which qualified her to work as a psychoanalyst. The Institute demanded that Mrs. Kemper cease this work. The couple refused to do what was asked and, as a consequence, both were dismissed.

After this, the Institute started trying to bring in another analyst, but they only succeeded in 1954 with the coming of Frank Philips and Emilio Rodrigué. The candidates then received great help through seminars and supervisions which were, of course, extremely necessary at this point. It is important to say that it have been these two training analysts who introduced, in a systematic way, Melanie Klein's ideas and concepts. Philips supervised seminars on Melanie Klein (28 hours), on Rosenfeld (9 hours), on Hannah Segal (8 hours) and Paula Heimann (2 hours). The technical seminars complemented the theoretical ones and amounted to a total of 54 hours of case discussions. Rodrigue supervised 20 hours of theoretical and technical activities.

While the Brazilian Institute had the help of Frank Philips and Emilio Rodrigué, Kemper's group went on with their scientific activities with the help of the São Paulo group. Dr. Kemper's candidates had supervision with Katrin Kemper and with the analysts Adelheid Koch, Theon Sparendis, Darcy Mendonça Uchôa and Professor Virginia Bicudo.

At the beginning of 1949, the Perestrellos came back from Buenos Aires, followed by Dr. Alcyon B. Bahia. At the end of 1950 Dr. Walderedo I. de Oliveira also returned. At this time, as Dr. Marialzira points out, 'there was already a division in three groups: Burke's, Kemper's and the Argentinian group.' These three groups followed different paths in terms of society grouping. Kemper's group became official, creating the Centre of Psychoanalytical Studies and being recognized as a study group by the IPA.

The "Argentinian group" founded the Brazilian Society of Rio de Janeiro having one full member and three associate members nominated by the Argentinian Psychoanalytical Association. Kemper's group was recognized as a study group during the Business Meeting of the 18th International Psychoanalytical Congress in 1953, under the sponsorship of the São Paulo Society. In 1955, during the International Psychoanalytical Congress held in Geneva, the study group was recognized as a society affiliated to the IPA. On September 29 of the same year the Psychoanalytic Society of Rio de Janeiro was founded having as full members Werner Kemper, Fábio Leite Lobo, Gerson Borsoi, Inaura Carneiro Leão, Luis Dahlheim, Noemy Rudolfer and as associate members Celestino Prunes, João Marafelli Filho, Zenaira Aranha and Inês Besouchet.

The so-called Burke group was dispersed at the end of 1953, with Dr. Burke's departure for London. Three of his candidates also went to London to continue their training at the British Psycho-Analytical Society: Dr. Domicio Arruda Câmara started his analysis with W. Bion, Professor Edgard de Almeida with M. Balint and Dr. Manoel Thomas M. Lyra with Paula Heimann. Drs. Luiz Werneck, Cortes de Barros, Mário Pacheco de A. Prado and Pedro Ferreira e Mariz stayed in Rio de Janeiro, frequently getting together for discussion of clinical cases and psychoanalytic papers.

Approximately at this time – 1954 – Dr. Décio Soares de Souza, professor of Psychiatry at the School of Medicine of Rio Grande do Sul, arrived in Rio de Janeiro from London, where he had completed his psychoanalytical training. Dr. Décio was then an associate member of the British Psychoanalytical Society; he was a Kleinian in his theoretical and clinical approach and had a very important role in the distribution of Melanie Klein's ideas in Brazil.

In 1956 Professor Edgard de Almeida came back from London, also as an associate member of the British Society. Before him, in 1955, Dr. Henrique Mendes had also returned from London after three years of training. In the same year those who were left from Dr. Burke's group went to São Paulo to ask for Dr. Koch and Dr. Marcondes's support to become affiliated to the IPA. The condition for this support to be given was the presentation of clinical cases, which, if approved, would give the candidate the title of full member of the São Paulo Society.

The first to present a case was Dr. Mário P. de A. Prado, in April of 1956. The title of his paper was "Clinical Observations on an Obsessive Ritual and Underlying Pre-Genital Mechanisms". The other three members of Burke's group presented their papers after the formation of the study group.

During 1956 Drs. Décio de Souza and Walderedo I. de Oliveira attempted to become training analysts of the São Paulo Society. The requirement was to present theoretical clinical papers and also give clinical seminars to the candidates. The requirements were fulfilled during 1957. In this way, with the group having as members analysts from a society linked to the IPA, there were conditions for the recognitioin of a Study Group, with the support of the Society of São Paulo. This happened in 1957 during the Business Meeting of the XX International Congress in Paris.

The founding of this new group happened on October 7 of the same year at an assembly held at Dr. Walderedo de Oliveira's consulting room, in the presence of 11 members: Alcyon B. Bahia, Danilo Perestrello and Walderedo de Oliveira (full members of the Argentinian Psychoanalytical Association), Henrique Mendes (full member of the Brazilian Psychoanalytic Society of São Paulo), Décio de Souza and Edgard de Almeida (associate members of the British Psycho-Analytical Society), Marialzira Perestrello (associate member of the Argentinian Psychoanalytical Society), Mário P. de A. Prado (associate member of the Psychoanalytic Society of São Paulo), João Cortes de Barros, Luiz Werneck and Pedro Figueiredo Ferreira (candidates at the end of their training in São Paulo).

The recognition of the study group as an IPA-affiliated Society happened during the Business Meeting of the 21st IPA International Congress in Copenhagen in 1959.

In Rio Grande do Sul, or to be more exact, in Porto Alegre, the pioneers of the psychoanalytical movement were Dr. Martim Gomes and Dionélio Machado.

Martim Gomes published two books in the early thirties, *Le Rêve* and *Aesthetic Feeling and Psychoanalysis,* and Dionélio Machado translated "Elements of Psychoanalysis" by Eduardo Weiss into Portuguese.

In his paper "Psychoanalysis in Rio Grande do Sul", Dr. Roberto Pinto Ribeiro emphasizes the importance of Celestino Prunes, who, as a professor of forensic medicine, gave an annual course on elements of psychoanalysis as an introduction to the study of criminology and forensic psychiatry. In the same paper Pinto Ribeiro also mentions Professor Décio Soares de Souza and his major role in the introduction of psychoanalysis in Rio Grande do Sul. After studying with Jules Massermann, Décio de Souza became Professor of Psychiatry at the Medical School of Porto Alegre in 1944. Until 1950 he gave courses there on psychoanalytical training. Then he moved to London to complete his psychoanalytical training. Dr. Décio's place in Porto Alegre was taken by Dr. Paulo Guedes, and Dr. David Zimmermann became the clinical director there. These two put the teaching of psychiatry on a firm psychoanalytical basis.

According to Pinto Ribeiro, "psychoanalysis appeared as a well-organized profession after Dr. Mário Martins had returned from Buenos Aires in 1947, the first officially trained analyst to practise this profession in Porto Alegre".

Mário Martins had completed his medical studies in 1933 and had been interested in psychiatry since then, particularly in the works of Freud, which, in 1944, caused him and his wife, Zaira Bittencourt Martins, to go to Buenos Aires to take up their psychoanalytical training there. Mário underwent analysis with Angel Garma, Zaira Martins with Celes Cárcamo, then going on to specialize in children's analysis.

With Mário Martins' return there were two reasons for the beginning of the official psychoanalytical movement in Rio Grande do Sul.

The first reason was the beginning of the analyzing of psychiatrists, who were to form the nucleus of the future psychoanalytical society.

The second reason was Dr. Mário's resumption of his activities as a psychiatrist in the "São Pedro" hospital, where he influenced and taught the psychiatrists working with him.

Investigation and research on a psychoanalytical basis were also begun by Dr. Mário Martins in Rio Grande do Sul. His publication, *A Contribution to the Psychoanalytic Study of Epilepsy,* was the result of his investigations from 1947 to 1952.

In 1949 Dr. José Lemmertz, who had been analyzed by Dr. Luiz Rascowsky, also returned from Buenos Aires. This led to the commencement of theoretical seminars and psychoanalytical technique as well as individual and collective supervision. Besides Mário, Zaira and Lemmertz, the first group included Dr. Paulo Guedes, Dr. Ernesto La Porta and Dr. David Zimmermann. They were later joined by Dr. Gunther Wurth, Dr. Roberto Pinto Ribeiro and Dr. José Maria Santiago Wagner.

Professor Celestino Prunes, the third founder, returned from Rio de Janeiro in 1952, where he had completed his training and his analysis. Two years later, in 1954, Dr. Ciro Martins returned from Buenos Aires, where he had completed his training and had been analyzed by Arnaldo Rascovsky.

Thus it was possible, in 1956, to found the Centre for Psychoanalytical Studies.

Recognition as a study group followed in 1961 at the 22nd International Psychoanalytical Congress. The study group was granted the status of component society at the 23rd International Psychoanalytical Congress, which was held in Stockholm in 1963.

The Theoretical Currents

Freud formed the basis of the theoretical currents that influenced psychoanalytical practice in Brazil. With the arrival of Dr. Koch in São Paulo in 1937 there began the practice of psychoanalysis within the official regulations of the IPA. The theoretical directions taken by the group at the beginning were based on Freud, which was due to the fact that Dr. Koch had been analyzed by Otto Fenichel, the author of the *Psychoanalytical Theory of Neurosis.* This was considered for many years the most comprehensive and perfect work on psychoanalysis.

The discoveries and influences of Melanie Klein, however, were soon to become noticeable in Brazilian psychoanalytical thought. Noemy Rudolfer da Silveira maintains that Dr. Mark Burke was one of the pioneers of

Kleinianism and that after 1948 Kleinian theory slowly and progressively acquired more and more significance in the scientific psychoanalytical works produced in Brazil.

In the fifties a number of Brazilians went to London to undertake their training with the British Society. Professor Décio de Souza was the first to complete his psychoanalytical training in London, where he acquired the qualification of psychiatrist for children and adults.

Later, Dr. Frank Philips and Professor Virginia Bicudo also went to London. The latter stayed there from 1955 to 1960. In 1969 Frank Philips returned to São Paulo, bringing with him Bion's ideas and their influences. In the seventies Bion's works were included in psychoanalytical training in São Paulo.

According to Virginia Bicudo, "the tendency of the inclusion of psychoanalytical theories characterizes the training of the psychoanalyst in the organization of the programs of the Institute for Psychoanalysis, by being oriented to Freud in the basic course, and later to Melanie Klein and Bion". This orientation is also expressed at the present-time in the statement of the same author in her book on the characteristics of the psychoanalytical production of the Brazilian Society of São Paulo (1987) when she says: "I have tried to characterize the Brazilian Society of São Paulo by including them within the framework of the theoretical referential theme which is based upon contributions of Freud, Klein and Bion".

As far as the Psychoanalytical Society of Rio de Janeiro is concerned, we can say that initially Freud's classical theory was predominant. Kleinianism was introduced by Werner Kemper, who had had contact to Paula Heimann, Otto Fenichel, Melanie Klein and Wilhelm Reich in Berlin. From 1967, texts of the English School appeared together with those of Freud. The theoretical influences of the seventies, however, seemed to be based on such authors as Winnicott, Fairbairn and Bion. Argentinian authors too, such as Garma, Knobel, Grinberg and Aberastury are mentioned in the papers presented by the Society of Rio de Janeiro. French authors are seldom mentioned.

From 1979 to 1984, according to participants at the Latin American Congress, Freud quotations have the upper hand in the papers presented, with a few from Bion and Winnicott, and the importance of Klein decreasing.

Latin American authors, such as Aberastury, Rascovsky, Aray, Garma, Grinberg, Abadi, Bleger and Racker appear more and more frequently. Some French authors, such as Green, Lagache, and Leclaire, were mentioned.

According to Dr. Inaura Carneiro Leão, the theoretical influences that form the fundamental principles of the Brazilian Society of Rio de Janeiro have three doctrinal axes: the influence of Freud, Melanie Klein and Donald

Winnicott. Other authors such as Paula Heimann and Michael Balint also had a certain influence with their theories, as well as the contributions of Bion and the decisive influence of the works of Hans Thorner.

Recently, according to Dr. Inaura, two theoretical doctrinal lines have attracted attention within the Brazilian Society of Rio de Janeiro: the drive theory, which places emphasis on the drives within the emergence of the normal or pathological structure, and the theoretical line, which is based on the development of the "self", proceeding from the primitive relations of the self with suitable self objects.

Finally, the scientific line of H. Kohut, whose growing importance is due to the work of Dr. Inaura Leão.

In Porto Alegre the theoretical influence on the Psychoanalytic Society is based on the scientific line of the Psychoanalytic Society of Argentina, as three of the four founders had received their training in Buenos Aires.

Freud's fundamental ideas were initially predominant for the founding group of Porto Alegre, although a growing interest in Melanie Klein's ideas was becoming noticeable. Even though none of the society's members had been analyzed in London, the influence of authors of the English School was considerable, due to the frequent visits of Argentinian colleagues such as Marie Langer, Willi Baranger, Leon Grinberg and Arnaldo Rascovsky.

In 1974 Herbert Rosenfeld visited the society in Porto Alegre. His ideas, which had already influenced some of the analysts there, spread with the growing interest in Bion's and Meltzers's ideas. Of the post-Kleinian authors Betty Joseph has a major influence on those who follow the theoretical-technical line initiated by Melanie Klein. Winnicott's ideas are of some importance for the scientists in the Society, more important than Kohut's ideas.

As far as the authors of the so-called ego-psychology are concerned, it should be emphasized that they are studied at regular intervals, which means that their influence is noticed in presented psychoanalytical papers, yet only as a further development of the Freudian idea.

It should also be emphasized that the growth of the Brazilian societies has been constant and that it has been particularly strong over the last two decades.

The number of candidates for psychoanalytical training is large, as is the influence of psychoanalytical thought within the various cultural and scientific fields.

This is a particularly noteworthy fact if we consider the difficult economic and social problems the country is suffering.

Yet they are not an obstacle to the growth of our science in Brazil.

References

ALMEIDA PRADO GALVÃO, L. (1967): Notas para a História da Psicanálise em São Paulo. *Revista Brasileira de Psicanálise* 1, 46–48.

BICUDO, VIRGINIA (1981): Contribuição de Melanie Klein à Psicanálise, segundo Minha Experiência. *Alter Jornal de Estudos Psicodinâmicos* 11, Brasília.

– (1987): As características da Produção Psicanalítica da América Latina. Relatório da Sociedade de São Paulo. Correio da FEPAL.

CHAGAS LESSA, P. C. / I. MILANI TAVERES / M. WESTERLUND MONTETEVA (1987): As características da Produção da América Latina. Relatório da Sociedade Psicanalítica do Rio de Janeiro. Correio da FEPAL.

LEÃO, INAURA C. (1987): As características da Produção Psicanalítica da América Latina. Relatório da Sociedade Brasileira de Psicanálise do Rio de Janeiro. Correio da FEPAL.

MENEGHINI, L. C. (1987): As características da Produção Psicanalítica da América Latina. Relatório da Sociedade Psicanalítica de Porto Alegre. Correio da FEPAL.

PERESTRELLO, MARIA ALZIRA (1986): Primeiros encontros com a Psicanálise. Os precursores no Brasil (1899–1937) *J. Brasileiro de Psicanálise* 35, No. 4, 195–208.

– (1987): História da Sociedade Brasileira de Psicanálise do Rio de Janeiro: *Imago.*

PINTO RIBEIRO, R. (1961): Psicanálise no Rio Grande do Sul. *Psiquiatria* 1, No. 4, 88–91.

SAGAWA, ROBERTO Y. (1989): Entre a alienação na Psioanálise e a Produção das Psicanálises. *Revista Brasileira de Psicanálise* 23, No. 3, 109–121.

Journals

Revista de Psicanálise do Rio de Janeiro
since 1991; Ed.: Dr. Moises Tractenberg
Dumará Distribuidora de Publicações
Av. Nossa Senhora de Copacabana, 435 – Conj. 207
CEP 22020 Rio de Janeiro RJ

Contribucões em Psicologia, Psiquitria e Psicanálise
irreg.; Ed.: Editora Campus (Subsidiary of Elsevier, North-Holland)
Rua Barao de Itapagipe 55, Rio Comprido, 20261 Rio de Janeiro RJ

Arquivos Brasileiros de Psicologia
since 1949; Ed.: Fundacao Getulio Vargas
C.P. 9052, 22250 Rio de Janeiro RJ

Institutions

Sociedade Brasileira de Psicanálise de Rio de Janeiro
(Brazilian Psychoanalytic Society of Rio de Janeiro)
Rua David Campista 80, 22261-010 Humanaitá, Rio de Janeiro, RJ
Tel./Fax: 55-21-537 1333

Sociedade Brasileira de Psicanálise de São Paulo
(Brazilian Analytic Society of São Paulo)
Rua Sergipe 441, 5°, Conj. 51, CEP 01243-001 Sao Paulo, SP
Tel.: 55-11-256 3106; Fax: 55-11-258 8353

Grupo de Estudos Psicoanalíticas de Pelotas
(Pelotas Psychoanalytical Study Group)
Rua Princesa Isabel 280, sala 1106, 96015-590 Pelotas, RS
Tel./Fax: 55-532-27 1610

Grupo de Estudos Psicoanalíticos de Porto Alegre
(Porto Alegre Psychoanalytical Study Group)
Rua Florencio Ygartua 409/202, 90430-010 Porto Alegre, RS
Tel./Fax: 55-51-330 3845

Grupo de Estudos Psicanalíticos do Recife
(Recife Psychoanalytic Study Group)
Rua Belarmino Carneiro 249, Torre, 50761-340 Recife, PE
Tel./Fax: 55-81-228 1756

Grupo de Estudos de Psicoanalise de Ribeirão Preto
(Ribeirão Preto Psychoanalytic Study Group)
Rua Rui Barbosa 1782, 14015-120 Ribeirão Preto, SP
Tel.: 55-16-625 4193; Fax: 55-16-636 7916

Dr. Germano Vollmer Filho, Av. Encantado 110, 90470-420 Porto Alegre RS

Canada

by Charles Hanly

Canada had an early opportunity to begin its development of psychoanalysis when Ernest Jones arrived in 1908.[1] But Jones did not come to Canada as a psychoanalyst nor for the purpose of establishing psychoanalysis in Canada. Jones came no less committed to neurology than to psychoanalysis. He only formed his total commitment to psychoanalysis after the disappointment of his hope for a career there in Kraepelinian psychiatry and after his renewed contact with Freud during his visit to the US in 1909 (Paskauskas, 1988). Jones was invited to Toronto as a neurologist and never held any official position as psychoanalyst. He did make efforts through his publications and through the organization of a Symposium on Psychoneurosis, during the meetings of the Canadian Medical Association, to inform his colleagues about psychoanalysis and its therapeutic potentials and to encourage their interest in it (Parkin, 1987). However, no study group was formed and no-one trained as a result of Jones's efforts. While in Canada, he did contribute to the formation of the American Psychoanalytic Association (APA) and served as its first secretary. The cultural and moral atmosphere of pre-World War One Canada made it difficult for psychoanalytic ideas to take root.

Psychoanalysis eventually took root in Montréal as a result of the work of a gifted teacher in an unlikely place, in the psychology institute of the faculty of philosophy at the University of Montréal. It was a pontifical university where Freud's work was on the index. The first effective teacher of psychoanalysis in Canada was not a neurologist, psychiatrist or psychoanalyst. He was a Dominican priest, a psychologist, father Noel Mailloux. He began teaching Freud using Fenichel's *Psychoanalytic Theory of the Neurosis* to a class of six students two of whom, Gabrielle Clerk and André Lussier, were to become psychoanalysts. During his education abroad,

1 I am indebted to colleagues for their help with this study and especially Constantinos Arvanitakis, Marie-Claire Belanger, Paul Finnegan, Paul Lefebvre, John Lorhenz, André Lussier, Alan Parkin, William Robinson, W. Clifford M. Scott, Daniel Traub-Werner.

Mailloux had gained some understanding of Freud's ideas and had the courage and enthusiasm to follow up his interest and to begin teaching Freud upon his return to Montréal. Mailloux, who wished to synthesize thomism and psychoanalysis, and who was not himself a psychoanalyst wisely sought an appointment for Daniel Lagache of Paris and when this failed, he arranged for the French psychoanalyst and psychology professor, Théo Chentrier, to join the psychology institute. Concurrently, a Spanish neuro-psychiatrist, Dr. Miguel Prados, came to McGill University in Montréal and, because of his interest in Freud, soon made common cause with Mailloux and Chentrier. In 1946 the "Montréal Psychoanalytic Club" was formed. For the first time in Canada, there was a forum for the study, discussion and exploration of psychoanalysis sustained by the committed leadership of Prados, Chentrier and Maillox and able to provide the basis for further development.

The work of Prados, Chentrier and Mailloux and the "Montréal Psychoanalytic Club" had two important results. Some psychologists and psychiatrists who were later to have an important role in the development of psychoanalysis in Canada were inspired to seek training in psychoanalysis abroad. An opportunity for collegial collaboration had been created in Montréal that could attract psychoanalysts from abroad. The silence about psychoanalysis had been permanently broken. The first of these instilled voices on behalf of psychoanalysis had been the voice of Father Mailloux (Lussier, 1987).

Thus from these first beginnings there sprang a two fold process of strengthening the place of psychoanalysis in Canada. Canadians who had gone abroad to train began to return to Montréal: Bruce Ruddick from New York, 1952; Jean Baptiste Boulanger from Paris, 1954; Clifford Scott from London, 1954; André Lussier from London, 1954; Nathan Epstein from New York, 1955. And independently of this process, which formed the main current of the early development of psychoanalysis, Alan Parkin returned to Toronto from his training in London in 1954 to play an important part nationally through his contributions to developments in Montréal as well as in the establishment of psychoanalysis in Toronto. In 1957, Irvine Schiffer returned to Toronto from Boston and, in 1961, Morton Berg from Philadelphia.

During this period, psychoanalysts from abroad also came to Montréal: Eric Wittkower from London, 1950; George Zavitzianos, from Athens, 1951; Alistair MacLeod, from London, 1951; Johann and Gottfriede Aufreiter from Vienna, 1954. In the meantime, Miguel Prados had been elected a member of the British Society in 1952. In these two processes, one is struck by the rich variety of influences from Europe, England and the US.

One is also struck by the fact that the development of psychoanalysis in Canada did not take the form of a colonization from abroad, because of the Canadians who, after training abroad, took a leading role in developing psychoanalysis and because the psychoanalysts who came from abroad became identified with psychoanalysis in Canada.

The question of colonization was not a trivial one. The American Psychoanalytic Association had an ambition to control psychoanalysis in North America. The APA showed every sign of wanting to make any Canadian society a component of the American rather than an independent member of the IPA. Here was a crucial issue in the development of psychoanalysis in Canada. The American Psychoanalytic Association did not accept non-medical analysts. This already had caused Mailloux and Chentrier to remove themselves from positions of leadership so that membership in the IPA could go forward, if need be, under the auspices of the American. The British Society which had always been prepared to act as sponsor of the Canadian group also happened to have a Canadian, Clifford Scott, as its president during this crucial period. Here was support for an independent Canadian Society. The IPA did not recognize the American claim over Canada and in 1957, under the British Society's sponsorship, the Canadian Psychoanalytic Association became a component society of the IPA.

As a result, the Canadian Society has been spared the problems of the law suit recently brought against the IPA and the American by US psychologist-psychoanalysts, a law suit, the settlement of which has yet further restricted the hegemony of the APA by providing access to membership in the IPA of non-APA groups in the US. More importantly, however, it has enabled psychoanalysis in Canada from the beginning to benefit from the contributions of non-medical psychoanalysts and in at least some of the ways that Freud (1926) envisioned. André Lussier is the most prominent of these, having been involved in the formation of the Canadian Society and its first training programme as well as later in the formation of the francophile Branch in Montréal.

Initially training was only available in Montréal. The seminars were scheduled so that candidates from other centers could attend. During the sixties a rapid expansion of psychoanalysis occurred. Some graduates of the Montréal based programme were now practicing in Ontario centers, especially in Toronto. Psychoanalysis had become more acceptable and prestigious in psychiatry and in Ontario medical schools. During the sixties psychoanalysts held chairs of departments of psychiatry in Ontario at Queen's University in Kingston, at the University of Ottawa, at McMaster University in Hamilton and at the University of Toronto. The return of Canadians to Canada from training centers abroad and the immigration of analysts continued. Some Montréal analysts moved to Ontario. In the sixties there was a sufficient number of analysts in Toronto to form a society.

In 1967 the constitution of the Canadian Society was reformed so as to provide for society and institute Branches. This reform was designed to accommodate the development of psychoanalysis in other Canadian cities but it was also a means of satisfying the need for a francophone society and institute in Montréal where French speaking Canadians could find training in their own language and, upon graduation, join a society for scientific exchange and professional advancement in French. As a result of this reform three Branches were formed in 1967, two in Montréal (French and English) and one in Toronto. Subsequently, Branches have been formed in Ottawa (1972), Western Canada (1978), Southwestern Ontario (1982), Québec City (1988) and Eastern Ontario (1989).

The Canadian Psychoanalytic Society

The Canadian Psychoanalytic Society has (1992) 366 members, of whom 25 are living abroad. The largest Branch society, the Toronto Psychoanalytic Society, has 108 members. Each of the Montréal Branches, the Québec English Branch and the Société Psychanalytique de Montréal, have just under 100 members. The Ottawa Psychoanalytic Society has 27 members and there are four smaller Branches: the Western Canadian Branch, with 12 members, the South Western Ontario Psychoanalytic Society, with 12 members, the Société Psychanalytique de Québec, with seven members and the Psychoanalytic Society of Eastern Ontario, with six members. Canadian analysts are concentrated in Toronto and Montréal with lesser numbers in Ottawa, London, Edmonton and Québec. One of Canada's most populous cities, Vancouver, has only three analysts, although a discussion group has recently been formed and it is likely that Vancouver will be the next major city in Canada to expand its psychoanalytic resources. Of the four maritime provinces, there is only one analyst in the province of Nova Scotia. There are still opportunities for pioneering work in the field of psychoanalysis in Canada.

The Branches exercise a great measure of autonomy in the management of their own affairs. The Canadian Society provides for common standards of admission to the profession in so far as the nominees of each Branch have to be approved for membership by mail ballot of all the members. The Canadian Society sponsors annual scientific meetings, and establishes and maintains common ethical and professional standards, although each Branch has responsibility for maintaining local ethical practice. The Canadian society provides for national committees to study common problems and to develop policies to deal with them. It acts on behalf of the profession in relation to the federal government just as the Branches deal with provincial matters. For example, a committee of the Candian Society successfully lobbied the federal government to exempt the services of non-medical analysts from the payment of a new federal goods and services tax. The national body maintains communication among the members of its Branches by means of a newsletter and the distribution of minutes of meetings and other information required for national policy and administrative decisions.

The four largest Societies, Toronto, Montréal English, Montréal French and Ottawa have training institutes that are Branches of the Canadian Institute of Psychoanalysis. As in the case of the Branch societies the institutes are given a maximum of autonomy compatible with the maintenance of common training standards. Each institute is responsible for selecting candidates, for monitoring their progress and deciding upon their suitability for graduation. Each is responsible for its curriculum. However, the credentials of a graduate of a Branch Institute are first reviewed by the Branch Society of which it is an institute and, if accepted, will be recommended for membership in the Canadian Society on the basis of the national ballot. A graduate could not become a member of a Branch Society without being a member of the Canadian Society. This national decision is in some respects *pro forma* in so far as there is a tradition of accepting Branch Society nominees. Only the clear, demonstrable evidence of inadequacy would move members of other Branches to vote against the nominees of a Branch at the national level. At the annual business meeting and prior to the mail ballot every member has the opportunity to review the credentials of all nominees. The possibility of rejection exerts an influence in the direction of maintaining a common national standard. As a result, membership is portable from Branch to Branch unless an individual has become professionally incompetent or unethical. The grounds for refusal of transfer of membership would also be grounds for expulsion.

A second key element in maintaining standards is the appointment of training analysts. Each Branch Institute is responsible for developing its own method for selecting training analysts and for nominating training analysts to the National Institute. Each nominee is required to circulate a clinical paper to the members of the National Institute. The nominations are reviewed at a business meeting of the National Institute and a report of the discussion and the Branch vote is included in the information for a mail ballot of all institute members. There is a mechanism whereby individuals deemed qualified but not nominated by a Branch Institute can be placed in nomination by the National Institute. Also the nominee of a Branch Institute may fail to receive the required two-thirds majority in the mail ballot. In that event, the nominee cannot become a training analyst in the Branch Institute which nominated her/him. As a consequence of membership in the Canadian Institute, the status of training analyst is portable from Branch Institute to Branch Institute.

However, this method of ensuring a national standard of training in Canada has had a flaw in it for some time. The method is premised on the principle of a national selection of training analysts who then serve as guarantors of the quality of training in so far as they are responsible for the training analysis and supervisions of all candidates as for the other training activities such as curriculum and seminars, candidate selection, progress and graduation. It is very widely, if not universally agreed, that the analysis a candidate receives as part of his training is the single most important element in the candidate's development as an analyst. Three institutes require that the training analysis be conducted by a training analyst. One institute, l'Institut Psychanalytique de Montréal, adopted a modified method some years ago. A candidate may choose as his analyst for his training analysis any analyst who has had five years of experience since becoming a member of the Branch and has been designated an *habilité.* The conduct of training analyses are no longer the responsibility of training analysts who continue to be responsible for supervision. This training innovation was intended to enhance the quality of the analysis candidates receive by removing from it the artifacts of training, to insure its privacy and to protect its integrity as an end in its own right rather than merely as a means to professional advancement.

The tendency to greater Branch autonomy and even isolation is illustrated by the fact that many of the issues debated within the French society of Montréal have not been discussed within the larger community of the Canadian Institution and Society since the changes were inaugurated by l'Institut Psychanalytique de Montréal. Nor has any attempt to evaluate this approach to the training analysis to see what could be learned from it by other Branches been made. The question as to whether or not it conforms to International Psychoanalytical Association requirements remains unexplored. It is unlikely that this situation is caused by the French-English fact, for the same would be likely to have happened if it had been one of the English speaking institutes that had adopted the innovation rather than the French institute. Branch autonomy is no less jealously guarded and reciprocally respected among Canadian analysts than is provincial autonomy by Canadians generally.

If few individual Canadian analysts other than the francophones have the linguistic skills required to keep abreast of publications in French and

English, there is a tradition in the English speaking societies of interest in European thought in translation. In this way the scientific life of the Canadian societies serve as a cross-roads or meeting place for the various currents in contemporary psychoanalysis. For example, although all of Canada's Lacanian analysts are francophone Québecers, the Toronto society has had a study group devoted to Lacan and some individuals continue an active interest in the clinical implications of some of Lacan's ideas. The cross-roads is even more in evidence, among the anglophone institutes, when it is a question of the influence of American ego psychology, British object relations and Klein. A project for a Canadian psychoanalytic journal was initiated and developed by Clifford Scott and Paul Lefebvre. But the energetic efforts to establish it of Jean-Yves Roy, who was to have been the journal's first editor, have not yet borne fruit. A journal devoted to Klein and object relations has been established despite the relatively small number of Kleinians and object relations theorists in Canada and the Société Psychanalytique de Montréal publishes a bulletin on psychoanalytic subjects. The Toronto institute experimented with a "three streams" curriculum with the aim of "giving equal time" to the classical, object relational and self psychological models. This effort to establish the cross-roads approach in the institute curriculum failed partly because candidates wanted more opportunity to study Freud than the plan would allow and because there were not sufficient numbers of teachers who were thorough students of object relations theory. It is nevertheless a good illustration of the importance and influence the cross-roads concept has had in Canada. Until recently the national scientific programmes were strongly influenced by the similar although somewhat different concept of a window on the world so that there was always a guest speaker from abroad along with Canadian speakers. A review of the history of recent choices of foreign speakers would show that the implementation of this policy over the years was strongly influenced by the cross-roads idea. A few names are indicative: Bowlby, Arlow, Green, Hartmann, McDougall, Rangell, Chasseguet-Smirgel. However, despite these and other examples that one could cite, contemporary schools of thought in psychoanalysis do not get "equal time" among Canadian psychoanalysts. The dominant orientation is Freudian classical psychoanalysis.

Theoretical Orientation and Publications

This feature of psychoanalysis in Canada is born out by the results of a survey of the orientation of members. All members were invited to communicate to me their theoretical orientation and publication. However, there were not enough responses to this request to use them otherwise than as a check on the adequacy of a second method adopted to get this information. A number of senior and less senior analysts were asked to survey the membership indicating the theoretical orientation of each member according to the following categories: Freudian (American or European), object relational (British or American), middle group (as in British middle group), Kleinian, self psychological, Lacanian, eclectic, unknown. Cross-checking with the individual responses, the judgments of the different members of the informal jury, and by some telephone calls to individuals suggested that the classifications were reasonably accurate. Most of the differences, which were surprisingly few, occurred in the more refined discriminations e. g. Freudian American or Freudian European.

The statistical results are presented as a reasonably accurate picture of the theoretical orientations of Canadian psychoanalysts: 61% Freudian, 10% Object rational, 9% Middle group, 7% Eclectic, 6% Kleinian, 4% Self psychological, 3% Lacanian. Of those who were classified Freudian in their orientation 71% were Freudian in the American fashion and 29% were Freudian in the European fashion. This division reflects the extent to which the influence of French (European) Freudian thought influences francophone analysts and the extent to which the same is true of the influence of American psychoanalysis on anglophone analysts. Only one analyst was classified by the *jurors* as Freudian (European) who was not a member of the Société Psychanalytique de Montréal. Also the two smallest groups are each limited to single Branch societies, the self psychologists to the Toronto Branch and the Lacanians to the Société Psychanalytique de Montréal. The other theoretical groupings are quite widely dispersed in the different Branches.

The dominance of classical psychoanalysis in Canada is also expressed in the curricula of the Montréal English and Montréal French institutes and less so in the Toronto institute. In the Montréal English institute, the first year is largely devoted to the study of Freud's major technical, clinical and theoretical works. The first year also includes the study of contemporary expositions, extensions, critiques, modifications and alternatives to the classical theory and this emphasis is greater in the second year which also introduces a sequence of seminars on the stages of individual development. Klein, objects relation theorists and self psychology are introduced along with a continuing study of Freud and ego psychology both in seminars devoted to development (phases of childhood and adolescent development) and to technique. The third year completes the seminars on development and then takes up a series of systematic theoretical, clinical and technical topics including female psychology, object relations theory, perversion, history of psychoanalysis, applied psychoanalysis, psychoanalysis and psychotherapy, psychosomatics, theory of affect and dream analysis. The reading lists for these topics draw widely from historical and contemporary sources with a continuing study of Freud's work. The fourth year continues the study of the history of psychoanalysis which is followed by a series of seminars on the alternative theories of Jung, Adler, Horney, Sullivan, the controversy between Klein and A. Freud, Bion, Lacan and Aulagnier. There are seminars on metapsychology and antimetapsychology, the scientific status of psychoanalysis. These are followed by a continuing series of seminars on the application of psychoanalysis in politics, religion, the arts and biography. The seminars conclude with a series on technique concerning termination and child analysis. Of course, throughout the last three years there are continuing case seminars to which the third semester is devoted. To this observer, an important feature of the Montréal English curriculum is the continuing work with Freud's contributions as old and new elaborations, alternatives and critiques are studied both in their own right and in relation to the classical theory.

The Montréal French institute has built the study of Freud and non-Freudian theories into its curriculum in a very imaginative way. The major Freud texts are studied in detail and in depth over the three years of the curriculum beginning with *The Neuro-Psychoses of Defence* (1894) and ending with *An Outline of Psychoanalysis* (1940). One is reminded of the "explication de texte" in the tradition of French scholarship which in the hands of an imaginative scholar opens a path to the clarification of the essential ideas of a text and their implications while at the same time preserving all of the nuances of their context, an approach that is especially appropriate to the Freud text. It is easy to imagine in this pedagogical choice the continuing influence of Père Mailloux in the didactic ideals of contemporary francophone analysts. In the fourth year the mandatory Freud sequence is devoted to systematic topics in Freudian thought. These topics are based on Freud texts with supplementary contemporary interpretive studies. Included have been the preconscious, the repetition compulsion, *The Project for a Scientific Psychology,* group psychology, psychoses and bisexuality. The topics may change; the principle is to take up texts that could not be included in the three year sequence in a way that emphasizes systematic, critical thought. The study of Freud's work is the basic element of continuity in the seminar work of the candidates.

The curriculum of the Toronto institute has three years of seminars, although a fourth year is being added in which candidates may participate in study groups or design projects of study in which candidates can follow up their own interests or make up gaps in their training somewhat along the lines of the Montréal French institute. The first year is largely devoted to Freud. It consists of theoretical seminars on dreams, phantasies and symptoms, drive theory, the structural theory, anxiety, conflict and defence and technical seminars on Freud's technical papers and case studies. Continuous case seminars begin in the third trimester and continue in the second and third trimesters of the second year and all trimesters of the third year concurrently with the theoretical seminars. The theoretical seminars in the third year include seminars on ego psychology, dreams, object relations theory and character. The seminars on technique in the first trimester include ego psychology and object relations perspectives on technique and child development with topics in ego psychology, Klein, object relations and self psychology. The third year seminars include self psychology, perversions, comparative psychoanalysis, termination and infant observation.

The Toronto institute curriculum has been more influenced by theoretical conflicts than have the others. One effort to solve the problem and to take into account the different theoretical orientiations within psychoanalysis was the "three streams concept" developed by Ian Graham in which the three streams would consist of self psychology, object relations and Freud. In any case, as mentioned above in a different context, because there was difficulty getting convinced objects relations theorists to man a seminar let alone a programme and because graduating candidates began to complain about the degree of their illiteracy in Freud, development in the direction of a thorough-going three streams curriculum stopped at one seminar on object relations theory and one seminar on self psychology. However, self psychology and object relations theory make their influence felt in other parts of the curriculum as well. The continuous case seminar that is concurrent with the self psychology theoretical seminar is conducted from a self psychological perspective. The technical implications of Kohut's theory are taught in the seminars on technique. A concluding seminar features a discussion of all three theoretical views with the addition of intersubjectivity which brings together Freud, Kohut, Fairbairn and Atwood and Stolorow.

Repercussion upon Public and Science

The development of psychoanalysis in Canada has been so rapid, partly because during the sixties Canadian psychiatry was busy catching up with the influence psychoanalysis already had in psychiatry in the US. The appointment of psychoanalysts to chairs of psychiatry in Ontario medical schools has already been mentioned. The same has been true of McGill and the University of Montréal. Never having caught up to the US, Canadian psychiatry has followed the US swing to organic, biochemical psychiatry with, perhaps, an even greater diminution of the influence of psychoanalysis in the medical schools and teaching hospitals because of Canada's late start relative to the US.

The rate of increase in the numbers of psychoanalysts has not, thus far, been greatly affected. This is in part because the provincial health insurance plans pay for analytic treatment by physician analysts and thus offer the prospect of a secure and prosperous livelihood. Training analysts whose services are insured by the health plan also use it to cover the costs of training analysis for candidates on the grounds that it is a therapy, as well as a requirement of training; for training requirements are not in themselves eligible for health insurance. In Québec, where psychoanalysis is not an insured service in the provincial health plan, the decline in medical applicants for training has tended to follow the US pattern, and, as in the US in the aftermath of the legal settlement, these places are being taken up by non-medical applicants. The numbers of non-medical analysts relative to medical analysts have always been much greater in Québec than in other provinces. Of the Toronto Society's 108 members only eight are non-medical. In Ontario there is a strong disincentive for non-medical analysts to apply because they will be confronted by an economic environment that provides analysis at no cost to the patients of medical analysts while the patients of non-medical analysts have to pay full costs. The economic environment is having an effect on the development of psychoanalysis in Canada. None of these effects are politically intended.

Psychoanalysis is not well identified or understood by politicians, ministers of health and their bureaucracies, except in the unusual case of the former Québec minister of health Camille Laurin who was himself a psychoanalyst and assisted the Québec psychoanalysts in excluding psychoanalysis from the insured services of the provincial health plan. It has been said that this decision on the part of the Québec analysts had three reasons; one was the wish to preserve the integrity and privacy of the analyst-patient relationship; a second was to avoid government control and interference; a third was to protect income, prompted by the belief, which may have turned out to be erroneous in the event, that a practice outside the system would be financially more rewarding because from the beginning the Québec health insurance plan prohibited extra-billing whereas in the other provinces extra-billing (charging the patient a sum in addition to the amount collected from the provincial insurance plan) was only recently prohibited by law. Some analysts have accepted the prohibition on extra-billing, others have continued it under the rubric of "non-insured services" (services in addition to the analysis required by the patient) as a means of imposing a measure of financial responsibility for his analysis on the patient and for financial gain. In the post-war period provincial governments have become heavily involved in financing university education and health. There has been a tradition of respecting the autonomy of the universities which have continued to make and implement academic policy without direct government interference. This approach also guides the health insurance schemes in so far as the doctor–patient relation is concerned. Thus a psychoanalytic treatment is covered so long as it is deemed necessary by patient and analyst. Whether provincial governments will be able to retain this policy in the face of increasing tax burdens is a political question only the future will answer. Medical analysts fear that, as a cost saving measure, psychoanalysis could be on a list of services from which insurance coverage is withdrawn. However, for the present, at least, the provincial health insurance schemes have made it possible for many more medical psychoanalysts to have full analytic practices than their counter-parts in the US.

Psychoanalysis has developed as rapidly as it has because of the appointment of psychoanalysts to departments of psychiatry at the major universities of Québec and Ontario and more recently of the prairie provinces. This influence became significant in the fifties; it greatly increased in the sixties and seventies and has been reduced by the swing back to organic psychiatry in the eighties and nineties. Nevertheless, psychoanalysts with psychiatric appointments still constitute the major stronghold of psychoanalysis in the Canadian universities.

These medical psychoanalysts have been instrumental in establishing and maintaining a psychodynamic point of view in psychiatry. But they have also played a fundamentally important role in the development of psychoanalysis in Canada thorugh the recruitment of candidates for training. These results have been accomplished through the involvement of analysts in the clinical institution of residents, courses of lectures which introduced psychoanalytic concepts and principles, contributions to hospital rounds and clinical conference and publications in psychiatric journals. There can be no question that psychoanalysis has only reached its current state of development as a consequence of the influences.

Psychoanalysis finds its way into the university faculties of the sciences and humanities largely through the individual academics who are both humanists, psychologists or social scientists and psychoanalysts. Their impact tends to be like that of Jones in Toronto at the beginning of the century. The presence of André Lussier in the psychology department at the University of Montréal, the same department where psychoanalysis had its first real beginning with the work and leadership of father Mailloux, could not resist the tide of experimental, cognitive, behavioral psychology which now dominates the department. There is nowhere in Canada a university that has a psychoanalytically based clinical psychology programme of the quality of, for example, the University of Michigan in Ann Arbor in which analysts from the local society play an active part. Psychoanalysis is not, on the whole, a subject of serious study or teaching in the psychology departments of the major Canadian universities. In the US it is not unusual for psychology-psychoanalysts to combine private practice with a professorship in psychology. In Canada it is very unusual and such a person is likely to be rather isolated.

The situation is much the same in the humanities and social sciences. Patrick Mahoney is a professor in the comparative literature department at the University of Montréal. Blema Steinberg is a professor of political science and Constantinos Arvanitakis holds appointments in both philosophy and psychiatry at McGill University. Marie Emond and Edward Hannah are professors of social work at the universities of Montréal and Wilfred Laurier respectively. Lise Monet is professor of philosophy at the University of Québec. The list could be considerably enlarged. However, it is characteristic that each of these analysts is working more or less alone in departments that are more or less, often less, interested in the advancement of psychoanalysis or applied psychoanalysis and, sometimes, with colleagues who are hostile to their endeavors. Hostility aside, the basic problem is that academic departments are interested in promoting their own discipline and they do not usually consider psychoanalysis to be a part of it. Consequently, there is no official encouragement from the departments to introduce psychoanalytic topics into courses or to do psychoanalytic research. When an analyst academic retires there is no incentive to replace him with another of his kind even if one could be found. For the most part, the only footing that psychoanalysis has in faculties of arts and sciences in Canadian universities relies upon these individual academics who teach it to students in so far as it applies to their primary academic discipline and who devote themselves to applied psychoanalytic research. Psychoanalysis is not recognized as a discipline in Canadian universities.

So far as I know, the only exception to this rule is the programme related to psychoanalysis in the broadest sense which is located at the University of Toronto. It grew out of courses on the history of psychoanalysis (Freud) and applied psychoanalysis taught for many years under the auspices of the philosophy department. Students had a right, with the approval of the faculty, to design a minor programme of five or six courses in a subject that was not available as a programme but which could be made up out of existing courses in the departments of the faculty. Soon more students were opting for self-designed programmes that would enable them to study psychoanalysis than were enrolled in many of the faculty's college based inter-disciplinary programmes. As a result, Trinity College sponsored a programme called "The humanities and psychoanalytic thought" along with the usual academic apparatus of director and committees. One can see at once in the expression "psychoanalytic thought" that this was not to be a programme with a core of courses on psychoanalytic theory that would enable students to use psychoanalytic ideas to study literature, history, philosophy and social science. Jung, Adler, Freud and Guntrip were to be of equal importance. A student could proceed through the programme without having studied anything of Freud.

There are also academics who develop an interest in psychoanalysis in addition to those who, as a consequence of it, become trained psychoanalysts and combine analytic practice with their academic appointment. Psychoanalysis also finds its way into the universities through their exploitation of psychoanalytic ideas in their research and teaching. I have no reason not to believe that the University of Toronto is representative of other Canadian universities in this respect where in a faculty of more than five hundred humanists and social scientists there are, perhaps, ten of whom this description is true. Of these a smaller number are serious scholars of psychoanalysis. In this assessment, I am excluding the fluctuating academic enthusiasm for the latest intellectual fashion which generates, for example, temporary interest in Lacanian literary criticism or in the psychoanalysis of hermeneutics. This is not to say that Lacan and hermeneutics are not worthy of serious study. It is rather to say that they have given rise to very fashionable but short-lived enthusiasms. Nor is it to say that these fashions do not have their use in disseminating psychoanalytic ideas. Curious and perceptive students are able to use all kinds of stimuli to find their way to serious enquiries. Even if Freudian psychoanalysis is not very well articulated, if it is distorted or if it is attacked, the good student will be able to take from the material what is useful and plausible and proceed beyond it to a study of the original.

There is a vernacular psychology that also silently evolves in our culture upon which psychoanalysis has had a considerable influence. The "common sense" psychology of the century's end is much more psychoanalytically informed than the "common sense" psychology of the beginning of the century. This silence is as congenial to psychoanalysis as the shared defenses of those who contribute to the definition of this vernacular psychology will allow. At its core is a tacit, mute recognition of the personal truth of the importance Freud's understanding of human nature attaches to sexuality (see also Moscovici, 1961). Freud, through his published work and the influence of his ideas on writers, artists, the healing professions, educators etc. has contributed more than anyone else to these changes in the vernacular psychology. This silence, concerning origins, which also inhabits the universities, is one that is congenial to the contributions of psychoanalysis to the study of the humanities and social sciences. In the long run, if psychoanalysis is to have a stable footing in the universities there must be departments or, at least programmes, devoted to teaching and research in psychoanalytic theory and its history and to applied psychoanalysis. These departments or programmes need to have in them in addition to academics who are autodidacts in psychoanalysis some professors who are fully qualified as academicians in a university discipline and as psychoanalytic clinicians. At the present time there is at best only one such programme at a Canadian university. For the present, the presence of psychoanalysis in Canadian faculties of arts and science is precariously sustained by those psychoanalysts who, in relative isolation, hold professorial appointments in departments of humanities and social sciences.

The above generalizations have some application to Canadian public opinion as well. The general public, while its great majority does not have the intellectual advantages of academics, neither does it suffer so much from their occupational hazard of intellectualization. However, if one were to base one's judgement on what the media considers the public's interest in psychoanalysis to be, one would have to conclude that Canadians are for the most part ambivalent. They are curious about psychoanalysis in general and about Freud in particular but what most interests them are denunciations of one kind or another. For example, a day long symposium organized by the Toronto Psychoanalytical Society devoted to psychoanalytic contributions to the understanding of aggression which was very well attended by the general public received little publicity in the press. Whereas a symposium organized by the Trinity College (University of Toronto) programme in the humanities and psychoanalytic thought which was largely devoted to criticism of Freud received headline treatment on a prominent page of Canada's national newspaper. The speaker or two who had constructive things to say about Freud and psychoanalysis went unreported. The attacks on Freud and psychoanalysis by Jeff Masson (a former professor of Sanskrit at the University of Toronto, graduate of the Toronto Psychoanalytic Institute and member of the Canadian Psychoanalytic Society until he lost his membership from his failure to pay membership dues) are always well covered by the Canadian media as are feminist critiques of psychoanalysis. Thus the enthusiasm for hostile criticisms of Freud's life and work which has acquired a recent vogue in the universities is shared by the media and, if the media is correct about public opinion, by the public, too.

Concluding Remark

However, this is by no means the whole picture. The psychoanalytic component of the vernacular psychology alluded to above keeps psychoanalytic ideas alive and at work in useful ways in many unrecognized and unacknowledged ways. One can hear psychodynamic psychiatrists expound a topic by first criticizing Freud and then proceed to present ideas that owe their origin to Freud. Modern ideas and practices of parenting and educating children have been strongly influenced by psychoanalytic ideas concerning individual development. Well planned, publicized and executed lectures, symposia and conferences devoted to a constructive, but not uncritical or uncontroversial, presentation of psychoanalysis are well received by the educated public. The Toronto Psychoanalytic Society extension programme offers courses that are always fully subscribed by health professions but also interested educated citizens. The Toronto Society's annual conference "A day on psychoanalysis" has been received with enthusiasm. The Société-Psychanalytique de Montréal has recently resumed its "Conference publique". The Montréal English Branch has an annual evening conference for mental health professionals. A course on psychoanalysis and modern art which the extension department of the University of Toronto thought might draw ten to fifteen people had an enrolment of more than two hundred and fifty. The out-reach programmes of seminars and lectures that are sponsored by the Branches have, on the whole, been well received by both fellow mental health professionals and the educated public.

The growth of psychoanalysis in Canada has been rapid but it has also been robust. Growth is likely to continue for some time not only in the new centers of opportunity such as Vancouver and Winnipeg, but in the cities in which psychoanalysis is now well established. New problems to solve will be posed by the provincial health insurance schemes. Much work needs to be done to find for psychoanalysis a secure place in the universities both in psychiatry and in the humanities and social sciences. A good foundation now exists for tackling these and other difficulties and challenges that the future may bring.

Eminent Persons

Alan Parkin is a classical analyst who has published studies on sleep, fetishism, states of enthrallment, literary biography, hermeneutics, working through, melancholia, masochism, mourning, narcissism and psychic structure. He has written a history of psychoanalysis in Canada.

Irvine Schiffer is a classical analyst who has written on conversion, psychoanalytic technique, a clinical book on the trauma of time and an applied psychoanalytic book on the psychology of charisma and groups.

Clifford Scott has written on depression, mania and mourning, aspects of technique, drive theory, obsessional rituals, sleep and narcissism over many years from a position that could, perhaps, best be characterized as that of the middle group although he has been the major spokesman for Klein among Canadian psychoanalysts. He is a patron, along with Horacio Etchegoyen of Argentina, of a new Canadian journal *Melanie Klein and Object Relations.*

George Zavitzianos has written from a classical point of view on the impostor, multiple functions of the ego, perversions and technique.

Charles Hanly has written from a classical point of view clinical and theoretical papers on drive theory, transference, narcissism, the nature of psychoanalytic knowledge and its testing, critiques of existential psychology and self psychology and on various topics in applied psychoanalysis. His authored books are on psychic determinsm and the nature of freedom and on method in applied psychoanalysis. His edited book is on psychoanalysis and philosphy.

Howard Bacal has co-authored a recent book *Theories of Object Relations: Bridges to Self Psychology* with K. M. Newman. He writes from a self psychology and object relations point of view.

Ian Graham has edited a book on the personal myth with chapters from differing points of view.

Sheldon Heath's book is on the therapist's vulnerability to depression from an object relational perspective.

Paul Lefebvre writes from a middle-group perspective. He has explored clinical and theoretical issues in psycho-somatics and in the psychoanalytic treatment of patients with severe physical problems.

Eva Lester has written on clinical and theoretical issues concerning pregnancy with an emphasis on object relations, on transference, countertransference and on developmental issue e. g. separation-individuation.

André Lussier's work is Freudian. He has published on censorship, the structural point of view, self-psychology, clinical treatment of physically handicapped patients, object relations, super-ego and ego ideal pathology and the perversions as well as more general theoretical studies.

George MacLean has edited a book on suicide in adolescence and children and with U. Rappen he has written a biographical introduction to a selection of the works of Hug-Hellmuth.

Patrick Mahoney has an American object relations orientation. He is the most published Canadian analyst. His work brings together his training as a literary scholar and as a psychoanalyst. He has written five books on Freud as a writer and on Freud's writings as literature; two of which are on the case histories of the Rat Man and the Wolf Man, some of which have been translated into German, French and Portuguese. He has also written papers on literary aspects of psychoanalysis, semiology and dreams and on topics in applied psychoanalysis.

James Naiman has written on the super-ego and acting out, testing interpretations, taxomania, psychic change, perversion and self-analysis from a classical point of view.

References

GOLDBERG, A. (1988): A Fresh Look at Psychoanalysis. The View form Self Psychology. Hillsdale: The Analytic Press.

MOSCOVICI, S. (1961): La psychanalyse, son image, son public. Paris: PUF.

LUSSIER, A. (1987): Le "feu sacre": de la psychologie a la psychanalyse. *Frayage* 3, 27-46.

PARKIN, A. (1987): A History of Psychoanalysis in Canada. The Toronto Psychoanalytic Society.

PASKAUSKAS, R. A. (1988): The Jones-Freud era, 1908–1939. In: Freud in Exile. Ed. Edward Timms/Naomi Segal, New Haven: Yale Univ. Press, 109–123.

Journals

Canadian Journal of Psychoanalysis
Revue Canadienne de Psychanalyse
since 1993; Ed.: Eva P. Lester, M. D.;
Becker Associates, 36 Bessemer Court, Unit 3, Concord, Ontario L4K 3C9

Melanie Klein and Object Relations
(original title: Journal of the Melanie Klein Association)
since 1983; Ed.: O. Weininger, Ph. D.
The Ontario Institute for Studies in Education
252 Bloor St. West, Toronto, Ontario M5S 1V6

Trans
Ed.: Dr. Dominique Sarfone
Case Postale 842, Succurdale Outrement, Montreal, Quebec H2V 4R8

Institutions

Canadian Psychoanalytic Society
Societé Canadienne de Psychanalyse
7000 Côte des Neiges, Montreal, Quebec H3S 2C1
Tel.: 1-514-738 6105; Fax: 1-514-738 6393

Professor Charles M. T. Hanly, Ph. D., 27 Whitney Avenue, Toronto, Ontario M4W 2A7

Chile

by Omar Arrué

Starting with Carlos Whiting in 1980, several different works by analysts have been published that deal with the historical development of psychoanalysis in Chile (Núñez, 1981; Florenzano, 1988; Davanzo, 1987; Piat, 1990; Arrué, 1988; Gomberoff, 1990; Ganzaraín, 1987).

In undertaking a similar task, I can hardly argue, given such a legacy, that I have insufficient material to enable me to arrange the major events and leading protagonists in the history of our Association in a neat temporal sequence, simply by cross-referencing the available information, collecting a few new pieces of data, and piecing together a historical outline. I must confess however that, from another vantage point, it strikes me as a more attractive prospect to handle this material in a way that transcends the mere outward actions of the protagonists, trying instead to trace out the connections between the more implicit aspects of events, while also attempting a historiographical appraisal of the publications cited.

Before entering directly into the subject-matter of our present enquiry, I feel I should put on record that I myself was privileged to undergo the first part of my clinical training in the 1960s, and that, as a result, I not only had as my instructors various members of staff attached to the Clinic of the University of Chile's Department of Psychiatry, a clinic of which Professor Ignacio Matte Blanco was the Director, but that, through being able to participate directly in the Clinic's activities, I had the opportunity to enjoy fruitful contact with what might fairly be termed the culmination of the first stage in the development of the Chilean psychoanalytic movement.

To return to our principal theme, an examination of the published material undoubtedly reveals that, although there are several items of historical background that can help explain the very existence of psychoanalysis in Chile, there is no doubt that it was between the mid-1940s and the mid-1960s that the psychoanalytic movement ostensibly arose, exhibiting strong early development, and proving extremely influential in the specialized area of psychiatry and related disciplines. The movement came into existence in the Department of Psychiatry of the University of Chile's Medical School, and was led by Professor Ignacio Matte Blanco in collaboration with a large group of medical doctors and mental health professionals. The members of this group had already been interested in psychoanalytic psychology and psychiatry for some time, while at the institutional level it was already being suggested that the group, in its capacity as a component part of the university, should involve itself in training, research, and the clinical care of the Chilean population. On a lesser scale, it was during this period that a psychoanalytic study group came into being in the Medical School of the Catholic University of Chile, as well as in the Psychology Departments of both the Catholic University and the University of Chile, the country's two leading institutions of higher learning.

The Clinic of the University of Chile's Department of Psychiatry had recently been presented with an excellently equipped modern building and, as I have already shown, its psychiatric teams, as well as its doctors and nursing staff, were able to rely on clinical psychologists, specially trained social workers, and other professionals, all of whom helped to create an especially favourable environment for the advances and initiatives of the up-to-date, comprehensive dynamic psychiatry of the time. From the outset, many members of the group became involved with psychoanalysis proper by integrating it into their teaching, research, and health care activities in the psychiatric field, the desire having been kindled in them to acquire psychoanalytic experience, to train as psychoanalysts, and to reach the stage where an independent scientific psychoanalytic body could be established with an identity of its own. This dimension of the Chilean psychoanalytic movement reached its culmination in the foundation of the Asociación Psicoanalítica Chilena (APC), and its subsequent official recognition, in August 1949, as a Constituent Association of the IPA.

During this period, opportunities for great advances were created by the confluence of interests of the leading protagonists, by the fact that they worked alongside each other in the Clinic for many hours each day, and by the many different kinds of opportunity that arose for stimulating interaction between the academic, psychiatric and psychoanalytic fields. As all who have written on this topic have pointed out, this period witnessed a notable output of research studies and published works, considerable growth in the number of trainees, including some from other Latin American countries who had come to Chile specifically to train at the Clinic, and the existence of an open-minded interest in different ways of tackling, among other issues, problems of mental health. This process appeared to reach its true culmination when we played host to our first international congress, the Third Latin American Psychoanalytic Congress, held in Santiago in 1960.

Considered in the light of the declared aim of this article, it was the events of this period, inspired by the staff of Dr. Matte Blanco's department, and the background of important circumstances against which they took place, that mark the birth of psychoanalysis in Chile. For this reason I feel that, if we are fully to comprehend the identity of the Chilean group, what makes it special, and how it differs from other psychoanalytic groups, if we are to appreciate its more positive aspects, and the more exciting of its potentialities, as well as some of it inner contradictions, we cannot afford to overlook the procreative role played in the emergence of the Chilean group by the academic and psychiatric worlds, as well as by the more narrowly circumscribed psychoanalytic milieu. More concretely, I am referring to the significance and influence that we can ascribe to the fact that psychoanalysis developed in close relationship with the universities, and to the immediate significance and subsequent ramifications of the fact that our group, right from the outset, made inroads into the field of psychosis and severe mental disturbance.

In many respects, Whiting's work "Notas para la Historia del Psicoanálisis en Chile" (Notes for the History of Psychoanalysis in Chile), published in 1980, is a well-documented, trustworthy and adequately 'disinterested' synthesis of the origins of the Chilean movement. It would nonetheless be fair to say that, considered as a means of shedding light on our chosen theme, it does call for some comment. Whiting tends to explain the history of Chilean psychoanalysis, for example, almost exclusively from the viewpoint of the Asociación Psicoanalítica Chilena, whereas it seems to me, as I have shown above, that psychoanalysis in Chile, at least as far as its origins are concerned, cannot be exhaustively dealt with solely from this perspective.

Although Carlos Whiting distinguished himself in our circles by being an analyst who believed in 'open consultation', who was equipped with an extensive repertoire of different forms of intervention, including psychoanalytic psychotherapy, and who was known to have assisted in the psychiatric training of scholarship holders, nonetheless the manner in which he refers to the relationship between psychoanalysis and psychiatry does occasion some surprise: "During this stage of the development of psychoanalysis in Chile (1943-1949), work was focused on the training of the psychoanalytic group, without neglecting the task of diffusion." This is open to question. To what does the phrase "without neglecting the task of diffusion" refer? The impression given is that it covers almost all the activities of Matte's department. If this is the case, then Whiting is certainly guilty of a lack of proportion. He continues: "The figure of Dr. Matte is central, since the greater part of the struggle to overcome the difficulties created by environmental influences fell upon his shoulders. Although diffusion was carried out at every level, it was focused principally on the stimulation of interest in analytic training, and in the selection of suitable candidates to undergo that training. Nonetheless, although the exhaustive theoretic-technical teaching of psychoanalysis was emphasized in the analytic training, this presupposes a psychiatric training as a prerequisite for clinical practice. To this proper formulation should perhaps be added *Dr. Matte's longstanding concern to integrate analysis and psychiatry*" (my italics). The difficulty stands out more clearly in this section of Whiting's text. Whiting certainly did undertake a satisfactory amount of diffusion, and as an Analyst Member of the APC he had access to, and collaborated with, several psychiatric institutions, perhaps in an attempt to stimulate interest in psychoanalysis and to select suitable candidates for training. Even so, diffusion was more a characteristic of a later period, since Whiting effectively carried out this type of activity in the psychiatric departments of the Salvador Hospital and the Hospital Psiquiátrico in the 1970s, when nuclei of psychiatric personnel from the university hospitals were formed, including Dr. Hernán Davanzo, Dr. Ramón Florenzano, Dr. Luis Gomberoff, Dr. Mario Gomberoff and others, among whom I must count myself, in my capacity as a lecturer at the Catholic University. As I shared the same aims, whenever the opportunity presented itself I ensured that the clinical training of successive classes of psychology students was focused on the psychiatric department at the Salvador Hospital. But to return to the point, I would not say that the activities of Whiting and his fellow analysts in the Matte Blanco clinic during those notable years 1943-1949 amounted to the "diffusion of analysis". On the contrary, I think that what we are concerned with here is the work of analysts who, besides studying and practising psychoanalysis, were also applying it to patients at the clinic and who were also psychiatrists and academics. The important point seems to me to be that, at this early stage of development, analysts were still making a clear distinction between psychoanalysis and psychotherapy, between psychoanalysis and psychiatry, between university-based or hospital-based institutions and scientific societies, and that, in the main, they were not experiencing any problems or contradictions with their professional image.

According to Whiting (1980), Ignacio Matte Blanco, who had already had some contact with psychiatry and (more particularly) with psychoanalysis during his analysis with Dr. Fernando Allende Navarro here in Chile, moved to London in 1933, where he remained until 1940, working initially as a Research Fellow in Physiology at University College. It is worth mentioning that, at the time in question, he was a lecturer in the Department of Physiology at the Catholic University. He subsequently established himself in the field of psychological medicine by undergoing training in neuropsychiatry at Northumberland House and, more extensively, at Maudsley Hospital. Following his arrival in London, he also underwent psychoanalytic training at the British Institute of Psychoanalysis. His training analyst (1940–1943) was Dr. Walter Schmideberg, and his supervisors were Anna Freud, Melitta Schmideberg, Helen Sheehan-Dare and James Strachey. Arturo Prat Echaurren (1990), an important founder figure of the Chilean psychoanalytic group, describes him quite explicitly as the initiator of the Chilean group, adding that, in 1940, Matte Blanco moved to Johns Hopkins Hospital, Baltimore, USA, and that he subsequently became an Assistant Professor at Duke University, North Carolina, between 1941 and 1943. Upon his return, a group interested in psychoanalytic psychology was formed, which used to meet both at its own premises, Bernarda Morín 440, and in the Psychiatric Clinic, which at this time was directed by Professor Arturo Vivado Orsini, who numbered among his collaborators Dr. Sergio Mujica and Dr. Carlos Núñez Saavedra. Prat Echaurren goes on to say that, during 1944 and 1949, a group of medical doctors underwent analysis with Matte Blanco, and that some of them made up the original group of the APC, which was officially recognized at the 1949 Zurich International Congress. Some months before that recognition was announced, and as a result of Professor Vivado's sudden death, Matte Blanco won an academic competition to become a Full Professor in the Department of Psychiatry of the University of Chile's Medical School.

As will be appreciated, according to the testimony of these founders of the Chilean analytic group, Ignacio Matte Blanco himself was already, at the time of his return to Chile, the master of a body of knowledge that integrated, at a high level, his abilities as an analyst, a psychiatrist and a university professor.

We should now be able to decide whether it was Matte Blanco who provided the initial impetus, and whether we can wholeheartedly agree with Prat Echaurren when he says that Matte Blanco was the initiator of the analytic movement in Chile. My own perspective is rather more wide-ranging. As we know, at such a level, no one can become a leader of a group if the members of that group have not themselves played an active part, both in the election of the leader, and in the formulation of the jointly agreed goals to which the group aspires, and which, it is envisaged, the leader will help it to attain. Put another way, no movement can come into existence without the necessary preconditions for its development. It is for this reason that I believe – and I am happy to repeat this – that the group that crystallized around Matte Blanco *was* very important, but that, if it succeeded, it was because it seemed to interpret or embody the scientific and intellectual interests that, with the characteristics indicated above, seemed already to be latent in the middle of this period. For this reason, we should not attribute the impulse to found the Chilean group exclusively to the personality of Matte Blanco, nor should we think solely in terms of 'personalities', the earliest of whom would be Germán Greve in 1910, and later - from 1925 onwards - Fernando Allende Navarro. Despite their degree of involvement, their training ability and their personal impressiveness, none of these people imparted sufficient impetus to Chilean psychoanalysis to bring into existence something that can be said to have had all the characteristics of an analytic movement.

The founder group, officially recognized as the Asociación Psicoanalítica Chilena at the Zurich Congress, which was held under the presidency of Ernest Jones, consisted of Dr. Fernando Allende Navarro, Dr. Ignacio Matte Blanco, Dr. Arturo Prat Echaurren, Dr. Carlos Whiting D'Andurain, Dr. María Rivera González and Dr. Adelaida Segovia Martin. The first committee featured Allende Navarro as President, Ignacio Matte Blanco as Secretary, and Prat Echaurren as Treasurer. In the period 1951-1953, Matte Blanco was President, Prat Echaurren Secretary, and Carlos Whiting Treasurer, and in 1953-55 Arturo Prat Echaurren was President and Dr. Ramón Ganzaraín Secretary. Arturo Prat Echaurren (1990) supplies a long list of individuals who, during this period, were involved in the activities both of the Psychiatric Clinic and in those of the APC, whether as graduate analysts or as trainees. Apart from the members of the founder group, especially worthy of mention are Drs. Sergio Rodríguez, Erika Bondiek de Guzmán and Julio Dittborn and, later, Hernán Davanzo, Fernando Oyarzún, Guido Solari, Victor Jadresic, Enrique Rosenblatt, Guillermo Altamirano, Ximena Artaza, Otto Kernberg, Ruth Riesenberg, Héctor Pauchard, Salvador Candiani, Bernardo Arensburg and Ester Infante. To this list we would have to add Dr. José Antonio Infante and Dr. Carlos Núñez Saavedra, who not only constituted the psychoanalytic group but also formed part of the teaching team in the Department of Psychiatry of the Catholic University's Medical Faculty. Núñez Saavedra headed this team in his capacity as Full Professor.

Returning to the origins of the movement, we would have to say that a great deal of credit must go to Dr. Fernando Allende Navarro, who played a role of decisive importance in being the first Chilean psychoanalyst and, perhaps, the most important of the movement's precursors. According to Dr. Whiting's account, Allende was born in Concepción in 1891, and studied medicine at the State University of Ghent in Belgium, receiving his doctorate in 1919 at the University of Lausanne in Switzerland. Initially interested in hygiene and parasitology, he later changed to neurology and psychiatry, eventually working with people as distinguished as Constantino von Monacov, Hermann Rorschach and Otto Veragout. In parallel, he also underwent psychoanalytic training in the Swiss transmission between 1920 and 1922, his training analyst and supervisor being Emilio Oberholzer. He was later elected a Full Member of both the Swiss Society for Psychoanalysis and the Paris Psychoanalytic Society. Immediately after his return to Chile, he revalidated his title of doctor of medicine at the University of Chile in 1926 with the thesis *El valor de la Psicoanálisis en la Policlínica. Contribución a la Psicología Chilena* (The value of psychoanalysis in the Policlinic. A contribution to Chilean psychology). Whiting (1980) comments that this was the first publication on analysis by a Spanish-speaking psychoanalyst, and that it is an excellent, clinically illustrated account of contemporary Freudian theory. Allende Navarro was widely recognized as a neuropsychiatrist in scientific and university circles, though he did not enjoy the same degree of success "with his analytic training, activities and publications, which were widely and strongly resisted". Conscious at times of meeting resistance from local scientific circles, he understood the need temporarily to abandon his principal focus of attention in order to work on diffusion. It was at this time that, after receiving a copy of Allende Navarro's first publication on psychoanalysis, Freud himself sent him a stimulating and affectionate letter congratulating him on, and supporting him in, his pioneering work.

Following a period characterized, according to Whiting, "by a struggle that was threatening to become both sterile and interminable", Allende Navarro "withdrew from the official scientific centres and societies", concentrating instead on his private practice and on his work as Director of two clinics. Apart from his analysis of Matte Blanco, his work of diffusion was principally focused on the training of several individuals, of whom the most prominent were the Jesuit priest Abdón Cifuentes (1878-1960), Dr. Ramón Clarés (1888–1946) and Dr. Manuel Francisco Beca Soto (1910–1958), all of whom were, in their turn, to undertake important work in one form or another on the diffusion of psychoanalysis in various scientific and cultural circles. Abdón Cifuentes was Professor of Theology at the Catholic University, Dr. Ramón Clarés was Head of Clinic in Professor Joaquín Luco's Department of Neurology, and Dr. Beca was Deputy Head of Clinic in Professor Arturo Vivado Orsini's Department of Psychiatry at the University of Chile, subsequently becoming the first Professor of Psychiatry at the Catholic University's Medical School (1950-1958). Apart from his own writings and those of his precursors, which have been enumerated by Whiting, the Revista Chilena de Psicoanálisis contains an important summary by Carlos Núñez Saavedra (1981) of Dr. Fernando Allende Navarro's personality and career, which may be amplified by the positive remarks frequently made by those psychoanalysts in our Association who were privileged to know him. His published works, and the information that I have just given, form the basis of my assessment of him as the most important precursor of the Chilean analytic movement.

Before Allende Navarro, the earliest evidence of the existence of psychoanalysis in Chile is associated with the figure of Dr. Germán Greve, who has the historic importance of having presented and published the first Latin American psychoanalytic work, during the first American International Congress on Medicine and Hygiene in Buenos Aires in 1910. This work, entitled "Sobre Psicología y Psicoterapia de Ciertos Estados Angustiosos" (On the psychology and the psychotherapy of certain anxiety states) involved an application of contemporary psychoanalytic concepts, and acquired a significant reputation, not only because of the surprisingly early date at which a Chilean doctor was applying the elements of psychoanalysis (he was in fact the first Latin American to do so), but also by virtue of the fact that Freud himself (1914) took notice of the work and discussed it in flattering terms in his "On the History of the Psychoanalytic Movement".

Whiting, who describes Dr. Germán Greve as possessing a multiple, anxious and achievement-oriented personality, tells us that he was of German ancestry, and that he was born in Valparaíso in 1869. In 1893, after qualifying as a medical doctor and pharmacist, he went to Germany, where he specialized in nervous and mental illnesses. After returning to Chile, besides holding important administrative posts in the clinical field, he devoted himself principally to private practice in neurology and psychiatry, fields in which he was considered extremely successful.

To synthesize, we would be justified in thinking that, apart from the notable figure of Greve Schlegel, it was the influence of Fernando Allende Navarro that was responsible for Chile's earliest and most comprehensive psychoanalytic experiences of any kind, and that prepared the ground for that institutional development which, by initiating the earliest interest in the group, finally gave birth to the psychoanalytic movement, now crystallized under the leadership of Ignacio Matte Blanco.

Before we move on to the events that occurred after 1966, we should perhaps detail the connections established during the Matte Blanco era between the psychiatric centres and the Schools of Psychology, connections that came about precisely because of the significance that the two kinds of institution were ascribing to psychoanalysis. Dr. Arturo Prat Echaurren was one of the first lecturers in the Department of Psychology of the

University of Chile, while the Catholic University's School of Psychology had, as its founder and Director, the distinguished Jesuit academic Hernán Larrain Acuña. It is certain that, after coming under the influence of Abdón Cifuentes, Larrain Acuña underwent a personal psychoanalytic experience during his postgraduate training in Germany. Upon his return to Chile, he set up, in the Catholic University's School of Psychology, a group of teachers that featured a full complement of psychoanalysts.

To continue with our historical account, it is a curious fact that, just after the Association had enjoyed a notable increase in membership following the Third Latin American Psychoanalysis Congress in 1960, internal conflicts began to make their mark, and the first signs of fragmentation had begun to appear. Most of the published material only hints at the nature of the problems that may have arisen. What is certain is that, some months after the Congress, most of the psychoanalysts, members of Matte Blanco's Department, left that institution. It has been surmised that they did so in order to dedicate themselves to the private practice of analysis, and to the task of strengthening the training function, and helping it to acquire a greater degree of independence through the APC's "Institute". In 1966, Ignacio Matte Blanco, who had remained in his post as Professor and Head of Clinic, left Chile and, with his wife (the analyst Luciana Bohn) and family, moved to Rome. For his part, in 1961, Otto Kernberg, who had already clearly demonstrated the extent of his influence upon the international scientific and institutional analytic field, emigrated to the United States, settling in Topeka, where he joined the institutions associated with the Menninger Foundation. Some years later, analysts from another group also moved there, and in 1963 Ruth Riesenberg moved to London, while Hernán Davanzo lived for several years in Riveirao Preto, in Brazil.

As I suggested at the beginning of this essay, I am not communicating the results of an inquiry into specific and possibly intimate aspects of the history of our scientific society. What I am interested in doing is giving an account of the main outlines of the story, and their more fruitful implications. The account that follows thus consists solely of a certain amount of background and a few hypotheses that have occurred to me quite spontaneously.

Regarding the reasons for Matte Blanco leaving Chile, those we have to hand include a longstanding ambition to return to Europe to work on themes that interested him, and an equally longstanding desire to take up permanent residence in Italy, a country with which he admitted to being profoundly in love. We would have to add to this the unfavourable conditions he had begun to encounter in Chile following the conflicts within the young APC and, more specifically, as I myself know, the very unsatisfactory conditions in the University of Chile's Department of Psychiatry.

An investigation into the causes of these latter circumstances would exceed the scope of this article, but the equivocations, and the attempts to discredit both Matte Blanco himself and psychoanalysis that arose within the clinic around 1964-1965, when most of the analysts had already been excluded from it, were very severe.

As I have said, towards the end of 1961 Otto Kernberg, in search of more favourable conditions for development, and having perhaps also been a protagonist in some of the scientific disputes within the early group, moved to Topeka with his wife Paulina Fisher, who was herself to continue with her specialization in child psychiatry and receive her psychoanalytic training at the Topeka Institute.

Towards the end of 1966, Ramón Gazaraín left Chile, also recruited by the Menninger Clinic. Apart from the professional reasons for his decision, it is perhaps worth mentioning that he had been Kernberg's analyst in Chile. Gazaraín, apart from his own duties as an analyst, also undertook very influential work in care and training, crystallized over several years of group experiences and psychotherapies in the University of Chile's Medical School, or through his work with graduates of the Catholic University's School of Psychology. Incidentally, his psychology teacher at the Colegio San Ignacio was the Jesuit priest Abdón Cifuentes, who, as we have said, had in his turn undergone analytic training and experience with Dr. Fernando Allende Navarro.

Finally, another person who left to join the group of Chilean analysts in Topeka and, in so doing, left a gap in the APC that was to remain unfilled for several years, was Dr. José Antonio Infante, although his departure took place later, was more cordial and, in the end, more beneficial, in as far as he was to make a 'round trip'.

As to the effects of all these events, we would first have to say that the fact that help was no longer forthcoming from Matte Blanco undoubtedly had an impact upon the group's purely scientific work and – as is clear – it led to a breakdown of the early connections between psychoanalysis, psychiatry and that form of academic aristocracy that, through its intrinsic merit and its traditions, was so strongly characteristic of the Chilean university world, connections in which, moreover, Matte Blanco had played such an effective part. An eloquent reference to, and illustration of, this latter point appears in the article by the distinguished psychiatrist and academic Fernando Oyarzún, entitled "La significación del Profesor Ignacio Matte Blanco en la Psiquiatria Chilena" (Professor Ignacio Matte Blanco's importance in Chilean psychiatry), published in 1990.

The gap created by the analysts who moved to the Menninger Clinic, besides having a further debilitating effect on the three-sided connective framework that we have just described, perhaps had an even greater impact upon the emotional climate of the group. Besides being involved in a sort of group emigration, this group of colleagues had succeeded in establishing closer links with the rising generation, either through one-to-one teaching, through therapeutic activities or through imparting psychoanalytic experiences to them.

Without considering the advantages that their presence must have brought to specific individuals, or the pleasant but ambiguous sensation we enjoy when, from time to time, we find ourselves meeting some of the most outstanding figures of the international psychoanalytic world, all these experiences of early fragmentation undeniably left their mark. Inevitably, both the reality of these experiences and the fantasies associated with them have helped to shape important aspects of the identity of the Chilean analytic institution. If we think of the group as an individual, what happened can be seen as a sort of traumatization through early separation and family breakdown, a 'family background' that, as well as connoting a fate of sorrow for the lost good, also becomes, as far as the area of aggression is concerned, a breeding ground for idealizations, counter-idealizations, feelings of devaluation, projection of oneself as a scapegoat, and so on.

The Members who, from the 1960s onwards, continued to be at the head of the Chilean psychoanalytic movement, taking especial responsibility for the transcendently important generative and training function now clearly focused within the APC, were Carlos Whiting, Ximena Artaza, Erika Bondiek, Hernán Davanzo, Carlos Núñez, José Antonio Infante, Ester Infante and Eva Reichenstein. For several years, Héctor Pauchard, Enrique Rosenblatt and Guillermo Altamirano were also involved. The last of these is worthy of a special mention since, in the field of child psychiatry and psychoanalysis, he spent several years directing the Psychiatric Department of the Luis Calvo Mackenna Hospital. This department, although much smaller than the original group, nonetheless exhibited the same three facets, in the style of the Matte Clinic, as well as bringing together a large group of psychiatrists, psychologists, candidates and future analysts.

Prat Echaurren (1990) says that, from its earliest days, the APC was sufficiently attractive at both group and individual levels to form connections with the leading international psychoanalytic figures and centres. During his time as President, he wrote to Melanie Klein to ask for the name of someone who could come to Chile to act as a training analyst, not only to provide theoretic-technical training to the members of the Chilean group, but also "to resolve the difficulties that were arising because of people having to work in the clinic alongside their own analysts". This enquiry led to Hanna Segal's name being put forward. Apart from the links that she had formed with Klein and her collaborators during 1950, she had also made contact in France with Lacan and Dolto with similar ends in view, as well as with Rascovsky in Argentina.

Prat acknowledges that all these efforts came to nothing, but it does suggest that he at least, along with certain other members who encouraged him, had pluralistic theoretical aspirations for the Association.

At the level of information exchange with other Latin American movements, apart from Davanzo's experience in Riveirao Preto, especially important were the activities undertaken from the 1950s onwards by Carlos Whiting and Ximena Artaza, who carried out supervisions and reanalysis in Buenos Aires. Worthy of special mention among the many contacts that they made were those with León Grinberg, Marie Langer and Heinrich Racker. Besides Ganzaraín's training visits, Dr. Erika Bondiek de Guzmán undertook similar activities by forming links with the Kleinian group in London.

The experiences that we have mentioned, besides contributing to the analytic enrichment of the people involved, also resulted in the group enjoying greater theoretic-technical progress, as well as a greater openness to new influence. On both the theoretical and technical side a strong Kleinian focus emerged, something that has been sustained up to the present day by a particular section of the membership, which, among other things, maintains a cordial exchange of scientific and institutional information with Ruth Riesenberg, our distinguished colleague at the British Psycho-Analytical Society.

Having discussed all these various factors, now is perhaps the moment to express an opinion on the motivating factors that led to changes in the essential character of the Chilean movement both before 1960 and after.

In addition to certain factors associated with specific members, I think that a crisis of growth caught our accelerated initial group unawares, and caused it to lose its cohesiveness. This crisis was probably exacerbated by the group becoming saturated with emotional catalysts resulting from the unsuitable conditions in which analytic experience was being acquired, and perhaps also from the frustrating situations that arose in the wake of differences in expectations and ambitions among the membership. Nonetheless, I think that one very central source of conflict may have been the difficulty that was experienced in absorbing and overcoming the relational strains between the group and its leader at a new stage of its evolution. Although inspired by different objectives, the group began to take an interest in developments beyond the confines of the Matte Blanco clinic. Apart from the experiences of Carlos Whiting and Ximena Artaza, Otto Kernberg had, before he finally moved to that country, spent time working at different psychiatric centres in the United States, and Ramón Ganzaraín had also made various trips to London for training purposes.

Growth led inevitably to a decline in idealization and, people being what they are, this provided a focal point for disillusionment and other conflicts. Nonetheless, I think that a more mature group would have been more successful in sustaining this decline in idealization, and more tolerance could have been shown in certain areas towards the devaluations that generally accompany such processes.

As in every group, other types of situation arose, some of which, as well as being natural or inevitable, were frequently expressions of a more general problem, or else acted as fuel to inflame other already existing situations. I am merely referring here to the fallout from certain erotic-sentimental situations and the vicissitudes of one-to-one training within the group, which, as we know, often leads to fragmentation, or at least to important transformations in the way groups are formed.

In dealing with all these topics, one might be forgiven for thinking that I am trespassing on a field that really has very little to do with the history of a scientific society. But one must not forget that I am recounting this institutional history from a dynamic perspective, to allow a better understanding of the relationship between origins and identity. In addition, to be able to discriminate between the real aspects of institutional identity and those that are based on a sort of family romance of that identity, one must necessarily tackle such considerations first.

Moving on to another stage of development, at which fragmentation was just starting, the institutional analytic group was focused principally on the APC, and the goal it set itself was the development of psychoanalysis and the establishment of proper training procedures. This involved revising statutory aspects of the Institution, fine tuning the Institute's curriculum, and carrying out didactic functions with a very strict regard for the total framework. In addition, given the theoretical influence of some of the training analysts who remained, and some of the responses to the problems created by the existing dynamic situations, making a fundamental commitment to psychoanalysis implied making a decision that was seen as being similar to a consecration. In this rather ideologized context, which was not however saturated with the disturbing effects of external events, and which offered a wide choice of training analysts, as well a high degree of stimulus towards the idealization of intellectual and scientific leaders, several generations were trained.

Under the leadership of Hernán Davanzo and Mario Gomberoff, however, several graduates and candidates continued to work in university teaching and hospital-based psychiatric care, seeking to maintain a psychodynamic focus while also trying to maintain links with other disciplines in the psychology and mental health fields. It was in just those centres where these two analysts worked as training analysts that there emerged most of the people who were interested in psychoanalysis, and who subsequently became candidates and, later still, colleagues. These activities were carried out principally in the Department of Psychiatry of the Salvador Hospital and in the Hospital Psiquiátrico de Santiago.

We have to say that, at this stage, from the beginning of the 1960s to the middle of the 1980s, the socio-political situation in Chile naturally affected the personnel of the Institution, sometimes very severely: at the group level, however, there do not seem to have been any major repercussions.

While all this was happening, there was another development, which arose at the same time as certain distinctive deficiencies. In general, the members who belonged to this generation of trainees felt a great deal of satisfaction, and were much prouder of the training analysis that they received. They were nonetheless prone to criticize, and tended to feel devalued through belonging to an association that was growing only slowly, in which the Training Analysts made little contribution to scientific publication, and in which there was so little participation in extramural work and involvement in the problems of the community. This situation became more acute when the candidates graduated, and had to develop a new type of relationship with their former trainers.

Those members who divided their time between analytic activity and activity of another institutional character felt, to say the least, that they were very ambiguously valued both in their university institutions and within the group, especially by those training analysts to whom one tends to attribute the official thinking of the APC. Within this group they therefore felt that their identity and quality as psychoanalysts were being questioned. This was, furthermore, a contradictory situation, since the candidates were subject to a strict requirement to undergo a long period of practice in a Psychiatric Department, before they began the Institute's Seminars and other course components of a medical character.

In the first part of this period, in addition to the group of training analysts to whom we have already referred, and those who in their capacity as graduates and candidates lived through the transition from one stage to another, the figure of Carlos Whiting is especially prominent. Although he was a quite outstanding figure within the group, and was probably one of the leading promoters of the trend to focus activities largely on the APC, he chiefly distinguished himself through participation in, and contacts with, other Latin American psychoanalytic institutions, through activities in psychiatric teaching departments, and through forming many friendships with the intervening generations. The outstanding contribution made by David Liberman was also partly due to his relationship-building management style: he organized seminars at various points in the APC's history.

In brief, Carlos Whiting went on to make a distinctive contribution to the identity of the Chilean psychoanalytic group. His openness to the various influences in the development of Latin American psychoanalysis, especially those emanating from Buenos Aires and Montevideo, permitted the assimilation of a different theoretic-technical body of knowledge, different not only in content, but also regarding the different connotation ascribed to that content. In addition, it must be remembered that he was the only Founder Member of the APC who remained a member of it, and who, being gifted with a personality that was remarkably free of resentment and delusions, managed to avoid becoming the object of any kind of idealization.

We can sum up the state of the group during these two early decades of fragmentation in the following manner.

If we ignore the energetic and sustained progress in the work of training, fine tuning and popularization, a trustworthy account of which may be found in Hernán Davanzo's work *Características de la producción psicoanalítica latinoamericana* (Characteristics of Latin American psychoanalytic production), published in 1987, a closer look at the distinctive characteristics of the group would reveal that, of first importance, was the situation arising from the image projected by that group of training analysts who might be identified as having a fundamentally Kleinian theoretic and technical orientation, and whose analytic identity seems to have been sustained through exclusive dedication to the practice of psychoanalysis proper, with the consequence that they were active entirely within the institution, and dedicated themselves solely to the analysis of candidates and to teaching in the Institute. In a way, we may feel that such a subgroup, from its distinctive vantage point of analysis proper, was guilty of undervaluing other types of activity, such as psychotherapeutic interventions, applied psychoanalysis, theoretical studies, and so on, and also that the members of such a subgroup tended to argue that the activities of the Association were fundamentally those of the Institute, and not *vice versa,* as was only fitting, since, in a sense, the Institute, as a training body, is an organ of a larger scientific entity (the Association). On the other hand, most of the members of this subgroup enjoyed undeniable prestige within the Association, and their reputation, seriousness and dedication meant that they tended to be chosen as training analysts by the candidates. Even so, these candidates, sometimes in a rather 'split' form, criticized their rigidity, their massive devotion to the framework, their limited interest in purely scientific work, and their apparent lack of professional interest outside the limits of the institution.

Elsewhere, there was an emphasis during this period on the activities of a broad spectrum of members trained by analysts from the university hospital tradition, who were involved with various psychiatric centres in which a large number of psychologists and psychiatrists had been gathered. For historical reasons, because of their community of interests and, in some cases, for reasons of friendship also, this section of the membership had links with, and was rather more under the influence of, North American psychoanalysis, especially that line that was transmitted by the former members who had emigrated to that country. This line was especially stimulated by the visit to Santiago of Otto Kernberg and Paulina Kernberg, who were invited to participate in various conferences on psychiatry and mental health. Apart from the more specialized theoretical aspects that these contacts nurtured, we should also point out that all these processes were facilitated by the superior degree of contact between psychoanalysis, psychiatry, psychotherapy and other related topics that characterized the development of psychoanalysis in the United States.

Preeminent among those analysts who were particularly notable for their institutional work outside the APC was Dr. Hernán Davanzo. He was the second analyst after Matte Blanco to attain the title of Professor at the University of Chile, and it was under his leadership at the beginning of the 1970s that the Department of Psychiatry was founded at the Salvador Hospital. Dr. Mario Gomberoff and Dr. Ramón Florenzano initially formed a team with him, later creating and leading their own teams. Dr. Luis Gomberoff particularly distinguished himself by being appointed Director of the Hospital Psiquiátrico de Santiago for a long term of office, something that allowed substantial growth to take place in Dynamic Psychiatry. Another line of development, integrating psychiatry and psychoanalysis, was chiefly sustained by Dr. Elena Castro, and was concerned entirely with the specialized area of children and adolescents.

Besides the outstanding managerial work of many of our colleagues, most of whom have held the title of Full Professor in the Medical Faculty of the University of Chile, we must also emphasize the important work carried out in the School of Psychology of the Catholic University. This institution, which was already based on a historical tradition connecting it quite specifically with psychoanalysis, began to emerge at the beginning of the 1980s through the enthusiastic and well-organized work of a group of analysts from the younger generation. After the University had conferred on me the title of Full Professor in 1980, and after I had graduated as an analyst in 1981, I again assumed a full workload at this institution. Having been able to rely on the involvement of colleagues like Jaime Coloma, Eleonora Casaula, Juan Francisco Jordán and Ramón Florenzano, a group was formed which led to a strong impulse towards further development in this area. Several recently graduated candidates and analysts formed part of this team. Additionally, many specialists from other fields have been able, through the training provided, to acquire a more worthwhile and more accurate impression of psychoanalysis, although they have chosen to spend their professional lives in lines of work other than psychoanalysis.

To this we must add the gradual development of a broadly based third section, composed of graduates and new analysts who, both independently and under the auspices of the Association, became seriously involved in the development of the scientific aspects of psychoanalysis and in the future of the Institution, without aligning themselves with any of the tendencies referred to above. Nonetheless, as a vehicle for old dynamic impulses, this 'diminished' group was nonetheless destined to be marginalized for a time, and to adopt an attitude of some passivity towards the tasks of the Association, an attitude that expressed itself in the scant interest that it displayed in joining the ranks of the Full Members, in becoming training analysts, or in filling executive posts within the organization.

What happened next is already recent history, and some of its effects on the identity of the group will probably only reveal themselves later. I cannot bring quite the same degree of impartiality to it as I have tried to bring to the preceding account, since a few years ago I became a member of the Committee of the APC. Even so, I feel that, over the last few years, the Institution has achieved substantial growth both in numbers and in scientific activity, something for which it seemed to have been preparing for some considerable time. It has shown itself capable of creating in our intellectual and professional milieus an impact and an interest in psychoanalysis such as had never occurred previously, and has also shown that it can confront quite critical situations without fragmenting. On the contrary, its ability to continue to resolve existing problems and emerge all the stronger for them, has been a cause for pleasant surprise.

A line of development that, despite being of recent origin, is perhaps especially relevant, is that of the present openness of the APC to the world of culture and to the study of scientific thought generally. Examples are the broadening and deepening of interest that, in a multidisciplinary and systematic format, we have recently undergone in collaboration with Jaime Coloma and a group of sociologists, dramatists and actors in the applied field of drama; Jaime Coloma's distinctive and quite outstanding participation in various other intellectual events in our milieu; the systematic line of research in the field of epistemology, bilogic and the thought of Matte Blanco, brought to a high level of accomplishment by, among others, Juan Francisco Jordán; and the notable refinements in the field of empirical investigation in psychoanaysis achieved in Germany by Juan Pablo Jiménez.

To conclude, I would like to emphasize that the account that I have just given is not intended to be a "History of Psychoanalysis in Chile", but merely a selective focusing on certain factors that, by virtue either of their early appearance or their weighty import, must be considered to have had a determining effect upon the distinctive characteristics of our professional identity. Consequently, I must own up to omissions and unjust inclusions in those cases in which I have been unable to produce evidence of all the positive contributions which various people have made, or where I have failed to show the destructive and disturbing actions of which others have been guilty. As I stated at the beginning, I have sought only to bring together those leading elements that seem to have had definite repercussions upon the character of our institution. Even so, I must confess that it has not been easy to concentrate on the topics with which I have dealt, and adequately to discuss them, without lapsing into formalized rhetorical self-idealizing approaches, into thinly disguised devaluations, or into melancholic or projective reproaches in respect of the group. But, while running the risk of equivocation, it has seemed to me important to undertake this present communication, not only as a bald statement of the facts, but also as an attempt to communicate the really worthwhile thing about the Chilean group, which is that its principal characteristics are not subject to splitting.

In concrete form, my conclusions are as follows:

– The best way forward for our Association is to follow our own inclinations, rather than trying to reflect the image of other groups, however distinguished they may be.

– The Asociación Psicoanalítica Chilena is the inheritor and bearer of a valuable psychopathological clinical tradition, and we should accept and cherish this distinctive characteristic.

– As is true of only a few other places in the world, psychoanalysis in Chile has been developed in close connection with the universities, via their departments of psychiatry and psychology.

– Despite initial difficulties, our institution has offered very satisfactory conditions for training analyses.

– Our Institute of Psychoanalysis allows a sound theoretic and technical training, although certain lines have not been developed, and we must accept in any case that no single line can ever entirely exhaust the possibilities of our discipline.

– Finally, we should clearly accept that what binds us together of our own free will is a scientific, professional and intellectual interest, that one cannot set limits to this interest, and that the existence of such an interest is inconceivable without coincidence or difference in ideas.

References

ARRUÉ, O. (1988): 40 años de Psicoanálisis en Chile. *Revista Chilena de Psicoanálisis en Chile* 7, 3–5

DAVANZO, H. (1987): Caracteristica de la producción psicoanalitica latinoamericana. Correio de FEPAL. São Paulo, 83–90.

FLORENZANO, R. (1988): Estrategias de desarrollo y la Asociación Psicoanalítica Chilena. *Revista Chilena de Psicoanálisis* 7, 20–28.

FREUD, S. (1914): Contribución a la historia del movimiento psicoanalitico. Obras Completas, Tomo XIV. Buenos Aires: Amorrortu Editores.

GANZARAIN, R. / H. DAVANZO / A. PRAT (1987): Origenes de la Asociación Psicoanalítica Chilena. Video. A.P.Ch.

GOMBEROFF, M. (1990): Apuntes acerca de la historia del psicoanálisis en Chile. *Revista de Psiquiatría* (Chile) 7, 379–389.

NUÑEZ, C. (1981): Fernando Allende Navarro. Editorial. *Revista Chilena de Psicoanálisis* 3, 1–7.

OYARZUN, F. (1990): La significación del Profesor Ignacio Matte Blanco en la Psiquiatría Chilena. *Revista de Psiquiatria (Chile)* 7, 375–378.

PRAT, A. (1990): Historia de la psiquiatria dinámica en Chile. *Revista Chilena de Psicoanálisis* 8, 5–8.

WHITING, C. (1980): Notas para la historia del psicoanálisis en Chile. *Revista Chilena de Psicoanálisis* 2/1, 19–26.

Journals

Revista Chilena de Psicoanálisis
since 1979; Ed.: Eleonora Casuala
Asociación Psicoanalítica Chilena

Institutions

Asociación Psicoanalítica Chilena
(Chilean Psychoanalytic Association)
Ramon Cruz 136, Ñuñoa, Santiago
Tel.: 56-2-272 7133; Fax: 56 2 271 8189

Prof. Dr. Omar Arrué, Pedro Lira 1881, La Reina-Santiago de Chile

China

by Alf Gerlach

Psychic Processes in Traditional Chinese Thought

After treatment with medicine had brought no improvement, a physician is said to have intentionally enraged and infuriated his King, whereupon the latter recovered.

A description of this psychotherapy is to be found in a traditional Chinese medical handbook from before the 4th Century B.C. The experiences collected until then were systematized from the 4th Century B.C. in the *Handbook of the Yellow Emperor for Internal Medicine* (Huangdi neijing) and in a commentary on it, the *Book of Ailments.* In the course of China's subsequent development there evolved, influenced by Oracle and Demon medicine, by Confucianism, Taoism and Buddhism, a "Medicine of Parallels" (Unschuld, 1980), which has forged Chinese ideas on mental processes up to this day. According to this, visible and invisible occurrences in the internal and external worlds of the human being (e.g. emotions, internal organs, climatic conditions, elements) are allocated to particular series of parallels and are mutually dependent on each other. Thus the dividing lines between internal and external, mind and body, are removed, and a change in one link in the series of parallels will directly affect the others.

The basis of this system of parallels is formed by the concept of Yin and Yang, the theory of the five elements as well as the idea of a reciprocal dependence of the micro- and macrocosm. The concept of Yin and Yang contains two opposite but nevertheless complementary categories which apply to the human body as well as the whole cosmos. When these two forces are in balance, health and well-being prevail. Yang stands for brightness, sunshine, heat, masculinity, positive, whereas Yin stands for the dark, wet, cold, femininity, negative.

The theory of the five elements allocates one of the five assumed basic elements – wood, fire, water, metal and earth – to all physical phenomena as well as to all occurrences in nature. Thus, for example, five basic emotional states (rage, joy, anger, sorrow, fear), five internal organs (liver, heart, spleen, lung, kidney), five climatic factors (wind, heat, humidity, dryness, cold) are distinguished, between which there are ordered relations and "parallels". In this way internal physical or mental occurrences can be expressed, described and understood in terms of the language used to describe events in nature. For disturbances of the sense of balance both external events such as special conditions of the wind, cold, heat, humidity or dryness are taken into account as the cause as well as emotional states of rage, joy, anger, sorrow and fear. It was presumed that feelings controlled the circulation of the various influences in the body: anger was said to increase energy excessively and to reverse its circulation, joy to restore its balance, fear to slow down or even interrupt the circulation. According to the principles of Yin and Yang the rule then as now was to live a harmonious and well-ordered life (cf. Gerlach/Wengler, 1990).

For the Chinese understanding of the human being the trains of thought described have remained decisive for thousands of years, despite the integration of Confucian, Taoistic and Buddhist philosophy. To the present-day the view of human feeling and thinking has been embedded in a belief in which the human being is seen as an integral part of nature, as a microcosm which merely reflects the laws of the macrocosm and which is dependent on the balance between the forces of Yin and Yang. At the same time it was perfectly possible for advances in knowledge to be integrated in the existing ideas. At the middle of this millenium, for example, the confrontation with Demon Medicine played a significant part in the understanding of mental disorders. Until then demons had been seen as having an independent external influence on human beings, but were now seen as being a product of the human mind. It is quite possible to compare the model then drawn up with the conflict-theoretical model in psychoanalysis, albeit with a basic integral interpretation of correspondence and synthesis. As an example Yü Po's critical examination of the assumption of a pregnancy caused by a demon is quoted (from *The True Tradition of Medicine,* Yixue Chengzhuan, 1515): "The following can be said about this matter: What one thinks during the day, one sees at night. When men and women are lustful and idle, then their fire blazes uninterruptedly in their liver and kidneys. If these people are shy as well, they will often dream about sexual intercourse. The so-called demon-caused pregnancy is therefore in reality a false pregnancy! The fact is there is no such thing as sexual intercourse with demons or pregnancies resulting from it. An ancient recipe says: Where thoughts drift unbound, desires will remain unfulfilled. But the white fluid of impurity forms, collects in the uterus and merges there to become a demon foetus. So if a woman's own blood and her own obscene seed fluid flow together, a lump will form, her breast and womb start to swell and it will look as if the women concerned are pregnant."

First Contacts: Psychoanalysis in Pre-Revolutionary China

Western medicine was first introduced into China in the 19th century and its spreading was due primarily to Christian missionary societies which hoped to achieve successes with the combination of medical and missionary activities. The first psychiatric clinic was opened in Canton in 1898. Until the end of World War II treatment consisted, as was internationally customary, mainly in the administering of tranquilizers, the application of hydro-therapy and of electric shocks. Patients in states of agitation were locked up and put in chains. In the first decades of this century further psychiatric clinics were opened in Shanghai, Peking and Nanking. Several medical colleges also started to include psychiatry and neurology in their curricula. In Shanghai it was especially the Austrian physician Dr. Fanny Halpern who devoted herself to the care of the mentally ill and opened a clinic for mental hygiene in 1940. Despite all these efforts there were fewer than 50 trained psychiatrists in the whole of China in 1949.

Until then a number of Chinese psychiatrists had studied in the USA and other Western countries. Their thinking was influenced primarily by the psychological school of Adolf Meyer. In north-eastern China, however, orientation to Kraepelin's classical psychiatry was predominant, and only in Peking, Cheng-du and Nanking had psychoanalysis been able to gain a foothold. From 1935 until 1939 Dr. Bingham Dai, a psychiatrist of Chinese origin, worked at Peking Union Medical College; he had received a psychoanalytically oriented training in psychotherapy from H.S. Sullivan in New York and from L. Saul in Chicago and passed on his experiences in the form of teaching, supervisions and training therapies to his colleagues. He had to give up his work following the occupation of Peking by Japanese troops and later worked in the USA (cf. Dai, 1984).

In 1948 Fritz Kobler, the director of the neuro-psychiatric clinic at the University of Nanking, published in the *Psychoanalytic Review* a psychoanalytical study of a case of "Koro", which he interpreted as acute castration anxiety and which in this form could only be observed in southern China.

For a short time Adolf Joseph Storfer, a member of the Viennese Psychoanalytical Society and since 1925 director of the "International Psychoanalytical Publishing House", was able to help spread psychoanalytical ideas in China. Although Storfer himself did not work as an analyst with analysands, since 1921 he had initiated major publishing activities in Vienna. He was, for example, a co-editor of *Imago,* which devoted itself to the application of psychoanalysis in other scientific disciplines and in art, as well as the founder of the *Psychoanalytische Bewegung,* for which he wrote numerous articles and reviews, and of the *Almanach der Psychoanalyse.* Until 1938 he was also the editor of the *Zeitschrift für psychoanalytische Pädagogik.* After leaving the Psychoanalytical Publishing House in 1938 he worked as a freelance writer; his etymological dictionaries *Wörter und ihre Schicksale* and *Im Dickicht der Sprache* are still of value today.

Storfer had to experience the pogrom night in Vienna before it became possible for him to leave the country. Not until November 1938 was he able to flee, via Bremen, to Shanghai, where approx. 18,000 émigrés, mainly from Germany and Austria, were able to find refuge between 1933 and 1947. Despite the difficult living conditions in the Japanese controlled part of Shanghai, where Storfer lived at first, on 1st May 1939 he started to publish a German-language journal for émigrés, called the *Gelbe Post.* Subscribers were mainly German-speaking émigrés in China and throughout Asia, but also Chinese academics, many of whom regarded German as the leading language of science (some medical lectures were given in German). The *Gelbe Post* was certainly one of the best journals for émigrés of that time; in the twice-monthly periodical there appeared numerous articles from the field of culture and the humanities, on thought and life in China, on attempts to integrate Jewish émigrés in east Asian culture and on psychoanalysis. Storfer was able to win German, Austrian and Chinese writers and scientists as contributors; from November 1939 the periodical, which had approx. 20 to 30 pages per issue, appeared weekly, in 1940 even twice weekly.

Alongside psychoanalytical originalia, such as "Die Psychoanalyse der chinesischen Schrift", "Der Judenhaß in der Welt", "Die Psychoanalyse in Japan", articles from psychoanalytical journals were reprinted as well as sections from Freud's works. These articles, which often created a direct link to east Asian intellectual history (e. g. "Ein Traum aus einem japanischen Roman des 11. Jahrhunderts") and to Chinese thinking and feeling, certainly reinforced an interest in psychoanalysis which continued to have an influence in Chinese academic circles even after psychoanalysis had been discredited in the 1950s.

Eventually Storfer had to give up the *Gelbe Post* for economic reasons and sell it to the leading competitor in Shanghai, the *Shanghai Jewish Chronicle.* After Japan had entered the war the Jewish émigrés were again threatened, and Storfer had to flee once more, this time to Australia, where he died in Melbourne in 1944 (cf. Bremm, 1990).

Between Curiosity and Condemnation: The Reception of Psychoanalysis in the People's Republic of China

After the great upheavals of the Chinese Revolution central political directives determined the further development of the sciences and of intellectual life in the People's Republic of China, founded in 1949. In the field of psychiatry the Revolution initially made drug abuse disappear. Psychiatric clinics were also opened in rural areas. The idea of prevention was paramount, and modern Western methods were to be combined with traditional Chinese medicine. Under the increased influence of the Communist Party, psychiatry, too, had to orient itself to dialectical materialism and, owing to the close scientific dependence on the Soviet Union, to Pavlovian ideas. Mental illnesses were understood to be a product of an impaired balance between stimulating and checking functions in the central nervous system. Under extreme pressure from the environment, but also under the influence of "wrong ideas", the ability to cope with irritations was understood to decline and to lead to an exhaustion of the functioning of the stimulating or checking processes. This explanation recalls the desired balance of Yin and Yang in traditional Chinese medicine and the undesired effects of states of exhaustion and may thus have contributed to the acceptance of Pavlovian ideas in the People's Republic of China.

Insofar as can be seen in the articles dealing with psychology and psychiatry in the Journal of the Chinese Specialist Society for Neurology and Psychiatry, in the *Acta Psychologica Sinica* (Journal of the Psychological Association) or in the *Chinese Medical Journal*, psychoanalytical thought was not introduced. Yet psychotherapeutic methods were tested, such as a "combined short therapy", which included both suggestive and appellative forms of the psychotherapeutic conversation, drugs, breathing exercises and shadow boxing. Attendant psychological research described this combination method, which is directed at a quick improvement to complaints, as superior to other isolated methods. Later it was also used for the treatment of high blood pressure, stomach ulcers and on schizophrenic patients. The psychotherapeutic "heart-to-heart talks" were directed solely at the good sense and the conscious efforts of the patient, for unconscious or preconscious psychic processes were considered to be non-existent. The patient was to be brought to a point where he would recognize and correct his false understanding of the causes of his illness and would see the changes in his physical functions as the result of his illness. Correct, "normal" consciousness and correct realization should then lead automatically to socially desirable behaviour and adjustment to society.

The People's Republic of China's break with the Soviet Union brought with it a dissociation from the Pavlovian School in the 1960s. At first the main accent lay on biological psychiatry. Then the Cultural Revolution brought grave changes for psychiatric care as well. The methods of Western psychiatry were radically rejected. Doctors and nursing staff were now to see themselves only as part of a collective that also included the sick. The medical model of diagnostics and therapy was pushed back in favour of an educational emphasis that used appeals to the self-confidence of the patients, education to social behaviour and "correct political consciousness". Ideological education was seen as the most important therapeutic element. In many clinics any treatment using drugs was banned and the doctors' status as leader and expert was abolished. Scientific research and exchange with foreign countries came almost to a complete standstill. Only with the fall of the "Gang of Four" in 1976 did the situation change, and since the early '90s, with the opening of the People's Republic to Western visitors and experts, the scientific exchange has started to grow again.

The numerous reports of Western psychiatrists and psychologists that appeared in the '80s in specialist journals provide, however, only an inexact picture of the present situation in Chinese psychiatry. Isolated impressions, difficulties in understanding and wishful thinking are too often in the way of any deeper insight. Even statistics on the number of beds or staff in individual clinics differ greatly.

Besides individual psychoanalysts who have discovered China for themselves as a country to travel to and who have been able to forge links to clinics, two working groups from the Federal Republic of Germany have established a systematized exchange of experiences with psychiatrists in China. Besides the imparting of psychoanalytical theory, clinical work in the form of Balint group work and case-related supervision has also become possible. Beyond the still customary ideological rejection of psychoanalysis, great interest is expressed here, under the protective cloak of the medical sciences, in making use of psychoanalytical understanding in psychotherapeutic applications.

Psychoanalysis is given considerably more attention in the cultural life of China than in psychiatry, albeit beyond the media run and controlled by the state. In Chinese bookshops approx. 30 psychoanalytical works can be found, which have been published more and more since 1985. S. Freud himself is represented with the *Interpretation of Dreams, Civilization and Its Discontents*, the *Three Essays on Sexuality, Totem and Taboo,* the *Introductory Lectures on Psychoanalysis* and the *New Introductory Lectures on Psychoanalysis;* a complete edition of his works is discussed again and again. More recent psychoanalytical authors have also been translated into

Chinese, as well as works by C. G. Jung and A. Adler and their pupils. There are even two different translations of E. Fromm's *The Art of Loving*, which circulate mainly among young Chinese. Indeed, the psychoanalytical publications enjoy a greater following among sociologists, literary scientists and other academics than among psychiatrists. Accordingly, the political campaigns of the Chinese government, the last one after the massacre in Tian-anmen Square in 1989, again and again include violent attacks on the influence of the writings of Freud and his successors, psychoanalysis often being mentioned and condemned in the same breath as existentialism.

Psychoanalysis and the Chinese View of the Human Being: An Outlook

Psychoanalytical observers of Chinese psychiatry underline their impression, too, that at present there is no psychotherapy in China oriented to unconscious conflict, to transference and countertransference and to insight. Insofar as psychotherapeutic methods are applied, they are oriented to behavioural therapy or use supportive techniques. E. D. Joseph (1984), who travelled through China for three weeks in 1983 with a group from the American Psychoanalytical Association at the invitation of the Chinese Medical Association, as well as H. C. Halberstadt-Freud (1991), who had the opportunity of a similar exchange of experiences in 1988/89, argue, however, that this circumstance is also connected with traditional Chinese orientation patterns, which exclude disclosures about one's own feelings and thoughts to a stranger as well as openness to sexual desires. Both the traditional picture of the human being, anchored for four thousand years, and the introverted family-oriented Chinese attitude which oriented more to conflicts of shame than of feelings of guilt would thus stand in the way of any spreading of psychoanalytical ideas.

On the other hand there is a series of psychoanalytical case histories about treatments of Chinese patients, which, while bearing the specific cultural background in mind, provide the opportunity for useful access to internal experience (Muensterberger, 1951, 1982). There are also detailed social-psychological studies on a psychoanalytical basis on the understanding of Chinese culture (see *References* below). Though not based hitherto on any broad clinical material the hypotheses move along the lines, for example, that Chinese children experience a longer and more intensive oral phase or that the solution of the Oedipal conflict is sought more in submission to the father than in aggressive rivalry with him.

In principle, M. L. Ng (1985) has posed the question as to whether psychoanalytical concepts are really so alien to Chinese thought as has been claimed, and emphasizes that his Chinese patients in Hong Kong were accessible to psychoanalytical understanding if the interpretations were offered in a language appropriate to them. It is precisely this integral way of thinking and feeling, referring simultaneously to both body and mind, that is so very close to the present position of psychoanalytical theory and practice. Instead of imposing Western concepts on Chinese terms it is important for the analytical therapist in his work with Chinese patients to make use of precisely this background as a means of access. Because of my own experiences in intimate talks with Chinese, I can, like E. Federn (1986), endorse this conviction; psychoanalysis, after overcoming an encrusted power system, would be able to provide important ideas not only in the context of its medical applications as psychotherapy but also for Chinese intellectual life.

References

BREMM, C. (1990): Die gelbe Post. *Das neue China* 17.

DAI, B. (1959): Obsessive-Compulsive Disorders in Chinese Culture. In: M. K. Opler (ed.): Culture and Mental Health, New York.

– (1965): Culture and delusional systems of some Chinese mental patients. *Int. J. Soc. Psy.* 6.

– (1984): Psychoanalysis in China before the Revolution. *Transcultural Psychiatric Research Review* Vol. XXI.

DIEN, D. S. (1983): Big Me and Little Me: A Chinese Perspective on Self. *Psychiatry* 46.

FEDERN, E. (1986): Letter to the Editor. *Int. Rev. Psycho-Anal.*

GERLACH, A. / B. WENGLER (1990): Wenn das Feuer in der Leber lodert und die Seele krank ist. Psychiatrische Aspekte in der traditionellen Medizin. *Das neue China* 17.

HALBERSTADT-FREUD, H. C. (1991): Mental Health Care in China. *Int. Rev. Psycho-Anal.* 18.

HSU, F. L. (1949): Suppression Versus Repression. *Psychiatry* 12.

JOSEPH, E. D. (1984): Psychiatry and Psychoanalysis in the People's Republic of China: A Transcultural View. *Transcultural Psychiatric Research Review* Vol. XXI.

KOBLER, F. (1948): Description of an acute castration fear, based on superstition. *Psychoanalytic Review* 35.

MUENSTERBERGER, W. (1951): Orality and Dependence. *Psychoanalysis in the Social Sciences* 3.

– (1982): Versuch einer transkulturellen Analyse. Der Fall eines chinesischen Offiziers. *Psyche* 36.

NG, M. L. (1985): Psychoanalysis for the Chinese – Applicable or Not Applicable? *Int. Rev. Psycho-Anal.*

TSENG, W. / J. HSU (1970): Chinese Culture, Personality Formation and Mental Illness. *Int. J. Soc. Psy.* 14.

UNSCHULD, P. U. (1980): Medizin in China. Eine Ideengeschichte, München.

WEAKLAND, J. H. (1950): The Organization of Action in Chinese Culture. *Psychiatry* 13.

– (1956): Orality in Chinese Conceptions of Male Genital Sexuality. *Psychiatry* 19.

Dr. med. Dipl.-Soz. Alf Gerlach, St. Avolder Str. 4, D-66117 Saarbrücken

Colombia

by Inga Villarreal

In Colombia institutionally organized psychoanalysis has been limited until recent years to its capital Bogotá. The by far most important and biggest group of psychoanalysts belong to the Colombian Psychoanalytic Society, which is the only organization of psychoanalysts recognized by the IPA as a Component Society. The second largest group is the Colombian Psychoanalytic Association, which functions as well in Bogotá. For many years small groups outside of these two organizations have been functioning, but mainly in an informal and discontinuous manner. Only during recent years some Lacanian groups have started activities, the most important of these resides in Medellin.

In the first place I will refer extensively to the Colombian Psychoanalytic Society, not only because it has been the fastest growing group, but also because it has been the main agent for the development of psychoanalysis in Colombia. Secondly, I will give a short description of the Colombian Psychoanalytic Association and as a last item I will mention some of the smaller groups.

1. The Colombian Psychoanalytic Society

The Colombian Society consists of 28 Full Members, 45 Associate Members and 10 Honorary Members (1992). Of the latter only one, José Francisco Socarrás, resides in Colombia. 68 members live in Bogotá, 2 in the United States and 4 in other cities. Of the total of 74 active members, 62 are physicians and 12 are psychologists.

The Activities of the Society and of its Members

On the average of once a month a scientific paper is presented. Since 1984 an annual symposium of about two days brings the Colombian colleagues together for discussing papers and clinical case materials presented by some of its members.

The Colombian Society has its own journal which appears at present three times yearly. The journal publishes original articles nearly all written by the membership. Lectures given by visitors and at times translations of interesting papers by foreign authors are included as well. The journal has been appearing without interruption since 1976.

Study groups bring together colleagues with common interests. At present two of these groups are functioning: The first one is called "Freud's thought in his work". It dates from 1981 and is held once a week, conducted by Guillermo Arcila, with 8 to 10 members participating. The second one is a weekly workshop, coordinated by Eduardo Laverde and functioning since 1988. Its aim is producing scientific contributions and a number of interesting papers have been the result. However, the continued postgraduate studies so necessary for the practising analyst have not been up to a desirable level. Plans to improve this situation are being discussed.

Most of the members of the Society are full-time practising psychoanalysts, some are professors of psychiatry or teach in faculties of psychology and some are active in mental health institutions.

Tendencies of Psychoanalytic Thought

The members of the Colombian Society are well informed about the theories of different schools of psychoanalytic thought as these are taught as part of the curriculum of the Institute. However, the teaching of Freud's works remains central and this is reflected as well in the importance given to Freudian theory in the scientific contributions of the Society members. Besides, Melanie Klein's writings have strongly influenced psychoanalytic thinking, which is especially noticeable in the area of child analysis. One of our Members, Carlos Plata, who trained in Argentina at a time when Kleinian thought was very influential in the Argentinian Psychoanalytic Association, reorganized the Institute's curriculum in the early sixties, including M. Klein's works in the teaching. Argentinian authors such as Angel Garma, Arnoldo Raskovsky, Leon Grinberg, David Liberman, José Bleger and Heinrich Racker have influenced Colombian analysts through their writings and some of them as well by visiting and teaching in Bogotá. Post-Kleinians such as D. Meltzer and W. R. Bion are studied in depth by some of the colleagues. D. W. Winnicott's theories have importantly influenced psychoanalytic conceptions as well. But not only the authors connected with the Kleinian School of thought have been influential. The writings of Heinz Kohut and Otto Kernberg, especially those of the former, are increasingly studied. French authors have not had the same importance although some articles are read in the seminars. A few colleagues are interested in Lacanian theories but these are not taught or put into practice by the members of the Society. The groups of Lacanian analysts which have started to develop have no connection with our Society.

Colombian analysts, exposed to different trends of psychoanalytic thought from the time they were candidates, are developing a more critical approach towards the different theories and nowadays a strict adherence to one model of thought is disappearing. Some of the colleagues prefer the one or the other scheme of theoretical reference in the papers they present to the membership but during the discussions a variety of different models are used and in my opinion we are reaching a post-school approach to psychoanalytic theory. In spite of the fact that some of the members of the Society have published articles in international journals and some have written books about psychoanalytic topics (Simon Brainsky, Carlos Plata and Guillermo Sánchez) we are still a long way from full creative maturiy. As to psychoanalytic technique, great importance is given to the analytic setting and we consider a frequency of at least four hours a week necessary for the development of an analytic process. Heinrich Racker's influence on the theory of technique has been basic. Nowadays, Horacio Etchegoyen's text on technique is used as well for teaching. The Spanish translation of the *Theory and Practice of Psychoanalysis* by Hans Thomä and Horst Kächele is being introduced and I hope that through this work German psychoanalytic authors will become more known in our Society.

The Colombian Psychoanalytic Institute

The Colombian Psychoanalytic Institute functions as a dependency of the Colombian Society and is at present (1992) training 14 candidates, of whom 8 are currently in their 3rd and 6 in their 1st year of the four year seminar programme. The Institute has 12 training analysts and one full member authorized to conduct collective and individual supervisions of cases. The teaching staff consists of 16 full members, including all training analysts, and some 12 full and associate members have functions as Assistant Professors. Applying the models Anne-Marie Sandler (1981) described for the functioning of the psychoanalytic institutes which belong to the IPA, ours is a "closed institute" with strict selection procedures before the candidate can start his training and a well defined curriculum.

The training follows the traditional model of the tripartite system. Training analyses are conducted with a minimum of 4 hours weekly and are usually very long, as the candidate has to have a minimum of two years of analysis before entering the seminar programme and has to remain in analysis during the entire duration of his training. This amounts usually to a total of seven to eight years but may be much longer as well. Training analysts are strictly non-reporting.

The minimum requirements for indivudal supervisions are a total of 200 hours with three different supervisors.

The general aims of the Institute are the following: To train psychoanalysts who will be able to practise psychoanalysis autonomously and capable to function on a theoretic-investigative level; to capacitate the future analyst to study psychoanalytic theory in a methodic, systematic and critic way; to promote the realization of personal contributions (Laverde, 1983).

The seminar programme is extensive. During eight semesters five weekly seminars of two hours duration each are taught. The seminar plan comprises three areas: Theory, technique and continuous case seminars. The area of theory includes: The study of selected works of Sigmund Freud throughout the 8 semesters; general theory of development, 4 semesters and models of theory, 4 semesters. The theory of technique is taught throughout the 8 semesters. Besides the extensive teaching of Freud's work, a total of some 40 hours each is dedicated to the writings of M. Klein, W. R. Bion and D. W. Winnicott and some 20 to the ones of Anna Freud, E. H. Erikson and R. D. Fairbairn. Other authors such as J. Bowlby, R. A. Spitz, E. Bick, H. Hartmann and H. Nunberg, and a variety of Latin-American authors are studied with a much lesser frequency. Two weekly seminars are taken up by continuous case seminars throughout the training. During the first two semesters these seminars deal with initial interviews taking into account questions of analyzability and the case evaluation from a psychoanalytic point of view. During the last year of training one of the continuous case seminars is replaced by a workshop in which each of the candidates presents a paper on one of his clinical cases, which he discusses with his peers under the guidance of a training analyst experienced in questions of the methodology of writing scientific papers (Laverde, 1983; Sanchez, 1990). This workshop allows the candidates to write their first paper with peer support and with the help of an experienced analyst. Until 1976 the candidates who had finished their training had to submit a scientific paper in order to be received as Associate Members of the Society. An important number of colleagues would not take this step and would remain graduates from the Institute but would not become members of the Society. After the requirement of the presentation of a scientific paper for Associate Membership was abolished, the difficulties were passed on to the next step: The Associate Members who graduated after this change in the Bylaws frequently would not present the required papers for full membership.

*History of the Colombian Psychoanalytic Society**

Freud's works were read by a select group of intellectuals soon after their appearance. However, access to his works was limited as the predominant cultural influence well up to the Second World War was France and transmitted largely through the French language. Only after Freud's works had been translated into Spanish by Luis Lopez-Ballesteros during the years between 1922 and 1934 and published nearly simultaneously with the *Gesammelte Werke* did they become more known in Colombia. This early and nearly complete translation of Freud into Spanish was due to the initiative of José Ortega y Gasset, the great philosopher and humanist influential in the cultural and literary renaissance of Spain, who wanted to open intellectual life in Spain to trends of thought from German culture. The translation of Lopez-Ballesteros is rather free with emphasis on a fluent classical Spanish. It preserves some of the beauty and profound appeal to the reader so characteristic of Freud's writings and, in spite of the serious flaws of the translation, it contributed greatly to the spread of Freudian ideas in the Spanish speaking world (Villarreal).

One of the Colombian intellectuals influenced by Freud's ideas was a, at that time, medical student: José Francisco Socarrás. Ever since he has played an outstanding role in the development of psychoanalysis in Colombia. José Francisco Socarrás first heard Freud being mentioned by his psychiatry professor. He included as early as 1929 the teaching of Freud's works in the faculties of psychology in two of the universities, thus becoming the first professor to teach psychoanalysis in Colombia. In 1930 he wrote his thesis on "Fundamental Principles of Psychoanalysis". In 1946 he travelled to France to specialize in psychiatry and psychoanalysis; his analyst was Paul Cenac and he supervised with Sacha Nacht and Pierre Bouvet. He took part as well, together with René Diatkine and others, in seminars held by Serge Lebovici about child psychiatry and child psychoanalysis. He became an Associate Member- and later a Full Member – of the Paris Psychoanalytical Society. He returned to Colombia in 1950.

Another very important figure basic for the beginnings and the development of psychoanalysis in Colombia is Arturo Lizarazo. Arturo Lizarazo left Colombia in order to study medicine in Santiago (Chile). He specialized in psychiatry and had his training analysis with the first Chilean psy-

* I want to express my thanks to Guillermo Sanchez Medina for letting me consult chapters V and VI: "Historia del Psicoanálisis en Colombia" and "Psicoanálisis en Colombia" of the manuscript of his book *Psicoanálisis ayer, hoy y mañana. Historia del Psicoanálisis* from which I obtained much of the data and could corroborate other.

choanalyst: Fernando Allende Navarro. Having graduated from the Institute of the Chilean Psychoanalytic Association, he returned in 1948 to Colombia and was the first one to start the practice of psychoanalysis in this country.

Soon joined by Socarrás he began to spread psychoanalytic knowledge to a wider community. These two pioneers encountered great resistances and at times were violently attacked by some of the most well known psychiatrists and by some priests as well. This opposition on the part of the latter, partly due to Pope Pius XII's pronouncements against Freud's ideas (Socarrás, 1981), had its historical importance in a country in which the official religion is Roman Catholicism and where especially the Jesuit community has had a profound influence on education. However, this opposition has not proved to be a lasting hindrance and already for many years a number of colleagues have been teaching psychoanalysis at the Jesuit University.

A Venezuelan colleague, Hernán Quijada, trained in Paris together with José Francisco Socarrás. Because of the political situation in his native country, which prevented him from returning, he worked from 1951 to 1956 as a psychoanalyst in Bogotá after which he left for Venezuela. There he has been an important figure for the development of psychoanalysis.

During the early fifties Socarrás, Lizarazo and Quijada and some of their first analyzands began to create a psychoanalytic group. This early group consisted of medical doctors and some professionals with a non-medical background. On May 6th 1956, commemorating the centenary of Freud's birthday, the Colombian Psychoanalytic Study Group was officially founded. However, at this moment the non-medical members were excluded from the group. The official founding members are: José Francisco Socarrás, Arturo Lizarazo, Tufik Meluk, Alfonso Martinez Rueda and Germán Saavedra Bayer. The Group decided to accept as the rules of the organization the Constitution and Bylaws of the IPA and, as well, to request the Sponsorship of the Psychoanalytical Society of Paris and the Psychoanalytic Association of Chile.

The three analysts trained outside of Colombia functioned as the first training analysts of the group while the remaining four founding members were candidates in the process of finishing their training (Socarrás, 1981). The IPA officially accepted the Study Group during the International Psychoanalytical Congress which took place in Paris in 1957.

By the end of 1958 Carlos Plata Mujica returned to his native Colombia after having trained in Buenos Aires in the Argentinian Psychoanalytic Association. His training analyst was Arnaldo Rascovsky. He joined the Study Group as a training analyst and he has been a leading figure in Colombian psychoanalysis ever since. He was not only influential in introducing Kleinian psychoanalysis in Colombia and organizing the Institute but he has had an important role as well in structuring the Colombian Society. On the international scene his most important achievements were a Vice Presidency of the IPA from 1973 to 1975 and the Presidency of COPAL, the former organization of the Latin American Psychoanalytical Societies and Associations, from 1971 to 1973. In 1959 Guillermo Sánchez Medina returned to Colombia after having studied psychoanalysis in Madrid and New York. His father, Antonio José Sánchez, was most probably the first Colombian to be analyzed, from 1928 to 1930 in Geneva (Switzerland) by Charles Odier. He transmitted his admiration for Freud to his children and two of them, Guillermo Sánchez Medina and Alfonso Sánchez Medina are training analysts of our Society. In 1960 Guillermo Arcila, who trained in Buenos Aires, was accepted as a member of the Study Group. However, due to his residing in a distant town (Manizales), he only could begin to take part in the teaching activities in 1967. In 1961 Mauro Torres returned to Colombia after having completed his training in the Mexican Psychoanalytic Institute. His analyst was José Remus.

In 1961, during the Edinburgh Congress, the Colombian Psychoanalytic Study Group was recognized by the IPA as the Colombian Psychoanalytic Society. This was mainly due to the efforts of José Francisco Socarrás with the support of influential French analysts.

The unity of the newly approved Society did not last long. As in other psychoanalytic groups, founded by colleagues trained abroad in Societies with different frames of reference of psychoanalytic thought, the integration process proved to be difficult. In the particular case of the Colombian Society the very different personal and political ideologies of the two leading training analysts, who had between them all but one of the candidates in analysis, played an important role as well. In 1963 the conflicts, manifestly due to radical differences of political ideology, broke out in the open. Arturo Lizarazo felt that José Francisco Socarrás was introducing his Marxist ideas into the teaching of psychoanalysis and Socarrás defended his position as to the importance of the teaching of Hegel's dialectic, applying the latter's concepts such as the synthesis of contradictions – for instance love and hate – in order to reach a more complete understanding of the theory and practice of psychoanalysis. In Socarrás opinion (Socarrás, 1990, personal communication), on a deeper level the conflicts were due to a lack of understanding on the part of Lizarazo and himself of the negative transferences which some of the candidates relegated the "founding father" who was not their training analyst. A lack of adequate selection procedures and the tensions caused by the responsibility for so many candidates most certainly contributed as well to these severe personal conflicts. Arturo

Lizarazo resigned from the Society and all his analyzands left with him. At this time the Institute was training two groups of candidates, the first one of 8 was about to finish the seminars, while the second group of 7 was in its third year. The author of this contribution belonged to this second group of candidates. The split of the Society involved the two candidate groups as about half of the participants of each group was in analysis with either one or the other of the two training analysts in conflict. The candidates chose to remain with their training analysts, regardless of their political convictions at the time of the split. A total of 10 members and candidates left the Society and founded the Colombian Psychoanalytic Association. Of these only one member returned, after three years, to the Colombian Society of which he has been a training analyst for many years.

The difficulties of the Colombian Society did not end with the split. Already in 1964 on the initiative of Socarrás, who had in the meanwhile arranged his differences with Lizarazo, talks about a possible re-unification started. However, the fact that the candidates who had left the Society and co-founded the Association had been given training functions from the beginning, proved to be one of the obstacles for the re-unification. Mauro Torres, who was in 1964 opposed to the reintegration, resigned in 1968 protesting the failure of the renewed attempts at reuniting the two groups. Some candidates left as well. In Socarrás' opinion (Socarrás, 1990, personal communication) Torres' resignation was much more due to his gradual drifting away from psychoanalytic theories. Shortly after, during this same year, Socarrás resigned alleging personal difficulties with one of the training analysts of the Society. The report of the President of the Society, Carlos Plata, to the membership states that "some ex-members and ex-candidates who have in common their disagreement about the exclusively psychoanalytical orientation of our Society" had resigned (Plata, 1969).

The sixties were marked by the split and the resignations. The main efforts of the remaining members of the Society were directed towards consolidating its structure and maintaining a functioning Institute in order to continue with the training in spite of the reduced number of available teachers and supervisors. High standards and strict rules for a training not contaminated by personal differences of the training analysts with a view to graduate well prepared analysts were implemented. In spite of the crisis situation the Colombian Society was in 1968 host to the Latin-American Congress.

As I mentioned before, during the founding of the Study Group non-medical colleagues were excluded from the projected training. The question of lay-analysis has been ever since an important issue and was discussed during the decade of the seventies again and again. In the end a compromise solution was reached. In 1979 the Colombian Society created a Center for the Spreading of Psychoanalysis whose main function was the training of non-medical professionals. In the beginning this Center was conceived for the training of child and adolescent psychotherapists but soon the teaching of adult analysis was included and finally the programme was equal in all aspects to the one of the Institute. This Center trained two groups of psychologists who became, after graduating, Corresponding Members of the Society. Our Constitution and Bylaws did not permit professionals with a non-medical background to become Associate Members. This discrimination was intensely debated by the membership of the Society and was finally abolished in March of 1990. The candidates who are at present in their third year of training constitute the first group in which physicians and psychologists are integrated and receive their training together. The resistances to the admission of psychologists expressed by some of the members related to fears of a loss of their identity as medical doctors. Some of the Latin-American psychoanalytic societies closed the entrance for non-medical students, probably under the influence of the rules for training in the United States. However, this trend has been reversed in all but one of them in recent years.

The years from the seventies onwards have been characterized by a rather slow but steady growth of the Society. International recognition of the Colombian Society as a traditional, solid group of analysts came with the election of Carlos Plata in 1973 as a Vice-President of the IPA. In 1976 the IPA entrusted the Colombian Society with the teaching of a group of 9 candidates in Venezuela, which could not be accomplished by the Venezuelan colleagues because of a crisis in their Association. The teaching activities were coordinated by Guillermo Sánchez Medina and carried out by four training analysts of the Colombian Society (Guillermo Arcila, Guillermo Sánchez Medina, Inga Villarreal and Luis Yamin) during 1977 and 1978. In 1977 the author of this survey was elected Vice-President of the IPA and has been active in different IPA assignments ever since.

In 1979 the Society started to open up more to the community by giving courses about psychoanalysis to medical doctors, psychologists and other interested groups.

Since 1980 a yearly meeting of all training analysts is held during which topics of specific interest for training are discussed.

The Colombian Society is due to its geographic location rather isolated even from other Latin-American Societies. Because of the difficult economic situation of the country not many colleagues can travel to Congresses. For a few years the plans for regional meetings with neighbouring Societies resulted in Symposiums with the Venezuelan Association. However, only three of these did finally take place. Throughout our history visitors have played an important role as a stimulus for the development of our Society. For many years the annual interchange programme of COPAL and later FEPAL (Federation of Latin-American Psychoanalytic Societies and Associations) in which a training analyst from another Latin-American Society visits for a week, holding seminars and conferences, have broadened our views. As part of this programme Colombian training analysts have taught in a number of Latin-American Societies as well. Other distinguished visitors such as Arnoldo Rascovsky, Angel Garma, Donald Meltzer, Leon Grinberg and recently Otto Kernberg, to name just a few, have had an important influence.

During the last years of the decade of the eighties the Society again suffered a crisis, however of minor proportion, and, at least in its manifest content, connected with our troubled history.

José Francisco Socarrás had been expressing his wish to reenter the Colombian Psychoanalytic Society already for some years. The older generation of analysts which had lived through the crisis situations of the sixties felt that to reinstate him as an Honorary Member was a gesture of gratitude and of recognition of his great merits for the Society and for the development of psychoanalysis in Colombia. However, some members of the younger generation of psychoanalysts – who hardly knew Socarrás – and one of the training analysts who started only during 1967 to take part in Society issues, violently objected to his readmission. After the election of Socarrás by a majority vote of the membership in 1988, they involved the IPA and the international psychoanalytic community alleging violations of the Constitution and Bylaws of the Colombian Society and, more importantly, stating that Socarrás could not be reintegrated as he is, in their opinion, not a psychoanalyst. This opinion is based on the argument that he had not been a Member of the IPA for many years. It is not my intention to go into the possible underlying motivations of this crisis. However, the manifest reason for this crisis, the return of a founding father after 20 years of absence, gives material for thought.

One of the great challenges to the Colombian Society in the more immediate future is the spread of psychoanalysis to cities outside of the capital. In Cali there is now a group of four analysts, three are members of the Colombian Psychoanalytic Society, one is a member of the Argentinian Psychoanalytic Association, and the planning for a well organized training in Cali is starting.

2. The Colombian Psychoanalytic Association

As I mentioned before, the Colombian Psychoanalytic Association is the second largest group of psychoanalysts in Colombia. It was founded in June of 1962 by ten colleagues who had left the Colombian Psychoanalytic Society. One of the founders, Arturo Lizarazo, was a training analyst and founding member of the Colombian Society, another one, Gustavo Angel, was a Full Member and the remaining were candidates who were about to finish their training in the Colombian Institute. However, Gustavo Angel returned after three years to the Colombian Society. All these colleagues became training analysts at the time of the founding of the Association. This turned out to be the main obstacle for the reunification with the Colombian Society when especially José Francisco Socarrás tried to get the two groups together again during the years from 1964 to 1968. After the failure of the attempts at reunification, the Association applied in 1969 for official recognition as a Component Society of the IPA, which was not granted.

The Association has at present (1992) 9 Full Members, 7 of whom are training analysts (all of them belong to the original founding group), 9 Associate Members, 2 Adherent Members (medical or non-medical non-practising analysts) and 3 Honorary Members. Only physicians can become Full or Associate members. Five colleagues of the Colombian Assication are Fellows of the American Academy of Psychoanalysis.

During their 27 years of existence the Institute of the Association has trained a total of 18 candidates. The study programme of the Institute requires: a minimum of 600 hours of personal and training analysis; four years of theoretic seminars, with a minimum of 20 per academic semester; and a minimum of 200 hours of individual supervision (Gonzalez, 1987). An important aspect of their activities has been a psychiatric clinic (Instituto Colombiano del Sistema Nervioso) with which they have a special arrangement for teaching. A programme of specialization in psychoanalysis as part of the specialization program for psychiatry of the Colombian School of Medicine started last year and three students are taking part in it. Besides the training programmes the Association publishes a bi-annual magazine, called *Psicoanálisis, Revista de la APC* which was published from 1977 to 1980 and has appeared again since 1987. The Association has held annual Congresses for the last 10 years to which Symposiums were added in 1987. Two Latin-American analysts of a Kleinian orientation and a number of North-American colleagues have visited the Association and have assisted in furthering their development. Since 1988 the Association has been seeking again to be affiliated as a Component Organization of the IPA.

3. Other Psychoanalytic Groups

For many years the training of psychologists was not possible in either of the two important psychoanalytic organizations and, as I mentioned before, the Association continues to be closed for non-medical professionals. This has led to the existence of many psychoanalytic study groups of psychologists, which function in a more or less informal and discontinuous way. The teaching is very often done by analysts of either one of the two psychoanalytic organizations in an individual manner. This has resulted in a situation in which a great number of professionals, nearly all psychologists, are using psychoanalytic theories and technique, calling it at times psychoanalysis, in their practices. The training of psychologists, now possible in the Colombian Society, should diminish much of this undesirable parallel training.

A group of a different kind functioned for a number of years in Cali. It was called the Freud Center and the leader was a philosopher, Estanislao Zuleta, who died recently. He tried to integrate psychoanalysis with philosophical and sociological theories of Marxism, existentialism and structuralism. An Associate Member of the Colombian Society, Oscar Espinosa, who resigned his membership in 1978, was active in this group.

Various Lacanian groups have started to function during recent years. The oldest of these is called: Los Carteles Psicoanaliticos de Medellin (the Medellin Psychoanalytic Cartels). They have been publishing for the last years quarterly pamphlets with short contributions of their members and translations of other Lacanian authors. The members of these groups have not had the kind of training which is, in my opinion, necessary to be able to practise classic psychoanalysis.

Psychoanalysis, in spite of the resistances to its theories which will always exist due to its very nature, is nowadays a well recognized scientific discipline in Colombia. A commitment to a high level of training, following IPA Standards, is the only possible way of dealing with the possible dangers of the upsurge of many informal and changing groups which might dilute the essence of psychoanalytic theory and practise.

References

GONZALEZ, M. (1987): *Academy Forum* Vol 31, number 4, pg. 16.

LAVERDE, E. (1983): *Curriculum del Instituto Colombiano de Psicoanálisis* (unpublished).

PLATA, C. (1969): Informe del Presidente de la Soc. Col. de Psicoan. a la Segunda Asamblea Ordinaria (unpublished).

SANCHEZ MEDINA G. (1990): Psicoanálisis ayer, hoy y mañana. Historia del Psicoanálisis. Bogotá: Divulgación.

SANDLER, A. M. (1981): The Selection and Function of the Training Analyst in Europe. Pre-Congress on Training, Helsinki.

SOCARRÁS, J. F. (1981): Psicoanálisis en Colombia. *El Tiempo.* Mayo 13.

VILLARREAL, I.: Problems in Translating Freud. Chapter of: Translating Freud. Edited by D. G. Ornston. New Haven/London: Yale Univ. Press.

Journals

Revista de la Sociedad Colombiana de Psicoanálisis
since 1976; Ed.: Guadelupe Ltds.

Psicanálise
since 1977; Ed.: Danilo Diaz Granados

Institutions

Sociedad Colombiana de Psicoanálisis
(Colombian Psychoanalytic Society)
Avenida 13 N° 86, Santafé de Bogotá D. C.
Tel.: 571-257 6224; Fax: 571-236 5149

Dra. Inga Villarreal, Carr. 2A 70-66 (Apt. 501), Bogotá

India*

by Sudhir Kakar

The historical context of Indian psychoanalysis is inseparable from the life and work of Girindrashekhar Bose (Sinha, 1966a/b). Born in 1886, Bose was the son of the chief minister of a small princely state in Bengal. Though he studied medicine and practised as a physician in Calcutta after graduating in 1910, Bose's intellectual passion was abnormal psychology. He learnt hypnosis and by 1914 he had begun to treat patients suffering from mental disorders by a technique closely akin, as he says, to Freud's original method, presumably the use of hypnosis, suggestion, pressing and questioning to recall memories and encourage associations. He had already developed some of his psychological ideas including the basic elements of his theory of opposite wishes, namely that for every expressed wish there is an opposite wish working in the unconscious, before the first English translations of Freud's writings reached Calcutta and made a strong impact on the young Bengali doctor's mind. A man of great energy and a good deal of originality, Bose immersed himself further in his psychological studies and in 1921 received the first Doctor of Science degree in Psychology awarded in India. Steeped in Hindu philosophy and the Indian cultural tradition, Bose had many other firsts to his credit: the first professorship of psychology at the University of Calcutta, a founder of the Indian Psychological Association and, for us the most important first of all, the architect of the Indian Psychoanalytic Society.

The founders' meeting of the Society took place in 1922 with Bose in the chair. Of the fifteen original members, nine were college teachers of psychology or philosophy, five – including two British – belonged to the medical corps of the Indian Army while the professional affiliation of the remaining member is intriguingly listed as "Secretary of the Jute Balers Association".[1] In the same year, Bose wrote to Freud in Vienna. After

* First published in *Revue Internationale d'Histoire de la Psychanalyse* 2 (1989), 499–503.

1 The notice of this meeting is in the archives of Indian Psychoanalytic Society in Calcutta.

expressing sentiments of respect and admiration for the Master's work, he informed him of the formation of the Indian society. Freud was pleased that his ideas had spread to such a far-off land and asked Bose to write to Ernest Jones, then president of the IPA, for membership of that body. Bose did so and the Indian Psychoanalytic Society with Bose as its first president, a position he was to hold till his death in 1953, became a fully-fledged member of the international psychoanalytic community. Although psychoanalysis attracted some academic and intellectual interest in the thirties and forties, mostly in Calcutta, the number of Indian analysts was still fifteen in 1945 when a second training centre, under the leadership of an Italian, E. Sevadio, was started in Bombay.

Cut off from the thrust and parry of debate, controversy and ferment of the psychoanalytic centres in Europe, dependent upon not easily available books and journals for outside intellectual sustenance, Indian psychoanalysis was nurtured through its infancy primarily by the enthusiasms and intellectual passion of its progenitor. In the informal meetings of eight to ten people held on Saturday evenings at the president's house – the house was to become the headquarters of the Indian Society after Bose's death – Bose read most of the papers and led almost all the discussions. Without the benefit of training analysis himself, it was Bose who "analysed" the other members in a more or less informal manner and otherwise endeavoured to keep their enthusiasm for psychoanalysis alive.

From my own experience of psychoanalytic institutes in different countries I would venture to say that the practice of psychoanalysis is not unlike that of performance of Indian classical music. The basic musical vocabulary may be shared yet each *gharana* or school has a specific, traditional way of elaborating and performing a *raga.* The musician has learnt this traditional way through personal instruction over many years from his teacher who, in turn, has learnt it from his teacher and so on. Similarly, the way we practise psychoanalysis is essentially learnt from our own training analysis and can often be traced to a particular psychoanalytic *gharana.* Such a *gharana* is not to be confused with a self-conscious school advancing a divergent theoretical position. All it means is that the practitioners belonging to a *gharana* share a particular style of psychoanalytic "performance". Coterminous with a training institute or even with a national boundary, the *gharana*'s original teacher can often be traced back to the first generation of analysts.

In any event, because of its relative isolation, Indian psychoanalytic practice has been decisively marked by the stamp of the first Indian analyst. Essentially, Bose's method is derived from the psychiatric practice of his pre-Freudian years, his theory of opposite wishes and his readings of

Freud's writings on analytical technique. In a short communication to the International Journal of Psychoanalysis in 1931, he described it as follows: "In contrast with the active therapy and the forced fantasy method of Ferenczi, the method has the following salient features. In suitable cases the patient is first asked to give his free associations to determine the nature of the repressed wish active at the time. He is then *ordered* [*itals.* mine] to build up wish fulfilments and fantasies with reference to the repressed wish, ultimately taking up the roles of the subject and the object in the wish-situation" (Bose, 1931). The patient was further instructed to repeat this at home and to report the resultant fantasies in the next analytic hour. In the session the patient reclined in an easy chair with his eyes closed, the analyst sitting at the back diligently taking notes of what he or she said. These detailed notes were more than an *aide-memoire* for the analyst. They were actively used in the process of analysis for breaking down resistance. "The record is of value also in removing the resistances of the patient who may be denying some of his former statements in spite of the assertions of the analyst to the contrary. A reference to notes brings about a conviction of the truth of interpretations much more" (Bose, 1948). As late as in 1966, the brochure published on the occasion of the silver jubilee celebrations of Lumbini Park, the mental hospital run by the Indian Society, in its photographic illustration of an analytical session, shows a patient sitting with his eyes closed on a folding canvas chair while the analyst behind him is bent over a notebook writing down his utterances.

The actively didactic stance of the Indian analyst, as he engages in a lively interaction with the patient, fits more with the model of the guru-disciple than the doctor-patient relationship. Elsewhere, I have pointed out some of the reasons for this greater activity on part of the Indian analyst: an absence in the Hindu philosophical and literary tradition of life-historical introspection so that the patient may have to be taught the kind of "psychological mindedness" needed for successful psychoanalysis; the traditional child rearing practices and ideology of social relations which emphasise a demonstratively close, 'symbiotic' mode of relating with significant others, expectations from which the analyst is not immune; the dominant Indian idiom in which words are only a small part of interpersonal communication, where the patient often craves for eye contact and seeks to complement the spoken communication with facial expression, hand gesture and bodily movement (Kakar, 1985).

When Bose instructs the patient on the direction his fantasy should take, he is not far removed from some of the meditative procedures used in the Hindu psycho-philosophical schools of self-realisation. Tantric visualization such as *nyasa* or the *yoganidra* of Raja Yoga come immediately to mind. They are techniques with which Bose, through his deep study of the Yoga's was thoroughly familiar.

There may be grave reservations in many about the content of the clinical material elicited by the active, didactic stance of the Indian analyst, a stance to which the analytic method of Bose has greatly contributed. One can legitimately wonder if the analyst's activity does not come perilously close to what a lawyer is forbidden to do in the courtroom, namely "lead the witness", increasing the chances of suggestion and thus adulterating the clinical data beyond salvation.

We know that ever since Freud, who was seriously concerned about the suggestion problem, analysts have tried to make sure that analytic technique, in contrast to other psychotherapies, minimizes suggestion to an extent where it can no longer be regarded as an alternative explanation. As Marshall Edelson reminds us, interpreting the defence rather than suggestions about what the patient is defending against, interventions calling attention to the patient's habitual way of resolving ambiguities in life and in the analytic situation, pointing out the context in which the analysand has difficulties in saying what he has on his mind, and calling attention to what needs further explanation, constitute the bulk of analytic interventions in the clinical situation (Edelson, 1984). These are relatively free from the taint of suggestion. Heightened didactic activity on the part of the analyst thus need not be *ipso facto* suggestive. The analyst can exhort, encourage and interact as much as demanded by the context in which he operates as long as he refrains from suggesting the contents of a defence or of an unconscious conflict till the patient himself discovers it in some form or other. The *public* record of raw data in psychoanalysis being notoriously limited, we have no way of knowing whether the pioneers of the Indian *gharana* (or, for that matter of any other school) rigorously followed the discipline of the analytic technique. We have also no overriding reason to doubt that they did not.

Well into the nineteen forties, the published work of Indian psychoanalysts shows a persisting concern with the illumination of Indian cultural phenomena as well as registering the "Indian" aspects of their patients' mental life. Mythological allusions to Hindu gods and goddesses like Shiva or Kali regularly crop up in case history reports where the mythology appears to be used by the patient for both defensive and adaptive purposes. Thus, for instance, T.C. Sinha, a student of Bose and later himself a President of the Indian Society, reports the case of a sixteen year old youth whose intense passive homosexual wishes were accompanied by the fear of pregnancy. He countered the analyst's reassurance that men could not become pregnant by referring to the example of the mythical Yuvanasva.

Though he had a hundred wives, the king Yuvanasva had no son and approached sages for remedy. Taking pity on him they performed a special ritual. A jug of water was made potent by recitals of mantras to be given to the queens to make them pregnant. Unknowingly, Yuvanasva drank of this water and after ten months gave birth to a child who came out of his body by bursting open the right side of his stomach. To protect himself from Yuvanasva's mythical fate, the patient now developed the fantasy of having his own penis inside his anus (Sinha, 1949).

By the nineteen fifties, however, the interest in comparative and cultural aspects of mental life as well as the freshness of the papers written by the pioneering generation of Indian psychoanalysts was lost. In the last twenty five years, Indian contributions, to judge from the official journal of the Indian society, have been neither particularly distinctive nor original. Even the best papers are little more than status reports on global analytic concepts or introduction to the theories of a few selected post-Freudians such as Klein or Bion.

Here I can only speculate on the reasons for this total divorce of Indian psychoanalysis from Indian culture and society. Psychoanalysis, in the sense of psychoanalytic concepts and theories which gain a large number of adherents among analysts at a given time and subsequently shape their clinical observations, is not completely independent of the historical situation of the analyst and his patients. Freud's postulation of the death instinct and increasing interest in the problems of human aggression after the carnage of the First World War, the magnified importance of object-relations theories after the re-assertion and renaissance of the values of the Counter-Enlightenment in Western societies since the late 1960s, are only two instances of the influence of the historical *Zeitgeist* on psychoanalytic theorising and practice.

In India, the last forty years have witnessed an ever-increasing pace of modernization and industrialization. The country has entered in a big way into the world market, both economic and intellectual, which is dominated by the First World. There has been a phenomenal rise of an urban, educated middle-class to which normally both the Indian analysts and their patients belong. A consequence of these related processes has been the uncritical acceptance by the middle class, itself the child of modernization, of Western intellectual models (of which Marxism is also one) with claims to universality. It is perhaps no accident that in Bombay, the most western of Indian cities, both geographically and spiritually, the younger generation of psychoanalysts are adherents of the Kleinian school which, with its focus on the universal aspects of the object – "good" and "bad" breasts, "good" and "bad" penises and so on – is perhaps the most universalistic of the many "relational" theories. But even in more traditional Calcutta on the eastern seacoast, any critical engagement with received theory has by now almost disappeared. This was not true of the early period of psychoanalysis in India. If psychoanalysis is any kind of illustration for the rest of Indian intellectual life, then it seems that when India entered the world market on a truly big scale after Independence, the Western colonisation of the Indian mind paradoxically became greater than was the case when the country was still a British colony.

The absence of the cultural idiom in case histories today, such as the patient's use of Indian mythology, are then not only due to a presumed increase in mythological illiteracy as a consequence of the modernising process. It may well also be due to the patient's sensing the analyst's disinterest in such material because of his committment to "deeper", universalistic models. Far from the intellectual founts of his professional existence, practising in a culture indifferent to psychoanalytic ideas and hostile to its view of the person, the Indian analyst may be tempted to idealise analytic "gurus" in distant, presumably more receptive lands, and uncritically follow their models in the smallest detail.

References

BOSE, G. (1929/1950): The Genesis of Homosexuality. Samiksa 4 (2), 1950, from 74.

– (1931): A New Technique of Psychoanalysis. *Int. Journal of Psychoanalysis* 12, 387-388.

– (1948): A New Theory of Mental Life. Samiksa 2, 108-205.

– (1949): The Genesis and Adjustment of the Oedipus Wish. *Samiksa* 3 (1), 222–240.

EDELSON, M. (1984): Hypothesis and Evidence in Psychoanalysis. Chicago: Chicago Univ. Press.

KAKAR, S. (1985): Psychoanalysis and Non-Western Cultures. *Int. Review of Psychoanalysis* 12, 441-448.

SINHA, T. C. (1949): Some Psychoanalytical Observations on the Siva Lingh. *Samiksa* 3, from 37.

– (1966a): Psychoanalysis in India. In: Lumbini Park Silver Jubilee Souvenir, 61–77.

– (1966b): Lumbini Park. In: Lumbini Park Silver Jubilee Souvenir.

Journals

Samiksa
Journal of the Indian Psychoanalytical Society
since 1946; Editor: S. Banerji
14, Parsibagan Lane, Calcutta 700009

Institutions

Indian Psychoanalytical Society
14 Parsibagan Lane, Calcutta-9
Tel.: 91-033-350 8788

Dr. Sudhir Kakar, C-22, Gitanjali Enclave, New Delhi 110017

Japan

by Keigo Okonogi

I. A Historical Overview

The history of psychoanalysis in Japan may be roughly divided into two periods: 1) the period before World War II; and 2) the period from the end of World War II to the present.

1. The period before World War II

The first Japanese document on psychoanalysis, an article by Kaison Ohtsuki entitled "The Psychology of Forgetfulness", appeared in a journal of psychological research in 1912. The same year, Kyuichi Kimura published "How to Detect the Secrets of the Mind and to Discover Repression", which introduced psychoanalysis as a scientific method of exploring people's thoughts.

Psychologists and educators introduced Freudian psychoanalysis in a variety of forms over the next ten years. The most notable effort was *A Lecture on Psychology,* written in 1914 by the psychologist Yoichi Ueno. While in the United States, Ueno had become acquainted with Freudian psychoanalysis through a lecture by Professor Stanley Hall of Clark University. On returning to Japan, he wrote *A Lecture on Psychology,* which included Japan's first systematic outline of psychoanalysis. It contained such chapters as: "The Origin of Psychoanalysis", "Psychoanalytic Therapy", "The Interpretation of Dreams", "Infantile Sexuality", "The Psychoanalysis of Mythology and Art", "Forgetfulness and Verbal Slips", "Wit", "Psychoanalysis and Education", etc.

From 1929 to 1933, two collections of Freud's work appeared in Japanese translation. Both were the work of a group headed by the literary figures Kenji Ohtsuki and Yaekichi Yabe.

On a visit to London in 1930, Yabe, a psychologist, met the president of the IPA, Ernest Jones. Yabe subsequently established the Tokyo branch of the IPA. Ohtsuki, a writer, later succeeded Yabe as president. The Association, however, promoted psychoanalytic theory to the general public only as a system of thought, without inviting the participation of psychiatrists. It thus never developed as an association of clinical psychoanalytic psychotherapists, and was finally disbanded after the Second World War.

In the domain of Japanese psychiatry and medicine, Freudian psychoanalysis was originally dismissed as a misguided theory of pansexualism. Kiyoyasu Marui became the first Japanese psychiatrist to study psychoanalysis as a theoretical system of psychopathology.

Marui went to the United States in 1919 to study with Adolf Meyer at John Hopkins University. Witnessing the influence of psychoanalysis on American psychiatry, he hoped to introduce psychoanalysis to the Japanese psychiatric community. After returning to Japan, he began teaching at the University of Tohoku in Sendai (in northeastern Japan). Psychoanalysis became the focus of his medical school lectures on psychiatry. Beginning in 1925, he also taught psychoanalytic theory to practising psychiatrists. Marui furthermore published psychiatric textbooks with a special emphasis on psychoanalysis. Psychiatrists who studied unter Marui became Japan's first generation of psychoanalytically-oriented psychiatrists, known collectively as the Tohoku School.

The Tohoku School flourished from the late 1920s to 1940. However, this school of psychiatrists led by Marui did not fully comprehend the techniques of psychoanalytic therapy. Rather, they understood psychoanalysis simply as a theory of psychopathology. On the basis of this understanding members of the Tohoku School presented papers focusing on a psychoanalytical understanding of neurosis in Japan at meetings of the Japanese Association of Neurology and Psychiatry. They also published the *Journal of Psychoanalytic Psychopathology.* However, the mainstream psychiatric circle in Japan at the time was characterized by a German Kraepelinian trend. Marui's small isolated group was continuously subject to harsh criticism. In 1933, nonetheless, Marui visited Freud in Vienna and received approval for establishing a Sendai Branch of the IPA.

Heisaku Kosawa, a student of the Tohoku School, began to question Marui, who taught only theory without understanding Freudian psychoanalytic therapy (which Kosawa himself had been studying directly from the works of Freud). In order to learn psychoanalytic methods at first hand, Kosawa left Japan to study at the Vienna Psychoanalytic Institute from 1932 to 1933. He received training analysis from Richard Sterba[1], and individual supervision on psychotherapy from Paul Federn.

1 It was in the latter half of the 1980s that Dr. Arnold Cooper told me of Dr. Sterba. According to Cooper, Sterba fondly remembered the days when he had performed psychoanalysis on Kosawa in Vienna, and wished to relate this experience to psychoanalysts in Japan. Sterba was at that time living in Detroit, where he had moved from Vienna. I strongly wished to record an interview with Sterba, since I felt such a document would be invaluable to the history of psychoanalysis in Japan. I began to make arrangements for a meeting. However, to my great disappointment, Sterba passed away before our plan was realized.

While in Vienna, furthermore, Kosawa visited Freud at his home at Berggasse 19 and interviewed him directly. He presented Freud with a paper explaining his theory of the Ajase complex, which he contrasted with the Western oedipal complex. (Kosawa's theory will be discussed more thoroughly in Part II.) Unfortunately, however, Freud does not appear to have evinced great interest in Kosawa's thesis.

After returning to Japan in 1933, Heisaku Kosawa, now at odds with Kiyoyasu Marui, opened a private clinic in Tokyo. Here he began practising psychoanalytic therapy as it was known in Europe and the United States.

With the outbreak of World War II in 1939, Japan became an ally of Nazi Germany – which regarded psychoanalysis as a dangerous, Jewish system of thought. Heisaku Kosawa came under constant surveillance from the special police. Nevertheless, he continued to conduct a private practice throughout the war.

2. *The period after World War II: The second-generation psychiatrists and the Kosawa School (the 1950s to 1960s)*

The end of World War II brought an influx of learning and culture from the United States, which greatly influenced all aspects of Japanese society including the field of psychiatry. It created a generation of young psychiatrists who sought to study the model of American dynamic psychiatry. They chose to receive training analysis and individual supervision from Heisaku Kosawa.

This group of psychiatrists who studied under Heisaku Kosawa became the second generation of Japanese psychoanalysts, known as the Kosawa School. Some leading members included: Takeo Doi, from the University of Tokyo; Makoto Takeda and myself from Keio University; and Shigeharu Maeda and Masahisa Nishizono, from Kyushu University. These young psychiatrists from the Kosawa School became members of the Japan Branch of the IPA.

After the death of Kiyoyasu Marui in 1953, Heisaku Kosawa had succeeded Marui as director of the IPA Sendai Branch. Through exchanges with Anna Freud and Heinz Hartmann, Kosawa later changed the name of the Sednai Branch to the Japan Branch. He then established its headquarters in Tokyo, a move approved by the IPA.

The Japan Branch of the IPA is known internationally as the Japan Psychoanalytic Society. Members of the Society have completed studies in training analysis based on rigorous international standards, as well as psychoanalysis through individual supervision. Psychiatrists who received training analysis from Heisaku Kosawa between 1950 and 1960 represent its core members.

At approximately the same time, from the end of the 1940s to the early 1950s, a study group for psychoanalysis was established by Heisaku Kosawa and professors of psychiatry from various universities. With this group as its centre, the Japan Psychoanalytical Association was established in 1955.

As far as its focus is concerned, the Japan Psychoanalytical Association should more correctly be called the Association for Dynamic Psychiatry. It was established by psychiatrists and psychologists with a psychoanalytical orientation. Although it includes "psychoanalysis" in its name, the Association has no specific eligibility requirements or standards for membership.

Membership in the Japan Psychoanalytical Association has grown steadily over the years. It is currently a major scientific organization with 1,500 members, roughly 70 to 80 percent of whom are dynamic psychiatrists. A number of clinical psychologists also participate.

The founding members of the Japan Psychoanalytical Association, like those of the Japan Psychoanalytic Society, received psychoanalytic training from Heisaku Kosawa. Psychiatrists who have studied psychoanalytic psychotherapy and dynamic psychiatry in the United States and Europe have also become members. The Association does not limit itself to any specific school of psychoanalysis; some members adhere to Freudian ego psychology; others advocate British object relations theory or the Kleinian school. In this sense, various schools cooperate to run the Association. Members who have joined after studying psychoanalytic psychotherapy abroad include: Akihisa Kondo, who worked with Karen Horney; Kenji Sakamoto, who studied under Clara Thompson; and Ikuo Miyoshi, who received training from Medard Boss of Switzerland.

3. The third-generation psychiatrists (the 1960s to 1970s)

In 1969, following the death of Heisaku Kosawa, Michio Yamamura succeeded to the presidency of the Japan Psychoanalytic Society and the Japan Psychoanalytical Association. The period 1960–1970 also witnessed the return of several Japanese psychiatrists from clinical training abroad. Kiyoshi Ogura, for example, returned to Japan after undergoing complete clinical training at the Menninger Hospital. Third-generation psychiatrists, who had completed training with second-generation psychiatrists such as Nishizono and myself, returned from shorter sojourns in England and the United States. Among these returning third-generation psychiatrists was

Tetsuya Iwasaki, who, after studying at the Menninger Psychiatric School, presented Otto Kernberg's theory on borderline personality organization and its treatment. He also translated the works of Hanna Segal, and introduced the Kleinian school of thought to Japan. During the same period, Joji Kandabashi, Sadanobu Ushijima and others received training from John Padel in London. They introduced the object relations theory of Winnicott to the Japanese clinical scene.

Boosted by the participation of these third-generation psychiatrists, psychoanalysis gradually gained importance in Japan and became a major influence in the field of clinical psychiatry. However, as mentioned before, Japanese psychiatry has traditionally possessed a German – more specifically a Kraepelinian and biological – orientation. This long established tradition within Japanese psychiatry resulted in a variety of conflicts with emerging psychoanalytic dynamic psychiatry. It was under these circumstances that clinicians with a psychoanalytic orientation in psychiatry, clinical psychology, and psychosomatic medicine gradually began demonstrating their leadership through the vehicle of the Japan Psychoanalytical Association.

During the period 1960 to 1970, many important psychoanalytic works were translated into Japanese, in a movement towards internationalization organized by the Japan Psychoanalytic Society under the leadership of myself. The third Japanese translation of Freud's collected works appeared. In addition, most of the leading works on ego psychology by Wilhelm Reich, Heinz Hartmann, Ernst Kris, Anna Freud, and Erik Erikson were translated into Japanese.

The most original research in Japanese psychoanalysis at this time was that of Takeo Doi. As will be discussed later, his theory of *amae* eventually received recognition not only in Japan, but also in the international psychoanalytic community.

In terms of clinical practice, it was during the period 1960 to 1970 that the diagnosis and psychotherapy of borderline cases, as well as classic psychoanalytic therapy, began to attract keen attention. Reflecting contemporary trends in Europe and the United States, psychoanalytic psychotherapists in Japan began actively performing psychotherapy for schizophrenic patients. Soon, psychiatric family study, particularly that of the schizophrenic family, became a theme of major importance. From approximately 1970, however, Japanese psychiatry came under the influence of the worldwide anti-psychiatric movement; as a result, numerous disputes occurred among various psychiatric societies and universities.

4. *The fourth-generation psychiatrists, and increasing international exchange (the late 1970s to 1980s)*

As disputes among universities and academic societies abated, a new wave of psychiatrists – who might be called the fourth generation – joined the established psychiatric community. This fourth generation, like the third, returned to Japan after studying psychoanalytic psychotherapy and dynamic psychiatry in Britain and the United States. Kuninao Minagawa, for example, received five years of training in psychotherapy at Michigan University from the Nagera group, focusing on the treatment of children and adolescents. Rikihachiro Kano returned to Japan after receiving training in psychoanalytic psychotherapy and dynamic psychiatry for three years at the Menninger Hospital in Topeka, Kansas. Osamu Kitayama received training in psychotherapy with a psychoanalytic orientation at the Department of Psychotherapy of London's Mousley Hospital.

During the 1980s, Japanese translations appeared of most of the essential works of object relations and Kleinian theorists: Melanie Klein, Michael Balint, Douglas Fairbairn, D. W. Winnicott, and Hanna Segal. The translation of Bion's work is still under way, although Leon Grinberg and Elizabeth Bianchedi's study *An Introduction to the Work of Bion* has appeared in Japanese.

From 1980 onwards, a growing number of psychoanalysts from overseas, particularly from the United States, began to visit Japan. Leading American psychoanalysts such as Cornell University's Otto Kernberg and Arnold Cooper conducted the first international seminar in Tokyo, on borderline cases and narcissism. Numerous psychoanalysts from other countries followed, resulting in a dramatic increase in the number of seminars and lectures held in Japan. Leading IPA analysts – including former IPA presidents Robert Wallerstein, Serge Lebovici, and Joseph Sandler, among others – came to Japan on various occasions to give lectures and organize seminars. Ramon Ganzarain visited Japan for the congress meeting of the International Association of Group Psychotherapy, Serge Lebovici, Robert Emde and Joy Osofsky for the IACAPAP, and Efrain Bleiberg for the Menninger Workshop Tokyo.

Following the IPA Congress in Hamburg in 1985, the Japan Psychoanalytic Society has implemented English-Japanese simultaneous interpretation at subsequent IPA Congresses in Montreal (1987), etc. The number of Japanese members taking part in the IPA Congress increases each year, and full-scale international exchanges with the IPA have been organized.

During the late 1980s, I became interested in reviving Kosawa's theory of the Ajase complex, seeking to integrate it with my own clinical experience and subsequent psychoanalytic research. Presented at a variety of international conferences, this new interpretation of Kosawa's theory has received widespread attention. Doi's concept of *amae,* presented at the IPA Congress in Montreal as well as the Amsterdam Congress (1993), has also attracted attention for its universal applicability. Osamu Kitayama has made original presentations at several IPA congresses, including the Psychoanalytic Congress in Rome (1989), the IPA Congress in Buenos Aires (1991), and the Amsterdam Congress 1993. His studies are beginning to draw worldwide interest as well.

II. Studies by Japanese Psychoanalysts

As studies by leading Japanese psychoanalysts frequently cited in overseas literature, I would like to introduce (1) Takeo Doi's theory of *amae;* (2) the Ajase complex theory, developed by Kosawa and later expanded by myself; and (3) Osamu Kitayama's *The Prohibition of Don't Look* and *Studies on Mourning.* In terms of chronology, I should rightly begin with Kosawa's Ajase complex. However, in order to include my own subsequent research on the Ajase theory, I will follow the order in which the studies drew international notice, and begin by discussing Doi's concept of *amae.*

The theory of amae: Takeo Doi

The first paper by Doi introducing the concept of *amae* appeared in an American speech journal (the 1956 Spring issue of *Western Speech)* under the title "Japanese Language as an Expression of Japanese Psychology". The relevant passage from this paper appears below.

"*Amaeru* [*amae* is its noun form] can be translated as 'to depend and presume upon another's love.' This word has the same root as *amai,* an adjective which corresponds to 'sweet'. Thus, *amaeru* has a distinct feeling of sweetness, and is generally used to express a child's attitude toward an adult, especially his parents. I can think of no English word equivalent to *amaeru* except for 'spoil', which, however, is a transitive verb and definitely has a bad connotation; whereas the Japanese *amaeru* does not necessarily have a bad connotation, although we say we should not let a youngster *amaeru* too much. I think most Japanese adults have a dear memory of the taste of sweet dependency as a child and, consciously or unconsciously, carry a lifelong nostalgia for it (p. 92)"

Thus, although *amaeru* has its primary locus in childhood, it may also apply to an interpersonal relationship between adults, if that relationship contains the same desire for dependency and belonging experienced by a child. Doi argued that the visibility or conscious recognition of *amae* might itself be a distinguishing factor of Japanese culture.

Doi furthermore discovered that an unfulfilled desire for *amae* lies behind *toraware* (a state of obsession in which a patient adheres to one idea to the exclusion of all others), often seen among patients of Morita *shinkeishitsu* or "nervousness" – the type of neurosis most prevalent among the Japanese. Doi later concluded that the psychodynamics of *amae* plays a central role in a variety of other psychiatric disorders as well.

Eventually, Doi came to assert that *amae* was not a psychology unique to the Japanese, but rather a universal psychology, appearing in other cultures as well. The psychology of keeping pets, for example, may be understood in terms of *amae.* Doi thus maintains that although the word *amae* originates in the Japanese language, the concept of *amae* possesses universal applicability and represents an important tool for psychoanalytic investigation.

In order to position his theory within the broader context of international psychoanalysis, Doi has compared *amae* with several existing psychoanalytic concepts. He writes:

"It has been my belief at the same time that this concept has a universal applicability inasmuch as the patient's transference can be interpreted in terms of *amae.* In other words, the concept of *amae* can lend itself to psychoanalytic formulation and may even complement the existing theories of psychoanalysts."

I would like to continue with another quotation from Doi:

"Amae agrees with object-relations theory and makes it more amenable to introspection precisely because *amae* and its vocabulary refer to inner experience. For instance, passive object love or primary love as defined by Michael Balint can be equated with *amae* in its pure form and as such, his concept becomes something quite tangible. In fact, Balint deplores the inadequacy of the word 'love' to catch its essence in nascency, and states as follows: 'All European languages are so poor that they cannot distinguish between the two kinds of object-love, active and passive.' (1965, p. 56) It is then remarkable that the Japanese language has this word *amae,* enabling the infantile origin of love to be accessible to consciousness. Incidentally, I began to correspond with Balint in 1962 and he confirmed, after reading some of my papers, that his ideas and mine were developing in the same direction. I also had the good fortune to discuss the matter with him personally when I went to London in 1964. I was furthermore delighted that he honored me later by citing my work in his last book, *The Basic Fault.*

In this connection, I would like to say a few words about the concept of attachment, which was introduced by John Bowlby into psychoanalysis from ethology, since it obviously covers the same area as *amae.* As is known, Bowlby sharply distinguishes attachment from dependence, saying that a child does not become attached to his mother because it has to depend on her. So he prefers attachment to dependence as a term, as the former can be more precise than the latter in describing behavior. He also mentions the negative value implications of the word dependence as another reason for avoiding it. Even so, it seems to me that he overlooks the fact that attachment involves a dependence of its own, as one necessarily becomes dependent on the object as far as one is attached to it. In this regard, *amae* definitely has an advantage over attachment precisely because it implies a psychological dependence in the sense mentioned above and unlike attachment refers to behavior. All in all, one can say, paradoxical as it may sound, that the concept of *amae* makes it possible to discuss what is not verbalized in ordinary communication, hence is something that remains totally unnoticed if you are speaking European languages.

Next, I would like to explain how the concept of *amae* can be related to narcissism, identification and ambivalence. *Amae* is object-relational from the beginning, therefore it does not quite agree with the concept of primary narcissism. However, it fits in very well with secondary narcissism, in fact it is particularly well-suited to describe whatever state of mind may be called narcissistic. Namely, of the two kinds of *amae*, primitive and convoluted, that I mentioned before, the convoluted *amae*, which is childish, wilful and demanding is surely narcissistic. As a matter of fact, if you suspect someone of being narcissistic, you may be sure that this person has a problem with *amae*. In the same vein, a new concept of self object defined by Kohut as 'those archaic objects cathected with narcissistic libido' (1971, p. 3) will be much easier to comprehend in the light of *amae* psychology, since 'the narcissistic libido' is none other than convoluted *amae*. Also, Balint's observation that 'in the final phase of the treatment, instinctual wishes, and to demand their gratification from their environment' (1965, p. 181) makes perfect sense, because the primitive *amae* will manifest itself only after narcissistic defenses are worked through by analysis."

Doi's *amae* theory has prompted numerous debates and discussions. I myself, for instance, have discussed adult perceptions of *amae* behavior in children. The concept of *amae* as represented by Doi is an intrapsychic emotional state experienced by adults, and it is also a mode of interpersonal relationship. It should be noted firstly, however, that Japanese rarely use the word *amae* subjectively, for example, in the sense, "I want to *amaeru.*" Rather, the word refers to someone else: "He or she is *amaeru*-ing", "is overly *amaeru*-ing" or "is resorting to *amae*". It is essentially a word used by an adult to refer to a child, or by an older or senior person to refer to a junior, describing the latter's emotions, or mode of interpersonal relationship.

Secondly, some adults experience negative feelings toward *amae*. They may want to prohibit or punish it in others, or they may feel ashamed and guilty of their own desire to *amaeru*. In certain cases, the mind may work to ignore or negate feelings of *amae*. In psychoanalytic terms, the conflict with the superego towards *amae*, or the defense of the ego against *amae*, generates a variety of emotions. Part of all of this mental process is then projected onto another person.

Finally, within the context of the parent-child relationship in Japan, the word *amae* frequently carries a sense of reproach: „Stop *amaeru*-ing", "See, your're *amaeru*-ing again", "I've had enough of your *amaeru*-ing", or "You're an *amaeru*-ing child".

2. *The Ajase complex: Kosawa and Okonogi*

The Ajase complex is an original theory developed by Heisaku Kosawa, and subsequently expanded by myself. Whereas Freud based his Oedipus complex on a Greek tragedy, Kosawa developed his theory of the Ajase complex from stories found in Buddhist scripture. The story of Ajase centers on the Buddhist concept of reincarnation.

Well known to the Buddhist world, Ajase's story appears with many variations in the scriptures of ancient India. These scriptures entered Japan by way of China and Korea from approximately 700 to 1000 A.D. Kosawa modeled his theory on the version of Ajase's story appearing in the *Kanmuryojukyo*, a Buddhist scripture centering on the salvation of the mother. In this instance, the woman saved by the Buddha is Ajase's mother, Idaike.

Wife of King Binbashara, the ruler of an ancient Indian kingdom, Idaike feared that as her beauty faded she was losing her husband's love. She consulted a soothsayer, who told her a sage living in the forest would die in three years' time, to be reborn as her son. However, Idaike was too anxious to wait three years, and desperate to have a child, she killed the sage. As he was dying, the sage cursed Idaike, telling her that, reincarnated as her son, he would one day kill the King. Idaike became pregnant at this moment. The unborn Ajase had thus already been murdered by his mother's egotism. Moreover, fearing the wrath of the sage reincarnated in her womb, Idaike attempted to kill her son by giving birth to him from the summit of a high tower. Ajase survived; however, having broken his little finger as a result of his fall, he was nicknamed "the prince with the broken finger".

Ajase passed a happy childhood. However, on reaching adolescence, he learned from Daibadatta, the enemy of Buddha, that his mother had attempted to kill him by giving birth from the top of a high tower, he had only a look at his broken little finger for proof. The Sanskrit word Ajatasatru means "broken finger" and "prenatal rancor" (a term to be discussed below). Disillusioned with the mother he had idealized, Ajase attempted to kill her. He was subsequently overcome by guilt, however, and developed a severe skin disease, characterized by festering sores so offensive in odor that no one dared to approach him – except for his mother, Idaike. Despite his mother's devoted care, Ajase did not readily recover; he even attempted several times to kill her. Seeking relief, Idaike went to the Buddha and told him of her sufferings. The Buddha's teachings healed her inner conflict, and she returned to continue to care for Ajase. Eventually, the Prince was cured to become a widely respected ruler.

This is the version of the Ajase story Kosawa wrote in the 1950s, based on the *Kanmuryojukyo.*

My own research has identified two fundamental aspects of the Ajase story as presented by Kosawa. I will also present, as a third point, Kosawa's own examination of guilt in the Ajase complex.

The mother's conflict between the wish for a child and infanticidal wishes

Queen Idaike wished to have a child in order to protect her status as queen and maintain her husband's love – she took the extreme action of killing the sage to achieve her desires. However, believing that the birth of the reincarnated sage would bring disastrous results, Idaike began to fear the child in her womb. She then attempted to kill her child by giving birth to him from the top of a high tower.

The story of Ajase illustrates two conflicting emotions on the part of the mother. On the one hand, she wishes to have a child in order to protect herself, and to achieve her own desires. On the other hand, projecting persecutory imagery and hatred onto her baby, she becomes fearful of the child's birth and attempts to kill him.

According to Serge Lebovici, such conflict depicts the mother's ambivalence concerning her bébé imaginaire. The egocentric conflict of the mother – her wishes both to have a child and to eliminate her baby – arouse persecutory anxiety through projection onto the child she carries. This unconscious maternal conflict appears clearly in the Ajase story.

The child's prenatal rancor and matricidal wishes

Ajase experienced rage towards his origins from the moment of conception. As a reincarnation of the murdered sage, that is, he desired to kill his mother even before his birth. In Buddhism, this anger experienced towards birth itself is termed *mishoon,* or prenatal rancor.

Kosawa compared the Oedipus complex and the Ajase complex as follows: "Freud's Oedipus complex originates in a conflict involving the libido, with the son's love for his mother and hatred for his father. The Ajase complex, on the other hand, concerns the more fundamental question of birth or origins." Kosawa further contended that whereas incestuous desire and patricide formed the core of the Oedipus complex, the Ajase complex centered on the themes of matricide and prenatal resentment.

Two types of guilt, and the mother's forgiveness

The paper Kosawa originally submitted to Freud concerning the Ajase complex bore the title *Two Types of Guilt* ("The Ajase Complex" was rather its subtitle). In this paper, Kosawa asserted the following. When a child makes a mistake or does something wrong, he or she first experiences guilt as a fear of punishment. However, human beings have another sense of guilt, which is of a higher dimension than mere fear of punishment. This second type of guilt is experienced when the child who fears punishment is forgiven his or her wrongdoing.

In terms of the Buddhist legend, Ajase suffered feelings of guilt when confronted by a minister with his desire to kill his mother. Shocked at his own contemplated matricide, he began to shake, and became deathly ill. Idaike, however, forgave her son and nursed him devotedly. Under his mother's care, Ajase experienced a more profound sense of guilt, one of heartfelt remorse.

Kosawa termed this guilt resulting from the forgiveness *zangeshin* or "repentance". He emphasized the need to differentiate between repentance and the guilt related to punishment. This "repentance" type guilt compares with Klein's depressive/reparative guilt. The Ajase story may thus be viewed as depicting the transition from a punitive to a reparative type of guilt. (Kosawa may in fact have read Klein's *The Psycho-Analysis of Children* before writing his thesis.)

Ramon Ganzarain, an American psychoanalyst who studied the Ajase complex, has delineated several defense mechanisms in its treatment of guilt: denial, confusion, etc.

3. Subsequent discussions of the Ajase complex

The mother's distress over losing paternal support

I once received the following remarks from Professor Theodore Lidz concerning the Ajase story. In his view, children should be raised by both parents; the conflict of the Ajase story originates in the father's declining an active role and leaving the child's fate in the hands of the mother. Ajase's difficulties, in other words, began with the mother's tragedy of losing her husband's – or, in a broader sense, a man's – support.

I believe this is a very important interpretation. One of the important themes of the Ajase complex is that, although children grow up in a triadic world of father, mother, and the child, a mother such as Idaike carries the burden of raising her child by herself. The world of the Ajase complex is therefore a dyadic world.

Lidz's interpretation is also relevant in light of the socio-historical background of the Ajase legend in Japan. Early Japanese Buddhism was highly influenced by Chinese philosophy. (As mentioned above, Buddhism arrived from India via China and Korea.) An essentially Japanese, popular Buddhism began to develop during the Kamakura era (1183–1333) – through the efforts of such priests as Shinran and Nichiren. One of the issues in popular Japanese Buddhism was the possibility of women's entry into the Buddhist paradise. Behind this issue lay the problem of guilt over infanticide, particularly abortion, since Japanese women have traditionally been assigned responsibility for disposing of unwanted children. The depiction of Idaike's salvation in the *Kanmuryojukyo* played an important role in assuaging mother's guilt over infanticide.

On the origins of the text of the Ajase complex

The Ajase story also appears in the *Nehangyo* quoted in the teachings of Shinran, the *Kyogyoshinsho,* with an emphasis on the father-son relationship and patricide as in the Oedipus complex. Kosawa, however, influenced by the *Kanmuryojukyo,* wrote his story as a uniquely mother-child story.

It is interesting to compare this textual history with recent Western studies of Freud's Oedipus complex. For example, attention has recently been focused on Freud's omission of certain aspects of the Oedipal story, particularly the conflict occurring between Laius and Jocasta before Oedipus' birth. Freud omitted this portion of the Oedipus myth and focused only on the conflict between the adolescent Oedipus and his parents, naming this is the Oedipus complex. If Freud had included the incidents surrounding Oedipus' birth, his story might have possessed a greater thematic similarity with the Ajase complex. From a cross-cultural perspective, one might suggest that Freud was influenced by the Judeo-Christian tradition, whereas Kosawa was heavily influenced by the oft-cited "maternal" aspect of the Japanese culture.

The Ajase complex of Sigmund Freud

Balmary and Krüll (1979) have proposed that one reason behind Freud's radical switch from the psychic trauma theory to the endogenic drive theory lay in defense mechanisms organized against the acknowledgement of his father's failures. They argue that, while married to his second wife, Rebecca, Freud's father had a relationship with a 20-year-old woman who became pregnant. This child was Sigmund Freud. After Rebecca's flight and subsequent suicide, Jacob married Amalia, Freud's mother. If this hypothesis is correct, Freud would have experienced extreme conflict concerning his existence as his parents' "imaginary baby".

Does the avoidance of origins and of the *"bébé imaginaire"* in Freud's Oedipal story represent a repression of the Ajase complex? Joan Raphael-Leff, a psychoanalyst based in London, has compared Ajase's mother Idaike in the Ajase story with Oedipus' mother Jocasta in the Oedipus myth. In her paper, Raphael-Leff contends that, like Idaike, Jocasta, too, displays maternal ambivalence, expressing both the desire to have a child and infanticidal wishes. Further study of the Oedipus myth in light of the Ajase complex might prove to be highly significant.

In sum, the origins of both Oedipus and Freud, as well as Freud's Ajase complex, have recently become the subject of study in the West.

The theory of the Ajase complex is thus not only applicable to Japanese mothers and children, it is a universal theme.

4. *The study of "On", the Japanese concept of debt or indebtedness, and of the "Don't look" prohibition: Osamu Kitayama**

As Osamu Kitayama states in "Metaphorization – making terms", the analyst's receptiveness to ambiguity is generally thought to be an essential part of his or her psychoanalytical practice. The interpretation of multiple meanings can effectively create a "bridging function" between personal metaphorical meaning and shared literal meaning. It appears that this ambiguous metaphor fails to function in the treatment of schizophrenics, who experience metaphor in literal terms. Some, however, can utilize metaphors, indicating positive signs (i. e., a non-psychotic part, an anal retentive tendency, creativity, ambiguity, tolerance, etc.).

Kitayama's paper concerns the transitional process from literal experience to metaphorical understanding in schizophrenic patients. In this process, the therapist's role of translating the patient's expressions, which are experienced literally, into metaphorical "here and now" events is essential. Among relevant technical issues, the appearance and usage of the "in-metaphor" and compound metaphor may play an important role in interweaving the words and meanings of the two persons in therapy.

Kitayama (1993) next analyzed several ambiguous metaphorical expressions in the Japanese language: for instance, the Japanese word *"on"*, which expresses obligation, debt, guilt, and love or kindness. Whereas the English concept of guilt is associated with punishment, *on* implies repayment or

* The following summary of his work was contributed by Kitayama.

"requital". It is interesting to note that concepts such as *oime, giri,* and *kari,* which also seem important to Japanese ways of thinking, share with *on* the core meaning of debt or indebtedness.

Intrigued by the importance of debt to Japanese motivational concepts, Kitayama (1985) investigated Japanese myths and folk tales, particularly tales of marriage between humans and non-humans, in order to relate them to his clinical experience. In one tale, the snake-wife, responding to the hero's demand, forfeits her milk-producing eyeballs. The most typical and popular legend is "A Crane's Repayment of Her Debt *(On)*". Below is an outline of the tale.

1) The hero rescues an injured crane, who, in the guise of a beautiful woman, then visits his home and offers herself in marriage.
2) The young woman is a talented weaver as well as a devoted wife. However, she prohibits the hero from watching her at work, since, in her original form as a crane, she is weaving cloth from her own feathers.
3) Unable to resist temptation, the hero ignores the prohibition of "Don't look" – only to see the young woman in her animal form.
4) He becomes frightened; the crane-woman feels hurt and ashamed. The two separate in the end.

The prohibition of "Don't look" is a taboo which, in a two-body relationship, *should be broken over time,* in contrast to the oedipal incest taboo, *the taboo to be kept.* Kitayama concluded that the tragic development of the above tale shows a sudden transition, in Kleinian terms, from the paranoid schizoid position to the depressive position.

Kitayama (1991) further argued that from the viewpoint of "environmental failure", "false charge" or "forced guilt" may occur when the infant is suddenly confronted with its causal relation to the fragile environment, and that maternal prohibition should be withdrawn gradually as the infant develops the capacity to tolerate causality. As an infant's feeling of indebtedness stems from the relative tension between his or her own destructiveness and the mother's survival, it is thus possible to speak of "forced" or "false guilt", generated in infants with masochistic caretakers.

Finally, Kitayama (1993) proposed the value of "indebtedness" as a psychological concept to bridge external charge and internal debt. When analyzing transference and repeated acting-out in the form of masochistic or suicidal behavior, we may discover a conscious or unconscious pathological accumulation of debt.

III. The Present State of the Japan Psychoanalytic Society

To restate briefly, on succeeding to the presidency of the IPA Sendai Branch in 1955, Kosawa changed its name to the IPA Japan Branch and relocated its headquarters to Tokyo. This IPA Japan Branch later came to be called the Japan Psychoanalytic Society. The Society is currently directed by psychiatrists who received training analysis from Heisaku Kosawa, Japan's first generation of psychoanalysts.

Michio Yamamura succeeded Kosawa as president of the Society, to be followed by Takeo Doi, and current president Masahisa Nishizono. I myself have served as secretary for many years. Sadanobu Ushijima is the current treasurer, and Tesuya Iwasaki the current chairman of the Education and Training Committee.

During the transition period between Kosawa's death and the start of training conducted by the first generation psychoanalysts, training analysis was not actively performed in Japan. The present membership for the Japan Psychoanalytic Society therefore remains quite small, with 18 active members and 13 associate members.

Eighty percent of the Society members live in the Tokyo area, with the remaining 20 percent in distant Fukuoka (in southern Japan) and vicinity. Although the Japan Psychoanalytic Society has not yet established a psychoanalytic institute integrating these two areas, it hopes to do so by 1994. Members, however, have not yet agreed whether to establish one psychoanalytic institute covering all of Japan, or two psychoanalytic institutes – one in Tokyo and the other in Fukuoka.

The Society intends to establish, by 1994, new regulations in line with the education and training criteria set forth by the IPA. It also plans to increase the number of training analysts, and to implement training analyses in accordance with international standards.

IV. Conclusion

The psychoanalytic theory transmitted from the Vienna Psychoanalytic Institute via Kosawa forms the mainstream of psychoanalysis in Japan. From the 1950s to the 1970s, the dominant trend received its greatest influence from the dynamic psychiatry of the United States.

Presently, there is a mounting interest in Japan for Kohutian self psychology as well as object relations theory, particularly the work of Melanie Klein, D. W. Winnicott, and W. Bion. Establishing the clinical applications of these theories has become a major challenge for numerous Japanese clinicians. The application of psychoanalysis to the fields of adolescent and infant psychiatry is also a focus of interest, and has been the topic of international meetings conducted in Japan. There is finally a growing trend to conduct psychoanalysis independent of either dynamic psychiatry or psychoanalytic therapy.

The number of patients receiving psychoanalytic psychotherapy has increased dramatically in the Japanese cities of Tokyo, Osaka, Fukuoka, Kobe and Hiroshima. There has also been a sharp rise in the number of private psychotherapeutic clinics operating in Tokyo, including five or six psychoanalytic psychotherapy clinics. These trends indicate potential for the future growth of psychoanalysis and psychoanalytic psychotherapy in Japan.

Japanese psychiatrists' and psychologists' study of psychoanalytic thought generated an encounter between Western and Japanese culture. Indigenous Japanese patterns of thought merged with the imported theory of psychoanalysis, paving the way for such theories as those of *amae*, the Ajase complex and the "Don't look" prohibition. These theories aid in understanding the mentality not only of Japanese, but also of people from other cultures; they furthermore promise to contribute greatly to psychoanalytic understanding itself. I sincerely hope that Japanese psychoanalysis will continue to make significant theoretical contributions to the international community.

References

BALMARY, M. (1988): L'homme aux statues. Editions Grasset et Fasquelle, 1979. Translation by Hiroshi Iwasaki, Tesugaku Shobo.

DOI, T. (1962): Amae: A key concept for understanding Japanese personality structure. In: R. J. Smith / R. K. Beardsley (Eds.), Japanese culture: Its development and characteristics. Chicago: Aldine.

– (1963): Some thoughts on helplessness and the desire to be loved. *Psychiatry Journal for the Study of Interpersonal Processes* 26.

– (1964): Psychoanalytic therapy and Western man: A Japanese view. *International Journal of Social Psychiatry* 1.

– (1973a): *The anatomy of dependence* (J. Bester, Trans.). Tokyo: Kodansha.

– 1973b): Psychotherapy as "hide and seek". *Bulletin of the Menninger Clinic* 37.

– (1988): On the concept of amae. *Infant Mental Health Journal* 13.

GANZARAIN, R. (1988): Various guilts within the Ajase complex (Translation by Okonogi, K.): *Japanese Journal of Psychoanalysis* 32, No. 2, 93–102.

KITAYAMA, O. (1985): Pre-Oedipal "taboo" in Japanese folk tragedies. *Int. Rev. Psychoanal.* 12, 173–186.

– (1987): Metaphorization – making terms. *Int. J. Psychoanal.* 68, 499–509.

– (1991): The wounded caretaker and guilt. *Int. Rev. Psycho-Anal.* 18, 229–240.

– (1993): On digesting ambiguous indebtedness. Presented at the 38th IPA Congress in Amsterdam.

KOHUT, H. (1971): The Analysis of the Self. New York: Int. Univ. Press.

– (1977): The restoration of the self. New York: Int. Univ. Press.

KOSAWA, H. (1953): Final Kosawa version of the Ajase story, in the translator's afterword, "Japanese version of Neue Folge der Vorlesungen zur Einführung in die Psychoanalyse, 1932".

– (1954): Two kinds of guilt. *Japanese Journal of Psychoanalysis* 1, No. 1.

KRÜLL, M.: Freud und sein Vater, München: C. H. Beck, 1979. Translation by Setsuo Mizuno, Shisakusha, 1987.

LEBOVICI, S. (1988): Fantasmatic interaction and intergenerational transmission. *Infant Mental Health Journal* 9, No. 1.

OKONOGI, K. (1971): Dr. Heisaku Kosawa as a great pioneer of Japanese psychoanalysis. *Japanese Journal of Psychoanalysis* 15, No. 6.

– (1978). The Ajase complex of the Japanese (1). *Japan Echo* 5 (4), 88–105.

– (1979): The Ajase complex of the Japanese (1). *Japan Echo* 6 (1), 104–118.

– (1991). Le complex d'Ajase. *Devenir* No. 4, 71-102.

– (1992): Amae as seen in diverse interpersonal relations. *Infant Mental Health Journal* 13, No. 1. Spring

POLLOCK, G. H.: Oedipus: The myth, the development stage, the universal theme, the conflict and complex, in: Pollock, G H. / J. M. Ross, (1988): The Oedipus papers. Int. Univ. Press.

RAPHAEL-LEFF, J. (1989): Freud, son of Jocasta. Invited paper presented to the International Conference on Prenatal and Perinatal Psychology, Amherst, Mass., August (unpublished).

– (1992): Mother of Ajase and Jocasta, 1992. Invited paper presented to The Tokyo Meeting of Infant Psychiatry, Tokyo.

ROSS, J. M. (1985): Oedipus revisited: Laius and the "Laius Complex", in: Pollock, G. H. / J. M.Ross (1988).

STERN, D. N. (1985): The interpersonal world of the infant: A view from psychoanalysis and developmental psychology. New York: Basic Books.

STOLOROW, R. D. / BRANDCHAFT, B. / ATWOOD, G. E. (1987): Psychoanalytic treatment: An intersubjective approach. Hillsdale, NJ: Analytic Press.

TAKEMOTO, Y. (1986): Amae as metalanguage: A critique of Doi's theory of Amae. *Journal of the American Academy of Psychoanalysis* 14.

YAMAMURA, M. (1975): Reviewing the 25 years of the Japan Psychoanalytical Association. *Japanese Journal of Psychoanalysis* 24, No. 4, 215–219.

Journals

The Japanese Journal of Psychoanalysis
since 1954; Editorial Committee of the Japan Psychoanalytic Society
Iwasaki Gakujutsu Publ. Co.
1-4-8 Kobinata, Bunkyo-ku, Tokyo

Japanese Journal of Adolescent Psychiatry
since 1991; Ed.: Japanese Society for Adolescent Psychiatry
c/o Neuro-Psychiatric Dept.
Keio University School of Medicine,
35 Shinanomachi, Shinjuku-ku, Tokyo

Japanese Journal of Psychotherapy
since 1974; Kongo Shuppan Publ.
Masumoto Bldg., 1-5-16, Suido, Bunkyo-ku, Tokyo

Imago
Seido-sha Publ., Ichise-Bldg., 1-29
Kanda Jimbo-cho, Chiyoda, Tokyo

Institutions

Nippon Seishin-Bunseki Kyoukai
(Japan Psychoanalytic Society)
c/o Neuro-Psychiatric Dept.,
Keio University School of Medicine
35 Shinanomachi, Shinjuku-ku, Tokyo
Tel.: 81 3 3353 1211
Fax: 81 3 5379 0187

Keigo Okonogi, M.D., c/o Japan Psychoanalytic Society

Korea

by Doo-Young Cho

1. Historical Development

Sigmund Freud and basic concepts of psychoanalytic theory were introduced to Korea in the 1930s from Japan through the following three avenues. The first one was the academic circle of philosophers at Seoul Imperial University, which had close connections with the universities in Japan. Because of its influence, many Korean university professors had maintained the attitude that psychoanalysis belonged to the domain of philosophy up until the 1950s. The second one was the literary critics, who introduced D. H. Lawrence together with Freud. It led many Korean intellectuals to the misunderstanding that Freudian theory was by and large about adult sexuality and sexual freedom up until the sixties. The third and the least influential one was the small number of psychiatrists at Seoul Imperial University Hospital, who had only read some review articles at an introductory level in Japanese journals. They were mostly Japanese and a few Koreans, and at that time they practised such therapies as Morita therapy, persuasion, suggestion, hypnosis, and abreaction, mainly based on their humanitarian concerns. Kraepelian descriptive psychiatry prevailed in Korea and Japan, and no one in Korea was able to use the analytic techniques in clinical practice (Yoo, 1962; Rhee, 1966).

Even for a considerable period after the end of World War II and Japanese withdrawal from Korea the main trend of psychiatry in Korea continued to be descriptive, with the total of psychiatrists numbering no more than twenty. Then Koreans were randomly exposed to analytically-oriented psychotherapy prevailing in the United States at private gatherings by two American psychiatric social workers working as consultants of the United States Army in Korea. Starting in the year 1948, psychoanalytic theory began to be formally introduced to the Department of Psychiatry at Seoul National University Hospital (formerly Seoul Imperial University Hospital) through English and Japanese editions of Freud's papers. Later on, a Korean-translation of Freud's works was initiated by Suk-Jin Yoo, then Assistant Professor of Psychiatry, with the collaboration of junior psychiatrists. The Korean War broke out around the time when a part of the translation was completed (Yoo, 1962).

The Korean War in 1950 was an epoch-making event for the introduction of modern dynamic psychiatry and psychoanalysis. That is, as the number of casualties from combat stress reaction and post-combat stress reaction increased among Korean soldiers, an inevitable urgent need for well-trained psychiatrists with special emphasis on dynamic psychiatry developed. Several Koreans, including Suk-Jin Yoo, began to receive such training from American army psychiatrists at the 121 Evacuation Hospital of the US Army stationed in Korea. Later another group of ten Koreans was trained in the same course. In 1952, the Korean Army established its own training center at the Capital Army Hospital in Seoul, headed by Yoo, where they taught some basic theories of psychoanalysis and its applications to clinical settings. The total number of trainees increased to forty, and these eventually came to be leaders in Korean psychiatry. Starting in the late fifties, after the war, more than two hundred young psychiatrists discharged from the military services went to the United States seeking postgraduate training.

On May 6th, 1957, Yoo and his associates held a "Symposium on Psychoanalysis" in memory of the 101st birthday of Sigmund Freud, which was open to the public, at the grand auditorium of the Seoul National University College of Medicine. Yoo and his associates made up 8 of the twelve speakers, while the other four were philosophy professors from four different universities. Two thousand persons attended the symposium. Although the audience, hungry to learn about psychoanalysis, was most enthusiastic, the "fever" did not last long. There was no one qualified to lead the psychoanalytic movement further.

The first publication of the Korean translation of a psychoanalytic book was the *Interpretation of Dreams* (Freud), in 1959, by Yong-Ho Lee, an English-major graduate from Yonsel University, who successively translated the *Introductory Lectures on Psychoanalysis* (Freud) and two monographs of Karl Menninger. Sang-Chang Paik was the first Korean psychiatrist among the translators: in 1961 he translated *Three Essays on Infantile Sexuality* (Freud).

In the early part of the sixties several hospitals in Korea began to offer intensive psychotherapy to their patients, and from the mid-sixties some university hospitals adopted an individual supervision system in psychotherapy for their trainees on a regular basis. In the seventies the practice of psychoanalytically-orientied psychotherapy had become wide-spread in Seoul, and in the eighties group and individual psychotherapy supervision systems were adopted by all the teaching hospitals, as psychotherapy was included as one of the compulsory subjects in the specialty board certifying examination. Meanwhile the general atmosphere became more favorable for the development of insight-oriented psychotherapy, with rapidly progressing urbanization and industrialization of Korean society, increased college and university enrolment reaching 1.2 million, and the annual income per capita jumping to 6,000 dollars (Cho, 1988).

Doo-Young Cho, then the Assistant Professor and currently Chairman of the Department of Psychiatry at Seoul National University College of Medicine, who finished his residency training at Cornell Medical Center, Westchester Division of New York in the late sixties and had been analyzed for two years by Alan Fraser of the New York Psychoanalytic Society, was the first to recognize the necessity of an organization for teaching Koreans psychoanalysis. From December, 1979 to February, 1980 he visited with Jacob Arlow, Marianne Kris, Arnold Cooper, and Edward Joseph (then, President of the IPA) of New York, Miss Anna Freud (then, Honorary President of the IPA) of London, and Keigo Okonogi and Tetsuya Iwasaki of Tokyo to discuss the Korean situation. All of them in return gave him their personal encouragements and blessings to initiate the first organized psychoanalytic movement in Korea. On May 6th, 1980, Cho along with five fellow psychiatrists, namely Seung-Hwan Oh, Eyong Kim, Hyun-Woo Kim, Dong-Soo Han, and Jin-Wook Sohn, founded the Seoul Psychoanalytic Study Group in Seoul. All of the members agreed upon the condition that "under no circumstance will anyone claim that he or she is a psychoanalyst unless the IPA authorizes him or her to do so, and every member shall be in personal analysis with an IPA-authorized training analyst". The group held book-reading seminars bi-weekly on Wednesday evenings for three to four hours. In the subsequent years membership steadily increased to twelve. In 1983, the group elected Cho as the first president.

Starting in 1984 the group has invited two to six analysts per year from abroad to Seoul to continuously provide up-to-date psychoanalytic knowledge and experiences for its members. Most of them have been English-speaking training analysts, and they have given two to twelve (eight an average) sessions during each visit. Specifically the group invited Masahisa Nishizono (Japan), Alan Fraser (USA) and Myunghee Kim (USA) in 1984, Normund Wong (USA), Kim Skoglund (Sweden) and Donald Cohen (USA) in 1985. Normund Wong (USA) and Edward Joseph (USA) in 1986, Takeo Doi (Japan), Dinora Pines (England), Normund Wong (USA), Collette Chiland (France) and Matthew Suh (Canada) in 1987, Keigo Okonogi (Japan), Sanford Gifford (USA), Robert Wallerstein (USA), Edward Joseph (USA) and Theodore Cohen (USA) in 1988, Myunghee Kim (USA) and Normund Wong (USA) in 1989, Joseph Sandler (England), Anne-Marie Sandler (England), Albert Solnit (USA) and James Strain

(USA) in 1990, Otto Kernberg (USA), Joseph Sandler (England), Anne-Marie Sandler (England), Arnold Cooper (USA), Myunghee Kim (USA), and Raymond Gehl (USA) in 1992.

Concomitantly starting in 1984, some junior members of the group went abroad for formal and informal analytic training. Dong-Soo Lee was the first one, who was trained at the Psychoanalytic Institute at the New York University Medical Center as a formal candidate from 1985–1991. He has been an associate member (academic associate) of the American Psychoanalytical Association since 1990. Heikyong Ha went to London in 1987, and she is presently a formal senior candidate of the "Freud Institute Zurich" of the Swiss Psychoanalytical Society. Moo-Suk Lee and Min-Cheol Park had partial personal analyses in London, each for 6 months in 1987 and 1989. Do-Un Jeong, as a candidate (special student) of the San Diego Psychoanalytic Institute, had two years of training with personal analysis during the period of 1988–1990. The sixth, Tae-Yul Lew, went to the United States in 1991, and has been a formal candidate of the Institute of the Philadelphia Association for Psychoanalysis since then. The seventh, Tak-Yoo Hong, has been a candidate (special student) of the San Diego Psychoanalytic Institute since 1991. Furthermore three native Koreans, who are associate or regular members of the IPA, joined the group between 1987 and 1988, namely, Myunghee Kim (USA), Matthew Suh (Canada) and Kim Skoglund (Sweden). As the group had grown and many had joined from other parts of Korea, the name of the group was changed to the Korean Psychoanalytic Study Group (KPSG) in 1989 (Cho, 1989).

The members of the KPSG have been attending IPA Congresses since 1985, and in 1993 fifteen attended the Amsterdam Congress. In 1991, at the Buenos Aires Congress, the KPSG was officially recognized by the IPA as one of the Guest Study Groups under the auspices of the IPA. The *Journal of the Korean Psychoanalytic Study Group*, published annually since 1990, written in Korean and English, has been carrying original articles, review articles, case discussions, and other appropriate writings.

2. The Present Psychoanalytic Study Group

As of now, the KPSG has 46 regular members (three of whom are members of other foreign societies, and another three of whom at present reside abroad for the purpose of analytic training) and seven temporary members. Two thirds of the members of the KPSG work as faculty at major medical schools in Korea, and the others are in private or hospital practices. The Admissions Committee recruits new members every two years. Usually a new member bears the status of a temporary member and in one and half years, on the recommendation of the Admissions Committee after careful evaluation of his or her ability and devotion, becomes a regular member. Because of the nation-wide geographical distribution of the membership and travel times of up to five hours one way, the KPSG is now considering dividing the group into three subgroups (Seoul, outskirts of Seoul, the other areas), in order to facilitate attendance and to allocate more time for in-depth academic activity.

The centre of the KPSG is located in Seoul, the capital city of the Republic of Korea, and its administration is taken care of by an Executive Council consisting of nine members (President, Vice-President, Past President, Secretary, Treasurer, Chairpersons of Education, International Liaison, Admissions, and Publication Committees). The president is elected by means of the vote of the assembly of regular members, and the president appoints other members of the Executive Council. The term is two years. The Education Committee has the task of preparing the programmes of scientific activity. The International Liaison Committee has the tasks of inviting teachers from abroad and communication with the IPA and other foreign societies. The Secretary manages the files and the lists of members, and publishes the roster and a gazette containing the reports of the assemblies.

The Journal of the KPSG has a circulation of twelve hundred: it is distributed to all the regular members of the Korean Neuropsychiatric Association (membership: approximately one thousand) and all of the university and college libraries in Korea. The KPSG has been holding an open lecture on psychoanalysis once a year in May for the members of the Korean Neuropsychiatric Association, and from 1993 it will be twice a year, in May and November.

The KPSG has been holding scientific meetings on every other Wednesday evening at 6:30–9:30 pm., with frequent additions of weekend seminars. In addition, temporary members are required to attend another regular scientific meetings, a kind of catch-up sessions, twice a month in their first year in the group, where senior members in rotation take leading roles. In order to organize its educational efforts more efficiently it has adopted regular curricula of the San Diego Psychoanalytic Institute of the American Psychoanalytic Association since 1991. Recently the scientific programme has been focusing on clinical case discussions. The present main goal of the KPSG is to have qualified training analysts, whom the IPA approves for training analyses of the members. Actually the KPSG has been struggling to invite one or two English-speaking training analysts from abroad for years.

3. Other Organizations of Psychotherapy

The KPSG at present only accepts psychiatrists who have completed one year of rotating internship and four years of residency training and have been board-certified as members. This is so because no other sectors of the Korean academic world, including psychology and the social sciences, have been able to offer the basic training needed by students to treat the mentally-ill, while psychotherapy training under group and individual supervision has been one of the mandatory subjects for every psychiatric resident in Korea since the 1980s. Naturally the KPSG has close relations with the Korean Neuropsychiatric Association, in which many of the KPSG members have been taking the important academic and administrative roles. For example, Doo-Young Cho was the forty-fourth president and the first chairman of the Scientific Planning Committee of the Association for three years.

Along with the KPSG there are four other academic groups dedicated to psychotherapy in Korea. The first one is the Korean Academy of Psychotherapists, organized in 1974 and led by Dong-Shik Rhee, who graduated from Kyungbuk National University College of Medicine in 1941, was the chairman of Department of Psychiatry at Soo-Do Medical College in the early sixties, and had his residency training at the Bellevue Psychiatric Hospital of New York City in the late fifties. He has an eclectic orientation, and tries to integrate Eastern Tao and Zen into Western psychotherapy. The Academy has close relations with the American Academy for Psychoanalysis and the International Federation for Psychotherapy. The Academy has more than one hundred members, one third of whom are psychologists and social workers, and it is going to host the 16th International Congress of Psychotherapy (ICOP) in the summer of 1994. Two of their members have joined the KPSG. The second one is the Korean Society of Analytical Psychology, the Jungians, founded in 1978 and led by Bou-Yong Rhi, who graduated from Seoul National University College of Medicine in 1959, trained at the Jung Institute in Zurich from 1963–1968, and is currently Professor of Psychiatry at Seoul National University, and by Zouk-Nae Lee, who graduated from Kyungbuk National University College of Medicine in 1963, trained at the Jung Institute in Zurich from 1970–1976, and is currently Professor of Psychiatry at Kyungbuk National University. The Jungian group has more than 120 members, one half of whom are non-psychiatrists.

The third group is the Korean Academy for Psychoanalytically-oriented Psychotherapy, founded in 1988 and led by Jae-Seung-Lee, who was trained at the William Alanson White Institute in New York from 1978–1982, and is currently Clinical Associate Professor of Psychiatry at Yonsei University. It has a Sullivanian orientation, and has thirty members, all of whom are board-certified psychiatrists and psychiatric residents. The fourth is an informal group of about forty members, of orthodox Freudian orientation, composed of clinical psychologists and university counsellers, led by Soon-Imm Yoon, a woman psychologist trained in West Germany in the eighties.

References

CHO, D. Y. (1988): Psychotherapy in Korea. In: Nishizono, M. /Yamamoto, J. (Eds.): Psychotherapy in Japan, Asia and North America. Tokyo: Kobundo, 1988, 195–218 (in Japanese).

– (1989): Reports to the International Psychoanalytical Association on Korean Situation (in English), Submitted to the President of the IPA.

KANG, S. H. (1990): Training and Development of Psychotherapy in Korea. *Psychotherapy and Psychosomatics* 53, 41–49 (in English).

RHEE, D. S. (1966): Concept and Attitude for Psychotherapy. *J Korean Neuropsychiatr Assoc.* 5, 9–11 (in Korean).

YOO, S. J. (1962): Historical Development of Korean Psychiatry. *J Korean Neuropsychiatr. Assoc.* 1, 55–66 (in Korean).

Journals

Journal of the Korean Psychoanalytic Study Group
(in Korean and English; summaries in English)
since 1990; Ed.: H.Y. Kim
I. K. Hwang Publ.

Institutions

Korean Psychoanalytic Study Group
c/o Dept. of Psychiatry, Seoul National University Hospital
28 Yongon-dong, Chongno-gu, Seoul 110-744, Korea
Tel.: 02-760-2450

Prof. Dr. Doo-Young Cho, c/o Korean Psychoanalytic Study Group

Mexico*

by Raúl Páramo-Ortega

Pre-History

As far as I was able to discover regarding the reception of Freud in Mexico, 1922 was the year in which Freud's name for the first time appeared in print in Mexico. The well-read provincial doctor, José Torres Orozco, had written an essay entitled "Freudian Theory in relation to mental illnesses". The periodical in which the article appeared was called *Mexico Moderno* (Vol. 2, No.1), whose editors included the *crème de la crème* of Mexican intellectuals, among them personalities who were to attain political prominence in Mexico: e. g. the communist Vicente Lombardo Toledano and the conservative lawyer Manuel Gómez Morín. The famous poet José Gorostiza also deserves to be mentioned. Torres Orozco was able to read Freud in the original without difficulty and a few years before he had even published some essays on Nietzsche, furthermore enjoying the fame of having read the library of the *Colegio Nicolaita* (Morelia) twice. Even though the article mentioned above did not contain detailed knowledge of Freudian thought, Torres Orozco nevertheless recognized the fundamental significance of sexuality for the human being. This was above all possible because he had grown up in an open and liberal atmosphere: his father, Don Mariano de Jesús Torres, was namely a well-read, versatile and distinctive personality who edited his own opposition newspaper *El Centinela* (against the dictator Porfirio Díaz (1876-1910)). Our provincial doctor, however, was more an isolated occurrence who did not start off a movement in Mexico. The positivist philosopher Samuel Ramos, who was a friend of Torres Orozco and was the next person to try to shed light on the conflictual identity of the Mexicans by using psychoanalytical tools, does not orient himself to Freud,

* This essay is a summary of the author's more detailed portrayal of this subject: Raúl Páramo-Ortega: Freud in Mexico. The History of Psychoanalysis in Mexico. Munich (Quintessenz) 1992 [in German]. At this point I should like to express my gratitude to Ms Marita Zimmer de Luengas for her collaboration and without whose invaluable assistance I would not have been able to write this paper in German, a language I only learnt later in life.

however, but decidedly to Adler, whom he briefly visited in Vienna in 1928 (Hernández Luna, 1982). Ramos also had a great influence on the well-known writer Octavio Paz. In 1950 Paz wrote an enlightened and still today fundamental book on Mexican identity, entitled *The Labyrinth of Loneliness,* which was translated into several languages. Octavio Paz, at that time still young and progressive, had in fact ideas that can be regarded as being a part of psychoanalytical thought. Curiously enough, the pioneer of psychoanalysis in Mexico, Santiago Ramírez, also wrote, independent of this, a noteworthy essay entitled *El mexicano – psicología de sus motivaciones* (1959). Mexico's identity was one of the first objects of research to be given special attention by Mexican psychoanalysts. In this connection two books by Francisco González Pineda must also be mentioned: *The Mexican – his psycho-social dynamics* and *The Mexican – his destructivity.* Both Santiago Ramírez and González Pineda come from the founding group of the Asociación Psicoanalítica Mexicana (APM), which is a component society of the IPA.

Freud's Late Reception in Mexico – a Hypothesis

Four interwoven factors were above all responsible for Freud's late reception in Mexico:

a) The obvious language barrier.
b) The breaking-off of diplomatic relations between Austria and Mexico, as well as scanty contacts to Germany and Switzerland.
c) The intense "Frenchifying" of Mexican culture.
d) Universal resistance to the new shattering insights brought forth by psychoanalysis.

Regarding a): Relations between Germany and Mexico were not particularly well-developed or not directed specifically to cultural matters but more to commercial ones. This applies to the period between 1900 and about 1950. Even the associations run out of an interest in culture (such as the Jewish lodge B'nai-B'rith, which in Mexico in the thirties published a bulletin in Yiddish, *In Kamf)* imparted no information on the Jew Sigmund Freud (cf. Zárate, 1986). Despite the fact that Freud himself was active in this association in Vienna (Jones, 1962, III, from p.151), no approaches were made to him.

Regarding translations, the first Spanish translation of Freud's work is dated as late as 1923, not in Mexico but in Madrid. In addition to this, the two most used translations (López Ballesteros and José Luis Etcheverry) contain numerous and fundamental errors.[1]

Regarding b): After the assassination of Emperor Maximilian in 1867 diplomatic relations between the Austro-Hungarian Empire and Mexico were broken off and not resumed until 1901 (Vavrik, 1989). These interruptions had an effect for many decades to come and only in the sixties do we find Mexican students interested in getting into contact with the German-speaking world. The first and second world wars were naturally an insuperable obstacle in the way of any possible cultural influence.

Regarding c): The first intrusion by France into Mexico's history was of a military nature, following the refusal of the president at that time, Benito Juárez, the wise Oaxakenian Indian, to repay Mexico's financial debts (1861). Thus Napoleon III decided, in 1861, to use his military power. From the beginning the French were very careful to secure their cultural influence, which was expressed, for example, in the founding of the Academy of Sciences (1864). Soon afterwards many Mexican intellectuals (above all medical doctors) went to France in order to widen their knowledge. They included the influential Gabino Barreda (1820–1881), himself a pupil of August Comtes, who later took on a leading position in the Mexican Ministry of Education. In the Medical School Daniel Vergara López (cf. Gortari, 1963) introduced both the French school of medicine as well as Pavlov's theories. For the Mexicans, Pavlov epitomized Europe.

Up to the present-day psychoanalysis in Mexico has, by and large, been influenced above all by the psychoanalysis of North America, France and Argentina (in that order; Argentina, incidentally, has also been considerably influenced by the French). It is therefore impossible to speak of these three influences having any kind of unity. By comparison, Freudian texts have come off badly. Moreover, opinions of Freud frequently appear in Mexican literature, which, due to poor translations, have nothing to do with Freud. Influence from the German-speaking world in terms of quantity is very small. To sum up, psychoanalysis is inevitably second-hand, so to speak.

1 See a number of examples of this in Páramo-Ortega et al. 1982 and Páramo-Ortega / Perez-Robles 1987.

Two Pioneers: Erich Fromm and Santiago Ramírez

The first attempts at institutionalization were made in the fifties. A number of psychiatrists, including Guillermo Dávia, José F. Diaz, Abraham Fortes, Raúl González Henríquez, and Alfonso Millán, who had heard about hypnosis, hysteria and the unconscious during a lecture trip by Pierre Janet (in 1925), knew that the psychoanalyst Erich Fromm was staying at a health resort near Mexico City and arranged to meet him. In the original group we find (among others and besides those mentioned above) Aniceto Aramoni, Jorge Derbez, Arturo Higareda, Armando Hinojosa, Ignacio Millán and Jorge Silva García (in alphabetical order). A little later, in 1951, Fromm was given a lectureship at the National University of Mexico (Universidad Nacional Autónoma de México, UNAM). Many prominent patients went to him and at the same time he also started to give seminars, above all for medical doctors who were interested in getting to know more closely and practising the new method of psychoanalysis (cf. Millán, 1965; Silva García, 1988).

Other medical doctors, who were not interested in the theory of a revisionist (Fromm) but more in so called orthodox theory, received psychoanalytical training at one of the training centres of the IPA.

Thus the pioneer Santiago Ramírez[2], who later epitomized Mexican psychoanalysis, went to Argentina (where Marie Langer was his training analyst). His friend Ramón Parrés, as well as Francisco González Pineda, Alfredo Namnum and Fernando Césarman went to the United States. Avelino González, Jaime Tomás, José Luis González Chagoyán, José Remus Araico and Estela G. de Remus went to Argentina. The ways of Rafael Barajas and Carlos Corona Ibarra led to Paris. The former lived after his return in Monterrey and the latter in Guadalajara. Fortunato Castillo decided to go to England, where he then settled. None of the first pioneers even thought of learning the original language of psychoanalysis, let alone of going to Germany, Austria or Switzerland. We must not forget, however, that psychoanalysis in the German-speaking world at that time was in the difficult post-war phase. The earlier golden age in Berlin and Vienna as centres of training was already past. No Mexican, as far as I am informed, had taken any notice of the "good times" in Berlin and Vienna. Thus psychoanalysis in Mexico (let it be mentioned once more) was decidedly influenced by the USA, France, Argentina and, to a lesser extent, England.

2 Santiago Ramírez died at the age of 68 on 14 April 1989 in Cuernavaca, Mexico.

The first two pioneer groups failed in their attempt to start a common movement. Power struggles, as nearly always, were an insuperable obstacle. So each group went its own way: the so called orthodox Freudians and the Frommians. After their return the former joined together and founded the Mexican Psychoanalytical Association (Asociación Psicoanalítica Mexicana, APM), which was officially accepted as a member of the IPA at the 20th IPA Congress Paris in 1957 (cf. Parrés / Ramírez, 1966). In the meantime this association has developed very well and grown stronger, today (1989) having 18 life members, 47 full and 16 associate members. The number of training candidates, according to official information, is 26 (Velasco, 1989). The APM has the training centre with the highest standards in the whole country. (Most of the candidates who do not come up to the required standards are – let's say tactically and *de facto* – referred to the recently opened *Centro de Estudios de Postgrado,* where they have the opportunity of gaining a *Maestria* in psychotherapy. This *Maestria* is officially recognized by the Ministry of Education). Originally the APM consisted almost entirely of medical doctors, with one exception, the psychologist Luis Feder, who later attracted attention with a number of investigations into the ambivalent affectivity of parents, under which children are frequently born. He coined the term "pre-conception phase" and also published quite a lot on creativity, acting out and committed incest. From the conflict between medical doctors and so called laypersons (there were of course other kinds of conflicts too) different branches came into being which were founded by members of the APM themselves in 1965: the Asociación Mexicana de Psicoterapia Psicoanalítica (AMPP), supported by Santiago Ramírez, at the beginning had only female psychologists as members (of these Raquel Berman later made a name for herself). Another offshoot worthy of mention is the Asociacíon Mexicana de Psicoterapia Analitica de Grupo (AM PAG, founded by José Luis González, Gustavo Quevedo and Frida Zmud in 1967), as well as the Instituto Mexicano de Psicoterapia Psicoanalítica para la Adolescencia (IMPPA), under the directorship of Armando Barriguete. The conflictual and momentous splitting away of the APM crystallized in the forming of the Sociedad Psicoanalítica de México (1978), led by Avelino González and Amapola González de Gaitán (see González de Gaitán, 1980), who later formed the Asociación Psicoanalítica Jalisciense in Guadalajara as an offshoot of the above mentioned association, led by Enrique Torres Acevedo and Manuel Fernández Villanueva. In Monterrey, the third most important city in Mexico, a study group which was recognized as such by the IPA was formed, a leading role being played by Rafael Barajas, Ricardo Diaz Conty and later Rubén Tamez Garza and Hernán Solís Garza.

The Frommian group overcame all its difficulties and became firmly established. At its training institute 93 psychoanalysts had completed their studies by the end of 1989. The number of teaching staff is 19 (see Silva García, 1988). The Instituto Mexicano de Psicoanálisis published a yearbook that propagated Fromm's humanistic psychoanalysis. The Mexican Psychoanalytical Circle (Circulo Psicoanalítico Mexicano, CPM) was founded by Armando Suárez and Raúl Páramo-Ortega in Mexico City in 1969. This has helped to reduce further the monopoly of medical doctors, although Páramo-Ortega, and Jaime Cardeña, who joined later, are both medical doctors themselves. Jaime Cardeña had completed training at the APM. Yet he was soon to view this association (APM) critically, which was why he made the decision to leave it. The founders mentioned above, Suárez and Páramo-Ortego, had in the tradition of their teacher Igor Caruso tried very hard to emphasize the socio-critical aspects of Freudian theory and its connection with sociology (of a Marxist slant) and ethology. They both saw themselves as true Freudians and were virtually the only and the first ones to seek to do their training in German-speaking countries. The present director of the CPM (1992) is José Perrés. According to official information the CPM has at present (November 1989) 74 training candidates and a teaching staff of 15. In Guadalajara there has been a branch of the CPM since 1987, led by two pupils of Armando Suárez, Fernando González and Juan Diego Castillo. The pendulum has swung so far in the other direction that nowadays hardly any medical doctors are to be found at the various training centres in Mexico. Only the APM continues to have almost only medical doctors in its ranks. In recent years – in my opinion rightly so – it has not been in principle opposed to psychology as a prerequisite for training, but opposed to qualitative shortcomings in the study of psychology. Freud pleaded for the inclusion of non-medical analysts, but the so called laymen of the pioneering period at that time had – compared to Mexico – a tremendously good educational background with which a Mexican diploma in psychology simply cannot compete. The logical consequence is that for some time now a doctorate (and not only a licence) in psychology as well as certain psychiatric experience have been called for. Added to this is the fact that – in view of the financial crisis over the past ten years – the study of medicine (much more expensive, longer and more demanding) is hardly possible. This is an insuperable obstacle for Mexican students, helping to bring about a drop in the standards of training candidates in psychoanalysis. The surfeit of psychotherapists of all descriptions in Mexico City has also caused many to move to other cities where they hope to keep their heads financially above water. The worst thing is yet to be mentioned: The flourishing of so called "psychoanalytical training centres", where many people try to save their difficult financial situation by "acquiring" a formerly highly esteemed profession (that of psychoanalyst). The laws governing the practice of any profession cannot keep up with the situation that is currently prevalent in all professions. And we must not forget that in Mexico a law is very often a useless law.

Catholicism and Psychoanalysis: the Lemercier case – from about 1960 until 1970

In the early sixties, the Belgian benedictine priest, Gregorio Lemercier, played an indirect, yet noteworthy rôle in Mexican psychoanalysis. Initially he had come to Mexico full of missionary Christian-Eurocentric zeal to found a monastery. Only by chance, namely that he had unexpectedly had a visual hallucination, did he come across psychoanalysis. The visual hallucination finally turned out not to be psychogenic, so to speak, but a symptom of cancer of the retina. At any rate, the friend he consulted (the psychoanalyst Santiago Ramirez) had advised Lemercier, besides the ophtalmological examination, to undergo psychoanalysis with Gustavo Quevedo. The personal analysis was so enlightening for Lemercier that he tried, full of enthusiasm, to apply psychoanalysis to the whole monastery. With the help of Frida Zmud and later of José Luis González Chagoyán, Quevedo applied psychoanalytical group therapy. Because of this Lemercier got into difficulties with the Vatican, in the end losing his struggle. The Vatican closed the monastery because it, perhaps rightly, feared that the spiritual vocation and/or even the Christian faith might be lost through psychoanalysis. Lemercier, on the other hand, maintained defiantly that psychoanalysis could and should only enhance the faith. After the break between the Vatican and Lemercier, the Belgian priest enthusiastically undertook, together with Quevedo, the Utopian-mystical project, Centro Psicoanalítico Emmaus, of applying psychoanalysis to everything one can think of (e. g. factories, hospitals etc.). The project was, however, tactically and technically, too out of touch with reality and at the same time so imbued with salvationist zeal and phantasies of omnipotence that it was quickly doomed to failure. Quevedo, who had been trained in Argentina, paid for this by becoming mentally unbalanced. He suffered from deep depressions at that time. A little later he died in a car crash, for which – in the opinion of many people – his state of mind was also to blame.

For all its tragic nature, a side-effect of the whole experiment "psychoanalysis in the monastery" was that it provided a tremendous impulse for the application of group therapy and for psychoanalysis in general. For the first time psychoanalysis came into the public eye and the analysts' consulting hours were heavily booked.

The Immigrants: From 1974 to the Present

In 1974 a wave of emigrants, mainly from Argentina, came to Mexico, fleeing from their politically and economically unsettled country. This emigration set a lot in motion, some of it not only of a positive nature. There were serious and well trained people who enriched the psychoanalytical movements in Mexico, but also, unfortunately, less serious people, who caused a certain amount of chaos in psychoanalytical identity. In no time many "Psychoanalytical consulting rooms" came into being. The influence from Argentina only increased the grave economic and spiritual crisis that prevailed in Mexico.

Among the emigrants there are some outstanding personalities, such as Marie Langer, Juan Carlos Plá, Ignacio Maldonado, Silvia Bleichmar, Frida Saal, Miguel Matrajk and Armando Bauleo, as well as the more controversial Néstor Braunstein, to mention but a few. Initially Braunstein was regarded very highly because of his fundamental book *Psicología: ciencia e ideología* (Braunstein 1975), but later took a controversial direction, as already mentioned. He was very active, publishing many books, and in the most recent phase has oriented himself decidedly to Lacan. He formed, with unusual financial support, the Centro de Investigaciones y Estudios Psicoanalíticos (CIEP). In this connection the Escuela Lacaniana de Psicoanálisis should also be mentioned, whose followers are almost entirely Argentinians. Irrespective of what the Lacanian school has to offer in terms of content, many psychoanalysts (or those who consider themselves as such) have looked for a new identity figure in the Frenchman Lacan. The figure of Freud as an ideal image was already occupied, so to speak, in their elected country Mexico. The situation of exile (a lack of roots, shattered identity, new surroundings, and precarious finances) was for some people more the basis of an opportunistic impetus to follow a modern direction in psychoanalysis (Lacan).

Psychoanalytical Literature

Mexican psychoanalytical literature is not extensive and has not in fact produced anything remarkable in terms of quality. Among the books published by members of the APM, however, there are some that are worth mentioning, though I shall naturally dispense with making a complete list: *La infancia es destino* by Santiago Ramírez (1959); *La técnica psicoanalitica* by Agustin Palacios, Santiago Ramírez and Gregorrio Valner (1963); *La práctica del psicoanálisis* by Marco Antonio Dupont (1988); also the book by Guiseppe Amara, *El hombre imposible: anatomia de un psicoanálisis* (1987).

I cannot go into Erich Fromm's extensive publishing activities in a summary such as this article. Beyond that, reference is made to the double issues 1 and 2, January–June 1984 (Vol. XVII) of the *Cuadernos de Psicoanálisis* (journals on psychoanalysis edited by the APM). They give us an invaluable view of psychoanalytical practice as the Mexicans see it, an amalgam, in fact, of Mexican and North American psychoanalyis. Regarding periodicals, it is important to mention that the Argentinian, Silvia Bleichmar, edited eight issues of a periodical of a very high standard during her time in Mexico (from about 1981 to 1987). The periodical is called *Trabajos de Psicoanálisis* (freely translated: *Working through psychoanalysis*). In it, French influences are apparent, above all the ideas of Laplanche. In Guadalajara the *Cuadernos Psicoanalíticos* (*Psychoanalytical journals,* 11 issues up to 1992) appear at irregular intervals. The editors are the small Sigmund Freud Study Group, who, as the name says, see themselves as Freudians. They emphasize the ideological-critical aspects of psychoanalysis (that is, psychoanalysis as a cultural theory) and have drawn attention to the poor Spanish and English translations of Freud's works. In Monterrey, again at irregular intervals, the periodical *Imago* is edited, and in Morelia *La Nave de los Locos (The Ship of fools).*

Summing up I should like to add that Mexico, in my opinion, is too close to North American psychoanalysis and too far away from European psychoanalysis (particularly from the German-speaking world – the language of Freud). Psychoanalysis in Mexico is of necessity a transcultural product. The grave economic and spiritual crisis in Mexico is of course also reflected in our profession. Psychoanalysis in Mexico represents a distinct kind of "therapeutically"-centred psychoanalysis, which, as Erdheim (1988, p. 9) says, "creates the unconsciousness in society which (the analyst) – seeks to reduce in patients".

References

AMARA, G. (1987): El hombre imposible: anatomia de un psicoanálisis. México: Siglo XXI.

BRAUNSTEIN, N. et al. (1975): Psicología: ciencia e ideología. México: Siglo XXI.

DUPONT, M. A. (1987): Raices e Identidad de una Institución Psicoanalítica Mexicana. En: La práctica del psicoanálisis, 55–67.

– (1988): La práctica del pscicoanálisis. México: Editorial Pax.

ERDHEIM, M. (1988): Die Psychoanalyse und das Unbewußte in der Kultur. Frankfurt/M.: Suhrkamp. [p. 9]

GONZÁLEZ, F. M. (1986): Notas para una historia del psicoanálisis en México en los años setentas. En: Psicoanálisis y realidad. México: Siglo XXI. [p. 75]

GONZÁLEZ DE GAITÁN, A. (1985): Reseña histórica de la Sociedad Psicoanalítica de México. *Gravida* 1, No. 1, 5–13.

GORTARI, E. DE (1963): La ciencia en la historia de México. México: FCE.

HERNÁNDEZ LUNA, J. (1970): José Torres Orozco – el último positivista mexicano. México (Edución del autor).

– (1982): Samuel Ramos. Bibliografía de su desarrolo intelectual, Morelia: Universidad Michoacana de San Nicolás de Hidalgo. [p 185]

JONES, E. (1962): Das Leben und Werk von Sigmund Freud, Band III, Huber Verlag, Bern, p. 151 ff. [The life and work of Sigmund Freud, Vol. 3. New York: Basic Books, 1957]

LANGER, M. / J. DEL PALACIO / E. GUINSBERG (1981): Memoria, historia y diálogo psicoanalítico. México: Folio Ediciones.

LEMERCIER, G. (1968): Diálogos con Cristo – monjes en psicoanálisis. México: Ediciones Península.

MILLÁN, A. (1965): Desarrollo de la Sociedad Psicoanalítica Mexicana y del Instituto Mexicano de Psicoanálisis. *Revista de Psicoanálisis, Psiquiatría y Psicología* 1, (sept-dic), 5–9.

PALACIOS, A. / S. RAMÍREZ / G. VALNER (1963): Psicoanálisis, La tecnica. México: Ed. Pax.

PÁRAMO-ORTEGA, R. et al. (1982): Muestrario de errores y limitaciones en la traducción al castellano de la obra de Freud. *Cuadernos Psicoanalíticos* 3, 3–36.

PÁRAMO-ORTEGA, R. / J. PÉREZ-ROBLES (1987): Nuevos errores de traducción en la obra de Freud. *Cuadernos Psicoanalíticos* 7, 19–28.

PÁRAMO-ORTEGA, R. (1992): Freud in Mexiko. Zur Geschichte der Psychoanalyse in Mexiko, München: Quintessenz.

PARRÉS, R. / S. RAMÍREZ (1966): Historia del movimiento psicoanalítico en Mexico. *Cuadernos de Psicoanálisis* 2, No. 1–2.

PAZ, O. (1950): El laberinto de la soledad, México: FCE.

RAMÍREZ, S. (1959): El mexicano – psicología de sus motivaciones, México: Ed. Pax.

– (1959): La infancia es destino. México: Siglo XXI.

– (1979): Ajuste de cuentas. México: Ed. Nueva Imagen.

Silva García, J. (1988): Erich Fromm in Mexiko 1950–1973. Bulletin 2 de la Internationale Erich Fromm Gesellschaft (Tübingen). Mimeo.

Torres Orozco, J. (1985): Ensayos sobre la patología del lenguaje, el tarbadillo, la neurastenia, la locura y la tuberculosis. Biblioteca de Cientificos Nicolaitas, Morelia (includes an essay by Samuel Ramos).

Vavrik, St. (1989): Cultural Attaché of the Austrian Embassy in México City. Letter to the author, march 3, 1989.

Zarate, G. (1966): México y la diáspora judía. Instituto Nacional de Antropología e Historia. México.

Journals

Cuadernos Psicoanalíticos
since 1977; Ed.: Raúl Páramo-Ortega
Grupo de Estudios Sigmund Freud, A.C.
Apart. Postal 6-203, Guadalajara 11650

Institutions

Asociación Psicoanalítica Mexicana, A.C.
(Mexican Psychoanalytic Association)
Bosque de Caobas 67, Bosques de las Lomas Deleg. Miguel Hidalgo, 11700 México
Tel.: 52-5-596 0009/7427; Fax: 52-5-596 7427

Asociación Regiomontana de Psicanálisis, A.C.
(Monterrey Psychoanalytic (Provisional) Society)
Angel Martinez Villarreal, 2626 Col. Lomas, Monterrey, N.I.
Tel.: 52-83-342 2686; Fax: 52-83-343 8036

Raúl Páramo-Ortega, Justo Sierra 2135, 44650 Guadalajara

Peru

by Hilke Engelbrecht and Alvaro Rey de Castro

The history of psychoanalysis in Peru, or to be more exact, of the influence of psychoanalytic thought on Peruvian intellectual circles, medical doctors and psychologists up to the founding of their own psychoanalytical society, occupies a special place when compared to other Latin American countries. On the one hand, Peru – in 1915 – was the first country in the whole Spanish-speaking world (in Latin America and Spain) in which psychoanalysis was introduced. These early contacts are verified by the correspondence between Sigmund Freud and Honorio Delgado, which we shall describe in Section 1. This correspondence gave Delgado the special privilege of being the first representative of psychoanalysis in Latin America, which is further underlined by Freud's mentioning of him in "The History of the Psycho-Analytic Movement" (Freud, 1914).

On the other hand, the Peruvian Psychoanalytic Society is the second youngest of the meanwhile fourteen psychoanalytical associations in eight countries in Latin America. Our essay therefore refers not only to the founding history of the Sociedad Peruana de Psicoanálisis, which began approx. 20 years ago, but includes the 77-year history of the reception of psychoanalysis, which has been marked by an interplay of encounters and misunderstandings.

The portrayal presented here will show that – at first – psychoanalytical ideas, and then psychoanalytical practice too, were introduced in Peru as early as the second decade of our century. Freudian ideas on general psychology soon appeared in academic discussion, but their practice remained restricted to therapeutic experiments within psychiatry, from which, however, they were to be banished about fifteen years later.

Their re-introduction and gradual consolidation in the fourties and fifties, initially once more within the framework of psychiatry as Dynamic Psychiatry, then as psychoanalysis in the narrower sense, came from medical doctors. During the seventies, however, the interest of psychologists in psychonalysis grew. Courses on psychoanalytical theory and analytical psychotherapy were included in the curricula of a number of universities, and at present (1992) ten of the twelve persons who are training to become psychoanalysts at the Peruvian Institute of Psychoanalysis are psychologists.

1. The Influence of Honorio Delgado

Let us turn at first to the "prehistory" of psychoanalysis in Peru, the period between about 1915 and the mid-thirties, which was dominated by the psychiatrist Honorio Delgado.

Delgado collaborated as a young psychiatrist with Hermilio Valdizán, the holder of the first and at that time only Peruvian professorship in psychiatry at San Marcos University. After Valdizán's death he took over this position – at the time he was 37 years old – which was to guarantee him decisive influence on the development of psychiatry in Peru for at least the next decade.

On 1st January 1915, *El Comercio,* a respected and traditional daily newspaper which still exists today, published in its New Year's issue one of the first articles in Spanish on the theme of psychoanalysis. Its author was Honorio Delgado and his article bore the title "Psychoanalysis". With the same title Delgado published four years later the first book in Spanish on psychoanalysis (Delgado, 1919).

These two works were only the beginning of a long series of publications on the theme of psychoanalysis, all of which it is impossible to mention here individually. By way of an overview we should like to show the changing tendencies of these works. In his first articles and books Delgado dealt enthusiastically with Freud's character and ideas: in 1926 he published a Freud biography, which in parts was similar to a hagiography (Delgado, 1990).

But already in the following year this enthusiasm started to wane, introducing the second phase, the gradual turning away from Freudian ideas. Delgado attended the International Psychoanalytical Congress in Innsbruck in 1927 and wrote: "The contributions were all mediocre, intended to clarify problems of detail, however justified the observations may have been individually. Not one single great revelation. Psychoanalysis has passed beyond the titanic age of *great* discoveries and the heroic element of ambitious hypotheses."

At this congress Delgado often met Ernest Jones, Wilhelm Reich, Sandor Ferenczi and Anna Freud; Jones made him an active member of the British Psycho-Analytical Society, so that Honorio Delgado, considered from a formal viewpoint, became the first Peruvian psychoanalyst, just at a time when his enthusiasm for psychoanalysis was starting to wane.

In this second phase, particularly clear in the first edition of *Psicologia*, which Delagado wrote jointly with the philosopher Mariano Iberico, his critical attitude towards psychoanalysis becomes more and more apparent (Delgado/Iberico, 1933).

Much later works that appeared after 1940 belong to the third phase, which is marked by open hostility towards psychoanalysis: *The Freudian Doctrine* (1940), *Freud seen from afar* (1950) and *Kraepelin and Freud, a hundred years after their birthday* (1956). Finally Delgado discards all the central concepts of psychoanalysis: the drive theory, transference, the method of free association, the training analysis etc. From being one of the major advocates of Freudian ideas he became one of their most bitter opponents.

In order to understand the briefly sketched development of Delgado's attitudes and ultimate turning away from psychoanalysis better, it is first necessary to consider more closely the phase of his seemingly total support of Freudian theory.

On the face of it he was a privileged representative of psychoanalysis. Besides his membership in the British Psycho-Analytical Society and his many pertinent publications, it is worth mentioning that Delgado met Freud on a trip to Europe in 1922. Already some years before a correspondence had begun which was to continue until 1934 (see Rey de Castro, 1990).

Freud frequently mentions the *Revista de Psiquiatria y Disciplinas Conexas* (Journal for Psychiatry and Related Disciplines), which was edited by Honorio Delgado together with the other major Peruvian psychiatrist of that time, Hernilio Valdizán. In *The History of the Psycho-Analytic Movement* (1914), in a comment added in 1924, Freud describes it as the organ of this movement. Furthermore, articles by Delgado in psychoanalytical periodicals existing at that time were quoted and even published (León, 1983).

These formal, apparently serious relations to psychoanalytical institutions enabled Delgado to speak on behalf of psychoanalysis, but later made his turning away from psychoanalytical attitudes in the Peruvian context all the more drastic. He then used his authority to condemn Freudian ideas.

Yet on studying his writings more closely, it is surprising how little of the psychoanalytical way of thinking he had in fact adopted. A few central Freudian concepts, particularly transference, were completely alien to him. We are surprised to discover in Delgado's works dealing with psychoanalysis an eclectic blending of concepts from Freud, Jung and Adler, preferably from the latter two. Just like Adler, Delgado never accepted the libido theory. Even his article from 1915 (Delgado, 1915) closes with the words:

"In fact, the libido concept, which is based on exclusiveness, is the most arbitrary concept in psychoanalysis; this is why, even among Freud's followers, a group of dissidents has come into being, led by Adler, who has created a more comprehensive theory, which, in our opinion is more compatible with psychic reality: the theory is that from earliest childhood every individual, in constant conflict with reality, has the tendency to confirm his personality and to impose his own rhythm on his surroundings; the influence of the cosmic, vital and social environment evokes in the psychic mechanisms of a person symbolic defence reactions with which he frees himself from the tension that the needs in him evoke."

There was very little left, even then, of the revolutionizing message of the drive theory.

It is of note that even an article by Delgado in German was published in a book edited by Adler: "Unterricht in der Philosophie des Lebens, begründet in der Individual-Psychologie" (1922).

A little later, however, Delgado dissociated himself from Adler as well. In the summer and autumn of 1927, after attending the International Psychoanalytical Congress in Innsbruck, he also attended the congress of the Adlerians (see Delgado 1927). He wrote: "[...] individual psychology has mingled with the popular movements. Before the congress discussed here, there was one on Socialist [!] individual psychology, led by one of Adler's most devoted pupils. These links between science and political parties can only redound to the dishonour of the representatives of the former. 'Quand la populace se mèle à raisonner, tout est perdu!' " (When the mob presumes to think, all is lost). The elitist attitude demonstrated here by Delgado was to grow stronger in the following years, eventually causing him to adopt positions that were close to the ideology of National Socialism.

Even in Delgado's few works referring to his psychoanalytical practice, we can read how far he was from a real understanding of the therapeutic process. If one takes into consideration that he had had neither the experience of a personal analysis nor continuous contact with other colleagues working in analysis, then it is hardly surprising. In various articles Delgado hints that he is attempting to conduct a self-analysis according to the Freudian example. An interesting anecdote, and at the same time typical of his naivity regarding psychoanalytical technique, is provided by Delgado's comments on his attempts at treating psychotics by means of psychoanalytical lectures. He writes enthusiastically of his methods and reports of fantastic cures (detailed description in Rey de Castro, 1990).

Despite this confusion in his attitude to practice and despite his later development to becoming an opponent of psychoanalysis, one cannot, from today's standpoint, deny Delgado the credit for awakening interest in Peru in psychoanalytical themes with his publications and, above all, with the periodical *Revista de Psiquiatria y Disciplinas Conexas,* which he co-edited with Valdizán and which appeared from 1918 to 1924.

In 1926, the periodical Mercurio Peruano devoted a special issue to Freud and psychoanalysis, whose authors, besides the psychiatrists Delgado and Valdizán, were more or less famous Peruvian intellectuals of the time, such as the philosopher Mariano Iberico. The appearance of the shortened translation of Freud's autobiography and of a chapter from *Group Psychology and Ego-analysis* in the same issue was also due to Delgado.

At about the same time a translation of "Resistances against Psychoanalysis" (Freud, 1925) appeared in the periodical *Amauta,* which was edited by the Marxist philospher José Carlos Mariátegu, and in the second and seventh issues Delgado published two articles. One of them, "Por qué nos gustan los ojos", had first appeared in German four years before in *Imago,* under the title "Der Liebesreiz der Augen".

As we can see, no clinical themes are to be found among these publications. Delgado, even at the time of his greatest enthusiasm for psychoanalysis, evidently did not strive for the training of other medical doctors to psychoanalysts.

In the mid-thirties an exception, Carlos Gutiérrez Noriega, appears as the author of a psychoanalytical case study (about a case of paranoia), which he presents as his PhD thesis; he also published psychoanalytical articles in the Revista de los Estudiantes de Medicina. It is not known where Gutiérrez acquired his psychoanalytical knowledge – he was probably an autodidact; he later turned to psychopharmacological research (see Rey de Castro, 1985).

When Hermilio Valdizán died in 1929 and left the only Chair in psychiatry in Peru empty, Delgado, hitherto the holder of the Chair in physiology, became his succesor. From this position he was to leave his mark on the development of Peruvian psychiatry in terms of his turning away from and his subsequent aversion to psychoanalysis.

II. The Influence of Carlos Alberto Seguin

Apart from a few isolated publications in the thirties (see above), psychoanalysis only attracted greater attention again through the influence of the psychiatrist Carlos Alberto Seguin, who, as a young man, had come into contact with Dynamic Psychiatry and psychoanalysis in Argentina and the USA, before returning to Peru. His first publication, in 1940, was already dedicated to Freud: *Freud, un gran explorador del alma* (Freud, a great explorer of the mind).

Although Seguin underwent analysis in New York for two years and at the same time attended courses at the New York Psychoanalytical Institute, he was evidently not interested in completing analytical training. What he later achieved in Peru had not been aimed at a psychoanalytical project in the real sense but at the introduction of a counter-model to traditional psychiatry as represented by Honorio Delgado at that time. In this way an, at times, passionate and polemic discussion came about which at any rate broadened the perspectives of Peruvian psychiatry, introduced psychosomatic medicine and reformed psychiatric care in some of the hospitals in Lima. Later Seguin came close to existentialist thought patterns; he himself considers *Amor y psicoterapia* (Love and Psychotherapy, 1963), in which he presents his conception of the therapeutic relationship, his most important work.

For the Peruvian context it is interesting that Seguin's influence on academic psychiatry was only temporary (approx. from 1954 to 1961), for at the university (there was at that time, in the fourties and fifties, only one medical school in Lima), the phenomenological school of Honorio Delgado continued to be predominant. Seguin, on the other hand, was building up a psychiatric training course for specialists at one of the hospitals administered by the state insurance system, the "workers' hospital", a course which has been very popular ever since and which has been and still is very open to psychoanalytical concepts. Within the framework of further education, a training course in psychoanalytical psychotherapy is offered.

Not only the four founding members of the Psychoanalytic Study Group, from which the Peruvian Psychoanalytic Society was later to emerge, but also a further seven members of the present institution were psychiatrists of the Seguin school before they turned to psychoanalysis. Meanwhile Seguin himself dissociated himself from the efforts to form a psychoanalytical institution in Peru: "Unfortunately, the time isn't ripe for the realization of the project which the enthusiastic Peruvian psychoanalysts of today have ventured on. The 'Golden Age' of psychoanalysis is over in the whole world; meanwhile, everything that is valuable about it (psychoanalysis) – and there is much – has been assimilated in the general store of knowledge of 'classical' psychiatry, and the exaggerations – of which there are many – are gradually being rejected by mature and experienced psychiatrists" (Silva, 1979).

Although Seguin's direct influence was restricted to psychiatry, he also made psychoanalytical ideas known by publishing many popular scientific articles in magazines, weekend supplements, etc.

At the same time another psychiatrist at San Marcos University was arousing the interest of some psychologists in psychoanalysis: Francisco

Alarco had held the Chair there since the late fifties and the themes he installed in the curriculum included: Interview and observation technique and Dynamic Psychology. For several years he had undergone training at the Psychoanalytical Institute in Chicago, which at that time was determined by Alexander's and French's ideas concerning corrective and emotional experience. Alarco's activities focused mainly on the university, and he was not interested in establishing practical psychotherapeutic training.

III. The Peruvian Psychoanalytic Society

In the late sixties the history of psychoanalysis in Peru entered a new phase – that of institutionalization. Between the setting up in practice of a single Peruvian analyst, trained in the British Psycho-Analytical Society, – Saul Peña – in Lima twenty years ago, and today, with the Peruvian Psychoanalytic Society (since 1987) recognized as an independent institution within the IPA, with 24 members and about 20 candidates (training participants), a lot has changed regarding the reception of psychoanalysis in Peruvian society in general and in psychiatry, psychology, the human sciences and the intellectual environment as a whole. But above all, the way analysts and candidates see themselves, has also developed considerably. The achievements and risks of this development will be briefly dealt with in the concluding remarks, as well as the situation of psychoanalysis in the present crisis in Peruvian society.

Initially it was thanks to the commitment of the first three analysts – Saul Peña, Carlos Crisanto and Max Hernández, who, having all been trained in London, worked in Lima from 1969, 1972 and 1974, respectively – that from the early eighties further analysts went to England and Argentina for training and that a few others returned to Lima after completing their training. The members of this "second generation", approximately in the order of their setting up in practice in Lima: Moises Lemlij and Gustavo Delgado-Aparicio (trained in London); Noel Altamirano, Alberto Péndola, Fernando Maestre and Pedro Morales (trained in Buenos Aires); César Rodriguez Rabanal and Hilke Engelbrecht (trained in Frankfurt); Jaime Heresi (trained in Caracas).

Although the variety of psychoanalytical schools and currents that left their mark on these Peruvian analysts during their training led to many confrontations after their return, the narrow-mindedness of restriction to one single direction within psychoanalysis was prevented.

In 1977 the Instituto Peruano de Psicoanálisis was founded, recognized as a training institute of the IPA. Alvaro Rey de Castro, the co-author of this article, is one of the first analysts to have been trained in Peru.

As is customary in the IPA, the Peruvian Psychoanalytic Society and the Institute were supported by a sponsoring committee for many years, which, with periodic visits, accompanied the process of institutionalization.[1] Due to this, but also due to the many personal and professional contacts of the analysts trained abroad, a productive exchange on an international level was guaranteed from the beginning.

An example of this that may be of interest to foreign, especially German readers is that, as early as 1977, Alexander and Margarete Mitscherlich spent two weeks in Peru during a lecture trip organized by the Goethe-Institute and that they did not only visit the recently formed study group of the psychoanalysts but also both gave public lectures which met with a great response.[2]

Apart from such highlights, the group of Peruvian analysts was, in those first few years of its existence, initially isolated from the context of the scientific discussion in the country and concentrated fully on the problems of consolidating its own institutions and building up the training institute.

An attendant phenomenon was that, although interest in psychoanalysis had grown in certain sections of society, it had not grown to the same extent in the discussion within medicine and psychiatry or the social science subjects. We believe that the analysts, because of their – albeit understandable – isolation in this phase of their history and because of their almost exclusive restriction to clinical work and training issues, partly had themselves to blame for the reproach of blindness levelled at them. During that time, for example, there were hardly any publications from members of the group.

This situation has changed radically since the mid-eighties. Not only have contributions by Peruvian authors appeared at international psychoanalytical congresses and at national psychiatric and psychotherapeutic meetings but there has also been a growing dialogue between psychoanalysis and the human sciences. The congresses and symposia organized by

1 The group of sponsors included: Serge Lébovici (Paris), Willy Baranger (Buenos Aires), Otto Kernberg (New York); and, at times, Inga Villarreal (Bogota), Leo Rangell (Los Angeles).

2 Other visitors who contributed to the scientific exchange with lectures and/or supervisions: John Bowlby, Adam Limentani (both London), Edward D. Joseph (New York), Horacio Etchegoyen, Carlos Mario Aslan (both Buenos Aires), Mechthild Zeul (Frankfurt/Madrid), Otto Goldschmidt, Ellen Reinke (both Frankfurt), Lorenz Böllinger (Bremen), Jürgen Habermas (Frankfurt), Helmut Dahmer (Darmstadt).

the Sociedad Peruana de Psicoanàlisis have helped this development, and their success, which is shown by the numbers of visitors and the attraction for foreign analysts and scholars, is testimony of the opening of the discussion of psychoanalysis in Peru.

Several events and publications are cited here as examples of this: in 1983 the periodical *Hueso Humero* devoted a whole issue to psychoanalytical topics; some of the authors were analysts (including Hernández, Rey de Castro, Rodriguez Rabanal), others were social scientists or arts scholars. In 1987 a conference was organized by the Universidad Catolica, at which historians, sociologists and anthropologists discussed interdisciplinary topics with psychoanalysts (see also Rey de Castro, 1983 and 1985).

Since 1988 the Peruvian Psychoanalytic Society has organized a congress every two years which, besides analysts, may be attended by psychologists, medical doctors, human scientists and students of these subjects. The topics of the first three congresses: in 1988: Psychoanalysis and Identity; in 1990: The Interest in Psychoanalysis – 77 years after; in 1992: From Listening to Interpretation – within the context of the current situation in Peru. The papers presented at these congresses are all published in book form (Sociedad Peruana, 1989, 1991), as are the contributions to the International Symposium on Myths which was organized in Cuzco in 1989 (Sociedad Peruana, 1989/90). The publication of the contributions at the 1st Symposium on Psychoanalysis and Education in 1991 will appear shortly.

In general, the development of psychoanalysis in Peru, a country organized on extremely centralist lines, is limited to the capital city, Lima. The above mentioned Symposium on Myths in Cuzco was almost completely organized from Lima, but with the collaboration of the Social Sciences Department of the University of San Antonio de Abad in Cuzco. In the second biggest city in Peru, Arequipa, cycles of lectures on psychoanalytical topics took place in 1989 (Tafur, 1990) and 1990, each of which was attended by about 70 people, in 1990 following the II. Psychoanalytical Congress; co-organizer was the Universidad Nacional San Agustin de Arequipa.

During the eighties the structure of the group of training participants at the Psychoanalytic Institute changed in favour of psychologists (for professional reasons and at the proposal of the sponsors of the IPA there was still an equal number of psychiatrists and psychologists admitted for training in the first two groups), social scientists and arts scholars: meanwhile two anthropologists, a sociologist, a linguist, a classical philologist and a priest with previous psychotherapeutic experience have been admitted for training.

General and interdisciplinary interest is also reflected by the attendance of about 300 people from home and abroad at the above mentioned interdisciplinary symposia on myths organized by the Peruvian Psychoanalytic Society in collaboration with the University of Cuczo in April/May 1989.

So interest in psychoanalysis seems to be growing within scientific circles. At the same time it seems remarkable to us that over the past few years the interest of scientifically active psychoanalysts in questions that go beyond clinical topics has increased, something that is borne out by the publications.

One could say that the majority of Peruvian analysts do mainly clinical work and do not publish, though a minority with scientific interests concern themselves, alongside their clinical work, which in psychoanalysis is of course the basis of research activity, with topics that belong to border areas between psychoanalysis and the social sciences or the humanities. Here are some examples:

A group of analysts has been collaborating for years with an anthropologist and a historian in the "Seminario Interdisciplinario de Estudios Andinos – SIDEA", investigating and interpreting ancient Peruvian myths and traditions. The results have appeared in several books and individual articles (e. g. Hernández, 1987).

Max Hernández wrote as the result of studies lasting many years a psychobiography of the Inca Garcilaso de la Vega, the chronicler of the epoch of the Conquista and one of the first and most famous mestizos. The book appeared, on the occasion of the events to commemorate the discovery of America 500 years ago, in a Spanish publishing house (1991).

Alvaro Rey de Castro has written about the "prehistory" of Peruvian psychoanalysis in several essays (1983, 1985, 1990) in which he elucidates psychoanalytical and historical aspects.

Finally, since 1982 a group of analysts, therapists and sociologists has been working in the "Centro Psicoanálisis y Sociedad" (Research Centre for Psychoanalysis and Society), headed by César Rodriguez Rabanal, on various research projects in the slums of Lima in order to investigate, while applying the psychoanalytical method, the psychology of poverty and violence and the unconscious dimension of conformity and survival mechanisms. The results of this research have been reported in several papers, contributions at congresses etc., in part also in German (Rodriguez Rabanal 1989, 1990), as some of the projects were funded by German foundations.

Scientific exchange between Peru and Germany, however, is not limited to the financing of research projects. The analysts trained in Frankfurt reported on contributions by German authors, especially texts on methodological and scientific theoretical questions by Alfred Lorenzer, Jürgen Habermas and Hermann Argelander. (A curious story in this connection was that, due to this orientation, a number of Peruvian colleagues confused the Sigmund Freud-Institute with the Frankfurt School (see Engelbrecht, 1992a)).

Publications of Peruvian analysts are evidence of this interest: several works by H. Engelbrecht on supervision and other methodological topics (see bibliography), an essay on the psychoanalytical first interview, going on from the works of Alfred Lorenzer and Hermann Argelander (Martinez, 1987), and an investigation into different note-taking methods during the analytic session for the investigation of countertransference (Escribens, 1989).

IV. Concluding Remarks

Summing up, it seems remarkable to us that in the twenties and thirties, despite excellent relations to the centres of psychoanalysis at that time and the generally heeded efforts of an individual scientist in Peru, no relevant group - in terms of numbers - of psychoanalytically active people came into being; that, on the other hand, in the last twenty years the number of psychoanalysts and candidates has risen from zero to almost fifty. And these of course are only the ones registered in the previously mentioned institution of organized analysts recognized by the IPA.

In addition there is a group of Lacanians and a fairly large number of analytical psychotherapists – mostly psychologists – who are more or less associated with the analytical institution. In 1982 and 1983 respectively, two training institutes were founded for analytical psychotherapy, the "Centro de Psicoterapia Psicoanalitica de Lima" and the "Instituto Sigmund Freud de Psicoanálisis Aplicado", both of which are headed by trained psychoanalysts, and in 1986 an Association of Psychotherapy for Children and Adolescents was founded, which publishes its own periodical.[3]

This *boom* – which, as will be explained below, is naturally full of risks – is particularly astonishing in view of the economic and political crisis and the instability, which, as we know, have intensified in Peru in roughly the same period. A deeper analysis of this theme would be beyond the scope of this essay – there has been no exhaustive investigation of this complex of questions as yet. Therefore it can only be assumed that, though Peruvian society in the twenties and thirties was relatively more stable than today's, there was no large educated middle class ready to receive psychoanalytical

3 *Transiciones, Revista de la Asociación de Psicoterapia de Niños,* No. 1, Lima 1990; No. 2, Lima 1991.

ideas and offers of treatment. Since the mid-thirties developments in Argentina, for example, have been quite different.

In the past two or three decades both interest in psychoanalysis and the need for psychoanalytical treatment have grown considerably, since, despite the deepening of the general crisis, a relative relaxation of previously still closed semifeudal structures in society has taken place.

At the same time there is a danger, however, that psychoanalysis, by restricting itself too much to its clinical tasks, could isolate itself from the major problems of the present and hence forfeit its social relevance. In our opinion the only way to avoid this risk is interdisciplinary confrontation, particularly with other human sciences, reflecting jointly on such themes that affect society in its present crisis. This includes above all investigation of the subjective factor in historical and social processes.

As we mentioned above, there are a number of encouraging signals in this direction. Only if psychoanalysis in Peru is ready to answer questions that go beyond the concerns of a limited social class, will it be possible to consider it a serious partner for discussion in the intellectual life of the country.

References

DELGADO, H. (1915): El psicoanálisis. *El Comercio* (1.1.1915).

– (1919): El psicoanálisis. Lima: Ed. Sanmarti.

– (1922): Unterricht in der Philosophie des Lebens, begründet in der Individual-Psychologie, in: Heilen und Bilden, ed. A. Adler / C. Furtmüller). München.

– (1927): Correspondencia de Europa. Dos congresos médico-psicológicos. *El Comercio* (1.11.1927).

– /M. IBERICO (1933): Psicología. Lima: Imprenta Hospital Victor Larco Herrera.

– (1940): La doctrina de Freud. Lima.

– (1950): Freud a la distancia. Lima.

– (1956): Kraepelin y Freud a los cien años de su nacimiento. Lima.

– (1990): Sigmund Freud, in: Freud y el psicoanálisis. Escritos y testimonio [First Vol. of the Collected Works of H. D.], ed. J. Mariátegui. Lima: Universidad Peruana Cayetano Heredia. Fondo Editorial.

ENGELBRECHT, H. (1988): El proceso de supervisión y el proceso psicoanalítico, in: Psicoanálisis e Identidad, *Biblioteca Peruana de Psicoanálisis.* Lima.

– (1990a): La intuición dentro de la metodología psicoanalítica. *Revista de la Sociedad Colombiana de Psicoanálisis* 15, No. 1.

– (1990b): Die Inszenierung der psychoanalytischen Situation der Supervision. *Psyche* 44.

– (1992a): Un malentendido honoroso: La Escuela de Frankfurt, el Psicoanálisis y el Perú, in: Encuentros y Desencuentros. Lima: Ediciones de la Pontifica Universidad Católica del Perú.

ESCRIBENS, A. (1989): Los diferentes registros de la sesión psicoanalítica, In: Psicoanálisis e Identidad. *Biblioteca Peruana de Psicoanálisis* 1. Lima.

FREUD, S. (1914): On the history of the psycho-analytic movement. S.E. 14.

– (1925): Resistances against psychoanalysis. S.E. 19.

HERNANDEZ, M. et.al. (Eds.) (1987): Entre el mito y la historia, Lima: Ediciones Psicoanalíticas Imago S.R.L.

HERNANDEZ, M. (1991): Memoria del bien perdido: Conflicto, identidad y nostalgia en el Inca Garcilaso, Madrid: Quinto Centenario/Ed. Siruela.

LEON, R. (1983): Honorio Delgado y el psicoanálisis. *Revista de Psicología* (Pontifica Universidad Católica) 1, No. 2.

MARTINEZ J. R. C. (1987): La primera entrevista psicodinámica: un enfoque clínico. Lima: Universidad Católica del Peru [degree dissertation].

REY DE CASTRO, A. (1983): Freud y Honorio Delgado: crónica de un desencuentro. *Hueso Humero* 15/16.

– (1985): El psicoanálisis en el Perú: Notas marginales, in: Debates en sociología. Lima: Ed. Universidad Católica del Perú.

– (1990): Las cartas de Sigmund Freud a Honorio Delgado, in: Freud y el psicoanálisis. Escritos y testimonio, ed. J. Mariátegui. Lima: Universidad Peruana Cayetano Heredia. Fondo Editorial.

RODRIGUEZ RABANAL, C. (1989): Cicatrices de la pobreza. Caracas: Nueva Sociedad. [German 1990: *Überleben im Slum*, Frankfurt/M.: Fischer]

– (1990): Psychoanalytische Gespräche mit Slum-Bewohnern in Lima. *Psyche* 44.

SILVA, M. (1979): Conversaciones con Seguín. Lima: Mosca Azul Ed.

SOCIEDAD PERUANA DE PSICOANALISIS (Ed.) (1989): Psicoanálisis e Identidad. I. Congreso Peruano de Psicoanálisis 1988, in: *Biblioteca Peruana de Psicoanálisis.* Lima.

– (1989/90): Mitos – universales, americanos y contemporáneos. Un enfoque multidisciplinario, in: *Biblioteca Peruana de Psicoanálisis.* 3 Vols. Lima.

– (1991): El Múltiple Interés del Psicoanálisis – 77 años después, in: *Biblioteca Peruana de Psicoanálisis.* Lima.

TAFUR, J. C. (Ed.) (1990): La Ciencia y el Saber Psicoanalítico. Lima.

Further Publications by the authors:

ENGELBRECHT, H. (1990): El Psicoanálisis como Método Científico, in: Tafur (1990).

– (1991c): Freud: Nuestro Totem?, in: El Múltiple Interés del Psicoanálisis – 77 Años despues. *Biblioteca Peruana de Psicoanálisis.*

– (1991d): El concepto de la comprensión Escénica de Alfred Lorenzer y 3 ejemplos de su aplicación en la práctica de supervisión. *Revista de la Sociedad Colombiana de Psicoanálisis* 16, No. 1.

– (1992b): El aporte de la supervisión a los procesos de integración en la formación psicoanalítica, in: Proceso de formación. De la multiplicidad a la integración. Lima.
– (1992c): Formación psicoanalítica: Cambio e incertidumbre, in: XIV Precongress for training analysts of the FEPAL, Vol. 1. Montevideo.
– (1994): Empathy – intuition – comprehension. *Melanie Klein and Object Relations* 12, No. 1. Toronto.
Rey de Castro, A. (1983): Freud y Honorio Delgado: crónica de un desencuentro. *Hueso Húmero* 15/16 (oct.–mar.), 5–76. Lima.
– (1987): El errático Dr. Freud: Freud and the Rat Man de Patrick Mahony. *Escritos* 3, No. 6, 30–32. Lima.
– (1990): La irrupción de la intimidad: una nueva mirada a los orígenes del psicoanálisis. *Escritos* 6, No. 8, 24–27. Lima.
– (1992): La noción de análisis en el psicoanálisis: química de un olvido. *Areté* 6, No. 1, 267–290. Lima.
– (1993): Del malestar en la escucha a la interpretación: hacia un ethos psicoanalítico, in: M. Lemlij (Ed.): De la escucha a la interpretación en el Perú de hoy. Lima: Fondo Editorial Biblioteca Peruana de Psicoanálisis, 280–295.

Journals

Revista del Centro de Psicoterapia y Psicoanalítica de Lima (CPPL)
since 1987; Ed.: Pedro Morales, José Gálvez 887, Lima 18

Transiciones. Revista de la Asociación de Psicoterapia de Niños
since 1990; Ed.: Victoria Pareja, Dellepiane 779, Lima 27

Institutions

Sociedad Peruana de Psicoanálisis
(Peru Psychoanalytic Society)
Tudela y Varela 470-1, San Isidro, Lima
Tel./Fax: 51 14 42 6362

Dra. Hilke Engelbrecht, República 941, Lima 27
Prof. Dr. Alvaro Rey de Castro, Tudela y Varela 138-603, Lima 27

Uruguay

by Mercedes Freire de Garbarino, Irene Maggi de Macedo and Juan Carlos Neme

Introduction*

The origins of psychoanalysis in Uruguay lie in the 1940s, while its course of development might be divided into two periods: the first, which we shall call the prehistory of the Asociación Psicoanalítica del Uruguay (APU), runs from about 1943 until either 1956 or 1961, while the second extends to the present-day. I have cited two different dates for the ending of the first period, since it was in 1956 that we acquired our legal personality, and in 1961 that we were formally recognized as an Association by the IPA. These two dates therefore mark the birth both of our own Association and of Uruguay's involvement in psychoanalysis at, respectively, national and international levels.

As I have said, it is from about 1944–45 onwards that psychoanalysis can properly be said to have existed in Uruguay. It was Dr. Valentín Pérez Pastorini who was to communicate to us both the corpus of psychoanalytic theory, and his own enthusiasm for, and dedication to, this field of knowledge. Dr. Pérez Pastorini was in charge of clinical training in the Department of Psychiatry of the University of the Republic's Medical Faculty.

To acquire further experience of psychoanalytic practice, he not only studied and applied the knowledge he had obtained, but made monthly or twice-monthly visits to Buenos Aires for his personal analysis, and to undertake supervisions of his patients. A psychoanalytic group already existed in Argentina, recognized by the IPA. Its analyst was Dr. Angel Garma, and its supervisors were Dr. Angel Cárcamo and Dr. Enrique Pichon Rivière.

Dr. Miguel Sesser underwent the same preparation, but his work had less impact, due, no doubt, to the distinctive nature of his personality. He was not attached to any particular hospital, and he carried out his work in isolation in his consulting rooms, without sharing his findings with his colleagues. As a result, he had no pupils or followers.

* by M. Freire de Garbarino, Founder Member and Full Member of the Asociación Psicoanalítica del Uruguay.

I should like to emphasize something which, though it has very little direct connection with the task in hand, is nonetheless important for a proper orientation within the cultural and scientific context with which we are dealing.

In Uruguay, psychology had several different starting-points, which together acted as a coherent but widely-spread network of focuses of interest. There is one date, however, which in my view, marks the first moment of unification. I am referring to the arrival in Uruguay of Emilio Mira y López, a Spanish Professor of Psychiatry. He came here to take up an appointment at the Instituto Normal de Pedagogía, where he worked for several years in the Institute's Laboratory. This was transformed into a major centre of psychological research, even though the Laboratory restricted its activities to the study of intelligence levels. To launch the Laboratory's work, which was carried out under the Professor's direction, anyone with an interest in this topic was invited to go and work there, subject to interview. I think this was probably the starting-point for the creation of the relevant psychological and scientific institutions and trade associations.

I thought it was worth mentioning this to underline the parallels in the development of psychology and psychoanalysis in Montevideo: the two subjects began to organize themselves and acquire scientific status at approximately the same time.

At the time of Dr. Pérez Pastorini's death, Dr. Rodolfo Agorio and Dr. Gilberto Koolhaas had already been in analysis with him for some years, and had been authorized to practise. Dr. Héctor Garbarino had also developed an interest in the subject, and had begun his personal analysis. He later continued his analysis with Dr. Rodolfo Agorio.

As time went by, interest in psychoanalysis in Uruguay greatly increased. At that time, interested parties tended to congregate around Dr. Agorio and Dr. Koolhaas. Señora Laura Achard, a Professor of Secondary Education, also joined the group, as, subsequently, did Dr. Juan Carlos Rey.

Dr. Fernando Taragano and Juan Pereira Anavitarte, a philosophy professor, were also analysed by Dr. Koolhaas.

I feel that psychoanalysis was, as it were, handed on from Dr. Pérez Pastorini to Dr. Agorio and Dr. Koolhaas, whose personalities were, however, markedly different from that of their predecessor. Though it is indisputably true that both Dr. Agorio and Dr. Koolhaas were men of considerable scholarship and wide reading, their transmission was nonetheless a good deal less enthusiastic and vivid than that of Dr. Pérez Pastorini, although it was, perhaps, calmer and more serene.

The group began to grow, although slowly. Within a short time it included both those I have already mentioned and the psychologist Marta Lacava. Under the impetus of the younger generation – which means, essentially, the writers of the present article – a study group on the works of Freud gathered around Dr. Agorio, a group which included Dr. Koolhaas, Laura Achard, Héctor Garbarino and Juan Carlos Rey. These were the people who had spent the most time in analysis, and who had already been authorized to practise.

This was the starting-point for our Association, since it was the first time that people who were dedicated to psychoanalysis had been united in a common endeavour. This was in about 1950. Within a short time, Dr. Fernando Taragano and Juan Pereira Anavitarte had joined the group. A little later, Marta Lacava and I also became members. Dr. Agorio was an outstanding member of the group. It was no accident that we used his home for meetings, and that all correspondence was forwarded to him. We had enormous respect for him and hung on his every word. He was a man of calm and balanced judgement.

At the time that Marta Lacava and I joined the group, the aim was not so much to study, which was something we preferred to do in small groups, as to find some way of organizing ourselves as a scientific institution, with a view to applying for membership of the International Psychoanalytical Association. Our reference point was the Asociación Psicoanalítica Argentina (APA), upon whom we were very dependent. All those of us who were authorized to practise had to pay monthly visits to Buenos Aires for supervisions with training analysts of the APA.

The IPA heard about us through the APA, and we were accordingly informed that we could not undertake any official activities until we had acquired a training analyst. We began an immediate search for one, but when this proved fruitless, we decided to adopt a different approach, one which the IPA had itself suggested, and which involved one of us going to live in a country where there already existed an Association recognized by the IPA, and making a career there. Laura Achard and Marta Lacava decided they would do this, and moved to Buenos Aires. Things were difficult for them there, but we visited them frequently. I well remember that one of Laura's patients followed her to Buenos Aires to continue her treatment. Laura used to attend to her in the little hotel room which she shared with Marta, who had to go out every time the patient had a session. This arrangement actually helped them, since neither of them had much money. Meanwhile, back in Uruguay, the rest of us went on hoping, in the anticipation that these circumstances would prevail for a further four or five years.

As it happened, Laura and Marta had to return to Uruguay at the end of the year, due to the difficult political situation. This was the era of Juan Domingo Perón. His government had problems with ours and there was a fear that, as subsequently happened, diplomatic relations between our two countries would be broken off. Laura and Marta were advised to return to Uruguay as soon as possible, since their position in Argentina was no longer considered secure.

This inevitably caused us a good deal of unhappiness, since it disrupted our plans. Not only had our colleagues' preparatory training been cut short, the rest of us were no longer able to travel for supervisions, except Héctor Garbarino, who had obtained an official passport and was therefore free to travel.

Accordingly, we went back to our original plan, which was to try to find someone who was willing to come and live in Uruguay. Amid the flurry of correspondence, we were surprised to receive a reply from London saying that Hanna Segal, who was thinking of emigrating, wanted to know what Uruguay had to offer in the way of opportunities. We engaged her for a month, so that we could investigate the possibilities of her moving here. She spent the whole of December 1952 with us.

Thus far, our group had functioned without any specific leaders. Although, of course, Dr. Agorio and Dr. Koolhaas were regarded as the movement's *maestros* and pioneers, there were no differences in rank between us when it came either to making decisions or putting them into effect. Dr. Agorio and Dr. Koolhaas identified with the group completely, and we all put our shoulders to the wheel.

After a month of intensive work with Dr. Hanna Segal, consisting of seminars, supervisions and clinical sessions, she decided not to remain with us since, although she thought the group was a good one, Uruguay's social and cultural milieu did not offer her husband, who was a successful mathematician, the sort of environment to which he was aspiring. Otherwise she would certainly have stayed with us, in which case she would have been able to make periodic visits to Buenos Aires, where the facilities of the APA were already on loan to us.

As can be imagined, a new wave of depression swept over the group. I think I should also point out that there were several psychoanalysts at this time who were obliged to participate in the group by correspondence, and who requested information, but then gave up.

This brings us to the end of 1953 and the beginning of 1954, when someone in Buenos Aires informed us that a French-trained senior analyst, who might also be available for training analysis, wanted to leave Argentina. The analyst in question was Willy Baranger.

We contacted him, and in November 1954 he settled in Uruguay. The eleven members of our group began analysis with him, while continuing to see their own patients. At the beginning of 1956, we all began theoretical seminars with him and his wife, Madeleine Baranger.

I should like to take the opportunity of placing something on the record about this period – from November 1954 to the middle of 1955 – during which Willy Baranger invited us to several meetings to draw up the regulations and negotiate the group's legal personality. We had to transform ourselves from a group which made decisions and implemented them in concert, democratically, to one which was willing to "do whatever might currently be in the mind of Señor Baranger". Remarks like that were quite common. I also heard people saying things like "In whose hands are we now exactly?", or "Who is this man, who takes our material off to Buenos Aires and goes around handing out details of our private lives?", or, more simply, "Who does he think he is?" We held clandestine meetings to plan what we were going to do next, and discuss just what it was we had become involved in. The meetings had to be *secret.* We had to try to avoid mentioning them in the analyses, since it was important that Willy Baranger did not find out about them. The very next day, of course, Willy Baranger would have all eleven versions of what had happened at the meetings, because the first thing we would do when we met him was to tell him all about them. The senior members of the group, Dr. Agorio and Dr. Koolhaas, did not, in fact, offer us any assistance. I remember that Dr. Agorio used to say, "You're crazy. After they've shown that they can achieve the impossible by pulling this off, then they'll just want to get rid of it". When the administrative meetings and seminars finally began, however, we found that we all contributed on an equal footing, albeit under the guidance of Baranger, a much younger person.

In September 1955 we signed the act of foundation. There were eleven of us: Willy Baranger, Madeleine Baranger, Dr. Rodolfo Agorio, Dr. Gilberto Koolhaas, Héctor and Mercedes Garbarino, Laura Achard, Marta Lacava, Juan Carlos Rey, Juan Pereira Anavitarte and Miguel Sesser. Dr. Agorio and Laura Achard were appointed President and Secretary respectively, with Mercedes Garbarino as Treasurer. In February 1956 we acquired our legal personality – and therefore our legal existence – in Uruguay. There then began a period of intense controversy with various groups in our intellectual and professional milieu, in particular with the psychiatrists. The opening chapter of our history at national level was to prove a very stormy one.

1956 and the beginning of 1957 were extremely difficult, due to a newspaper campaign accusing us of making illegal use of medicine. The attack was targeted directly at our non-medical members. I say *directly,* because the underlying attack was aimed at psychoanalysis itself. The press had pounced on the subject and sensationalized it, every article being eagerly devoured and gossiped about by the general public. Banner headlines appeared on the front pages, such as "The idea is that the analyst falls in love with his patient". Meetings were held at the various medical and legal societies to discuss the situation. Finally, the Uruguayan Medical Association intervened, and it was they who settled the matter, finding in our favour, and thus restoring calm.

The Professor of Psychiatry in the University of the Republic's Faculty of Medicine, Dr. Fortunato Ramírez, joined the seminars. Several Argentinian analysts also used to visit Uruguay each month, and they joined us in individual or group supervisions, and theoretical and clinical seminars. Attending these sessions were Enrique Pichón Rivière, Arminda Aberastury, Rebe Alvarez de Toledo, Jorge Mom and Emilio Rodrigué. In 1956, our journal began publication under the editorship of Dr. Koolhaas.

In 1957 the IPA, on the recommendation of the APA, recognized us as a study group under the APA's own patronage. One month before this recognition was received, Juan Pereira Anavitarte was killed in an accident. This was an extremely sad event for us, for he was one of our youngest and most brilliant members. Also present at the seminars was the man we used to call the "solo navigator" or the "man of the two generations", Luis Enrique Prego. In 1957 he became our colleague and, subsequently, our pupil.

In 1958 we started organizing our own seminars. The first seminar group included Luis Enrique Prego, Marta Nieto, Jorge Galeano and Olga Alfonso. This was also the year in which we rented our first premises.

In 1961, at the Edinburgh Congress, we were recognized by the IPA. At this point our "prehistory" can be said to have finally ended.

To explain what happened next, I think it is important to understand another very sad loss, which occurred during the period when the Barangers were still with us. This happened in 1965.

In the previous year, 1964, we had appointed the first training analysts, Laura Achard, and Héctor and Mercedes Garbarino. At the end of 1964, Willy and Madé Baranger announced that they would be returning to Argentina the following year, since they felt that the Association could now manage on its own.

This was a truly painful separation for us, and I think that this was the moment when we saw just what an important role they had played within the group. Obviously, they left behind them a void which we found hard to fill. In 1965, the Association was faced with the task of preparing for the

XII Latin American Congress in 1966. I think this helped us to work out the grief caused by the loss of the Barangers. We all prepared for the Congress, chaired by Héctor Garbarino, with great enthusiasm. Also attending, at our invitation, was the President of the IPA, Dr. P. J. van der Leeuw. Our Association had already achieved recognition in Latin America and Europe. We had come of age.

Restructuring*

It was around this time that the candidates and graduates began to take an active part in our institutional life. This was a creative period, in which members undertook a thorough questioning of existing procedures in search of new modes of functioning, ones which would allow for even greater achievements. This was hard work, since the constant changes created a climate of uncertainty, resulting in meetings and debates in which quite different models would be discussed, one of which was subsequently to be chosen as conspicuously the best.

Information on this subject has been drawn from the 1972 report of the Education Committee, of which Marta Nieto was the Director, and from the report presented at the Pre-Congress of training analysts in Rio de Janeiro in 1974. We will confine ourselves strictly to the matter of the training of candidates, since the spirit of the review which was undertaken infuses all the Institute's various procedures and arrangements.

The process of change, which was experiential in character, started slowly after years of work and reflection at different levels – notably within the framework of a study group on educational problems – and initially focused on specific areas of training, especially at the level of theoretical education.

The conclusions of this review were:

- that educational methods should focus on the discovery of, and reflection upon, what psychoanalysis really is, and that the backbone of the learning process should therefore be a rapprochement with the discoveries of Freud, taking full account of the vicissitudes he underwent in his discovery of psychoanalysis and its specific field of study, the unconscious.

* by I. Maggi de Macedo, Full Member and Associate of the APU, and J.C. Neme, Associate Member of the APU.

- that education can lead to the acquisition by students of an analytic cast of mind, resulting in the development of a distinct sensitizing in their own practice;
- that every task should be accompanied by critical reflection upon what is being done;
- that all those involved in the training process should be active participants both in "doing" and in "thinking how to do".

Candidates' training consists of three main areas: personal analysis, seminars, and supervised psychoanalytic practice. These three areas are arranged in a temporal sequence in relation to the starting-point of the individual candidate's studies, thus forming several stages.

What is expected of the candidates? They are expected to acquire two forms of knowledge: theoretical knowledge, acquired through study, essential to the formation of a rich and logically structured referential scheme – the backbone of which is, we believe, the assimilation of Freud's thought in its major formulations – and experiential knowledge, acquired chiefly through the personal analysis. These two forms of knowledge must be brought together and synthesized through a careful linking of theory and practice.

Assessment of each stage in the training process, and of the candidates' degree of application to each separate function within each stage, is based on two criteria: the candidate must display both interest and ability. In each case it is the subject himself – whether prospective student, student, graduate, ordinary member or full member – who must take the initiative and apply for the next stage of membership, the Institute's role being limited to mirroring the candidate's own image, something which will lead, as a natural consequence, to acceptance, postponement, or rejection.

It is the Institute's desire that candidates assume full individual responsibility for their own efforts and initiatives, without them delegating any decisions.

Admission: Admission to the Institute begins with an application by the interested party who, after a series of interviews, learns from the Education Committee whether or not he or she may begin theoretical studies.

Theoretical Seminars: These seminars last four years. They are planned by the panel of teachers with the approval of the Education Committee, in accordance with a specific model which is not, however, rigid, but which is prepared afresh for each generation. This enables revisions and modifications to be made according to the results obtained. Care is also taken to maintain a precise temporal sequence, and a careful synchronization with the different points to be learned.

The seminars are compulsory (four each year, two each semester, two hours weekly for each seminar) and focus in particular on a study of Freud.

In the second semester of the second year, students begin the study of the English School of Melanie Klein, which enriches the candidates' understanding of psychosis, perversion and child analysis.

The seminars in the third and fourth years are geared to specific themes, such as the Oedipus complex and psychosis, and embrace and synthesize different points of view, Freudian, Kleinian and Lacanian.

In one of the fourth year semesters, the candidates have the opportunity to suggest themes which they would like to study in greater detail.

In these seminars, the aim is that teachers and students undertake a joint exercise of teaching/learning within a dynamic process which is both methodical and rigorous.

Evaluations are made in each seminar, with the aim of discussing the type of training being offered and the progress which each candidate in the group is making. Another element in the evaluation consists of the preparation of a dissertation on a topic to be chosen by the candidate from those featured in the course, which is then discussed within the group. In this way, opportunities are created for carrying out new tasks, developing new fields of interest, synthesizing knowledge, deepening appreciation of a particular aspect, or increasing a candidate's orientation towards research.

At the end of each year, the teachers decide which candidates may continue with their studies, which ones need to repeat a year, and which ones have to give up altogether.

As for both psychoanalytic technique and its theoretical basis, the aim is that the candidates should find these things out for themselves by rooting themselves in sound theoretical concepts, as well as in the effective management of the unconscious which they have achieved during their personal analysis and in the supervisions.

In this way, we avoid turning out mere technicians, and produce analysts capable of thinking for themselves, and of undertaking independent research.

Supervisions*

From the second year onwards, candidates may ask if they can begin supervised psychoanalytic practice. It is those teachers with whom they have

* by I. Maggi de Macedo and J.C. Neme

studied during their seminars who will advise the Education Committee whether they agree with this initiative, based on an assessment of the candidates' work during the seminars.

Two curricular supervisions are undertaken, lasting a minimum of two years each, and one child supervision, with joint evaluations by supervisor and candidate to determine whether work should be interrupted for a change of supervisor or whether, on the other hand, the candidate can continue with his or her existing supervisor.

The supervisors are in the best position to appreciate the candidates' manner of working – by which is understood their management of the unconscious – and, apart from the analysts themselves, are also the ones who are best placed to stimulate an analytic habit of thought, through the linking of theory and practice. The supervisions play a decisive role in the candidates' promotion to the rank of analyst, since it is these which will reveal whether the candidates have the necessary qualities to become fully-fledged analysts.

Once the supervisions and the seminars have been approved, the candidate is then promoted to the rank of graduate *(egresado).*

We would like to take this opportunity of underlining the basic elements in the restructuring:

- following the restructuring, candidates and graduates acquired their own representatives on the Education Committee, which was also composed of representatives of the training analysts, the supervisors, the teachers, and the Director of the Institute, who was elected by the Institute's General Assembly.
- the analyst was only there to analyse, and was not to interfere in any way in the candidates' applications at the different stages of their curriculum.
- if the theoretical bases of the seminars were, of course, essentially Kleinian, the reflection and study group work, which formed an integral part of the different levels of study within the Institute, resulted in the training becoming increasingly orientated towards a rapprochement with Freud's discovery of the unconscious, taking full account of the discovery's various vicissitudes.

The hard work and reflection involved in this restructuring of the teaching/learning process was to have an impact far beyond the frontiers of the APU. It has even had repercussions within the University, specifically within the Faculty of Medicine, where a group of analysts are hard at work integrating Medical Psychology into the Faculty's new study programmes. Achieving this goal has meant that analysts, as well as psychologists and psychiatrists with analytic training, now play an integral part in the Medical Faculty's basic academic cycle.

This has meant that existing methods of informative education have been challenged by a process of formative education, in which teacher and student are active participants in a mutually enriching process.

Unfortunately, political factors in the institutional life of the nation were to interrupt this rewarding experience, which was, among other things, helping students to achieve a greater measure of continuity in their academic careers, since the scheme had been extended to involve working with students at clinical level, i.e. just as their hospital courses were starting. In this context, our efforts were focused chiefly on the investigation of the student/patient relationship.

As we have just said, however, not long after the restructuring had been planned and carried out, Uruguay underwent a period of military dictatorship, a very painful experience both for the country as a whole and for our own Association, which lost several valuable members, who had taken an active part at every stage of the restructuring process. The Association went through a period of work and study in the shadows, suffering severe persecution.

At the Pre-Congress of training analysts in Mexico in 1978, a paper was presented entitled "El Instituto como lugar de la letra y de la ley. Cómo puede participar el Instituto en la patología del Proceso Didáctico" ("The Institute as the context of Literality and the Law. How is it that the Institute can participate in the pathology of the training process?"). This paper revealed the anxieties of our Association when confronted with an attitude of permanent criticism. The psychoanalytic institution, once it has acquired a measure of power, will become dependent upon the use which it makes of that power, in that it may drift either in the direction of the most productive viewpoint, which would involve the active participation of its members, or, alternatively, towards one in which the will of its members may become paralysed through blind submission to a model which they are obliged to follow.

The country has recently regained its democratic values, something which is reflected in the way in which psychoanalysis has become a part of modern life. The number of members has grown, and there has been an increase in scientific activity. Two journals are published twice a year, the *Revista Uruguaya de Psicoanálisis* and *Temas.*

The Association also publishes the *Biblioteca Uruguaya de Psicoanálisis*, in which the following volumes have already appeared:

Vol. 0: Las ratas. Un recuerdo de infancia de Paco Espínola. Daniel Gil, 1986.
Vol. 1: El juego en psicoanálisis de niños. Compilation, 1986.
Vol. 2: Estudios sobre Narcisismo. Héctor Garbarino, 1986.
Vol. 3: Psicoanálisis grupal de niños y adolescentes. H. Garbarino, M. F. de Garbarino, G. M. de Pizzolanti, 1986.
Vol. 4: El cuerpo, el lenguaje, el inconsciente. Gilberto Koolhaas.

Journals

Revista Uruguaya de Psicoanálisis
since 1956; Ed.: Asociación Psicoanalítica del Uruguay
Canelones 1571, 11200 Montevideo – c.c. 813
Tel.: 571-257 6224; Fax: 571-236 5149

Temas de Psicoanálisis
since 1983; Ed.: Asociación Psicoanalítica del Uruguay
Canelones 1571, 11200 Montevideo – c.c. 813
Tel.: 571-257 6224; Fax: 571-236 5149

Institutions

Asociación Psicoanalítica del Uruguay
(Uruguayan Psychoanalytic Association)
Canelones 1571, 11200 Montevideo – c.c. 813
Tel.: 598-2-407418; Fax: 598-2-480439

Psic. Mercedes Freire de Garbarino, Br. Artigas 1339, 11200 Montevideo
Psic. Irene Maggi de Macedo, Soca 1247, 11300 Montevideo
Dr. Juan Carlos Neme, Br. Artigas 88, Apto. 102, 11300 Montevideo

USA

by Edith Kurzweil

Introduction

The history of American psychoanalysis is not only rooted in its beginnings and in the personalities of those who introduced it into specific disciplines and to the public, but in the American way of implanting new ideas and customs. These include a propensity to appropriate unusual concepts and practices and to adapt these to current assumptions; the habit to simplify and popularize by many and the reaction against this habit through scientificalization by a few; the need to moralize and apply scientific advances quickly for the betterment of society; and to do so pragmatically and systematically. In the case of psychoanalysis, these tendencies kept sway over the development itself: as new uses were being suggested that contradicted established ones, each time with the customary fanfare in the media, new associations would be formed to further these uses by like-minded people which – as Tocqueville already noted – is yet another American practice. Eventually, psychoanalytic applications would have many faces, would take root in psychiatry and psychology, and occasionally would turn into a caricature of the original.

In the early years, while Freud himself was broadening and altering his theories, some American psychoanalysts, all of whom were hampered by a lag in available translation – would hold fast to Freud's initial and more familiar concepts (later, these would be called the topographical theory) whereas those who just had been in Vienna or Berlin would advocate and propose Freud's more recent reformulations. But because psychoanalysis was being championed by psychiatrists, psychologists, social workers, theologians and anthropologists, and each of the protagonists would highlight specific components of Freud's thought, psychoanalytic ideas would develop in line with disciplinary priorities which, ultimately, would show less and less affinity with the central tenets of others. Sometimes, two or more advocates' distinctive pursuits would rejoin each other, or recombine, and organize yet another psychoanalytic or pseudoanalytic association.

I am certain that readers in Germany are familiar with Ulrike May's excellent overview of "Psychoanalyse in den USA" (1976), which essentially emphasizes – correctly – the fact that nowhere else was psychoanalysis welcomed as openly or as broadly as in America, and that at least in the beginning this acceptance was due to the endorsement of the widely acclaimed "progressive movement" – in a country whose constitution almost recognizes progressivism as a national goal. In *Freud and the Americans* (1971), Nathan Hale, Jr. not only provides a lively portrait of American society and its acceptance of psychoanalysis before 1917, but demonstrates the underlying reasons for the affinity between the promises of psychoanalysis and the Americans' civilized morality – that stood against immorality, bad habits, prostitution, charlatans and unscrupulous faith healers.

Within the American context it was inevitable that individuals who favored psychoanalytic ideas would band together to create formal associations, that is, legal entities which would further the exploration and dissemination of these ideas. This held true also for competing models of psychoanalysis. Consequently, groups of psychoanalysts (or of would-be psychoanalysts) who might start by working with schizophrenics, neurotics or therapeutic groups, would tend to set themselves against those whose psychoanalytic agendas differed from their own. Thus, we cannot underestimate the fact that psychoanalysis took root in a society which, in 1932 for instance, had over 318,000 patients in state mental hospitals; that the 56,000 patients in New York State alone cost the taxpayers over $ 45,000,000; or that one-eighth of the expenditures of the State of Massachussetts went for the care of the mentally ill (Beers, 1935, 319). This situation, together with Beers' projection that the population in these institutions would be growing by 14,000 every year, and that the mentally handicapped were responsible for the large growth in crime and suicide rates, accounted among other things for the mounting popularity of the Mental Hygiene Movement. Inevitably, as psychoanalysis was being institutionalized, it would be inserting itself into this increasingly professionalized society. And the inevitable rivalries between these professions, also, would be responsible for the inordinate vehemence among Freud's followers. They not only would defend their own versions of therapy and/or theory and thus organize around ever "smaller" theoretical issues, but would keep their eyes and ears on competitors in rival organizations. In this ever more factionalized climate, the history of each faction as well would be recounted in a fairly biased manner.

On top of that, the intellectual divide between Freud and Alfred Adler, between Freud and Carl G. Jung, and the later differences he had with Otto Rank and Sandor Ferenczi, primarily over clinical methods, were being transposed into the American psychoanalytic milieu. The ensuing discussions which included these so-called deviants' ideas, often in public fora such as the New School for Social Research, further muddled the deliberations and practices. However, the very existence of the lively polemics which criss-crossed and opened up controversies about therapeutic techniques and the impact of psychoanalysis on psychiatry and society, about the application of theoretical and metapsychological concepts, and about the importance of an analyst's personality on his/her analysand, in turn helped keep psychoanalysis in the news – often negatively – after Stanley Hall, a psychologist, had invited Freud to speak at Clark University in 1909.

I. The Early Phase

Freud's immediate impact was determined, or at least influenced, by the diversity of the Americans who attended his lectures, and by the caliber of some of them. Among his listeners were A. A. Brill, who at the age of fourteen had left Vienna for New York, who had studied medicine and then gone to Zurich to work with Jung, and who, subsequently would be Freud's American translator; the psychiatrist Adolph Meyer, a native Swiss who had helped found the National Committee for Mental Hygiene dedicated to eradicating mental disorders; the anthropologist Franz Boas, who had already demolished doctrines of racism; the Boston Brahmin James Jackson Putnam, one of America's foremost neurologists; the introspectionist psychologist Edward Bradford Titchener; the psychologist and philosopher William James; and Emma Goldmann, the anarchist leader. Apparently, the heterogeneity of this group as well as its aura of expectancy inspired Freud to give an extended synthesis of psychoanalysis that was singularly appropriate for the Americans: he simplified psychoanalytic theory, emphasized practicality and optimism, and the viability of sublimation. By concentrating on examples of trauma and catharsis, he appeared to stress the efficacy of psychoanalytic treatment, and he exaggerated the potential of rational choice. He also took a bold yet highly ambiguous stand on reforming conventional sexual morality. This appealed to those who were pushing for a new approach to mental disturbance, at a time when psychoanalysts had not yet dealt with the vicissitudes of sexuality, narcissism, the death instinct, or the division of the personality into id, ego, and superego (Hale, 1971, 6). Had these concepts been developed, the Americans might have been less enthusiastic.

Clearly, the American's enchantment with psychoanalysis had inspired Freud to jump to radical generalizations and to organize scattered insights into a coherent and brilliant synthesis (Hale, 1971, 14). By stressing the idea that repressed unconscious wishes may result in neurotic symptoms, and defining sublimation rather vaguely, he encouraged simplistic interpretations of psychoanalytic theory and superficial applications. Unwittingly, in the Clark lectures, Freud took stands on issues that were preoccupying many Americans – on the relation between mind and body, heredity and environment, and on how physicians ought to treat their patients. Although he could not have known of the strange links between American popular and professional cultures, or of the speed with which new ideas tended to spread, he appeared pleased with the press coverage, although not with the inevitable simplifications and hyperbole with which psychoanalysis was being disseminated.

According to Emma Goldmann, Freud had proved that sexual repression had crippled the intelligence of women. The neurologist Morton Prince, who had developed his own psychodynamic theories, advocated the publication of psychoanalytic contributions even though he had a certain amount of scepticism. James Jackson Putnam, already before Freud's visit, had reported about the psychoanalytic treatment of hysterics. But he had argued that "consciousness, including the subconscious, was the ultimate reality" (Hale, 1971a, 133).[1] Other investigations into functional psychiatry, psychopathology, and psychological problems of childhood sexuality (linked to clinical observations by Boris Sidis, Edward Cowles, and Adolph Meyer) had prepared doctors to listen to what Freud would tell them. So, while the professional and cultural climate had been ripe for Freud, his lectures, in turn, contained enough ambiguity for people to interpret them in whatever way they pleased. Freud felt vindicated by this success. But soon afterwards, upon his return to Vienna, he wrote to Putnam that "most people demonstrate that they do not intend to accept anything new; [...] I know that you are free of such habits of mind, and therefore I assume that gradually you yourself will become convinced even of what may at the moment still appear inconceivable" (Hale, 1971b, 90, Dec. 5, 1909). Yet in his eagerness to promote the movement, Freud complimented Putnam for having begun to practice psychoanalysis. And he marvelled at the Americans' ready welcome. They all described cases that invariably corroborated his theories, and they almost outdid the Viennese disciples in dismissing critics as neurotic, ignorant, and unable to master the psychoanalytic method.

1 Hale also found that no single view of the unconscious was yet accepted: in 1908 Morton Prince, Hugo Munsterberg, Pierre Janet, and Alfred Binet had debated six common definitions without reaching agreement.

The psychoanalysts' righteous and overbearing attitudes, in turn, fomented opposition in the culture at large. Every journalist, philospher, medical celebrity, and religious leader now defended his turf against encroachment by psychoanalysis in the popular media. Havelock Ellis, though appreciating Freud's importance, argued that sexual intercouse was a private matter, but that sexual liberty would foster independence. Vice commissioners testified that the social evil (prostitution) was ubiquitous, particularly in cities, and was furthered by foreigners, drinking, and dancing. However, that sort of disapproval also united the friends of psychoanalysis, and the public polemics themselves helped spread the doctrine.

Some of the American followers, many of them doctors, maintained personal relationships with Freud through correspondence. He analyzed others on long walks during congresses and "supervised" their cases by mail. In their practices as well as in their public statements, the American disciples mostly focused on the curing potential of psychoanalysis. And because they were trained in specific, professional specialties, they were adamant in their opposition to crackpots, quacks, and mental healers who claimed to be psychoanalysts.

The Americans' acceptance triggered Freud's ambivalence. He was pleased, even though he could no longer control the direction of the movement, or the appeal of his disciples' more superficial and "palatable" approaches, in view of the extensive press coverage, and of the propensity to accept and try out miracle cures. As Hale noted:

> "Between 1915 and 1918 psychoanalysis received three-fifths as much attention as birth control, more attention than divorce, and nearly four times more than mental hygiene. The popular image of the cause of neurosis had discarded environmental stress, had strengthened the existing emphasis on trauma located in childhood, and had added the menace of suppressed sexual and aggressive desires. The unconscious had become a Darwinian Titan and dream analysis the road to its taming" (1971a, 397).

Since public interest in mental healing now included psychoanalysis, journalists asked the Freudians about their cases. Eager to proselytize, some of them would brag of miracle recoveries. Ultimately, reporter's clichés were being wedded to exaggerations and heightened by enthusiasm. By the early 1920s, psychoanalysts in the New York area went so far as to offer courses on sexual hygiene and on the "newer psychology" in extension classes, summer schools, and "girls' colleges" (Hale, 1971a, 398–400).

It is impossible to ascertain to what extent Freud had anticipated that his Viennese charm, together with a simplification of the theory, would seduce his American listeners. Nor is it clear to what extent the American cultural climate imposed itself on psychoanalysis from the very beginning. We do know, however, that Freud, Ferenczi and Jones stayed in touch with a number of their American hosts after their initial visitis. In fact, after Freud urged them to organize outside the Psychopathological Association instead of setting up a branch within it, Brill founded the New York Psychoanalytic Society (NYPS), in 1911.[2] The New Yorkers were granted autonomy at the Third International Congress of the IPA in 1914 – a situation that would inordinately influence psychoanalytic development. James Jackson Putnam set up the Boston Psychoanalytic Society in 1914. And already in 1909, George H. Kirby and William Alanson White, who were associated with St. Elizabeth's hospital in Washington, DC, had paid attention to psychoanalysis; and so had Clarence P. Oberndorf, who was working at the Manhattan State Hospital. They too founded an organization in 1911, the American Psychoanalytic Association (APA) (Hale, 1971a, 318).[3] Although most of the founders of the APA were doctors, they did not explicitly restrict membership to physicians.

For the most part, the Americans' disciples were learning about psychoanalysis by reading, as well as from proseletyzing analysts, neurologists and psychiatrists – who had studied in Vienna and Zurich, and later on in Berlin. Their social background differed from that of the Europeans in that most of them were from a slightly lower social rank than the average business-man, and only a small proportion were Jewish; and becoming doctors had meant upward mobility. Most of them had bachelor degrees as well and, until the late 1920s, they entered the profession after a self-analysis – helped by reading, discussion, and correspondence. At the outset, we recall, Freud had encouraged these means of "training", but soon had recommended that everyone copy the Zurichers – the first ones to require that analysts be analyzed. (Soon, this would be stipulated by the American, but not yet by the New York Psychoanalytic Association.)

Given this ad hoc training, it is no wonder that Freud and the Americans would disagree strongly over the question of lay analysis. As we know,

2 Among the fifteen founding psychicians were: A. A. Brill, George H. Kirby, Maurice Karpas, C. P. Oberndorf, L. Bish, Frederic J. Farnell, Ernest M. Poate, J. Rosenbloom, William C. Garvin and Charles Ricksher.

3 The early members included John T. MacCurdy, a student at Johns Hopkins Medical School; Adolph Meyer, clinical director of the Insane Hospital at Worcester; James Jackson Putnam, a distinguished specialist in nervous diseases; G. Lane Taneyhill, a Johns Hopkins instructor in neurology; A. A. Young from Omaha, who had studied in Zurich; and Ernest Jones.

Freud expected knowledgeable lay healers to be admitted into psychoanalytic organizations in order to raise the ethical and intellectual level of these groups, and to turn psychoanalysis into more than a medical specialty. In a letter to Pfister, on November 25, 1928, he would write that he perceived a "secret link between the *Lay Analysis* and the *Illusion.* In the former [he] wish[ed] to protect analysis from the doctors and in the latter from the priests [... in favor of] a profession which does not yet exist, a profession of lay curers who need not be doctors and should not be priests" (Meng/Freud, eds., 126, [Nov. 25, 1928]).

European Freudians and American psychologists have been quoting and requoting this passage to discredit the ensuing American "medicalization". But they frequently tend to forget that Freud, too, was opposed to the type of lay analysis that began to be practiced in America. Though he felt flattered by the American reception, he worried about the facile applications: "Americans came too easily by truths others had struggled to discover [...] and were too easily satisfied with superficial appearances" (1926a, S. E. 20, 179–258). Indeed, the American analysts' patients were more diversified than the Europeans: they saw a greater proportion of factory workers, secretaries, and poor artists. Still, most of their hours were filled by middle- and upper-middle class patients. They soon had their own publications and often printed daringly speculative articles in the *Psychoanalytic Review,* founded and edited by William Alanson White and Smith Eli Jelliffe in 1913. *(The Psychoanalytic Quarterly* was started only in 1933, in order to feature the more "orthodox" contributions.) At first, the Americans' organizations and their interactions not only were most heterogeneous, but also very informal: they kept scant records, particularly when compared to Rank's *Minutes* or the detailed logs of the Berliners. (American notices appeared in the *Zeitschrift.*) All of these informalities were bound to create problems when psychoanalysis became institutionalized.

After World War I, the discrepancies, particularly in training requirements, led to differences between the APA and the IPA. Soon, the APA began to push for independence. This attitude was sparked partly by anti-German feeling and partly by the wish for autonomy. As White put it when proposing a vote for separation, American psychoanalysts had to free themselves "from the Pope in Vienna". While White's motion was defeated, many of the Americans did realize that they weren't keeping up with psychoanalytic developments, and knew rather little about clinical practice. Hence, they asked Freud to spend six months in New York giving courses and conducting analyses. When he refused, a number of the Americans went for analyses in Vienna or Berlin. They allegedly were overwhelmed by the rigor, the sophisticated concepts, and the new clinical techniques.

To keep up, American psychoanalysts made other efforts: in 1924, the Boston society which had been dissolved in 1918, reconstituted itself; and they set up the Washington Psychoanalytic Association. But the Americans were not yet aware that the Europeans were far from united. They did not realize that Melanie Klein had left for London because she had strayed from the Berliner's interpretations of Freud's death instinct, and from their understanding of the onset of the primal anxiety that triggers neurosis; or that Rank was already distancing himself from the training practices the Berliners were perfecting.

Instead, Rank had unwittingly upset the Americans when he presented them with "a new viewpoint, introduced by me," and when he argued that short-term psychoanalytic therapy often was preferable to in-depth treatment, and could be most effective (Lieberman, 1985, 229). At the time, American Freudians felt pressured on the one hand by the many quacks and healers claiming to do brief "psychoanalyses" and on the other hand by the Europeans' push against lay analysis and short-term therapy:[4] they were unaware that Rank and Ferenczi were increasingly deviating from Freud's method – by gearing their analyses less to uncovering traumatic events in the patient's past than to the activity of the psychoanalyst – that is, to the therapeutic dialogue. (This approach soon would be incorporated into Harry Stack Sullivan's interpretive psychiatry). Freud, who in the beginning had been less orthodox, now backed the Berliners and their followers, so that by 1924, he officially rejected Rank's ideas and became estranged from Ferenczi a few years before the latter died in 1933. But his American paragones got whiffs of these disputes belatedly, and then in a fairly partial and distorted way.

II. The 1930s

At the beginning of the 1930s, when American psychoanalysts realized they had to undergo training, they made quantum leaps. Now they began to establish training programs. Increasingly threatened by impostors and charlatans, whom the public was unable to distinguish from bona fide psychoanalysts, they felt pushed to build up their associations. Medicalization, they argued, though keeping out a few qualified humanists, was a lesser evil than the proliferation of wild practices: at least they could insist on uniform

4 Even theologians and religious sects like the Emmanuel movement adapted psychoanalysis to their own ends (Michel, 1984).

professional criteria. Thus the Freudians called upon the training commission of the IPA to resolve this issue. But they failed to realize that the IPA could control access to membership, but could not possibly influence the American policymakers who had the last word on who would be allowed into the healing professions.

In 1926, for instance, after the New York society had asked the New York State Board of Charity for permission to establish a psychoanalytic clinic, the state, supported by a powerful physicians' lobby, passed a law forbidding non-medical people to practice medicine. This meant that lay analysts, whatever their training, would be barred and that the APA, which did have a few lay members – at first was denied its request for a psychoanalytic clinic. In 1927, Bertram Lewin, who presided over the New York Council on Professional Standards, convinced his fellow analysts that he was not trying merely to gain his own ends but was responding to pending legislation: were lay analysts admitted to the New York Institute, it might be closed. (Franz Alexander and Karl Menninger soon talked of similar conditions in Chicago.) Still, legal statutes could not decide whether medical training is necessary for, or improves, the practice of psychoanalysis, although these did regulate access and restrict membership.

These issues have remained central and have continued to dominate the profession. Then, it did not help that Ferenczi, while visiting New York, held private seminars which non-doctors could attend and that his listeners later on would call themselves psychoanalysts. (Rank and Adler did the same.) That was why this topic divided the participants of the Tenth International Congress in Innsbruck, in 1927: 28 papers were presented "on the question of lay analysis". The controversies reached their peak when Anna Freud, referring to herself, wanted to know whether a regular lay member of the Wiener Psychoanalytic Verein could be admitted to the APA or the NYPS and Oberndorf said "no" (1953, 136). But the "victory" by America's medically trained analysts did not stop organizational disagreements. For Americans continued to go to Vienna or Berlin to become lay analysts and thereby could circumvent American rules. (Among others, Esther Menaker [1989] has written about this epxerience.) They finally forged a truce within the IPA after the Europeans agreed not to train lay candidates who had not already been approved by an American society, and the Americans promised to "consider" accepting non-doctors.

By 1929, a number of local societies (New York, Boston, Washington, and Chicago) began to hold seminars, to offer theoretical courses to candidates, and to institute control analyses. To that end, they invited a number of Europeans to teach. Among them were Sandor Lorand, Franz Alexander, and Sandor Rado. In 1931, the New York Psychoanalytic Institute

(NYPI), modeled after Berlin's, was opened. Brill became its president. In 1932, the first German analysts, led by Karen Horney, moved to America.[5] During the following year the APA was dissolved and reconstituted as a federation of local organizations. This federation had few functions because training and membership decisions would be made by the "locals", and analysts who were accepted by a local society automatically would become members of both the APA and the IPA. The latter was to have ultimate authority and to approve every decision taken by the APA's Council on Professional Standards. Eventually, the rifts between the Americans and the Europeans widened. Therefore, at the International Congress in Marienbad, in 1936, the Americans announced that they would veto any resolution that in any way addressed American issues.

The Europeans, however, were losing their hold as a result of political events. As more and more of them were coming to America as émigrés, they softened their views in response to the dislocation they had undergone: they were both grateful to and at the mercy of their hosts and became more cognizant of the American milieu. Earlier differences diminished as they cooperated for the sake of psychoanalysis and as the "former Europeans" started to realize that they had underestimated the weight of local conditions and the Americans' preference for pluralistic control – for federation over centralization.

By 1938, the APA had formulated its own rules for "minimal training of physicians" at psychoanalytic institutes and societies; it spelled out proper conduct for its members; and it prohibited the training of laymen, although these rules could be amended with the consent of local organizations. The Americans then submitted their resolutions to the IPA and declared that in the future they would cooperate on scientific matters alone. In practice, this meant that they would admit a few select lay analysts, namely those whose reputations towered over those of their American colleagues. Among them were Ernst Kris, Siegfried Bernfeld, Erik Erikson, Otto Fenichel and Theodore Reik. But Reik did not cotton to being accorded the special status of "honorary member", and by 1948 started his own Society – that would school psychologists in psychoanalysis. His graduates, of course, would receive the requisite psychoanalytic training but would lack the M. D.

5 Horney was invited by Franz Alexander to help train analysts in Chicago, but moved to New York two years later. Alexander had come to the University of Chicago in 1928 as Visiting Professor of Psychoanalysis. But the institute he founded was independent of the local psychoanalytic association.

European events soon transformed the American organizations, and the sudden influx of European analysts changed the composition of the APA. The presence of bona fide Freudians allowed for the creation of new teaching institutes, so that between 1939 and 1946, Washington-Baltimore, Topeka, Philadelphia, and San Francisco, became training centers, and other cities started societies. Moreover, the influx of famous European analysts increased the demand for psychoanalysis. Still, it did not take long before the controversies over lay analysis that had been played out between the IPA and the APA surfaced within the APA itself. And the ensuing chaos set the stage for many of the subsequent splits in the American groups which, in addition, were instigated by specific individuals who responded to specific issues. (The history of each society, I have been told, would fill a book.) Yet, in spite of the various defections (see below), by the end of the war the APA reported the following growth in membership:[6]

Year	Number of APA Members
1932	92
1938	157
1940	192
1942	230
1944/5	247
1946	273

III. The Émigrés Come to America

Long before 1945, a number of early disciples were going their own way. Among them was Harry Stack Sullivan who, together with E. Hadley, and L. Dooley (all members of the Washinton-Baltimore Psychoanalytic Society) had founded the W. A. White Psychoanalytic Foundation in 1933 – and which he would use as a base to launch an interdisciplinary journal, *Psychiatry: Journal of the Biology and the Pathology of Interpersonal Relations,* in 1938. Sullivan, who by and large is remembered for advocating "interpersonal relations" based on an amalgam of the social self postulated

6 From R. P. Knight: The Present Status of Organized Psychoanalysis in the United States, *Journal of the American Psychoanalytic Association* 1, No. 1–4 (1953), 207, Table 1.

by William James and George Herbert Mead, also was a strong proponent of Psychiatric training as a prerequisite to psychoanalytic practice, and of curing schizophrenia by means of psychoanalysis (Green, 1962, 276). S. Ely Jelliffe, another "eclectic", responded in yet another way: he corresponded with both Freud and Jung well into the late 1930s, long after they had come to be at intellectual and political loggerheads. It is interesting to note that as late as February 9, 1939, Freud wrote to him matter-of-factly that he was "by no means happy to see that Analysis has become the handmaid of Psychiatry in America and nothing else" (McGuire, 1983, 279).

But the émigrés for the most part were coming to New York, and their first contact was with the members of the NYPI – who were physicians working with psychiatrists rather than physicians identified with psychiatrists. Now, they also would incorporate theories on their recent trauma. Thus they realized, soon after they had been rescued – by means of introspection and observation – that just like biological organisms, only the most adaptive (though not all of them) had been able to escape the Nazis. But the psychoanalysts among them were in the unique position to penetrate to the psychic elements of differential adaptation. By analyzing the relevant mechanisms, they not only would get closer to understanding what contributes to personality formation and structure, but would further the reputation of psychoanalysis as well as their own. In fact, the newcomers felt themselves propelled toward exploring the innermost core of character and its connections to biology in line with the scientific criteria Americans valued, and with their own (changing) links to culture – links which they kept investigating as they were moving from Vienna and Berlin to Paris and New York.

Like other refugees from Hitler, the Freudians had been traumatized. But unlike most of the others, they could use their discipline to examine their responses to this trauma. And unlike most other German and Austrian (and later on Czeck, French and Hungarian) middle-class and professional Jewish émigrés, the psychoanalysts were joining colleagues, many of whom they had known in a rather closely knit international association. Thus they were in a position to ask for and receive the sort of personal assistance from Americans most of their countrymen tended to lack. Moreover, the more enlightened of the American Freudians appreciated the émigrés' theoretical sophistication and experience in treating patients and in training candidates. So, aside from the human concerns, the leading Americans, such as Lawrence Kubie and Bertram Lewin, were aware of the professional advantages they might reap by inviting and collaborating with the émigrés. In that sense, their former proximity to Freud was useful; and it would be even more so when, soon after his death, reminiscences would be invoked also to clarify theoretical points.[7] Ultimately, friendship and the customary American humane instinct to save people suffering from political repression or natural disasters came together in the efforts to rescue these colleagues.

Lawrence Kubie was the power behind The Emergency Committee on Relief and Immigration. He went to Washington immediately after the Austrian Anschluss. On March 19, 1938, under the auspices of the American Psychoanalytic Association, and in his role as Chairman of this Committee, he wrote the following letter to all the members, and enclosed a solicitation form:

> Detailed and trustworthy information is now available on the situation in Austria, both from Dr. Ruth Brunswick (who telephoned from Paris immediately on arriving there from Austria early this morning) and from the State Department in Washington where various officials were interviewed by the Chairman of this committee [Kubie] yesterday. Some official advice from the State Department is worth heeding.
>
> The information from Austria indicates the seriousness of the local situation in Vienna, – with carefully organized confiscation of property, minute searching of private homes, etc. Apparently, however, this is done with official formality and not with mob violence. No physical violence has been suffered by our friends to date, although they have been searched, minutely questioned, and some properties and money at the Verlag have been confiscated. Through diplomatic channels efforts are being continued to win a special permission for Professor Freud to leave. These efforts are being conducted largely through Dr. Ernest Jones who is still in Vienna.

In the course of his visit to the State Department, Kubie apparently had learned that the government wanted to help but advised caution: "No amount of haste will enable anyone to escape [legally or illegally] on whom the new regime has already centered its resentments." And because "no legal travelling permits are being issued anyhow, [...] there are certain advantages in delay, such as avoiding the destruction and confiscation of valuable papers, [and] of physical violence to refugees en route." Kubie went on to detail the reasons why State Department officials suggested that affidavits and moneys be transmitted through them. He continued:

> It is extremely difficult for anyone in the State Department to indicate a definite amount of money as the basic amount required to guarantee a year's support for an immigrant. They recognize that people coming in with fine medical and psychiatric reputations, with specialized skills which can be put to immediate use, can expect in a short time to be earning at least a part of their own living. For such people they de-

7 *The Psychoanalytic Quarterly* 9 (1940), no. 2, was dedicated to reminiscences about the influences of Freud, mostly by those who had known him – both émigrés and Americans.

> mand less in the way of a guarantee than for those whose future economic security is less certain. The only approximation which I could get, was that for a family of three or four, who could not be expected to earn any material sum of money within a year, they would want a guarantee of about $5,000.

In a follow-up letter of March 31, 1938, Kubie reported that "the situation in Vienna looks, if anything, more distressing than before." He noted that very few Austrian Jews had been able to leave, and that all those who would leave were allowed to take with them no more than 20 shillings ($4). He went on to say that affidavits had been secured for a large number of psychoanalytic colleagues in Austria, but that much more money would be needed "for food, shelter, and travelling expenses for those who get across the border [... as well as] living expenses during the first months of their arrival."

Four weeks later, the "psychoanalysts who desire to emigrate to the USA "would receive a three-and-a half, closely typed "bulletin of information", advising them of the legal regulations surrounding the practice of psychoanalysis in America which, essentially, was "defined as the practice of medicine" – in whatever state the question had been raised. This meant that psychoanalysts had to "secure licenses for the practice" of medicine before practicing psychoanalysis"; that they had to consider the fact that in many states non-citizens were barred; that they had to pass an English exam; that due to overcrowding (on the East Coast) newcomers would have to endure "a certain amount of isolation and loneliness", but that they would receive advice and financial support. The rules of the American Psychoanalytic Association about the training of candidates (in accepted institutes) were outlined, along with the exception for "well-trained laymen". Information about procuring visas and travel money, and a questionnaire that would enable the Americans to assess potential émigrés, were appended. (The Minutes of the New York Psychoanalytic Association, during the second half of 1938, repeatedly mention Kubie's admonition – backed by Sandor Radó – to be cautious, and to heed the advice of their contacts in the State Department not to make waves, and to be patient.)

These details demonstrate that 1) the American psychoanalysts were inordinately intent on aiding their colleagues (Kubie, along with Bertram Lewin as treasurer and Betty Warburg as secretary, carried on a formidable amount of work while continuing to practice psychoanalysis); 2) and that the émigrés who had been distinguished individuals had been reduced to helpless, dependent beggars: they had to adapt, to rely on hand-outs until they passed their medical boards and their English exams. At the time, they did not know that the psychoanalysts' Emergency Committee was affiliated with the National Coordinating Committee for the Resettlement of Foreign Physicians which did not have unanimous backing by the profession. Nor that doctors around the country, who feared for their livelihoods, had passed exclusionary laws in all but New York, New Jersey, Connecticut, Massachussetts, Maryland and Ohio. From Kubie's "Memorandum on the Problem of Refugee Physicians" we learn that fear that these states as well might succumb to such pressure led him to urge émigré physicians not to "remain in our eastern seaboard states".[8]

By November 22, 1938, twenty-nine individuals had arrived – two neuropsychiatrists, three lay analysts, two medical students and twenty-two physicians who had been "members of one of the recognized European [psychoanalytic] societies". To avoid further legal restrictions, Kubie argued also that it was essential for them, at first, to spend some time in New York: that is where they find friends; can take the Medical Boards most promptly and enjoy most reciprocity; can join tutoring groups; and "for many who have been tragically disturbed by the uprooting and the enforced transplantation of their lives, immediate further migration becomes psychologically and emotionally impossible, arousing great anxiety and depression and endangering the ultimate happy adjustment to this new environment".

Clearly, Kubie's psychoanalytic explanation for the émigrés' preference for New York also was an attack on his colleagues in medicine, many of whom maintained that they could not absorb so many doctors without causing unemployment to native physicians. But Kubie and his committee actively tried to find jobs for the newcomers. Among others, they sent Rudolf Ekstein, "a partially analyzed psychologist", to teach at the Crouch School in New Hampshire; they found a medical internship for Dr. Margaret Hitschmann at the New England Hospital; and they filled a position in the School of Social Work at Chapel Hill.[9]

Thereby, the émigrés spread psychoanalytic ideas. Still, these pressures must have daunted all but the strongest among them. To survive after having escaped Hitler, they continuously had to adapt. Inevitably, the stress must have influenced their thinking, must have led them to confuse

8 See especially the files of Paul Federn (Library of Congress, Washington, D.C.), The files of the Emergency Relief Committee at the library of the Payne Whitney Clinic in New York, among others.

9 Letter of May 18, 1939, to Dr. Warburg, about two openings in Chapel Hill, for a "psychiatrically trained man" to teach normal psychology and behavior study to first year social work students and abnormal and clinical study to more advanced students.

personal, familial and societal issues. But the psychoanalysts would have to explore these issues also on the most abstract psychoanalytic levels. Those who were theoretically inclined as well as "adaptable", such as Heinz Hartmann, Ernst Kris und Rudolph Loewenstein, soon found that the existing theoretical paradigms were not entirely adequate.

IV. Insurmountable Controversies Leading to Splits

By then, the "medicinalization of psychoanalysis not only had been enacted legally, but had become a fact of life; and the émigré analysts interacted with physicians, mostly with psychiatrists, and thus would lean ever more heavily on scientific language. And psychoanalytic ideas increasingly were penetrating American culture. Again, thanks to the records and activities of Kubie's Committee, we learn that proportionately few physicians fell victim to Hitler's destruction of the Jews; that proportionately many received visas before the American quota was exhausted. Is it possible, I now wonder, that the theory about "the guilt of the survivors" toward those who perished in the death camps was triggered not only by the overall guilt of having remained alive while so many millions of Jews had been systematically exterminated, but by the fact that special efforts had been made to save physicians, and that among these the psychoanalysts had been the most fortunate: their early rescue had contributed to the exhaustion of the quota and by implication to "preferential treatment". This is particularly clear from the extensive correspondence of, for instance, Paul Federn, whose inordinate efforts to get his family to Amercia failed. (I am not arguing that the notion of guilt is to be discarded but that the psychoanalysts were the only ones to turn it into a theory.)

To give a summary of the political and cultural atmosphere the émigrés were dropped into, and to surmise how they might have apprehended it, is nearly impossible. But a letter Kubie wrote to Edward Glover in London, on November 2, 1939, might give us some clues:

> The psychological situation here with regard to the war is full of paradoxes. You can hardly find a man in any walk or stratum of life who does not feel at least that it is to our interest for the democratic allies to win; and in most cases they will go as far as to say that it is vital to us. Instead of deducing from that the conclusion which seems to me to be unavoidable, namely that in that case it is both indecent to stay out and to our interest to go in at once, they rationalize our inactivity by an endless series of excuses, – the allied blunders since the war (shutting their eyes to our own), the suspect position of the Chamberlain government with regard to possible Nazi-Fascist leanings; the fascistic developments in France (or their suspicions of them);

the three thousand miles of intervening ocean; etc. etc. Around every dinner table the fight wages; with the majority somewhat uncomfortably silent, – and the main battle coming between some articulate proponent of our neutrality, and some equally articulate proponent of intervention.

If Kubie, whose close relatives were not endangered, felt this way, how must the traumatized émigrés have taken to, and judged, the indifference of most of the citizens in their new country?

Hartmann stated after arriving in America, and after a scant two-year stay in Paris, that "adaptation to social structure and cooperation is essential to humanity" ([1939[1958, 31). He proceeded to explore the relevant mechanisms of such "adaptation" by focussing on intrapsychic conflict and the resulting integration and coordination of contradictory drives, in line with Freud's postulates in *The Ego and the Id* (1923). Such an approach was acceptable to the native Freudians: it appealed to the American scientific ethos; and it was bound to help psychoanalysis take hold among New York doctors. In addition, this sort of emphasis promised to explain some of the issues the leading social scientists were trying to solve.[10] By 1950, Hartmann would go on to argue for the creation of a common conceptual language for the social sciences, in order to define sociological problems in terms of their psychological meaning and, vice versa, to formulate psychological ones in direct relation to the social structure.[11] The following year, at a meeting of the Psychoanalytic Section of the APA, Talcott Parsons, the foremost American sociologist who would dominate his own discipline until the late 1960s, stated that the influence of psychoanalysis had "deepened and enriched the understanding of human motivation and had become pervasive in the social sciences".[12]

Only fifteen years before, Rudolf Loewenstein, who would become Hartmann's coauthor of the most central concepts in so-called American ego psychology, and which for at least twenty years would come to overwhelm psychoanalysis worldwide, – after having left Berlin and before coming to the United States – had taken what we would consider the most

10 Hartmann, Heinz (1944): Psychoanalysis and Sociology, op. cit., *Essays on Ego Psychology. Selected Problems in Psychoanalytic Theory* New York: International Universities Press, 19.

11 Hartmann Heinz (1950): The Application of Psychoanalytic Concepts to Social Science, *Essays on Ego Psychology* 90 . *Selected Problems in Psychoanalytic Theory.* New York: International Universities Press.

12 Parsons, Talcott (1951): The Superego and the Theory of Social Systems, in: Persons (1964), 17 [Reprinted from *Psychiatry* 15, no. 1, Feb. 1952].

standard "biological" approach, which he had based squarely on the Oedipus complex (Cénac/Loewenstein, 1936). How did Loewenstein get from his classification of the four phases in the development of male sexuality that "normally consitute the genital automatism" – desire, erection, ejaculation, orgasm – to his "pertinent propositions for interdisciplinary co-operation"? (p. 5) How come that already by 1949 he was accepting and defining "instinctual drive not [as] identical with the one used in animal psychology, but [as] a construct particularly designed to describe the phenomena of conflict in man which psychoanalysis studies?[13] Simply put, what had led him to broaden the notion of "biology"?

Loewenstein's metamorphosis, I believe, developed in the context of what my sociological colleagues would call his life experience – of the adaptation to his intellectual environment which, in turn, was being altered by the increasing appropriation of psychoanalytic notions by physicians. Hartmann had addressed questions of adaptation already before he left Vienna, and now began to speak of "the subject's relation with and adaptation to reality" as a necessary indicator of mental health. He held that adaptation was emotional *and* biological. (For Loewenstein, who was rescued late and spoke no English but nevertheless had to conduct psychoanalyses to support himself and his family, I was told, "listening" took on a new dimension.)[14] But all the psychoanalysts who had been forced to leave Europe and thus the cradle of their discipline, began to evolve psychoanalysis from a new existential situation – from their responses to American reality and to their exodus. Since they were in the habit of explaining their personal experiences psychoanalytically, these were bound to permeate their theories.[15]

These experiences included: 1) the shock of being delegitimated as psychoanalysts and as human beings; 2) of being victims of a virulent, racially-based anti-Semitism; 3) of being helped to escape on the strength (mostly) of being physicians who could get jobs in hospitals; 4) of being penniless;

13 Ibid., 6. He quotes Heinz Hartmann, Ernst Kris, Rudolph Loewenstein, Notes on the Theory of Aggression. *The Psychoanalytic Study of the Child* 3/4 (1949), New York: Int. Univ. Press.

14 Reminiscence by Hedda Bolgar. Loewenstein told her that he was forced to take on patients while his English was still extremely deficient. So he learned by listening, by waiting with interpretations.

15 In an interview with David James Fischer (*Society*, March/April 1991, 69), shortly before his death, Bruno Bettelheim recalls that Freud told him: "Heinz has to put on his glasses which change all clinical experience into adaptation." However, Hartmann did not develop this concept into a central theory until after his exodus.

5) of having to learn English – the tool of their trade; 6) of having to penetrate a struggling profession; 7) of being ignorant of American society and politics; 8) and of expecting to provide tools to help defeat Hitler. In the process, they: 1) furthered their professional acceptance by stressing what they had learned in close proximity to Freud; 2) adapted to their host country as quickly as possible; 3) and pursued the "scientific" aspects of psychoanalysis as they thought Freud might have done. All of them, finally, judged America with a view from the couch. But it did not take long before these views would diverge.

The first person to institutionalize a major disagreement was Karen Horney. Instead of focussing on the intrapsychic conflicts due, among other things, to cultural influences, she and her followers focussed increasingly on the primacy of cultural factors, and thus appealed, also, to a much more general public than Hartmann and his collaborators.[16] Horney in particular, increasingly relied on Freud's sociological observations rather than on the more technical ones, and these dovetailed with some fairly popular findings the anthropologist Margaret Mead was calling "preconscious".[17]

Within the New York Psychoanalytic Institute, which had become Horney's home, the ensuing theoretical controversies were coming to a head. Ostensibly, disputes were about the training of candidates alone. But what future psychoanalysts learn has enormous significance for the direction of both the theory and the movement. The fires had been smoldering for a long time. Essentially, Horney, as well as Harry Stack Sullivan, Clara Thompson and William V. Silverberg were opposed to Kubie's, Radó's Fritz Wittels's and Bertram Lewin's clinical 'L'orthodoxy'. She accused them of being domineering and argued: 1) that it is often more productive to address a patient's present in order to understand his/her past rather than

16 Edith Kurzweil (1990): The New York Psychoanalysts Between 1933 and 1943. *Revue internationale de l'histoire de la psychanalyse* 5, (1992), 243–258.

17 See "discussion of Dr. Mead" [8. III. 42] in Dora and Heinz Hartmann papers, Library of Congress, Washington, D.C.: "If Dr. Mead's presentation was so particularly interesting to us, it is not only so because of the 'objectivity' of the method. Equally important is the fact, that in the choice of the material, in her ideas about what is relevant and what not, and in the few interpretations she gave, Dr. Mead relies upon psychological ideas that agree with the experiences and concepts of at least the analysts among us. There is no approach wholly accepted (?) to our theoretical concepts and it is preferable to state explicitly the concepts she relies upon, rather than using them preconsciously. "Common sense" questions and answers, though some people like them better, at least in this field, as being allegedly less prejudicial than a theoretical fundament, are as a matter of fact far more dangerous to the objectivity of our findings; they cannot as easily be controlled as the explicit use of theoretical actions can."

begin with getting insight into this past; and 2) that the thrust of what was taught to psychoanalytic candidates was culture-bound rather than universal. Her opponents maintained that she was teaching her own views and that training candidates were not being introduced to the classical Freudian concepts they considered crucial to psychoanalysis.[18] Kubie commented, again a letter to Glover, on November 22, 1939, on the compromise he had helped forge:

"I think I hinted to you that this [new] curriculum was the fruit of a pretty violent struggle, in the course of which I was quite unwillingly erupted into the presidency of the Society and into the midst of a rather unpleasant scrap. The situation which lay behind it was briefly that we were developing four cliques not only among the Society members, but among the students: a group of students who were under exclusive Horney influence, – another group under exclusive Radó influence, – and a group that had a more general classical training. Each group was more or less hermetically sealed from the other, and you can imagine how much confusion, lopsided and inadequate training, and mutual distrust and hostility all of this generated.

This curriculum was designed in order to insure some kind of reasonable orderliness in the sequence of the students' studies, and to make it certain that every student would have to be exposed to all possible influences."

As we know, Horney resigned on May 1, 1941, after being informed that she no longer could train candidates. America entered World War II half a year later. By then, her books, *The Neurotic Personality of Our Time* (1937) and *New Ways in Psychoanalysis* (1939), had made an enormous impact not only on intellectuals but on a large number of the general population. Basically, she did not emphasize the biological bases of life circumstances, and the role of childhood affection. Furthermore, she denounced her opponents' "theoretical paths [... as leading] into blind alleys [... and as] a rank growth of abstruse theory and a shadow terminology (p. 21). And she immediately started her own organization, the Association for the Advancement of Psychoanalytic Training. The separation was acrimonius and had other repercussions, especially on the Washington-Baltimore Psychoanalytic Institute, which led her to collaborate more closely with Sullivan. The latter created the William Alanson White Psychoanalytic Institute (together with Clara Thompson, J. Rioch Bard, D. Rioch and E. Fromm), which would separate from the Washington School of Psychiatry in 1946. (Soon, Horney and Fromm would part company as well.)

By that time, neither Franz Alexander, Karen Horney, Sandor Radó, Felix and Helene Deutsch were any longer émigrés: they had come to

18 Kurzweil (1990), op. cit. (n. 16).

America before the Austrian Anschluss, and Horney was not even Jewish. But within the medical profession their foreign accents as well as their European background defined them all, as did psychoanalysis – although via increasingly separate paths. Outside their profession, they not only expected to apply their scientific expertise to questions relating to individual adaptation, ego-development and psychosomatics, but to morale during wartime, and the cure of war neuroses. So, aside from the clinical and theoretical differences, they offered different suggestions for interventions in the culture at large. And both camps suggested psychoanalysts help fight the war.

In 1943, Horney's Committee on the War Effort issued bulletins on, for instance, the "Dynamic of Group Panic", and the "Understanding of Individual Panic". Horney stated:

> We must vigorously reject the idea that panic is inevitable [...] the high morale of the English after Dunkirk, was to a great extent, the reaction to catastrophe. Imminent danger and fear brought people together and led to an increased mutual respect and the realization that they needed each other. [...] Therefore in our long-term planning for emotional stability, we must foster and facilitate the whole idea of inter-relationship in home life, school life, business life, social life, community life. [...] The enemy tries every device to make people feel *helpless!* We must use every device to make people feel *helpful!*[19]

The members of the New York Psychoanalytic Society, on the other hand, resolved to intervene more clinically. They decided to extend the functions of the Committee on the Emergency Service Fund (even though emigrants no longer were arriving) in order to assist "the men now in the armed forces [... upon their] return to civilian life". And they supplied psychoanalyses of Hitler[20] and other studies predicting behavior under conditions of war.[21]

On July 5, 1944, the New York Psychoanalytic Society held a meeting on "how to assist in the war effort". Essentially, they discussed means of applying clinical knowledge to "interview returnees and those otherwise involved (wives, sons and daughters of soldiers in the armed services)". They proposed to enlarge their already established clinics, and conceptu-

19 Karen Horney (1943): Bulletin 3 of *The American Journal of Psychoanalysis* – Committee on War Effort.

20 Walter Langer (1972): *The Mind of Hitler.* New York: Basic Books. At the time, this was a classified report and thus not published.

21 See, for instance, Kurt Eissler (1960). Kurt Lewin's various studies of stress and of leadership in groups.

alized "war work" as clinical intervention – a replay of what had happened at the time of the First World War, when the Freudians had begun to deal with war neuroses.

This habit of generalizing from one-on-one therapy among the émigrés – all of whom belonged to the American Psychoanalytic Association, and most of whom were physicians – *did* represent a close continuation of Freud's earlier practices. (Whether or not this was useful is a moot point.) This emphasis itself was furthered by, and in turn furthered, the need to extend what soon came to be called American ego psycholgy. Now, many psychoanalytic research projects were set up in hospitals, child guidance clinics and other institutions. Paradoxically, as these projects took hold and their findings were incorporated into the general psychological lore, "the power of theorizing failed to equal the power of [Freud's] clinical insights", so that Hartmann would remind his colleagues that "'good' hypotheses aided his discoveries as well as their meaningful interrelation".[22] But none of this could have happened without the greater acceptance of psychoanalysis by increasing numbers of patients. It is safe to assume that the "culturalists" were in the forefront of these forays.

V. The Scientific Theories Become Central

In order to understand the increased parsing of psychic mechanism which the more and more complex inquiries engendered, to pinpoint where the environment "entered" the psyche, the so-called classical psychoanalysts reexamined and refined Freud's structural theory (id, ego, superego). But they also appropriated the Amercian scientific ethos, and the language of medicine. Because personality structure is formed between birth and the Oedipal period (here would be their central theoretical advances and disagreements) they engaged in empirical studies of the young, and used the theoretical perspectives they were perfecting to understand their adult patients.

Actually, the majority of Hartmann's publications between the time he left Vienna and the end of the Second World War were on cultural issues. However, by looking through the Dora and Heinz Hartmann files in the Library of Congress, I found contributions for symposia, and all sorts of notes, many of them in a shorthand I could not decipher; and typed copies of participations at meetings – all of them indicating his parallel concern

22 Hartmann, op. cit. (n. 10), 1950. "Mutual Influences of Ego and Id", p. 181.

with the scientific side of psychoanalysis. For instance, on 6. XII. 1941, (shortly after his arrival) Hartmann spoke at a symposium on instincts, elaborating on Robert Waelder's contribution which held that "the term instinct in psychoanalysis means something very different from what it means in other branches of science". In fact, Hartmann maintained that "instinct" has a double meaning: in addition to the genetic relation between animal instinct and human drive, there is a "relation between animal instinct and human Ego-function". On 7. III. 1942, in another discussion with Waelder, he spoke of classes of instincts, and of the importance to show "by which concrete psychical means the 'biological program' of 'self-preservation' gets realized". And in an undated note, he went into the "Ego-Id differentiation" and its consequences to the understanding of instinctual drives in men.

Thus Hartmann's seminal much cited work of 1946, which he published together with Ernst Kris and Rudolph Loewenstein, and which set out to integrate the many strands of empirical research that had been undertaken during the preceding six years by *all* the Freudian psychoanalysts, represented much of his thinking during his exodus. This paper would be acepted as the most important contribution first to guide further studies and then to deviate from them (Hartmann/Kris/Loewenstein, 1946). The authors began by describing the status psychoanalysis had attained:

> Psychoanalysis has developed under social conditions rare in science [...] The situation of the 1940s is hardly reminiscent of the period of early teamwork; large groups of psychoanalysts work in ever looser contact with each other and the diffusion of psychoanalytic concepts in psychiatry, their extension into psychosomatic medicine, social work and various educational and psychological techniques opens up new vistas of developoment (p. 11).

Eager to bring all the modifications and reformulations of Freud's theories under one roof, Hartmann, Kris and Loewenstein tried to integrate early hypotheses and later shifts and emphases and to address "problems of ego development and superego formation" (1946, 13). And they expected to clarify psychoanalytic terms from a structural perspective by separating them from and subordinating them to questions of libidinal development. They also maintained that the concepts of id, ego, and superego were already *in incubo* in some of the formulations of the 1890s – which indirectly would "delegitimate" the theoretical foci of opponents who stressed the simpler, "topographic" distinctions such as conscious and unconscious. By demonstrating that recently accumulated empirical data *did* fit into Freud's "three centers of psychic functioning (characterized by their developmental level, their amount of energy, and their interdependence at a given time)", they further justified their claims (p. 14). Their relation to Freudian orthodoxy was to be the subject of many subsequent controversies. But Freud himself had not been clear: in *Beyond the Pleasure Principle* (1920), he had concluded that "the ego is the true reservoir of the libido", and two years later had reversed himself to "recognize the id as the great reservoir of the libido". According to Strachey, Freud had envisaged two processes: (1) original object cathexes go out from the id to the ego indirectly; (2) the whole libido goes from id to ego and reaches objects only indirectly (S. E. XIX, 63–66).[23]

In any event, Hartmann, Kris, and Loewenstein chose to read Freud in the following way:

1. They stayed away from biological correlations and from Freud's parallels between the psychic and the central nervous systems – because Freud had once said that he preferred using psychological terminology until an adequate physiological vocabulary would be available (1946, 15).[24]

2. They considered the use of metaphoric language as non-scientific, because "metaphor infringes on meaning and anthropomorphizes the structural concepts".

3. They decided to "replace the word 'ego' in Freud's text by the word 'self'", because Freud had used the term ambiguously, sometimes referring to the whole person, sometimes to his psychic organization.

4. Instead of speaking of superego approval and disapproval, they concentrated on degrees of tension between psychic mechanisms. Such an approach was to lead towards a developmental model of ego control. Child studies had yielded much empirical information on the effects of toilet training – of stimuli influencing conflicts between elimination and retention, the child's attempts to control, and the mother's requests – and they expected to systematize these data. Because Freud's own metaphors had led them to understand the part anthropomorphism plays in introspective thinking, the authors said they would use his structural concepts and would separate them from the drives (pp. 17–21).

5. They held that the defense mechanisms controlling instinctual drives take root toward the end of the first year; and they found that by then the

23 In a superficial way, objects are people and object relations are interpersonal relationships – although these concepts refer to unconsciously "internalized" meanings and potential interpretations inducing the subject to behave in a certain way.

24 The English translation of *Jenseits des Lustprinzips* into *Beyond the Pleasure Principle,* for instance, it has been argued, fails to render Freud's meaning correctly and yet is taken at face value. The crucial word here is *jenseits,* which could be translated as "on the other side of" – which also could imply "on the other side of life".

child's lasting object relations (to mother) were in place. In this "newfound security", they noted, anxiety was taking on new shapes (p. 27).

6. After establishing that defenses were central, they concentrated on specific ego defenses – to cope with id impulses, the outer world, and later with the superego. Now, repression was thought to demarcate sharply the boundaries between id and ego (pp. 28–29). (This was why in the 1950s and 1960s American candidates would be taught that the analytic focus *must* be on defense mechanisms.)

7. They described the "replacement" of the pleasure principle by the reality principle as a learning process that transforms libidinal energy into aim-inhibited libidinal energy. And this process, they noted, enriched the child's inner world (p. 30).

8. Summarizing Freud's ideas on superego formation during the Oedipal period, the authors wanted to explain how early (and rigid) moral conduct becomes differentiated. Hence they distinguished the child's identification with the idealized parent (his perception was altering along with maturation) from the psychic energy that gets sublimated and used in idealization, and from the internalized aggressive attitudes, which were found to be the energy behind superego demands.

9. Unlike Freud, who thought that personality development was more or less complete at this point, Hartmann, Kris, and Loewenstein expected existing psychological structures to be modified by development itself. (This supported Piaget's theory of children's moral development – from moral "absolutism" to differentiation – via a gradual adjustment of superego functions during latency.)

10. As adolescents look for support outside the family, the authors continued, they may choose a new set of ideals. In this process, the condition that had accompanied superego formation in the first place – rebellion – was said to be reactivated. And this situation was found to trigger changes in identification.

11. But the superego, the authors now declared, also takes its clues from cultural forces, which impinge on its functions. And they maintained that when social values change rapidly and new ones do not replace them, or when "new ideals of conduct do not supplement the older structure of the superego", individuals become compliant (pp. 34–35).[25]

25 They also noted that conformity arises in adolescence and stated that questions of mass psychology and fascism are rooted at this juncture. But they did not explain how they got from observations of specific adolescents to social phenomena.

In conclusion, Hartmann, Kris and Loewenstein stated that they had relied on data based on 1) the reconstruction of life histories in psychoanalytic observation; 2) the study of regressive phenomena in neuroses and psychoses; 3) observation of children; 4) on historical and anthropological knowledge. Now, they urged that these hypotheses be tested in studies focussing on, for instance, the communication between the child and the mother in the pre-verbal stage, on reactions of mother and child to toilet training – in order to explain the earliest processes of differentiation as well as "retrospective investigation" in the psychoanalysis of adults (p. 36). And these were the recommendations they would make to the Europeans at the first meetings of the IPA which took place in Zurich in 1949.

The Horney contingent was less programatic; and her followers were unable to create as strong an organization, or as cohesive a following. Basically, the members of her group had different agendas and interests from one another, and the notion that culture shapes personality inevitably led them into various areas of inquiry. In addition, dissent increased when she refused to teach lay people. Soon, Harry Stack Sullivan left and started the William Alanson White Institute; and William Silberberg departed as well. However, not all of those who at first had remained in the NYPA remained loyal. In 1942, allegedly in protest against the prevailing "authoritarian tendencies", the Center for Psychoanalytic Training and Research was formed at Columbia University – led by Abram Kardiner and Sandor Radó. And Erich Fromm published *The Fear of Freedom* (1942), which would have much influence on the public. His former association with the Frankfurt School was played out in his view that authoritarianism could be fought only by free individuals in a totally open, democratic (or socialist) society; and in attempting to understand how potential fascists (in democracies) may turn into practicing ones. Thus already before the end of World War II, American psychoanalysts had institutionalized many of their theoretical disputes: doctors and psychologists could be psychoanalysts, although only the former (depending upon their local affiliation) could belong to the APA and the IPA.

VI. Psychoanalytic Ideas Take Hold

In 1947, David M. Levy, who had sent a questionnaire to candidates at the time of Horney's departure from the New York Pschoanalytic Institute, and who soon thereafter had joined Radó and George Daniels at Columbia University, wrote a little book on *New Fields of Psychiatry*, demonstrating their enormous expansion – along with the influence of psychoanalysis.

Child guidance, he stated, had been non-existent until after the Institute for Juvenile Research, starting in 1920, followed the ideas of Adolph Meyer, Alfred Binet and Freud. Since then, a "specific" psychiatric approach had spread. Terms like "maternal overprotection" and maternal rejection" had become accepted – for children who are examined "socially, psychologically, psychiatrically and medically" – in several hundred child-guidance clinics around the country (p. 32). Levy summarized accumulated knowledge that could predict recidivism which could then be used by lawyers in defense of criminals and against them by parole boards.[26] And he outlined the many collaborations with social work, with educational, industrial and military psychiatry – most of it initiated by émigré psychoanalysts or their students – and especially by the military occupying the former Third Reich. In this context, a typed memo in the Hartmann files is of interest. For Hartmann refers to:

> the preliminary conference called by the Conference on Germany After the War, and held on April 29th and 30th [1944], [which] struggled through to an agreement as to the need for a fairly fundamental change in the character structure of the German people. The present typical structure, based upon a *status* concept (superiority-subordination), was found to exhibit a peculiarly dangerous dualism of dominance-subordination on the one hand, and individualism-romanticism on the other. We are asking the educational panel to help us determine what specific things can be done in German education to change this character structure into one more compatible with the sound ends of an orderly society.

And Hartmann went on to prepare specific questions he wanted the participants to be ready to answer – about education in general, pre-school environment, adult education, etc. Clearly, neither Hartmann nor his colleagues saw a rift between cultural/societal and theoretical/clinical issues. Instead, they considered the hundreds of so-called scientific investigations into the functions of the ego as relevant to the application of psychoanalysis.

26 Already in 1935, Beers had noted that "the National Commission for Mental Hygiene had carried out research, largely financed by the Rockefeller Foundation". As a product of the Mental Hygiene Movement, child guidance came into its own, and moved to the forefront of the movement (p. 332). In 1932, there were 674 clinics that provided services to juveniles (p. 333), and many of these were sponsored by psychiatric clinics as well as attached to hospitals, dispensaries, welfare bureaus, boards of education, colleges and universities, visiting nurse associations, medical schools, community chests, foundations, courts, probation services, mental hygiene societies, etc. (pp. 333–334).

Among such studies was, for instance, Edith Buxbaum's "The Role of a Second Language in the Formation of Ego and Superego". She found that two English-speaking boys of German backgrounds lost their conspicuous accent during their analysis, even though Buxbaum herself had a heavy accent: by rejecting the influences of American culture they had expected to win their father's approval – a defense against unconscious castration fears. Thus she postulated a "pathological accent" as similar in ethology to slips of the tongue, stuttering or misuse of words, and she argued that these may be employed as "additional defense mechanism[s], reinforcing repression, and also as a means of weakening the strength of the superego" (Buxbaum, 1949). René Spitz, in both the first and second volume of *The Psychoanalytic Study of the Child*, reported on the treatment of severely disturbed children at a Foundling Home. He examined the consequences of deprivation of maternal care, maternal stimulation and maternal love, and of severe isolation; and he demonstrated the psychosomatic damage these conditions tended to inflict: seriously impaired resistance to disease, a high rate of mortality, and eating disorders. This study dovetailed with Anna Freud's on "Infantile Feeding Disturbances" – which arise as byproducts of early feeding habits and the mother's notions of what constitutes an adequate feeding regime during specific phases – the oral, oral-sadistic or anal, or the fantasies of the phallic phase – associated to pleasure in eating, or its loss (Hartmann/Kris/Loewenstein, 1946, 19–32). And Anna Maenchen commented on the fact that unlike Anna Freud and Dorothy Burlingham in England, psychoanalysts in America had little opportunity to observe the impact of the war on the developing superego, although young boys often were affected by its ideological aspects, and by the absence of their fathers (pp. 257–262).

I could go on quoting other studies. But what distinguishes them all is the ironclad adherence to Freud's structural model of 1923, and its scientific ethos. For roughly twenty years such longitudinal studies as Margaret Mahler's on individuation and separation, René Spitz's on infants, and Robert Bok's on adolescents, were kept going – alongside the more culturally (and literarily) orientied studies. Franz Alexander's psychosomatic Institute in Chicago, though not precisely in the mainstream, kept attracting medical talent as well. All of these endeavors, in turn, encouraged more psychoanalytic investigations by many native Americans who had become psychoanalysts. Some, such as Charles Fischer cooperated with psychiatrists and neurophysiologists in dream studies at, for instance, Mount Sinai Hospital in New York. Many investigations were being supported by the National Institute of Mental Health, and by other agencies trying to find out more about child development in order to ensure healthy growth, or to prevent crime and delinquency. Clearly, questions of individual adaptation (to institutions, environment, changing conditions) remained as central as the rational, scientific approach to clinical studies which had to be maintained in order to receive funding. And because these were the Freudians who, after 1945, would bring psychoanalysis back to Europe, that is, to the IPA, their ideas would dominate for many years, thus keeping their hands on the rudder of the discipline.

In fact, the model of "ego-psychology" remained central until the late 1960s, and spread to the general public as well. The foremost proponent of this trend was Erik Erikson. A former artist who had been analyzed in Vienna by Anna Freud and had been accepted into the APA as "honorary member", he investigated cultural questions such as the socialization of American Indian children, and individuation in the course of the entire life cycle. Erikson's theoretical thrust was a hybrid of ego psychology and cultural adaptation, especially insofar as he played down the force of the early incorporation of its environment by the infant. But he always avoided breaking with his colleagues in the Boston Society or the APA. As he himself noted, his ideas were easier to understand and more palatable to the general public than those of the ego psychologists, and thus his book on *Childhood and Society* (1950) was a best seller. In any event, by the time the émigré psychoanalysts had become citizens, they not only had shaped American psychoanalysis but the new direction in psychiatry, and had spread psychoanalytic ideas to the culture – to practices of child rearing, social work and general medicine. Ultimately, the Freudians would influence the general thrust of the social sciences, the study of literature, and the prevalent beliefs about the roots of the psyche as well.

Under the circumstances, it is impossible to assign "credit". To what extent did Horney, Radó and Kardiner, and an increasingly large number of anthropologists and sociologists, turn into analysands and then into proselytizers? And did the dissatisfied patients – no matter whom they were dissatisfied with – spread interest in Freud's ideas when they knocked them? Certainly, as time went on, more and more intellectuals and academics were talking the psychoanalytic language even when they were not undergoing an analysis. By the 1960s, as Philip Reiff demonstrated, America had become the therapeutic society *par excellence.*

VII. Psychoanalytic Thought Becomes Ubiquituous

Although psychoanalysis was proliferating and penetrating American culture, only the psychoanalysts belonging to the IPA were in a position to cooperate formally with former European Freudians immediately after World War II. In fact, some of them, with the encouragement of the American forces of occupation, were instrumental in helping resurrect the former institutes, and to reestablish the discipline.[27] Consequently, psychoanalysts in, for instance, the Bundesrepublik (West Germany) and France have been under the impression that within America itself these were the only people spreading Freudian theory and therapy. (One could argue this point, if one accepts that ego psychology alone counts.)

Instead, the many "defectors", beginning with those around Horney, Silberberg, Thompson, Sullivan, Fromm, and those who disagreed with them, as well as the majority of psychiatrists and physicians in hospitals and clinics, increasingly were introducing psychoanalytic thinking. Furthermore, psychoanalysts of all denominations were analyzing psychologists and social workers who, in turn, would do some sort of therapy with patients in hospitals and outside. All of them contributed to the massive penetration into the culture.

After some time, these practitioners would band together and form associations. Some of these were formal, others informal; some were registered, others were not. These conditions proliferated, for the most part, in the large cities, although New York would far outstrip the organizational networks which began to proliferate in Chicago, Los Angeles, San Francisco and other large urban centers. And even the most "orthodox" Freudians had analysands who would become lay practitioners: some of them would adapt the theories and practices of one or another of the "defectors". By 1959, Walter Bromberg, in *The Mind of Man: A History of Psychotherapy and Psychoanalysis,* pointed out that psychoanalytic training had become indispensable for psychiatrists using psychological principles in their treatment, but that they were "depart[ing] from orthodox psychoanalytic techniques" due to their high costs and large demand. For the establishment of psychotherapeutic clinics throughout the country had led to greater demand. One center in New York, Bromberg went on, had been providing 30,000 hours of psychoanalytically oriented treatment for the last years. In such settings, he stated, some therapists were using the brief treatment introduced by Franz Alexander; others had not discarded "Jung's plea [for] the integrative power of mankind": yet others were heeding Horney's admonition to stress social factors; still others were focussing on the effect and

27 See, for instance, Geoffrey Cocks (1985), Edith Kurzweil (1989), but most of all, the *Bulletins* of the IPA, where membership numbers, the creation of new institutes and societies are recorded.

dynamics of their patients' interpersonal relations; and a few were stressing the "common sense" approach so congenial to the American temperament (pp. x–xi). In this cacophony of theoretical and therapeutic approaches the *eclectic* therapist emerged: "These are men trained in the basic sciences of neurology, psychodynamics, and psychobiology who utilize all aspects of neuropsychiatry in their therapy [... and their] tolerance for all theories and practices [... were] the hope of the profession" (p. xi).

In *The Freudians,* I focussed on those who remained with ego psychology alone. (See Appendix "A" for the member institutes of the APA.) But when surveying *psychoanalysis* in the US, one cannot leave out all the other practitioners who not only helped provide the climate for the classical Freudians to flourish in, but their patient population as well and, subsequently, relationships between them and these "deviant" therapists. Given the private and privileged contact between analysts and their analysands, these connections, for the most part, would not be publicly acknowledged, and certainly not in print. Examples abound. For instance, in the Freud archives in Washington, D. C., I came across a long correspondence between Kubie, who has been depicted as the central protagonist in the "ouster" of Horney from the NYPI, and Oliver Kerner, one of the most prominent Freudian psychologists in Chicago. Thus I found out that Kubie had been inordinately encouraging to Kerner, had advised him on how to manage entering psychoanalytic training. (One must assume there were others.) Also, many of the stalwart members of the NYPI were analyzing and supervising psychologists belonging to Theodore Reik's National Psychoanalytic Association of Psychologists, and later to the Freudian Society – one of *its* "deviant" offsprings. During that period, social workers who were being schooled by some of the psychoanalysts holding administrative positions in hospitals, began to practice what they were learning not only inside the hospitals but in private practice as well. Moreover, wives of American classical Freudians were getting psychoanalytic training and supervision: though they could not become members, they hung around their institutes and received referrals; some of them joined non-medical groups.

Of course, we can argue that these practices had been going on ever since Freud's break with Adler – both inside and outside the profession. But whatever those who remained at the periphery of ego psychology would be doing, most of them were not counted as members of associations or of the profession. And even if official membership figures had been available, these would not indicate multiple memberships, and would not include the informal groupings, and the many therapists who either don't belong to any association or work as guidance counsellors in schools and universities (with or without training), who do group therapy, or have come to child guidance via schools of education. Still, even the psychoanalytically trained psychologists who joined to the American Psychological Association did not organize separately until 1978.

VIII. The New Theoretical Landscape

During the 1970s, Freud's theories of narcissism moved center stage. But whereas among German Freudians these contributions might be applied to explorations of extreme authoritarianism, and their French colleagues might look to the consequences of the narcissistic desire for the penis as the symbol of omnipotence or power, their American peers focussed on the narcissistic aspects of the ego – often as unexpected consequences of permissive upbringing. In *On Narcissism* (1914c) Freud had argued that the infant at first is indiffernt to the external world, so that pleasure and satisfaction are primarily autoerotic. In *Instincts and Their Vicissitudes* (1915c) he had held that the infant acquires unpleasurable objects from contact with this world. Thus by taking in (introjecting) pleasurable environmental stimuli and casting out (projecting) unpleasurable ones "the *original* 'reality-ego'" was said to change "into a purified pleasure-ego" (S. E. 16, 136). But this was a hypothesis rather than scientific evidence: both the mechanisms of Freud's formulations and the role and fate of early narcissism were yet to be revealed by infant research. Among the profusion of American investigations on this subject, Margaret Mahler, a member of the NYPI, conducted one of the most extensive empirical research projects.

Originally a pediatrician directing a baby clinic in Vienna, Mahler at first worked with autistic children. By drawing on psychoanalytic observations and comparing these children to normal ones, she concluded that autism and symbiotic childhood psychosis develops in children who have not experienced their mothers emotionally and thus suffer from ego deficiencies. By 1959, she had a team of researchers who were observing the intimate interactions between normal mothers and their infants. They analyzed unfolding mother-child relations in tandem with the children's emerging sense of self, and thereby started to differentiate between the subphases of the separation-individuation process. Soon this focus on development led Mahler's associate Manuel Furer (1967) to perceive "identification with the comforter" as indicative of future superego formation, and to conclude that such identification "increases the child's capacity to bind its aggression and helps bring about the required reaction formation" (pp. 277–280). Together with John B. McDevitt, Mahler looked at the connections between adaptation and defense and learned that a child's character traits are determined by its adaptive style and its defensive behavior, which "gradually become internalized as more or less successful defense mechanisms" (1979, 100). Stressing sensitivity to separation from birth to about three years, Mahler conceptualized loneliness, vulnerability, and helplessness from the perspective of the "reality-ego". Hence she was observing phenomena Melanie Klein had located at an even earlier unsonscious level, and that Piaget had ascribed to cognition. Her co-worker Anni Bergman maintained that Mahler, like Freud, observed "cognitive structures that develop in relation to the self (selves) and important object representations", and she noted that her "developmental lines [... and] cognitive structures" were not Piaget's (1985, 251). Indeed, Mahler's concern with separation and individuation belonged to American ego psychology.

So did the work of Heinz Kohut. But while Mahler's "self" was rooted primarily in Freud's 1914/15 contributions, Kohut, a former Viennese neurologist who graduated from the Chicago Institute of Psychoanalysis after the Second World War, basically took his theoretical point of departure from Freud's 1917 works. This meant that like Melanie Klein, whose views remained anathema in American psychoanalytic circles, he took Freud's death instinct seriously and that *his* self developed from a more unconscious – or metaphsychological – level than Mahler's. So, what to her was individuation to Kohut was the establishment of an autonomous self.

Kohut had noted that children tend to make up for the "unavoidable shortcomings" of maternal care and the concomitant primary narcissism either by evolving a *grandiose* and exhibitionist *self-image,* or by creating an *idealized parental imago.* As the gleam in the mother's eye mirrors the child's exhibitionist display, he found, the child's self-esteem and grandiosity get inflated. Consequently, for Kohut narcissitic disorders would begin as soon as the baby was born. Depending upon the severity of the child's misperceptions, it might start to suffer from temporary or permanent self-fragmentation, or from self-self-object failures (unsuccessful integration of early experiences) that engender feelings of emptiness and loneliness. Hyman L. Muslin (1985) summarized these exceedingly complex psychodynamics:

> When the cohesive self breaks down or becomes fragmented, in response to a self-object rupture, it may [...] maintain a state of *chronic frustration* (protacted fragmentation disorders, borderline personalities), [...] may repair itself, [...] (episodic fragmentation), may reequilibrate itself with newly developed defenses against self-object bonds (narcissistic personality disorders), [...] or may focus on drives that are salient in the current developmental phase [...] as a manifestation of a regressive reaction (neurotic syndromes) (Muslin, 1985, 213).

Because these narcissistic structures are bound to show up in the transference neuroses, Kohut reconceptualized the psychoanalytic method of curing them. He had noticed that earlier experiences of both grandiose self and idealized parental imago are mobilized during the *idealizing transference* and that the vissicitudes of narcissism could be alleviated by strengthening ego functions (1971, 28). But this meant that the analyst had to break through his patient's extraordinarily resistent walls of defenses against infantile (oedipal) wishes by providing large doses of approval during the working-through process. Such patients, however, continue to be particularly fearful of regression to early traumatic events and their accompanying rejection, Kohut maintained, and therefore construct many obstacles within the "mirror transference" – which alone can handle the nearly insurmountable frustrations and discomforts brought on by the analysis itself. Even the most skilled analyst, Kohut continued, may have difficulty in dealing with a patient who suddenly idealizes him and just as suddenly turns on him. The analyst, he cautioned, may overlook his own intolerance to the release of narcisssistic tensions: but he will be compensated when watching such a patient's "growing self-esteem and realistic enjoyment, and the unfolding of moderate achievement, humor, empathy, wisdom and creativity" (1971, 199).

Kohut's conceptualization of the self was useful to the social scientists and philosophers with whom he cooperated in Chicago, and to others who wanted to explain the "looser morals" of the younger generation and the glorifications of the self by what became known as the "me-generation". But these theories, and the therapeutic practices these would entail – that is, the focus on narcissistic disorders rather than on ego disorders and psychoses – were challenges some Freudians refused and others would address only reluctantly.

Among them was Otto Kernberg, – who had left Vienna as a child and had become a psychoanalyst in Chile, and who introduced his version of object-relations theory (an amalgam of the ideas of Edith Jacobson, Melanie Klein and Angel Garma) to the Americans. He did not believe that narcissistic personalities were seriously threatened by massive disintegration. Instead, he saw them as suffering from a combination of pathological condensation of real self, ideal self and object structures; of repression and dissociations; of devaluation of object representations and blurred superego boundaries. At the risk of oversimplifying a very complex theory, I think it can be said that these are roots of their grandiose selves (Kernberg, 1976, 116).

Kernberg disagreed primarily with Kohut's notion that narcissistic investment and object investment start out together and then evolve independently. Instead, he maintained, both normal and pathological narcissism always is rooted in the relationship of the self to object representations and external objects, as well as in the struggle between love and aggression. Basically, Kernberg held that individuals continue to expand their *intrapsychic* structures from the moment they are born. Insofar as these derive from the interactions between mother and child, psychoanalysis can uncover their social roots: but this does not equate object relations and interactive behavior. Like Freud in *The Ego and the Id* Kernberg linked the origins of ego and superego *and* those of the id to the very earliest object relations. Reminding his colleagues of the biological determinants of psychic phenomena, he suggested that they account for such distinctions as the anthropologist, N. Tinbergen, had made between consummatory and appetitive behavior,[28] as Konrad Lorenz had noted in the "instinct movements" of animals responding to temporal needs, and as John Bowlby had shown in his "planned hierarchy" of flexible responses (1976, 89).

Kernberg for the most part retained Freud's tripartite structure of ego, id and superego for analyzing the oedipal period and applied object relations theory to describe infant development (Carsky and Ellman, 1985, 259–260). Thus he used the Kleinian theories of splitting and projective identification for the so-called low-level defenses and derived repression and isolation for the so-called high-level defenses from ego psychology. In order not to relativize the various concepts, Kernberg (1976) postulated "units of internalized object relations as subsystems [... that] integrate both drives and psychic structures" and placed instincts at the level of a "suprasystem of the personality at large" (p. 86). Thereby, he could account for neurophysiological and neuropsychological factors and could "integrate" the Kleinians' schizoid and depressive phases as well as Mahler's developmental theories.

Kernberg himself "specialized" in "borderline" adults – individuals who manifest rapidly fluctuating, and contradictory, ego states and whose transference reactions quickly move from idealization and love to rage and hatred. But whereas Kohut traced such behavior to its narcissistic roots, Kernberg located it in the process of splitting during early infancy, and in the reenactment of primary process behavior. This diagnosis, in turn, led Kernberg to differentiate three types of internalization – object-images or object-representations, self-images or self-representations, and drive deriva-

28 According to Kernberg, "internal factors such as internal sensory stimuli from the highest level central nervous system (that is, "motivations") either determine overt response or control the threshold of the response to external stimuli; external factors, in turn, may activate internal factors."

tives or particular affective dispositions. He then constructed a very detailed model of developmental stages – normal autism (first month of life), normal symbiosis (third or fourth to sixth or ninth month), differentiation between self and other (six to nine months to eighteen to thirty-six months), and integration of contradictory representations (from the end of the third year through the oedipal period). Narcissistic disorders are said to be rooted in this stage, and the formation of a healthy personality in the next one. Furthermore, Kernberg distinguished between high-level and low-level character pathology and explained why the "boderline personality organization" as such was stable, though chracterized as ego pathology. He suggested that analysts focus on prospective patients' self-understanding, their relations with others, and their grasp of reality. And he recommended that most narcissistic disorders be treated by psychoanalysis – with modifications and supportive treatment when indicated – and that patients with specific syndromes be hospitalized.

By integrating the Kleinians' bad and good objects and the depressive position, Kernberg broke American taboos; and by accusing the Kleinians of imprecision and of having neglected Freud's structural concepts, he bridged the ever widening theoretical gaps and to some extent brought Klein's ideas into the Americans' discussions, though through a backdoor. Kernberg's knack to automatically translate the meanings of analytic terms by taking account of their users' background, as well as his preoccupations with pathology rather than neurosis, struck a chord among social scientists and literary scholars who increasingly were looking to theoretical views that were being expounded abroad, among Parisian Lacanians and Frankfurt scholars.[29]

Nevertheless, notions of self resembled more closely the preoccupations within the culture, even though these did not enter into the the discussion about the unconscious elements Kohut was concerned with. For example, Christopher Lasch's *Culture of Narcissism* (1978), which had become a bestseller, had been extrapolated to a large extent from Kohut's work – in order to explain "emotional shallowness, fear of intimacy, hypochondria, pseudo-self-insight and promiscuous pansexuality". Other popularizations of these complex theories, and at times their fusion with Asian notions of self, were

29 At the Jerusalem Congress in 1984 Kernberg explained, for instance, that while object relations always refer to the relationship with a significant other, for Fairbairn this represented the shift from "infantile" to "mature" dependence allowing for cooperation with a perceived separate object; for Jacobson it was the ability to acquire "true object relationships"; and for Alice Balint it was the replacement of "egoistic love" with "altruistic love."

being discussed by students in anthropology and sociology, and so were those that converged with the debates in the increasingly popular women's movement and with the general therapeuticalization of the society. Though simplifying psychoanalytic concepts they nevertheless helped to get them into the mainstream.

In the ensuing theoretical bedlam, someone like Kernberg stands out intellectually, particularly for his grasp of the many competing theories. He traces his own formulations of ego splitting to Freud's observations of "love turning to hate" (1984) and defines object relations more broadly than Anna Freud (1936) and thus more in line with Melanie Klein. (Sometimes he seems perilously close to Lacan's dialogue between the self and the Other.) He has argued that the objects of both Kohutians and Sullivanians are stuck within the psychic apparatus – where structures so readily get fixed and replayed; he has maintained that the ego psychologists' structures are conceived at too high a level of abstraction and thereby "cause" conflict between drives and libido; he has traced his own theory from Mahler, Fairbairn, M. Klein, and Edith Jacobson. In essence, Kernberg is a kind of ubiquitous presence, on the highest level of abstraction – while contributing to clinical techniques for dealing with narcissistic and borderline patients.

Inevitably, Mahler's, Kohut's, and Kernberg's contributions, and those of their epigones and interpreters, appealed to some of the psychoanalytic psychologists as well, and would be discussed not only in terms of theories but in terms of their adaptability to therapeutic practice. That Kohut and Kernberg did not shun professional contact with people outside their own organizations, of course, not only helped spread their ideas but narrowed the gap between practices of the members of the institutes affiliated with the APA and those of "outsiders". Many, but far from all of them, were lacking medical credentials. And because psychoanalytic thought had become as widespread as the culture of the movies, and ever more people were accepting notions of the unconscious, it began to make less and less sense for those who were practicing therapists to belong to hierarchically layered institutes. And it bothered the non-medically trained psychoanalysts because they all were on the lower rungs of this hierarchy, sort of second class citizens.

IX. The Psychologists Demand Recognition

In 1981, the non-medically trained psychoanalyst Reuben Fine took inventory of the American psychoanalytic panorama. He held that in the midst of enormous growth and fratricide the psychoanalytic vision had persisted and had made continuous progress (p. 502) – in comparison to competing approaches by both experimental psychologists and psychiatrists. When Murray Meisels recounted the "History of the Division of Psychoanalysis, 1978–1988", he recalled that in 1978 Fine had been the one to collect signatures at the Annual Meeting of the APA in order to start a psychoanalytic division within that society – Section 39. It was granted the following year.[30] When a similar proposal had been made ten years earlier, psychologists had been afraid that such a move might set up new training institutes. Thus they had voted to organize a research group instead: Psychologists Interested in the Study of Psychoanalysis (PISP). In fact, this is precisely what happened after 1979, and what caused yet more antagonisms and hostilities among non-medical Freudians.

As Meisels recounts, the first rift occurred between those who expected to enforce standards similar to those of the IPA and the APA (these later formed the Division's Section I), and those who did not want to define any specific requirements. Section I maintained that psychoanalysis (as opposed to psychotherapy) consisted of at least three weekly sessions (the APA and IPA required four to five). Those who were against such a "traditional" standard – these included persons whose experiences were in social work, education, Adlerian, Jungian, interpersonal and ad hoc therapies – not only insisted on less rigorous rules but took longer to agree on what they stood for. Now, the battles over standards of training, and over the admission of "lesser trained" but practicing members became mindboggling. So, when Section I finally accepted thrice-weekly meetings as standard, the others perceived them as engaging in credentialling, and therefore attacked them. Actually, Section I did accept psychologists of all theoretical stripes as long as they went along with their "frequency/intensity dimension". Since 55 percent of psychoanalytic psychologists were located in New York, the arguments, too, were centered there, and those who accepted twice weekly treatments soon organized Section V. Another problem arose over questions of grandparenting or equivalency of training by experienced psychologists, and yet another about whether or not these psychologists ought to

30 Murray Meisels, "History of the Division of Psychoanalysis, 1978-88", in M. Meisels/ E. Shapiro (1990).

be allowed to perpetuate such training. This battle got to be every bit as divisive and nasty as the fights among Freud's early disciples, and those of the NYPI in the early 1940s. The local chapters outside New York, states Meisels, were fairly outside this brouhaha. Instead, they bemoaned the lack of training opportunities they had been suffering from, due to the exclusionary policies of the APA. However, after the formation of Division 39, a network of local chapters began to emerge, organized by Oliver Kerner of Chicago.

By 1984, reports Meisels, the Division's major agenda had shifted from the issue of standards to those of local training. During that year, a few members – Bryant Welch, Nathan Stockhamer and Ernest Lawrence, who felt that the refusal to train psychologists by the APA, the IPA and the Columbia University contingent, constituted restraint of trade. They filed a suit on March 1, 1985. And a representative of the "less-traditional viewpoint", Helen Block Lewis, became Division president. For the first time that December, representatives from chapters around the country met *en force.* They raised funds and began to push for a political power base within the Division, for what became Section IV – the Section of Local Chapters. Because psychologists in Michigan, Chicago, Denver, Dallas, Washington, D.C. and Boston for the most part had been analyzed, trained and supervised by members of the local institute of the APA, and depended on these, and on hospitals, for referrals of patients and for professional contact, they tended to move around the fringes of the regional medical society. Consequently, their theoretical focus was informed by ego psychology, and within the Division they seemed to be the natural allies of Section I, at least in terms of standards. However, they also wanted to adhere to non-traditional forms of training, and to compete openly with the traditional Freudians for patients. Thus the members of Division 39 engaged in internecine battles on the optimal number of hours, and years, it takes to train the "perfect analyst", and on how to assure that this person turns into the perfect practitioner. We recall that this had been the bane of every psychoanalytic group around the world. Should the training analyst report to the institute about the progress of the candidate? Are training analyses effective with such reporting rules? Or, is the bad reputation of the training analysis due to the reporting factor which itself is – or is not – the cause for the second analyses of psychoanalysts? How come the "perfectly-analyzed analyst" often achieves less-than-perfect results? Are transference neuroses ever neutralized or just relatively detoxified? Etc., etc.

While these questions were being pursued, the lawsuit was being settled. The IPA always had admitted non-medical Freudians, and now the leading members of the APA, the Columbia group, and the NYPI maintained that they had planned in any case to accept more psychologists. In other words, the members of Division 39 got their way. But this happened after their own training facilities had mushroomed. And any victory led to yet another round of squirmishes: each local society had to decide whether or not to apply for membership in the IPA (it certainly added prestige) – which meant that some of their "less-trained" members might not qualify, and that they all would have to adhere to rules not everyone was comfortable with. Once more, the Freudians were in pitched battle. The doctors' organizations had to decide on whom to accept and under what conditions, and the lay analysts on the conditions they would agree to.

At their meetings in April 1991, some of the leading non-medical analysts disagreed on whether the minimum pychoanalysis consists of three or four hours. Inevitably, those among them whose reputations rest on their publications, such as Louise Kaplan, Esther Menaker, Marion Oliner and Ruth Lax, or those who have been editors, such as Marie Coleman Nelson, Norman Kaplan or Martin Shulman, are bound to rise to the top of the new organizations. In the end, however, each practitioner will defend the pracices he or she is comfortable with. The ultimate problem, for everyone, will be to fill patient hours as more and more people enter the profession. Some are more convinced than others that good analysts need a maximum of training; others point out that fewer and fewer people can afford such intensive treatment. Still, to fill one's patient hours depends, once again, on the good will of colleagues who refer patients.

In the meantime, poorly trained or non-trained charlatans continue to pretend they are doing psychotherapy, psychiatrists increasingly employ drug therapy, and experimental psychologists claim to be psychoanalysts. And once more the members of the American Psychological Association are debating whether or not to require therapists to be licensed after they receive a doctorate – in order to ban impostors. Should they succeed, persons without *clinical* training could not be prevented from seeing patients. *Plus ça change, plus c'est la même chose.* In 1927, this was the situation that "inspired" Freud to write *On the Question of Lay Analysis.*

What is to be done, now that the culture is permeated with a Babel of psychoanalytic languages – of therapies of the self, of self-psychology, encounter and self-help groups, etc. – by more and more people who refuse therapies that threaten to penetrate to the unconscious? And unlike Freud's lay healers, who came from the arts and humanities, and who had a broad general, classical background, their American descendants, for the most part, lack what the French sociologist, Pierre Bourdieu, calls cultural capital. These factors conspire in rejecting what Freud called "the gold of psychoanalysis". When not being repudiated, it is being devalued, although talk about the unconscious has become chic, particularly by people outside the therapeutic profession. Still, some dedicated therapists insist on continuing in Freud's tradition. Whether or not they will be able to stem the tide remains to be seen.

References

BEERS, C. W. (1935): A Mind That Found Itself. New York: Doubleday.

BROMBERG, W. (1954): The Mind of Man: A History of Psychotherapy and Psychoanalysis. New York: Harper.

BUXBAUM, E. (1949): The Role of a Second Language in the Formation of Ego and Superego. *Psychoanalytical Quarterly* 18, 279–289.

CARSKY, M. / ST. ELLMAN (1985): Otto Kernberg and Object Relations Theory. In: Beyond Freud. A Study of Modern Psychoanalytic Theories. Ed. J. Reppen. Hillsdale, N. J.: The Analytic Press.

CÉNAC, M. / R. LOEWENSTEIN (1936): Mechanisme des inhibitions de la puissance sexuelle chez l'homme. *L'Evolution Psychiatrique* 3, no. 5, 5–25.

COCKS, G. C. (1985): Psychoanalysis in the Third Reich: The Göring Institut. New York: Oxford Univ. Press.

EISSLER, K. R. (1960): The Efficient Soldier. In: The Psychoanalytic Study of Society. Ed. W. Muensterberger / S. Axelrad. New York: Int. Univ. Press, 39–97.

ERIKSON, E. H. (1950): Childhood and Society. New York: Norton.

FINE, R. (1979): A History of Psychoanalysis. New York: Columbia Univ. Press.

– (1981): The Psychoanalytic Vision: A Controversial reappraisal of the Freudian revolution. New York: Free Press.

FREUD, A. ([1936] 1933): The Ego and the Mechanisms of Defense. In: The Writings of Anna Freud. Vol. 2. New York: Int. Univ. Press.

FREUD, S. (1914): On Narcissism. An Introduction. S. E. 14, 69–102.

– (1925): Instincts and their Vicissitudes. S. E. 14, 109–140.

– (1923): The Ego and the Id. S. E. 19, 1–66.

– (1926): On the Question of Lay Analysis. S. E. 20, 177–258.

FROMM, E. (1942): The Fear of Freedom. London: Routledge and Kegan Paul.

FURER, M. (1967): Some developmental aspects of the superego. *Int. J. Psychoanal.* 48, 277–80.

GREEN, M. R. (1962): The Roots of Sullivan's Concept of Self. In *The Psychoanalytic Quarterly* 36, 271–282.

HALE, N. G. Jr. (1971): Freud and the Americans. New York: Oxford Univ. Press.

– (1971a): James Jackson Putnam and Psychoanalysis. Cambridge: Harvard Univ. Press.

HARTMANN, H. (1939): Psychoanalysis and the Concept of Health. *Int. J. Psychoanal.* 20, 308–21.

– ([1939] 1958): Ego Psychology and the Problem of Adaptation. New York: Int. Univ. Press.

HARTMANN, H. / E. KRIS / R. M. LOEWENSTEIN (1946): Comments on the Formation of Psychic Structure. *Psychoanal. Study Child* 2, 11–38.

– (1951): Some Psychoanalytic Comments on "Culture and Personality". In: Psychoanalysis and Culture. Ed. G. Wilbur / W. Muensterberger. New York: Int. Univ. Press.

HORNEY, K. (1937): The Neurotic Personality of Our Time. New York: Norton.

– (1939): *New Ways in Psychoanalysis.* New York: Norton.

– (1943): Bulletin 3 of *The American Journal of Psychoanalysis* – Committee of War Effort.

JACOBSON, E. (1946): The Child's Laughter. In: Hartmann / Kris / Loewenstein, p. 40.

– (1950): Development of the Wish for a Child in Boys. *Psychoanal. Study Child* 5, 139–52.

KERNBERG, O. F. (1976): Object Relations Theory and Clinical Psychoanalysis. New York: Aronson.

– (1984): The Influence of Projective Identification on Countertransference. Paper presented to the First Sigmund Freud Conference, Jerusalem, May 27–29.

KOHUT, H. (1971): The Analysis of the Self: A Systematic Approach to the Psychoanalytic Treatment of Narcissistic Personality Disorders. New York: Int. Univ. Press.

KUBIE, L.: Correspondence. Library of Congress, Washington, D. C.

– : Records of the Emergency Committee. Library of the History of Psychiatry, Cornell Medical School / Payne Whitney Clinic.

KURZWEIL, E. (1989): *The Freudians: A Comparative Perspective.* New Haven: Yale Univ. Press. [German 1993]

LANGER, W. (1972): The Mind of Hitler. New York: Basic Books.

LASCH, C. (1978): The Culture of Narcissism. New York: Norton.

LEVY, D. (1947): New Fields of Psychiatric. New York: Norton.

LIEBERMAN, J. E. (1985): Acts of Will: The Life and Work of Otto Rank. New York: Free Press.

MAY, U. (1976): Psychoanalyse in den USA. *Tiefenpsychologie* 2, 482–527.

MCGUIRE, I. A. (1982): Jelliffe: His Correspondence with Freud and Jung. Chicago: Chicago Univ. Press.

MAHLER, M. S. / J. D. MCDEVITT (1979): Observations in Adaptation and Defense *in statu nascendi.* In: The Selected Papers of Margaret S. Mahler. Vol. 2. New York: Aronson.

MEISELS, M. / E. SHAPIRO (Eds.) (1990): A History of the Division of Psychoanalysis, 1978–1988. New Jersey: Erlbaum.

MENAKER, E. (1989): Appointment in Vienna.

MENG, H. / E. L. FREUD (Eds.) (1963): Psychoanalysis and Faith: The Letters of Sigmund Freud and Oscar Pfister. New York: Basic Books.

MICHEL, S. (1984): American Conscience and the Unconscious: Psychoanalysis and the Rise of Personal Religion, 1906–1963. *Psychoanalysis and Contemporary Thought* 7, No. 3, 387–421.

PARSONS, T. ([1952] 1964): Social Structure and Personality. New York: Free Press.
REIFF, P. (1966): *The Triumph of the Therapeutic.* New York: Harper.
SPITZ, R. A. / L. M. WOLF (1946): Anaclitic Depression: An Inquiry into the Genesis of Psychiatric Conditions in Early Childhood. *Psychoanal. Study Child* 2, 313–42.
SULLIVAN, H. S. (1953): The Interpersonal Theory of Psychiatry. New York: Norton.
WALKER, N. (1957): A Short History of Psychotherapy in Theory and Practice. New York: Noonday Press.

Journals

American Academy of Psychoanalysis. Journal.
since 1973; Ed.: Guilford Publications, Inc.
(Dir.: Morton B. Cantor)
72, Spring St., 4th Fl., New York, NY 10012
Tel.: 1-212-413 9800, Fax: 1-212-966 6708

American Journal of Psychoanalysis
since 1941; Ed.: Plenum Publishing Corp.
(Dir.: Dr. Mario Rendon)
233 Spring St., New York, NY 10013
Tel.: 1-212-620 8047

American Psychoanalyst Quarterly. Newsletter
since 1991; Ed.: American Psychoanalytic Association
(Dir.: Dr. Arnold Richards)
365 Broadway, Hillsdale, NJ 07642
Fax: 1-201-666 2394

American Psychanalytic Association Journal. Monograph
since 1953; Ed.: American Psychoanalytic Association
(Dir.: Dr. Arnold Richards)
365 Broadway, Hillsdale, NJ 07642
Fax: 1-201-666 2394

American Psychoanalytic Association Workshop Series
since: 1985; Ed.: American Psychoanalytic Association
(Dir.: Dr. Arnold Richards)
365 Broadway, Hillsdale, NJ 07642
Fax: 1-201-666 2394

Association for Psychoanalytic Medicine. Bulletin
since 1961; Ed.: Association for Psychoanalytic Medicine
(Dir.: Dr. Elizabeth Auchincloss)
4560 Delafield Ave., Bronx, NY 10471
Tel.: 1-212-874 0070

Contemporary Psychoanalysis
since 1964; Ed.: William Alanson White Psychoanalytic Institute
(Dir.: Arthur H. Feiner)
20 W., 74th St., New York, NY 10023
Tel.: 1-212-873 0725

Institute for Psychoanalysis Newsletter
since 1932; Ed.: Chicago Institute for Psychoanalysis
180 N. Michigan Ave., Chicago, IL 600601
Tel.: 1-312-726 6300

Journal of the American Psychoanalytic Association
since 1953; Ed.: International Universities Press
(Dir.: Theodore Shapiro); Journal Department
59 Boston Post Rd., Box 1524, Madison, CT 06443-1524
Tel.: 1-203-245 4000

Modern Psychoanalysis
since 1976; Ed.: Center for Modern Psychoanalytic Studies
(Dir.: Phyllis W. Meadow)
16 W 10th St., New York, NY 10011
Tel.: 1-212-260-7050

National Psychological Association for Psychoanalysis Bulletin
since 1950; Ed.: National Psychological Association for Psychoanalysis
150 W 13th. St., New York, NY 10011
Tel.: 1-212-924 7440

National Psychological Association for Psychoanalysis. News and Reviews.
since 1970; Ed.: National Psychological Association for Psychoanalysis
(Dir.: Harvey A. Kaplan)
150 W 13th. St., New york, NY 10011,
Tel.: 1-212-924 7440

New York Psychoanalytic Institute Kris Study Group. Monographs
since 1965; Ed.: International University Press
(Dir.: Dr. Edward Joseph)
59 Boston Post Rd., Box 1524, Madison, CT 06443-1524
Tel.: 1-201-245 4000

Psychoanalysis and Contemporary Thought
since 1978; Ed.: International University Press
(Dir.: Leo Goldberger)
59 Boston Post Rd., Box 1524, Madison, CT 06443-1524
Tel.: 1-201-245 4000

Psychoanalytic Books
since 1990; Ed.: Psychoanalytic Books, Inc.
(Dir.: Joseph Reppen)
211 E 70th ST., New York, NY 10021
Tel.: 1-212-628 8792

Psychoanalytic Crosscurrents
since 1985; Ed.: New York University Press
(Dir.: Leo Goldberger)
70 Washington Sq. SO, New York, NY 10012
Tel.: 1-212-998 2575, Fax: 1-212-995 3833

Psychoanalytic Inquiry
since 1980; Ed.: Analytic Press, Inc.
(Dir.: Dr. Joseph D. Lichtenberg)
365 Broadway, Hillsdale, NJ 07642
Tel.: 1-800-926 6579, Fax: 1-201-666 2394

Psychoanalytic Psychology
since 1984; Ed.: (American Psychological Association, Division Psychoanalysis), Lawrence Erlbaum Associates, Inc.
(Dir.: Bertram J. Cohler)
365 Broadway, Hillsdale, NJ 07642

Psychoanalytic Quarterly
since 1932; Ed.: Psychoanalytic Quarterly
(Dir.: Dr. Sander M. Abend)
175 Fifth Ave., Rm 210, New York, NY 10010
Tel.: 1-212-982 9358

Psychoanalytic Review
since 1913; Ed.: National Psychological Association for Psychoanalysis, Guilford Publications
(Dir.: Martin Shulman)
72 Spring St. 4th Fl., New York, NY 10012
Tel.: 1-212-431-9800, Fax: 1-212-966 6708

Psychoanalytic Study of Society
Eds.: L. Bryce Boyer, Simon A. Grolnick
365 Broadway, Hillsdale, NJ 07642
Tel.: 1-201-666 4110, Fax: 1-201-666-2394

Psychoanalytic Study of the Child
since 1945; Ed.: Yale University Press
(Dir.: Dr. Albert J. Solnit)
92 A Yale Sta., New Haven, CT 06520
Tel.: 1-203-432 0940

Chicago Psychoanalytical Literature Index
since 1958; Ed.: Chicago Institute for Psychoanalysis
(Dir.: Glenn Miller)
180 N. Michigan, Chicago, IL 60601
Tel.: 1-312-726 6300

Institutions

The American Psychoanalytic Association
309 East 49th Street, New York, NY 10017
Tel.: 1-212-752 0450
Fax: 1-212-593 0571

Accredited Training Institutions

Baltimore-Washington Institute for Psychoanalysis
Suite 102, 14900 Sweitzer Lane, Laurel, MD 20707
Tel.: 1-301-792 80 60

Boston Psychoanalytic Society and Insitute, Inc.
15 Commonwealth Avenue, Boston, MA 02116
Tel.: 1-617-266 0953

Chicago Institute for Psychoanalysis
180 N. Michigan Avenue, Chicago, IL 60601
Tel.: 1-312-726 6300

Cincinnati Psychoanalytic Institute
3001 Highland Avenue, Cincinnati, OH 45219
Tel.: 1-513-96 8886

The Cleveland Psychoanalytic Institute
11328 Euclid Avenue, Cleveland, OH 44106
Tel.: 1-216-229 5959

Columbia University Center for Psychoanalytic Training and Research
722 West 168th Street, Box 63; New York, NY 10032
Tel.: 1-212-927 5000

Dallas Psychoanalytic Institute
P.O. Box 270156; Dallas, TX 75227
Tel.: 1-214-388-6335

Denver Institute for Psychoanalysis, University of Colorado School of Medicine
4200 East 9th Avenue; Denver, CO 80262
Tel.: 1-303-270 7776

Houston-Galveston Psychoanalytic Institute
5300 San Jacinto; Suite 145; Houston, TX 77004
Tel.: 1-713-524 0790

Institute of the Philadelphia Association for Psychoanalysis
15th Asaphs Road; P.O. Box 36; Bala Cynwyd, PA 19004
Tel.: 1-215-839 3966

Los Angeles Psychoanalytic Society and Institute
2014 Sawtelle Blvd.; Los Angeles, CA 90025
Tel.: 1-310-478 6541

Michigan Psychoanalytic Institute
16310 West 12 Mile Road; Suite 204; Southfield, MI 48076
Tel.: 1-313-559 5855

New Orleans Psychoanalytic Institute, Inc.
3624 Coliseum Street; New Orleans, LA 70115
Tel.: 1-504-899 5815

New York Psychoanalytic Instiute
247 East 82nd Street; New York, NY 10028
Tel.: 1-212-879 6900

Philadelphia Psychoanalytic Insitute
111 North 49th Street; Philadelphia, PA 19139
Tel.: 1-215-471 2575

Pittsburgh Psychoanalytic Institute
401 Shady Ave., Apt. B204; Pittsburgh, PA 15206
Tel.: 1-412-661 4224

Psychoanalytic Institute of New England, East, Inc.
P.O. Box 762; Needham, MA 02192
Tel.: 1-617-449 8365

The Psychoanalytic Institute, New York University
Medical Center
400 East 34th Street and First Avenue; New York, NY 10016
Tel.: 1-212-263 6243

St. Louis Psychoanalytic Institute
4524 Forest Park Blvd.; St. Louis, MO 63108
Tel.: 1-314-361 7075

San Diego Psychoanalytic Institute
1010 Turquoise Street; Suite 320; San Diego, CA 92109
Tel.: 1-619-488 0687

San Francisco Psychoanalytic Institute
2420 Sutter Street; San Francisco, CA 94115
Tel.: 1-415-563 5815

Seattle Institute for Psychoanalysis
4020 East Madison Street; Seattle, WA 98112
Tel.: 1-206-328 5315

Southern California Psychoanalytic Institute
9024 Olympic Blvd.; Beverly Hills, CA 90211
Tel.: 1-213-276 2455; 272-7620

Topeka Institute for Psychoanalysis
Box 829, 5800 SW Sixth Ave.; Topeka, KS 66601
Tel.: 1-913-273 7500

University of North Carolina-Duke University Psychoanalytic Training Program
UNC School of Medicine, Dept. of Psychiatry
Rm. 237, GB 7160, Wing C; Chapel Hill, NC 27599-7160
Tel.: 1-919-966 3379

Washington Psychoanalytic Institute
4925 MacArthur Blvd., N.W.; Washington, D.C. 20007
Tel.: 1-202-338 5453

Western New England Institute for Psychoanalysis
255 Bradley Street; New Haven, CT 06510
Tel.: 1-203-562 2103

Edith Kurzweil, Ph.D., Professor at Rutgers University, One Lincoln Plaza, New York, N.Y. 10023

Venezuela

by Nora Zambrano de Nava

Historical summary of our Association

In 1987 we presented a paper about the psychoanalytic movement in Venezuela at the Symposium of FEPAL held in April 1987 in Sao Paulo, Brazil which was published in *Correio da FEPAL* in August 1987.

The historical part of the cited work was based on Dr. Juan Olivares' paper "Breve Reseña histórica de la Asociación Venezolana de Psicoanálisis", published in the review *Psicoanálisis* of our Association in 1984.

Summarizing our history Dr. Olivares records that in the decade which corresponds to the years 1950–1960 the two first Venezuelan psychoanalysts who received their training abroad came back to our country: Dr. Hernán Quijada returned from France and Dr. Guillermo Teruel from England.

Dr. Olivares affirms that at the end of 1961 the first Psychoanalytic Study Group of Venezuela was formed by Dr. Manuel Kizer who was trained in Argentina, Dr. William Hobaica trained in France and Drs. Antonio García, Fernando Acuña and J. Araujo trained in Chile.

Later, Drs. Cesar Ottalagano of Argentina, Julio Aray, Hugo Domínguez, Juan Olivares and Hans Voss trained in Argentina, Antonio Briceño trained in Mexico and Nicolás Cupello trained in England, were integrated in this first Study Group which was officially accepted by the IPA at the International Congress held in Copenhagen in 1965.

Dr. Olivares also describes in his paper the following important facts:

For the period 1965–1967 Dr. Hernán Quijada was elected as President of the first Board of Directors of the First Psychoanalytic Study Group.

In 1966 the IPA named the Sponsoring Committee of the Study Group. It consisted of Drs. Grinberg and Langer of Argentina, Namnum of Mexico and Dahlheim and Koch of Brazil.

For the second period (1967–1969) Dr. Manuel Kizer was elected President of the Group. Dr. Guillermo Teruel, who became a training analyst in 1966, was elected Director of the Insitute.

Dr. Kizer became a training analyst in 1967 and Drs. Hugo Domínguez and Antonio Garcia in 1969.

In July 1969 the First Venezuelan Psychoanalytic Study Group became an Association at the International Congress of Rome.

For the third period (1969–1971) Dr. Guillermo Teruel was elected President and Dr. Manuel Kizer Director of the Institute. In this period the training activities of our Institute started.

In the same period our Association was visited by Drs. Rangell as President of the IPA, Parrés and González of Mexico, Martins of Brazil, Bleger, Kalina and Rascovsky of Argentina.

In July 1971 our Association was recognized as a Component Organization of the IPA at the Congress in Vienna.

In this period the Venezuelan Psychoanalytic Association organized the Ninth Psychoanalytic Latin American Congress held in Caracas in July 1972. The Organizing Committee consisted of Drs. Teruel, Kizer and Olivares.

For the Fourth Period (1972–1974) Dr. Hugo Dominguez was elected President and Dr. Antonio García Director of the Institute.

In 1973 the first group of the Venezuelan Institute graduated, consisting of Drs. Jesús Fuenmayor, Serapio Marcano, José Meliá and Alejandro Sanz.

Between 1973 and 1974 we were visited by Drs. Virginia Bicudo, David Zimmerman from Brazil, Luis Yamín from Colombia, André Green from France, Donald Meltzer from England, David Liberman from Argentina and Edward Joseph from the United States of America.

In 1974 for the fifth period Dr. Antonio García was elected President and Dr. Hugo Domínguez Director of the Institute.

In 1975 arose the first internal crisis, which divided our Association into two groups, A and B, presided over by different boards of directors.

In July 1975 during the International Congress in London the IPA named a Site Visiting Committee which visited Caracas to study this crisis.

After the IPA intervention our Association was visited by the IPA authorities, Drs. Lebovici, Widlöcher and Joseph in February 1976.

This crisis ended in May 1977 through an arrangement between the two groups, A and B, which elected a board of directors presided over by Dr. Joan Olivares. During the crisis the Site Visiting Committee suspended our Institute's training functions. Later on the same Committee supported the candidates' request made to the Colombian Psychoanalytic Institute, to continue our training programs.

Four training analysts, Drs. Luis Yamín, Guillermo Sánchez Medina, Inga Villarreal and Guillermo Arcila, re-opened the Venezuelan Psychoanalytic training under their direction.

After the International Congress held in Jerusalem, nine candidates (the second group from our Institute) graduated. Dr. Edward Joseph and the four cited Colombian training analysts attended the ceremony in Caracas (1978).

After this crisis, for the period 1980–1982 Dr. Julio Aray was elected as President of the Association and Dr. William Hobaica Director of the Institute. This board of directors had five members instead of three.

For the period 1982–1984 Dr. Serapio Marcano was elected President and Dr. Juan Olivares Director of the Institute.

For the period 1984–1986 Dr. Carlos Valedón was elected President and Dr. Juan Olivares Director of the Institute.

In January 1986 the Site Visiting Committee ended their functions and Drs. Edward Joseph and Inga Villarreal visited our Association for the last time. Both of them were named Honorary Members of the Venezuelan Psychoanalytic Association in acknowledgement of their work with us during 10 years.

From then to now:

For the period 1986–1988 Dr. Nora Zambrano de Nava was elected President of the Association and Dr. Addys Attías de Cavallín, Director of the Institute. For the period 1988–1990 Dr. Julio Aray was elected President and Dr. Nora Zambrano de Nava Director of the Institute.

At the moment our Association is confronting a new crisis (the second one) due to the resignation of 15 members who decided to separate from the Venezuelan Association in order to form another Psychoanalytic Group.

Theoretical Influences Integrated in Our Psychoanalytic Thinking

The most important theoretical influences reflected in our daily practice come from the different psychoanalytic schools where our founders were trained. Freud's works are the essence of our fundamental psychoanalytic orientation. Melanie Klein's concepts came to our Institute through the Venezuelan analysts trained in England and also from those trained in Argentina. That is the reason why the Kleinian School plays such an important role in the clinical perspective of our daily work.

Other English authors we study in our training are: Heimann, Riviere, Isaacs, Fairbairn, Kyrle, Rosenfeld, Winnicott, Balint, Bowlby, Segal, Meltzer and Bion. The French School is also important in our training process. We refer to André Green, Joyce McDougall and Janine Chasseguet-Smirgel.

Lacanian concepts have become interesting to some members of our Association but only as a perspective for scientific discussion without altering our traditional setting.

The Argentinian School has also influenced our psychoanalytic way of thinking. We consider it a very central and coherent line of development in Latin American psychoanalysis. Many of our founders were trained in Argentina. The most important authors studied in our Institute are: Racker, Liberman, Grinberg, Bleger, Rascovsky, Garma, Pichón-Rivière, Aberastury, Kalina, Baranger, etc. The American school of psychoanalysis has had some influence on our training. The authors of the American school of ego psychology and other psychoanalytic tendencies read by us are: Hartmann, Kris, Loewenstein, Rapaport, Mahler, Jacobson, Kernberg, Greenson and Erikson. From his own perspective, Heinz Kohut has allowed us to have a wider and better understanding of the narcissistic elements of psychoanalytic patients.

Questions that Currently Arise in Our Daily Practice and also About the Content of our Writings

The main local questions about our daily work are related to our observations on the psychoanalytic process and also on the goals of the psychoanalytic treatment of our patients.

In relation to the number of the weekly sessions of our psychoanalytic treatments there are several factors which we are obliged to consider at this moment.

From the technical point of view we can observe the reluctance of the majoriy of our patients to accept from the beginning a weekly number of sessions which is more than the patients themselves consider convenient for them.

It frequently happens that the patients reject the analysts' suggestions about this matter. Because at the beginning the patients feel those suggestions to be an imposition, they need some time to discover, with the analysts' help, the best way to establish a more facilitating setting for the development of the psychoanalytic process.

As we have noticed, the early establishment of the psychoanalytic setting (5 or 4 weekly sessions) tends to produce manifestations of resistances like: 1) Abandoning the treatment; 2) Looking for other kind of therapies; 3) Increasing of acting out, negative therapeutic reactions of fears to lose the secondary gains.

Due to the fact that the majority of Venezuelan psychoanalysts is concentrated in the capital city Caracas, patients coming from the interior of the country need special therapeutic arrangements for their analytic settings.

In general the official periods of hours in our country are very long. The patients have a very short time to engage in psychoanalytic treatments with an appropriate setting from the beginning.

The current economic situation of our country and the fact that the psychoanalytic setting consists of a long-term treatment cause many patients to consider psychoanalysis a very costly therapy for them.

At this time, people in general prefer the quicker and more active therapeutic methods before considering psychoanalysis a useful kind of treatment.

All of these facts have led us to take them into account, so we consider that at this moment in our country it seems convenient to let the patients initiate their analytic treatments with the number of sessions (1 or 2) they can emotionally and responsibly accept, in order to progressively increase the number of sessions according to their personal evolution, working first through their more urgent conflicts, to let them find their own need to go deeper in the analysis of the latent content, and eventually adding the required number of sessions for the analytic purpose.

This attitude on the part of the analyst prevents the arising of the before mentioned patient's resistances as a reaction to consider the analyst's suggestions as authorative impositions.

We also think that the same attitude to openly discuss the benefits and the disadvantages of other therapeutic treatments and techniques is also positive in building up a true confidence on the part of the patients in the analytic setting.

From this point of view it is important to let the patients take their time from the beginning to propose the convenient arrangement, taking into account their daily work and the long official periods of working hours in our country, especially now when we are suffering an economic crisis.

On the other hand this attitude has allowed us to re-discover the fact that the psychoanalytic work essentially depends from the technical point of view on the maintenance of the analyst's psychoanalytic vertex and on the patient's capacity of being analyzable.

In relation to the quality of our writings, we consider that they reveal not only our theoretical psychoanalytic framework but also the psychoanalytic perspective of our cultural characteristics.

Venezuelan Psychoanalytic Association

The Venezuelan Psychoanalytic Association has celebrated every year the "Jornadas Sigmund Freud" since 1980 and since 1987 every month we have had the Cineforos. Both events are very successful.

In 1987 our First Venezuelan Psychoanalytic Congress was held in Caracas. We have an active participation in the Psychiatry and Clinical Psychology Post Graduate Courses.

We also have published since 1984 our Review *Psicoanálisis*. Many of our members have made interesting contributions.

Some of our members have also published their own books on psychoanalysis: Dr. Julio Aray has published several books like *Aborto: Estudio Psicoanalítico, Manías Tristes, Sadismo en la Enseñanza, Senderos del Alma.* He also contributed to the book *Niveles Profundos del Psiquismo* with other authors like Arnoldo and Matilde Rascovsky.

Dr. Rafael E. López published *Inteligencia afecto y nivel social, Símbolo y mutación, El niño y su inteligencia, Dios es una mujer.*

Dr. Guillermo Teruel published *Diagnóstico y tratamiento de parejas en conflicto,* Dr. Hugo Domínguez: *Temas del Psicoanálisis* and Dr. Alfonso Gisbert: *Psicoanálisis, itinerario de una cienca.*

There is also a Caracas Psychoanalytic Society as a new provisional Society of the IPA consisting of 19 full members and 4 associate members (in 1994). The original Venezuelan Psychoanalytic Association has 45 members and our external as well as our internal activities have been developing in a positive way.

References

OLIVARES, J. A. (1984): Breve reseña histórica de la Asociación Venezolana de Psicoanálisis. *Psicoanálisis* 1, 117-124.

ZAMBRANO DE NAVA, N. (1987): Las características del desarrolo latinoamericano. In: Correio da FEPAL, 105-110.

Journals

Psicoanálisis
Revista de la Asociación Venezolana de Psicoanálisis
since 1984

Institutions

Asociación Venezolana de Psicoanálisis
(Venezuelan Psychoanalytic Association)
Apart.de Correos 6161, Carmelitas, Caracas 1010
Tel.: 58-2-781 8102; Fax: 58-2-781 1953

Sociedad Psicoanalítica de Caracas
(Caracas Psychoanalytical (Provisional) Society)
Calle Norte, Quinta ILD-MOM, Urb. Santa Sofía, Caracas 1061
Tel./Fax: 58-2-986 8498

Dra. Nora Zambrano de Nava, Calle Centro, Qta. Nora, Urb. Santa Sofía, Caracas 1060

Psychoanalysis against the Grain (Argentina, Chile, Nicaragua, Cuba)

by Erika Danneberg

The majority of German-speaking psychoanalysts who could only avoid physical extermination through Hitler's fascism by fleeing were faced with a double threat: as psychoanalysts and as Jews, some of them as Social Democrats or Communists as well. They could only take very little with them in the way of books or manuscripts. But more important was the refugee's baggage they could carry in their heads, something that could not be lost: the beginnings of a socially and politically committed psychoanalysis of the Left from prefascist times. It is owing to them that psychoanalysis today is a part of the "Latin American identity" of Latin American intellectuals, as I was able to hear at conferences in Cuba on "Marxist Psychology and Psychoanalysis".

At the time of fascism in Europe Latin American countries were preferred destinations for left-wing European émigrés. In the majority of the at best nominal "democracies" of the Southern Continent, with their artificial borders handed down from colonial days, rebellions and military coups were the political order of the day. The countries which let in the refugees were not "lands of freedom". But they offered refuge from fascism and war.

What had come over the Atlantic with the émigrés was at first classical psychoanalysis for an educated and wealthy middle and upper class. But the Europeans also brought political and professional experiences with them, of which at the beginning they could only make little use: experiences from the psychoanalytical ambulatoria in Vienna and Berlin, experiences, too, as politically persecuted or, like Marie Langer, as a doctor in the Spanish civil war.

In contrast to fascism in Europe, the socially and politically deeply split societies of their countries of refuge allowed the émigrés to choose which side they wanted to join. Insofar as they had studied for an intellectual profession, they were given, relatively soon, the opportunity to become members of a privileged white upper class, and the traditional rules of their professional training provided the analysts among them with an additional legitimation to keep away from political struggles. They could do their peaceful work in the classy ghettos of the urban upper and middle classes, without having to side openly with those in power. Yet this was only true as long as the split in society was expressed "only" in social protests, in hunger marches or in trade union struggles. With the transition to fascist dictatorships on the one hand, to an armed struggle for a more just distribution of the wealth created by society on the other, the "apolitical niches" became smaller and smaller: neither patients from the ranks of left-wing fighters seeking help nor, say, DINA, the Chilean gestapo, stopped at the analysts' doors.

My theory is that precisely this extreme polarization between a military that was in bondage to foreign countries for the protection of a small bourgeoisie that was in bondage to foreign countries – and a broad resistance rooted in the people, supported developments to place traditional domains of the ruling classes – the church, schools, the health system – at the disposal of the oppressed and their struggles: the "theology of liberation" against the official church, the "pedagogics of liberation" against the schools for the rich, and, against an elitist medicine for the rich, the many attempts to create alternative health institutions for and by the people, in which psychoanalysts, too, made major contributions with their theoretical knowledge and their correspondingly modified techniques.

Psychoanalytically inspired work in the service of large sections of the people can be divided according to the sociopolitical situation of the respective countries into three areas, each with different working conditions:

1. Attempts towards democratization of traditional institutions (universities, hospitals and other health facilities, psychoanalytical training institutes etc.) in countries where, under great pressure "from below", with the support of, say, active trade unions, a certain relaxation in the structure of the power apparatuses provided freedoms for the beginnings of a "civil(ian) society". Example: Argentina in the "short spring" (Marie Langer, in conversation) before the takeover by the military.

2. Psycho-social help for the victims and relatives of victims of fascist dictatorships. An important area in these programs is the scientific-theoretical and practical therapeutic treatment of the after-effects of persecution, torture, prison and exile, which continue even after the (nominal) end of the dictatorships and are reinforced by the efforts of those still in power, who even resort to seemingly lawful measures to bury the crimes of the past by ordaining "forgetting". Examples: Brazil, Uruguay, Argentina, Chile.

3. Support of victorious freedom movements in the building up of psycho-social institutions. Examples: Nicaragua, El Salvador.

Short Spring in Argentina

Marie Langer became a symbolic figure for psychoanalysis of the Left, not only in Latin America. In 1942 she, a young émigré from a no longer existing Austria, with psychoanalytical training in Vienna, was a co-founder of the Asociación Psicoanalítica Argentina (APA). For more than twenty years she helped to build up this association, as a training analyst, later as the president of the APA, too. Fascination with the new task and fear of attracting negative attention in the host country caused her for a time to consider her political past as a member of the illegal Communist party of Austria and as a doctor in the International Brigades in Spain as "past". But as early as the 1950s the "suppressed social feeling of guilt" led her to psychoanalytical work with groups and, together with Emilio Rodrigué, to the forming of the Asociación de Psicología y Psicoterápia de Grupo, which brought her first difficulties with the APA.

In the 1960s, as an activist in a committee of solidarity with Vietnam, Marie Langer returned to political life. From then on she no longer felt obliged to choose between her "two loves" – psychoanalysis and Marxism.

The emergence of the intellectual left in the late sixties did not stop at the psychoanalytical training institutes either. Marie Langer calls the Paris May a key date for the movement, which could also be felt among the young members and candidates of the Argentinian association. In 1969, at the 26th Congress of the International Psychoanalytical Association in Rome, training candidates organized an alternative congress with not only professional topics: Democratization of the psychoanalytical training institutes and re-evaluation of the revolutionary, cultural-critical roots of psychoanalysis. Marie Langer attended it. Platforms were subsequently formed which, according to regional circumstances, were to continue dealing with the controversial topics.

In Argentina, but also in Italy and in Switzerland, the results were radical: the Zürich Platform – later the Psychoanalytical Seminar – and the Plataforma and Documenta in Buenos Aires split from the IPA because of grave differences regarding the admission to psychoanalytical training, the curriculum and the right of co-determination of candidates, as well as relating to the position of psychoanalysis and psychoanalysts in societal-political processes. The movement, which had first become public in Rome, also led to consequences within the IPA. These included, at an organizational level, recognition of the international candidates' organization as well as, in the scientific-theoretical field, renewed and intensified concern with problems of training analysis, lay analysis and countertransference.

In Argentina the separation of the Plataforma and the Documenta from the APA took place in 1971, after the 27th International Psychoanalytical Congress in Vienna. It was Marie Langer's last appearance as the representative of the APA; her lecture "Psychoanalysis and/or Social Revolution" did not appear in the *International Journal of Psychoanalysis,* which traditionally publishes all congress contributions – "lack of space" was the official reason.

Plataforma separated from the APA in a period of strong social movements, marked by the uprisings in Cordova and Rosario, the emergence of guerilla groups and militant, class-conscious trade unions. The declaration of withdrawal, directed by the signatories "a los trabajadores de Salud Mental" (to the workers in mental health) leaves no doubt that the Plataforma people, contrary to previous psychoanalytical practice, were taking a stand in these political struggles. In a traditional component society of the IPA that must have sounded like a call to revolution: a declared rejection of political abstinence, which until then, more or less explicitly, had been a part of the foundations of psychoanalytical identity. But the colleagues who in 1971 separated from their psychoanalytical association without giving up their psychoanalytical identity were not primarily concerned with revolutionizing psychoanalyis – even if criticism of the undemocratic admission and training procedures in their institutes may have initiated the protest for some. When they declared their withdrawal they were part of a movement which had seized the whole country. The militant sectors of the population, with which the signatories of the declaration expressed their solidarity, were not the ideal of impatient intellectuals, they were socio-political reality in the Argentina of the late sixties and early seventies. The modest revolutions in psychoanalysis, just like the incomparably greater social revolutions, also need a revolutionary situation in order to be able to develop.

The long and difficult process of breaking away had already begun in the sixties and was inseparably bound up with professional developments as well as ones in society as a whole. As early as 1964 there had been a mass influx of APA members into the hitherto arch-conservative Argentinian Association of Psychiatrists (Féderacion Argentina de Psiquiatras, FAP). With Emilio Rodrigué, who in 1969 became president of the FAP Buenos Aires, a strong group of young left-wing psychiatrists acquired leading positions which enabled them to exercise influence on health policy in the psycho-social field.

Issues of health policy, if they are oriented to social requirements, are always issues concerning the training of the required specialists, too. The APA, like most psychoanalytical associations, only admitted psychiatrists for training. Against this there now arose, from 1971, in cooperation with the Association of Psychologists and Psychiatrists and with the substantial assistance of Marie Langer and other Plataforma members, a training program for medical doctors and psychologists/psychagogues and, subsequently, a coordination centre for activities in the psycho-social field and all the professional groups involved in it. In this way the medical doctors' monopoly was broken, the way to interdisciplinary cooperation at the service of broader, non-wealthy sectors of the population was opened.

The "Coordinadora de Trabajadores de Salud Mental" pursued in its training and research centre clearly defined trade unionist and political goals, with an interdisciplinary research program and a curriculum born by psychoanalysis and Marxism. Left-wing psychoanalysts had conquered a wide field of professional and political opportunities for extending their influence.

This development had become possible since 1971 due to a relaxation of the dictatorship under the pressure of the Peronist masses and left-wing guerilla groups as well as to the electoral victory of the Peronists in 1973. Marie Langer called this period "our short spring".

It was very short and eventually had to bow to one of the bloodiest dictatorships on the Southern Continent. Soon after the electoral victory in 1973, after the much cheered release of political prisoners in Buenos Aires, Pinochet's military coup in Chile, the murder of the elected president Salvador Allende, just like the murder before of Torres in Bolivia, showed how limited the room for freedom was, how close the threat of naked fascism with massive North American support was. The training and research centre of the "Coordinadora" was overcrowded with Chilean and Bolivian refugees, who were without accommodation or welfare. Despite growing pressure from the Triple A – Asociación Argentina Anticomunista – the colleagues from the Coordinadora continued with their work: at the university, at the hospital, in ambulatoria and in health centres. The psycho-social approach of these efforts produced an intensified development in group psychotherapy.

After Perón's death the terror of paramilitary fascist groups increased. Trade unionists and well-known left-wing intellectuals were at the top of the murder lists of the death squads: Marie Langer, too, at that time the president of the Association of Psychiatrists. At the end of 1974 she had to go into exile for a second time, this time to Mexico, a second time on the run from the fascists.

The military dictatorship drowned the short Argentinian spring in blood. But the experiences that the left-wing psychoanalysts collected with the opportunities for applying our science in the psycho-social field have not been lost. For a second time they were carried in the refugee's baggage of the émigrés, further developed in the next host country, ready for the next assignment: in the next revolutionary situation – in Nicaragua.

Psychoanalysis under Terrorism in Chile

Between the Argentinian experiment and the work of psychoanalysts in Nicaragua there was almost a decade and it was marked by fascist dictatorships in many Latin American countries. The example of Chile, where terrorism as a declared state doctrine under the label of "National Security" was to last longest (1973–1989), shows impressively how, under conditions of extreme social polarization, programs and techniques have been developed alongside classical psychoanalysis, and in part from it, which attempt to give social-therapeutic answers to social traumatization. Similar material is known from Brazil and Uruguay, too.

In extremely polarized societies it becomes clear – this is also true of "normal" democratic societies – that external reality is not the same for all the citizens of a country, of a city – therefore not for all analysands either. The external reality of a young apprentice whom we treat on a sick certificate is substantially different from that of a student from a wealthy family. Under the conditions of a dictatorship the difference in the external reality of a militant opponent to the regime from that of a sheltered, "unpolitical" daughter of the middle classes – and from the external reality of the analyst – is even more extreme.

Jiménez describes these different realities and how they are perceived as "intersubjective reality, socialized reality, the world of our direct experience". In contrast to the internal reality derived from the Unconscious, this external social reality would be the area of intersubjective agreement between analyst and patient. Yet since, under a dictatorship, social reality is not the same for all people and at every moment, he comes to the conclusion "that many analyses and psychotherapies in Chile can proceed perfectly normally."

A condition for the "normal" course of psychoanalytical work would therefore be that a large degree of intersubjective agreement regarding the social reality between patient and analyst allow the latter to guarantee a setting in which he can keep his neutrality. But Jiménez qualifies this: "In Chile there are times today (he is referring to the protest days of the opposition/E. D.) when it is not possible to maintain analytical neutrality and when the political ideological conflict breaks into the analytical session like an earth-quake".

It is clear that the requirement that the analysts remain neutral cannot be met under extreme social conditions. Even if analyses under these conditions proceed "perfectly normally", I would, as an analyst, ask myself the question of whether the cutting out of the "social drama" was not to be attributed more to denial, that is to say, defence, than to the readiness to do serious analytical work on the phenomena of internal reality. But of more weight is the fact that the analyst's fear of those directly affected in this drama denies those help who need it the most. Should we therefore disclaim competence in extreme socio-political situations because they threaten to break through our classical setting? Or can we develop techniques and settings which make our psychoanalytical experience useful to the victims of oppression to the oppressed?

To answer this question positively – offensively – seems important to me not only for the people who, under extremely traumatizing social conditions, need psychotherapeutic and psycho-social help – but also for the way we see ourselves as analysts, who have to be increasingly prepared to come across such conditions – not only in the Third World. It is a feature of extreme social polarization that the niches of neutrality – not only of analytical neutrality – get smaller and smaller. Juan Pablo Jiménez, who defines the conditions under which psychoanalytical work seems possible to him so exactly, also speaks of the danger of this work becoming a flight from socio-political reality: thus there is a danger of complicity by retreating to a seemingly unpolitical working area, as in many highly specialized professions, but it suggests itself particularly to us psychoanalysts because the internal reality of our patients is the legitimate centre of our professional interest and exceeding this area easily arouses the suspicion that we are no longer "proper" analysts.

Under these conditions it is not surprising that the organizations which in Chile, in Brazil, in Uruguay and other Latin American countries offer psycho-social help for victims of political repression do not bear the label "psychoanalytical", although many of their staff used to be or still are analysts and the programs in treatment technique and the psychodynamic approach do not deny their psychoanalytical roots. As an example of many similar institutions I mention the Chilean CINTRAS/Centro de Investigación y Tratamiento del Stress (Centre for Stress Research and Treatment), "stress" being the euphemism allowed under the dictatorship for torture.

CINTRAS is the "Chilean model" of medical-psychological and psycho-social assistance for persons who have been victims of violations of human rights. The centre was founded in Santiago de Chile in 1985, in a period of a recent increase in political confrontation, as the latest in a series of institutions – such as the Solidarity Curacy and FASIC (a foundation for social assistance of the World Council of Churches) –, which had concerned themselves for almost a decade with offers of relief for victims of political repression. The psychiatrist Carlos Madariaga, one of the initiators of the centre and today a member of its management committee, in his contribution to a seminar on mental health and human rights in Santiago, says a coinciding of historical and personal motives led to the forming of Cintras:

> "There are in fact two reasons for our formation: first the reference to a personal situation, exile, which two of our compañeros experienced; while working on their own project of regaining a foothold in Chile they eventually became cofounders of the institution. The second, more general reason is the objective necessity to increase the scope of our psycho-social assistance in order to meet the growing needs in the face of increased repression. That was what made us decide to devote 70% of our arranged hours to clinical therapeutic work, a criterium to which we have adhered to this day."

Already this report on motives makes it clear that the approach is different from the one we are familiar with in psychoanalysis in the isolation of the consulting room. Here the question is reversed – and perhaps it has thus been put on its feet: at the beginning there is no particular setting which is suitable for particular patients (and under particular social conditions) – and for other patients simply less or not at all suitable.

Here there is at the beginning a concrete socio-political situation that affects the therapists just as much as their clients – and the colleagues from CINTRAS have to (want to) try to meet a standard which they – not at all in a "neutral" way – experience as their own matter.

In addition to clinical work there is also a research program, always very close to concrete experience, focusing on the rehabilitation of people who have undergone extreme traumatization. By way of Hans Keilson's concept of sequential traumatization, which leads us into the abyss of our own past, we in Europe can also find a very direct way to the work of the Chilean colleagues.

Of course, such a project cannot do without the (not only financial) support of international organizations. The fact that it comes mainly from human rights' organizations underlines the social-therapeutic – the societal-political dimension of CINTRAS' work, which goes beyond the fate of individuals. It is based on the realization that the traumatization which was practised systematically for almost two decades was not an individual one, however painful it was for countless individuals; that here a people, a society as a whole, was traumatized in each individual, and that the individual wounds can only heal when the societal context has been restored.

The period of transition to democracy, which is what the Chileans call the situation of their country under President Aylwin, at least offers the opportunity to make the truth about the crimes committed under the dictatorship public – but Pinochet, who is still the supreme commander of the armed forces, is making sure that the known guilty persons are not called to account. The amnesty law, decreed by the Supreme Court in mid-1990, is, quite within the meaning of sequential traumatization, a fresh setback in the painful process of mourning work that should lead to individual and societal recovery. The work of the CINTRAS people will not be finished for a long time.

"Nicaragua, Nicaraguita ..."

Nicaragua, Nicaraguita – the title of the love song for Nicaragua with which one of the greatest folk singers of this country so rich in poets and singers has also reached the European and North-American centres. Hardly any other people's movement in Latin America has received so great an echo, so much solidarity and – love, in the industrialized countries, too. And not only from "romantic adolescents". Many highly qualified specialists – economists, ecologists, agronomists, engineers, medical doctors, teachers, social workers – all have lent their support to the difficult reconstruction process after the victory over Somoza. Many of them are still in the country today, after the change of government.

The team with which Marie Langer started to work in Nicaragua in 1981 consisted of twelve psychoanalytically trained colleagues of Argentinian, Mexican and Chilean nationality and called itself "Equipo Internacionalista de Salud Mental México – Nicaragua".

The invitation to do this work had come from the Nicaraguan government, which, with the victory of the Sandinists, had set itself the task of "improving the living conditions of the people in all areas". At the centre of these efforts, which were soon to be hampered by another rekindling of the war, was an agrarian reform in favour of the landless peasants, free admission to all educational institutions for all, supported by a literacy campaign run mainly by young people, and a free health system.

The invitation to cooperate on the Salud Mental project – it went first to the emigrated Argentinian psychoanalyst Sylvia Bermann – flowed from the wise judgement of the planners at that time, which even today, and perhaps today even more so, cannot be valued highly enough: a new conception of health and illness, the way they are determined by socio-economic and socio-cultural factors, and a new view of the human being as an integral psycho-physical whole set in a social context. This approach has made it possible for a country with a completely destroyed economy, at the end and, soon again, in the middle of a merciless war, to allow itself a project which in many rich countries is still far from being realized due to a lack of the necessary political will: Salud Mental. In line with the project's inner logic the Nicaraguan planners did not seek support for it from the organ-medical psychiatrists and psychologists but from the psychoanalysts, who had declared their solidarity with them and who were able to bring in their Argentinian experiences with professional work at the service of the people.

For many years the "Equipo Internacionalista", which after the death of its coordinator renamed itself "Equipo Marie Langer", has provided this support in its monthly working visits from Mexico. A number of European doctors and psychotherapists have followed their example.

A reason for the Nicaraguan health project was the understanding that a society moving towards solidarity needed different doctors from the logically profit-oriented ones of a small wealthy upper class. This had soon led to a restructuring of the study of medicine – "Axis Study-Work". The integral view of the human being, upon which all the programs were based, also called for a new definition of the doctor-patient relationship as an integrating element of every therapeutic treatment. And it was soon clear that "therapeutic treatment" was not only the affair of medical doctors – and not only because there were not enough of them to meet the needs of the whole population, as far as the most remote regions. Nurses, social workers, members of health brigades – they were all involved in this. And they all needed support in order to become conscious of their role as acting persons in the health process – especially in Salud Mental.

Marie Langer and her Equipo, with their psychodynamic approach and their experience of work with therapeutic and didactic groups, were able to help with the further training of "trabajadoras y trabajadores en Salud Mental". And they were able to provide impulses with their work in the General Hospital at León that went beyond the training of specialists: towards community work and Prevención Primaria.

Salud Mental was a national project that grew organically out of the objectives of the revolution. Also the idea of working mainly with group techniques in Salud Mental was not ready-made in the minds of the Internacionalistas when they arrived from Mexico. With it they were reacting to the situation they found of the people, as had been described to them by the Nicaraguan planners: the tremendous pressure on a person, after years of fighting against the dictatorship and a hard won victory, in the face of new threats, the necessity – and the impossibility – of coming to terms with the loss of so many loved ones, when at the same time all their energies are needed to defend what has been gained and to start anew; the divisions running through families – the problems in the relationships between the men returning from fighting and the young, self-confident women who have relinquished their traditonal role – the problems of the mothers bringing up children alone, of the many orphans, of the war-disabled – this excess of burdens, which express themselves in physical complaints, psychosomatic and mental illnesses, which cannot be cured by the quick administering of pills or overcome with so few doctors.

"Why don't you work with groups?" the Internacionalistas from Mexico asked. It was the appropriate technique in view of the national situation. The task of the Internacionalistas was only to show "how to do it".

None of the Nicaraguan colleagues had ever had the opportunity to experience the psychoanalytical process themselves – with the exception of the training director at the Psychiatric Hospital in Managua, who had studied in Paris before the Revolution. It was therefore a question of jointly applying and developing methods of further training that went beyond the imparting of theoretical knowledge. There were Balint groups for medical doctors and nurses, therapeutic groups with co-therapists and observers, and supervision talks which placed transference and countertransference, the doctor-patient relationship, often reflected in the therapist-supervisor relationship, at the centre of experience and perception.

The Equipo México-Nicaragua and all the others who collaborated as Internacionalistas with different theoretical and technical approaches in Salud Mental could not and did not want to introduce "classical analysis" or any other, in European terms, "classical" school, to Nicaragua. In this context I know from my own experience how much I owe my Nicaraguan colleagues in the difficult work of constantly checking what we brought with us for its usefulness under Nicaraguan conditions and modifying it wherever necessary.

And today? What has remained after the neo-liberal starvation of the people – and of the state health service too? There is no memorial plaque in Nicaragua for the Austrian/ Argentinian/ Mexican – the Internacionalista Marie Langer. But I know some small health insitutions there that are still functioning where her picture hangs on the wall, where a group room bears her name and where young psycho-therapists, who were trained by Marie Langer and her Equipo, work. To live on, not only in people's memories but also in the daily work of Nicaraguans, is better than any memorial plaque.

Cuba

In Cuba things developed differently. Twenty years before the victory of the Sandinists over the Somoza dictatorship the Cuban revolution's encounter with psychoanalysis proved to be more negative than had been the case in Nicaragua. In Batista's Cuba there had been analysts – in contrast to Managua, where people with money who needed psychotherapeutic help went to Miami or other North American centres. This lack of local professionals had the positive consequence that the Sandinist government was able to turn to left-wing psychoanalysts without an incriminating past when it approached the task of building up a psycho-social service appropriate to the needs of the people.

The Cuban psychoanalyists did not encourage the Revolution to include them in their health planning. They were, according to statements by Argentinian colleagues, "poorly trained and corrupt", and after the victorious Revolution had left their country. So Cuba's negative attitude towards psychoanalysis was not simply a copy of Soviet patterns but was based on its own experiences.

Thanks to the patient work of Juan Carlos Volnovich this rejection of psychoanalysis changed, gradually leading to a more open attitude towards it. The Argentinian psychoanalyst with Plataforma experience had found refuge in Cuba from the military dictatorship in his country and, with his work in a childrens' clinic, had gained the trust of his colleagues and the Cuban authorities. His intensive as well as cautious preparatory work led to the "Encuentros (encounters) of Marxist psychology and psychoanalysis" at the University of La Habana. In four conferences to date (1986, 1988, 1990 and 1992) an exchange of ideas of left-wing psychoanalysts from many Latin American and a few European countries with Cuban colleagues has got started, creating a greater feeling of trust between the two groups. Marie Langer was able to co-initiate the first meeting. At the second meeting we remembered her. The fact that such meetings have been possible and, hopefully, will continue to be possible, speaks for the openness of this island, which is blockaded since so many years.

What remains?

Even under "normal" social conditions, our own personal circumstances in life also play a role in the decision of whether we wish to work with a patient or not: our appointments' diary, our financial situation, specific scientific interest, the experience of being able to handle some personality structures better than others. In extreme situations of a political kind the decision to work with a politically threatened patient bears much greater weight: he is a risk factor for anybody who has anything to do with him – even more so for his analyst, who can be expected to be in possession of information.

No-one, of course, can demand of analysts, by referring to our "professional ethics", that they should behave "heroically" in the face of an absolutely real and by no means only, as Jiménez formulates it, "assumed" danger. In such situations we must honestly ask ourselves whether we are able and willing to take on this risk with all its possible consequences.

The documented experiences of Chilean, Argentinian and Uruguayan colleagues, but also those of Marie Langer and her "Equipo Internacionalista", as well as my own in Nicaragua, have confirmed for me again and again that the working alliance in a strongly politicized and polarized social environment is of the utmost importance. What is sufficient in "normal circumstances" – insofar as the working conditions in Western democracies can claim to be normal : the patient's hope, based for the most part on information he has received before and confirmed by our moderate benevolent manner during the preliminary conversations, that "his" analyst will understand him, has sufficient experience and will not abuse the power of his position as a helper, this preconditioned trust cannot be brought about in extreme conditions if we do not convey to the patient, without making grandiose declarations, the feeling that we at least understand his collective life project, even if we do not share it. With this I don't mean that in the first session under these conditions the political positions of both should be stated, let alone discussed. I mean we should be conscious more of the many non-verbal signals which patients pick up, not only with their preformed propensity for transference, but which they also piece together to form a picture, coloured by transference, of the real person with whom they may – or may not – form an alliance.

Under social conditions which are atypical for our customary psychotherapeutic work it is particularly important to distinguish between acting out and action, between internal and external reality, to recognize the great importance of patients' socio-reality in their real life as well as in their intrapsychic development process. If patient and analyst experience external reality in very different ways, if the analyst does not know the values that constitute the patient's life project in society, this dialectic process between internal and external world, between past and present, will hardly succeed.

David Becker (1992), a member of the Latin American Institute for Human Rights and Mental Health/ILAS, defines his conduct in his work with the victims of the repression very clearly: "As a therapist it wasn't a question of being neutral but of taking up a position. That is, to make clear that, for me, dictatorship was dictatorship, that the father had been killed and had not been a criminal".

That work of this kind calls for techniques different from classical ones often leads in discussions within psychoanalytical associations – insofar as they take place at all – to the question of what all of this has got to do with psychoanalysis. Nicaragua taught me that I need all my psychoanalytical knowledge and all my psychoanalytical experience to do useful work as an analyst in non-classical settings.

Does this mean that left-wing psychoanalysis helps itself to the fund of classical theory without developing it further with new insights from new working fields? It seems to me that especially Latin America has provided and still provides a variety of experience which certainly belongs to the wide field of psychoanalysis. If it is difficult to integrate, this is due not only to the geographical and cultural distance from the classical centres of psychoanalysis in Europe and the USA but also to a virtually phobic behaviour on the part of these centres with regard to the way psychoanalysts deal with (external, social, political) reality.

The fact is that analysts who become committed, also with their therapeutic work, to the socio-political struggles in their countries live more dangerously than their (politically) abstinent colleagues, who only concern themselves with the internal reality of their patients. They live all the more dangerously, the more threatening external reality becomes for patient and analyst. The inadmissable mingling of analytical and political abstinence provides an illusionary way of creating an analytical shelter from which the threatening political reality remains excluded.

Even Freud succumbed to this illusion with his ban in the thirties. We should know better with our historical experience. The ban did not save the Psychoanalytical Movement in Europe from its extermination by fascism, but it did do lasting damage to the foundation of psychoanalytical identity. The basic rule for patients, to say everything that comes into their minds, even if it seems unimportant or is embarrassing – this basis of the working alliance also contains an identity-forming requirement for analysts: they too, by the same token, have to be ready and capable of hearing everything that comes into their patients' minds, even if it threatens in reality not only the person on the couch but also the one behind the couch. If this readiness is restricted, for whatever reasons, the psychoanalytical identity is endangered along with the psychoanalytical process.

So psychoanalysis of the Left may not only be a part of their Latin American identity, as Latin American intellectuals assure us, but also a contribution to a new definition of psychoanalytical identity.

References

ARREGUI DE AZPIROZ, M. R. (1991): SERSOC Uruguay. Werkblatt. *Zeitschrift für Psychoanalyse und Gesellschaftskritik* 26, 7–20.

BECKER, D. (1992): Extremtraumatisierung in der Klinik und im gesamtgesellschaftlichen Prozeß, in: Seelenmord, Wien, Mitteilungen des Instituts für Wissenschaft und Kunst 47/1.

“FEHLLEISTUNG” Drittes lateinamerikanisches Treffen über marxistische Psychologie und Psychoanalyse – 1990 La Habana, Cuba. Bericht der columbianischen Delegation. Werkblatt. *Zeitschrift für Psychoanalyse und Gesellschaftskritik* 24/25 (1990), 122–126.

FREIRE, P. (1973): Pädagogik der Unterdrückten. Bildung und Praxis der Freiheit. Reinbeck bei Hamburg: Rowohlt.

FÜCHTNER, H. (1992): Politische Folter, Psychoanalyse und gesellschaftliche Macht. Anmerkungen zu einem brasilianischen Beispiel, in: Seelenmord, Wien, Mitteilungen des Instituts für Wissenschaft und Kunst 47/1.

GALEANO, E. (1973): Die offenen Adern Lateinamerikas. Die Geschichte eines Kontinents von der Entdeckung bis zur Gegenwart. Wuppertal: Peter Hammer.

HÖFER, B. / DIETERICH, H. / MEYER, K. (1990): Das fünfhundertjährige Reich. Emanzipation und lateinamerikanische Identität: 1492–1992. Bonn: Pahl-Rugenstein Nachf.

JIMÉNEZ DE LA JARA, J. P. (1991): Einige Überlegungen zur Praxis von Psychoanalyse und Psychotherapie in Chile unter der Militärdiktatur. *Psyche* 2/91

LANGER, M. (1986): Von Wien bis Managua. Wege einer Psychoanalytikerin. Freiburg: Kore.

– (1987): Das gebratene Kind und andere Mythen. Freiburg: Kore.

– (1988): Mutterschaft und Sexus. Körper und Psyche der Frau. Freiburg: Kore.

LANGER, M. / MALDONADO, N. (1983): Nicaragua Libre. Ein Lichtblick für Lateinamerika. Spanisches Manuskript.

MADARIAGA, C. (1992a): Tortura y proceso salud – enfermedad, in: Derechos Humanos, Salud Mental, Atención Primaria: Desafío Regional. Santiago de Chile: CINTRAS / Rehabilitation Center for Torture Victims – RCT – Copenhague.

– (1992b): Verschwundene in einer ländlichen Gemeinde. Psychische und psychosoziale Leiden / Ein Behandlungsansatz auf der Grundlage einer Gruppentherapie, in: Seelenmord, Wien, Mitteilungen des Instituts für Wissenschaft und Kunst 47/1.

– (1993): CINTRAS y la Experiencia Chilena en Salud Mental y Derechos Humanos. Santiago de Chile, Reflexión 6/18, 24–28.

VOLNOVICH, J. C. / WERTHEIN, S. (Eds.) (1989): Marie Langer – mujer, psicoanálisis, marxismo. Buenos Aires: Editorial Contrapunto.

Journals

Reflexión
Derechos Humanos y Salud Mental
1992/93
CINTRAS / Centro de Investigación y Tratamiento del Stress
Eulogia Sánchez 064, Providencia, Santiago de Chile

Werkblatt
Zeitschrift für Psychoanalyse und Gesellschaftskritik
Mühlbacherweg 5, A-5020 Salzburg

Dr. Erika Danneberg, A-1140 Wien, Hackingerstraße 46/2/5/15

Further European Countries (Supplement to Volume I)

Bulgaria

by Toma Tomov and Nikola Atanassov

A major fact about psychoanalysis in Bulgaria is that World War Two with communism thereafter managed to eliminate effectively all psychoanalytic activities in the country. This paper will attempt to provide an answer to why this happened with the belief that the journey to the answer may turn out to be as revealing of the Bulgarian scene as the answer itself.

One reason why this approach to presenting psychoanalysis in Bulgaria may appear intriguing is that the rest of Eastern Europe, notably Hungary, managed to keep psychoanalytic practice (or a semblance of it) going even during the times of harshest animosity towards the intangibles of human nature. So the question is whether there is something peculiar about Bulgaria which has rendered psychoanalysis dispensible for a period of 50 years in this particular cultural space of Europe.

The Setting

The paper will first of all attempt to outline the social and cultural setting in the country during the twenties and thirties when Bulgaria was still very much in the making. Having re-emerged in 1878 on the map of Europe after 500 years of history as a province of the Ottoman empire, Bulgaria had managed by the twenties to have more than its share of the bitterness which goes with autonomy. It had lost wars to all its neighbours. It had had bad luck with its first choice of an imported crowned head and had reconciled grudgingly to its second one. It had experienced the price of accelerated economic development as the only way to catch up with rapidly advancing capitalist Europe. It had discovered the vicissitudes of political life and had wasted its best minds in political fightings.

In this process of building up an identiy a recurrent theme was the making of a choice from among the European powers of a partner to affiliate with and thus secure access to guidance and protection. For a newly fledged democracy, which had shed blood to break away from the oppressive dominance of an Asian guardian, it was only natural to be preoccupied with this concern. Russia was the chief contendent for the role. Its main advantage was a long history of a relationship with Bulgaria which had on record an indisputable Bulgarian contribution in that it had exported the cyrillic alphabet and had played a role in channelling Christianity to Russia. Asking help from Russia, therefore, did not necessarily imply recognition of being in the dependent position: it could just as readily be seen as a return for a favour done in earlier times.

Furthermore, the Russian kings had for centuries supported a steady input of Russian culture to Bulgaria mainly by securing educational opportunities for young Bulgarians at the schools of Moscow, Odessa, St. Petersburg and Kiev. Upon their return these people would typically become teachers or priests and would share their sentiment for Russia with their students. And finally it was Russia that declared the war on Turkey in 1876 and brought about the liberation of Bulgaria.

What made Russia less attractive as a partner in comparison with the Western powers at the beginning of the century was its technological backwardness. Industry was the key to development and the indisputable lead of Western Europe over Russia in that respect directed the flow of young men, blessed by their families to experience foreign ways, towards Leipzig, Vienna, Geneva and other Central European cities. Unsurprisingly, the majority of the professors who established the University of Sofia as an academic institution in those years were graduates from German schools. French came to be accepted as the politically correct language for social interaction. The role of the Alliance Francaise in this development was crucial: French stayed the most widely studied foreign language in Bulgaria for a number of years.

Geneva was generally believed to be the best place for young Bulgarians to socialize internationally for at least three reasons: French and German were equally of use there: the Swiss experience of a young, small and disciplined state was attractive as a model which Bulgaria could follow; being a centre of Russian emigration Geneva provided some of the flavour of pre-Soviet Russia which many missed in Bulgaria.

One could summarize by saying that the decades that saw psychoanalysis emerge in Europe were for Bulgaria a time of hectic growing of links to the West thus balancing old emotional ties to Russia and compensating the after-effects of oppression and the lost sense of time that goes with it. In the course of this healthy process of integration to the rest of the world Bulgaria had, among many other novel experiences, its first encounter with psychoanalysis. Two related aspects of this cultural context need to be considered in some detail, as in our view, they highlight why psychoanalysis could not acquire other than a marginal status in Bulgarian culture. These are the prevailing social attitudes during those years of early capitalism and the accompanying development of the Bulgarian language.

"Languaging" about Success

Experience of success was easily, though unidimensionally available to the generation of our grandparents: generally it took a few years of studying for a trade abroad followed by a coming back to implement a particular skill or knowledge in an immensely backward country. The dominance of outer, physical reality over inner experiential reality had been continually ascertained through a mode of living called upon by the historical imperative to catch up with the industrial world.

This attitude of mind did not predispose to the hermeneutics of suspicion, the trend in Western thinking from which psychoanalysis was inseparable. Doubts and disillusionment were set in store for the next generation of Bulgarians, that of our parents. They were the ones who would have probably challenged the simple unidimensional view of successful living, which their parents espoused, by finding that there was more to life than just conquering territories and by discovering eventually psychoanalysis. Doubtful they became but were forced to live their adult years under communism which would not allow experimenting with ideas and language. So the generation of our parents was prevented from taking issue with the values of those before them, who could justly be regarded as pioneers. Among the many missions that they failed to accomplish on the Balkans vis-a-vis Western civilization was the transfer of psychoanalysis.

Not surprisingly the incipient play with language on the part of the Bulgarian literary elite of the thirties had not spread enough by the time the war began for recursive structures to develop that could provide a vehicle for rendering the highly metaphoric constructs of psychoanalysis in Bulgarian. The representatives of the natural sciences from among the Bulgarian pre-war intelligentsia could not dream of even considering that languaging had something to contribute to facts. Years ago when one of us was still a student at the Medical School in Sofia, a professor in psychiatry, who inspired profound reverence, while polemizing with fictional psychoanalysts, uttered a shattering argument: "[…] and they could not help admitting to never actually having seen a single castration complex!" What he meant was that while schizophrenia was amply visible walking round the wards of the psychiatric hospital the case with the castration complex was far from established in that indisputable manner.

To summarize, neither the pathos nor the language of doubt had penetrated Bulgarian culture deeply enough prior to World War Two to provide a setting for psychoanalysis to grow roots. And yet it doubtlessly had a presence in this country.

Psychoanalysis in Bulgaria: Unrecorded History.

In 1921 the Psychological Society in Sofia was founded. Its members were Nikola Krestnikov (professor in psychiatry), Nikolai Popov (professor in psychiatry and neurology), Ivan Kinkel (professor in sociology), Mladen Nikolov (doctor in psychology), Spiridon Kazandjiev (associate professor in psychology), Mihail Dimitrov (assistant professor in psychology), Dimitar Bochev (lawyer). (See below for details.) There is no written record found of the deliberations of this group, nor has its official registration under the law been possible to trace (Atanassov; Kinkel; Milenkov/Popov; Stoev). This society must have stayed outside the main stream of conventional academic life.

Two of its members, N. Krestnikov and M. Nikolov, analysed patients (Kinkel, 1922). Since no written record of their method of work nor any of the protocols of their sessions with patients were preserved it is hard to know precisely what their approach was. According to Kinkel (1922) they applied "the method of Freud and Jung". Referring to a report by M. Nikolov on his work with patients Kinkel indicated that M. Nikolov used the "100 key words of Jung". This could be taken to mean that no distinction was made between free associations in the sense of Freudian analysis and the association experiment in the sense of Jungian analytical psychology. At their meetings the members of the society discussed cases and commented upon each other's work. It appears that they were practising peer supervision. There is no evidence that any of them underwent personal analysis or that the issues of transference and countertransference were dealt with. A patient who was presented with expansive delusion was also subjected to analysis (Kinkel); this at the time when Freud himself considered the analysis of "narcissistic neurosis" impossible.

This group published psychoanalytic texts in philosophical, educational and general culture journals. Their publications were seldom concerned with clinical topics; they dealt typically with broad cultural issues (e.g. religion, sex, art) for the explanation of which they recoursed to psychoanalytic concepts. For example, A. Iliev, a philosopher, after having spent two years in Vienna upon his return published extensively on psychoanalysis and art only to distance himself from psychoanalytic thinking shortly after. Nevertheless, the texts published were provocative enough to invite responses, usually of devastating criticism on the part of main-stream academic psychology and clinical psychiatry. Typical in this respect were the articles of M. Dimitrov in *Filosofska Missl (Philosophic ideas).*

From the perspective of the present day these psychoanalytic texts and their critical reviews equally strike as been written in an objectivist language and structured in line with expectations deriving from positivist science. Psychoanalytic structures are typically talked of as if they have a substantive realitiy. Languaging, and for that matter thinking in Bulgaria at that time had apparently not yet attained the status of activity intended to structure reality for a better fit with it.

A lot of effort was dedicated by the group to disseminating psychoanalytic ideas by way of public lectures, popular writings and presentations. B. Isaev himself gave over 400 talks on various psychoanalytic topics to the general public. Active in this vein were also I. Kinkel, M. Nikolov and L. Roussev. M. Nikolov translated *The Unconscious* and *On Psychoanalysis: Live Lectures* (published in Bulgarian in 1927) and A. Andreev translated *The Introductory Lectures on Psychoanalysis* (published 1947) and the biographical essay *Sigmund Freud* by Stefan Zweig.

Ivan Kinkel's *On the Psychological Basis and Origins of Religion* was published in 1922 in German in *Imago* on the suggestion of Freud, to which attests a letter addressed to Kinkel by Otto Rank (Kinkel). A critical review of this paper was published the next year by von Hern.

Not all members of the group contributed psychoanalytic writings. S. Kazandjiev, for example, published within the experimental tradition of Wilhelm Wundt. N. Krestnikov (1929) developed a therapeutic technique of his own which he called "reproduction" and which was akin to hypnosis in spite of his claims that he was strongly influenced by psychoanalysis.

It is not known how long the Psychological Society in Sofia stayed functional. By the early thirties, it is reported (Stoev; Andreev), a psychoanalytic group of considerably innovated membership became active again (see below for details). Once again the evidence is anecdotal and inferred from publications in learned and popular journals.

Psychological Society in Sofia, 1921: Membership List

Dimitar Bochev, lawyer.
Ivan Kinkel, born 1883, graduate of social science and philosophy in Leipzig and Zurich, member of the International Psychoanalytical Association, professor at the Faculty of Law, University of Sofia.

Mihail Dimitrov, assistant-professor in psychology at the University of Sofia.
Spiridon Kazandjiev, born 1882, graduate of psychology in Leipzig, doctoral degree from Zurich on the psychology of Wilhelm Wundt, associate-professor in psychology at the University of Sofia.
Nikola Krestnikov, born 1880, graduate of medicine in 1904, specializes with Bechterev in St. Peterburg and Dejerine in Paris, a founding professor of the medical school in Sofia.
Mladen Nikolov, born 1881, graduate of philosophy, doctoral degree in psychology from the University of Berlin, private psychoanalytic practice in Sofia.
Nikolai Popov, professor in psychiatry and neurology.

The Bulgarian Psychoanalytic Group of the 30s

Andrey Andreev, psychiatrist.
Buko Issaev, graduate of law in Sofia and administration in Vienna, lawyer.
Ivan Kinkel (see Psychological Society in Sofia/92).
Ilia Lingorsky, psychiatrist.
Mladen Nikolov (see Psychological Society in Sofia/92).
Lyuben Roussev, psychiatrist.
Lyubomir Roussev, born 1902, studies in Vienna, graduate of philosophy and education in Sofia, specializes in Berlin, school-teacher.
Naiden Sheytanov, born 1980, graduate of philosophy, history and philology in Leipzig and Prague, school-teacher.
R. Tsalomonov, psychiatrist.

Psychoanalysis in Present-Day Bulgaria

Confused ideas about psychoanalysis as a practice different from psychotherapy and psychiatry plague the mental health scene in Bulgaria today. Problems of professional identity, training, accreditation, standards and the like are enormous, which should not come as a surprise given the fact that psychotherapy and psychoanalysis have never had any academic or professional standing in this country. Individuals who have strayed from the prescribed behaviour for state employees in the socialist health service and have aspired to mature professionalism as psychotherapists have often chosen to flee the country in the past.

Psychoanalysts of Bulgarian origin with established practices abroad (typically George Kamen from the USA and Nikolay Kolev from Sweden) may consider coming back to Bulgaria after the political change only to discover that missing contextual structures render psychoanalytic work impossible.

Schools of psychotherapy such as psychodrama, family therapy and group therapy and group relations have managed to gain a footing in Bulgaria largely since 1986 as a result of a consistent effort on the part of the Neuroscience and Behaviour Research Programme and a group of young professionals who lobbied to attract international support. Response came from various centres of good international standing, notably the Institute of Anthropos in Athens, The University of Lundt (Sweden), The Psychodrama Academy, Stockholm (Sweden), Psychodrama, Berne (Switzerland), The Grubb Institute, London, and others.

The strategies deployed in virtually all of these collaborative projects have in common the serious consideration given to the cultural, organizational, structural and various other aspects of the Bulgarian context. This enabled ingenious flexibility and innovation in the transfer of technologies.

It is against this background that the absence of psychoanalysis on the Bulgarian mental health scene became conspicuous. Action was taken in 1992 by a group of six founding members who came to establish officially the Bulgarian Psychoanalytical Society. None of the founding members has had personal analysis. The group developed contacts with the International Psychoanalytical Association, with the Centre for Psychoanalytic studies at the University of Kent, UK, and with the Johann-Wolfgang-Goethe University, Frankfurt am Main, Germany, Activities aimed at meeting the needs for information, for relevant literature and for training and education of the members of this group were undertaken with the kind support of David Reason and Robert Young from the University of Kent, Peter Kutter from the Goethe University, who presented lectures on psychoanalysis in 1990, and from others.

The collaboration with the Centre for Psychoanalytic Studies at the University of Kent evolved into an academic programme which the recently founded (1992) New Bulgarian University in Sofia endorsed as one of its pioneering projects in the field of human development. It is the mission of this University to invest in individual growth and development by adopting teaching methods which are experientially based and by evolving an academic environment which encourages autonomy and self-exploration.

History and experience of previous generations invite careful consideration as to which will prove the winning strategy for bringing psychoanalysis to Bulgaria. It certainly is an ambitious project to attempt to found a new tradition in an ancient culture replete with traditions, few of them friendly to aliens.

A very clear message from prior attempts of psychoanalysis to gain footing in Bulgaria is, that, given the unpopularity of introspection in the Balkans, psychoanalytic ideas stand little chance to thrive in these lands if divorced from the method of psychoanalysis. This clearly speaks in support of a strategy that would invest in training Bulgarians as analysts, in contrast to a far less demanding exercise of only providing for psychoanalytic studies in these lands.

Psychodrama, family therapy, group therapy and the like, unreconciling as psychoanalysis may be to unorthodoxies, do blaze a trail in the case of Bulgaria and do contribute to a context receptive to psychoanalysis. Recognizing this invites a measure of flexibility on the part of the international psychoanalytic community, when considering the case of Bulgaria and psychoanalysis.

Bulgarian Psychoanalytic Society, 1992: List of Founding Members

Nicola Atanassov, clinical psychologist, Institute of Psychology, Bulgarian Academy of Sciences, Sofia, (secretary).

Dimitar Dochev, philologist, New Bulgarian University.

Emil Georgiev, historian, Centre for the Study of Democracy.

Nadia Polnareva, child psychiatrist, Department of Psychiatry, Higher Medical Institute, Sofia.

Toma Tomov, psychiatrist, Department of Psychiatry, Higher Medical Institute, Sofia.

Lyubomir Zhivkov, psychiatrist, medical director, City Psychiatric Dispensary, Sofia, (chairman).

References

ATANASSOV, N. (1992): The psychoanalytic movement in Bulgaria between the world wars (unpublished manuscript).

KINKEL, I. (1922): Zur Frage der psychologischen Grundlagen und des Ursprungs der Religion. *Imago* 8, 1, 23–45, 197–241.

KRESTNIKOV, N. (1929): Die heilende Wirkung künstlich hervorgerufener Reproduktionen von pathogenen affektiven Erlebnissen. *Arch. Psych. und Nervenkrankheiten* 88, 3, 369–410.

MILENKOV, K. / CH. POPOV (Eds.) (1983): Founders of Bulgarian psychiatry, Sofia: Medizina i Fizkultura (in Bulgarian).

STOEV, S. (1969): Freudian psychology and how it was overcome in Bulgaria, Sofia: BAN.

Institutions

Bulgaria Psychoanalytic Society
see list of founding members above!

Dr. Toma Tomov, Associate Professor; WHO Collaborating Centre for Research and Training in Mental Health 15, Dim. Nestorov St.; Sofia 1431
Nikola Atanassov, Mladost 1, Block 131a, Sofia 1750

Croatia

by Eduard Klain

Introduction

When writing about the historical development of psychoanalysis in some country or some region one should, in order to avoid any misunderstanding, define what one means by psychoanalysis and psychoanalyst. This may seem unnecessary for many people will say that it is well known what psychoanalysis is and who a psychoanalyst is. But history has proved that different people have quite different associations to the words psychoanalysis and psychoanalyst. It is often considered that a psychoanalyst is a person who likes psychoanalysis, someone who reads and writes about it, or that psychoanalysis is any psychotherapy with elements of depth psychology. Freud warned that such an opinion was dangerous for psychoanalysis, stating once that the most dangerous enemies were the inner enemies. Therefore I want to emphasize at the beginning that I am going to write about the development of psychoanalysis in Croatia, psychoanalysis primarily as a therapy of free associations as founded by Freud, and I shall also mention the use of psychoanalysis. For me, as for most after all, a psychoanalyst is an adequately trained expert applying psychoanalysis in treating the patients. Besides psychoanalytical therapy and psychoanalytical training, I shall deal with the wider use of psychoanalysis in Croatia, first of all its influence on psychotherapeutic theory and practice and the practice in psychiatry. In our milieu psychoanalysis largely influenced both psychotherapeutic education and education of the medical students and postgraduate students in various psychiatric branches. In our country psychoanalysis has developed, which is seldom found in the world, in institutions, and it has also influenced our culture. We as analysts have had a need to popularize psychoanalysis among intellectuals and the wider public.

The Historical Development or Psychoanalysis in Croatia

a) The Period before World War Two

The development of psychoanalysis in Croatia is linked first of all with one name, and for a long period of time only with one name. It was Dr. Stjepan Betlheim, who was born in Zagreb in 1898 in a Jewish family of textile merchants. He finished his medical study and specialization in neuropsychiatry in Vienna, Berlin and Paris, as was usual then. He became familiar with psychoanalysis in Vienna, and there he was in training. He had his first training analysis with Paul Schilder for a year, then with Sandor Radó through 18 months. He had supervision with Karen Horney in Berlin and with Helen Deutsch in Vienna. In 1928 he became a member of the Viennese psychoanalytical society, and this membership lasted until World War Two. Between 1928 and 1935 he worked as a neuropsychiatrist in a Zagreb hospital, and from 1935 to 1941 he worked in the station for Mental Hygiene. Through all this period till the beginning of World War Two he had psychoanalytic patients in private practice. One of his patients became later a psychoanalyst in Great Britain, and many years later one of his patients from that period came to me to analysis. From 1938 to 1941 he had Lizzi Rosenberger, Ph. D., in training analysis, which was interrupted by the war. Today she is a member of the Israeli Psychoanalytic Association in Tel Aviv. In this period Dr. Betlheim wrote about psychoanalysis and from his Viennese period before 1928 comes his known paper on parapraxes in Korsakoff's psychosis written by him and H. Hartmann and quoted by Freud in his *Interpretation of Dreams*. Quite often he gave lectures about Freud and psychoanalysis in the adult education centres, and he also conducted a study group on psychoanalysis with a few progressive intellectuals in Zagreb. The war interrupted Dr. Betlheim's work and he fled to the partisans and stayed with them until the end of the war in 1945.

b) The Period after World War Two

After the second world war Croatia, largely destroyed during the war, became a part of the communist Yugoslavia. Conditions for psychoanalysis were practically non-existent. There were many psychiatric patients and very few psychiatrists. Psychoanalytical tradition was poor, and the communist regime was very suspicious of psychoanalysis, regarding it as a bourgeois product which might be dangerous for the working class. Immediately after the war we find Dr. Betlheim as a military doctor in the Psychiatric Hospital Kovin near Belgrade, treating, with a group of psychiatrists, partisans suffering from posttraumatic stress disturbance which then manifested itself in convulsive attacks. Dr. Betlheim and Dr. Hugo Klajn, also a psychoanalyst, wrote together about that treatment and research. An important year for the development of psychoanalysis in Croatia is 1948, when Professor Betlheim came to the Neurologic and Psychiatric Clinic of the Medical School in Zagreb as an assistant in his fiftieth year. Full of zeal and enthusiasm exceptional for his age, he gathered a group of young and curious psychiatrists to whom he showed psychodynamics of psychotic patients and with whom he had long conversations about psychoanalysis. That was the core of the future psychotherapeutic department. At the same time Betlheim continued to study Korsakoff's psychosis at the female psychiatric department, of which he was the head, and wrote an important paper about neurotic symptoms in psychotic patients. We would stop with historical description in the year 1953, when the first psychotherapeutic department at a clinic in former Yugoslavia was founded. One more thing should be noted: in 1952 Dr. Betlheim became a direct member of the IPA, as is evident from Heinz Hartmann's letters.

Psychotherapeutic Department of the Neurological and Psychiatric Clinic of the Medical School in Zagreb

In 1953 Dr. Betlheim founded the outpatient department for psychotherapeutic treatment of neuroses within the Neurological and Psychiatric Clinic, in the basement of the hospital, occupying a few gloomy rooms in a very busy corridor. But the spirit and enthusiasm of Dr. Betlheim and his collaborators made them do great psychotherapeutic work in such inadequate conditions.

a) Psychoanalytic Treatment

After the war Dr. Betlheim had no private practice because it was not allowed by the law. He treated the patients psychoanalytically at the Psychotherapeutic Department, as did his closest associates, who were also trained in psychoanalysis by him. Due to a great number of patients and many duties neither Dr. Betlheim nor his closest collaborators could devote much time to psychoanalytic treatment of their patients, so most of the patients were treated by psychoanalytically oriented psychotherapy. Two things should be emphasized here. First, the regime, although it neither favoured nor appreciated psychoanalysis, made us no difficulties in treating the patients, long-lasting analyses were even paid by the social insurance. I remember, for instance, that I had a female patient in analysis over eight years, three to four times a week, and our social insurance regularly settled the accounts. The other problem, or a characteristic, of psychoanalysis in an institution, concerns the poor motivation of the patients who do not pay themselves and who often come to treatment during their working hours. That has remained an unsolved problem which we sometimes analyze together with our patients.

b) Psychoanalytic Training

In a certain way our psychoanalytic education started even before 1953 when Dr. Betlheim talked about psychoanalysis to his collaborators and showed them with psychotic patients phenomena of regression etc. Systematic theoretical education of his closest associates began at the end of the 1950s, when they started to present and study Freud's cases, informed on topics from psychoanalysis, and once a week, in a kind of group supervision, presented the patients treated with analytical psychotherapy. In the late 1950s and in the 1960s Professor Betlheim decided to begin training analyses with his closest associates. First he had in training analysis Dr. Duška Blažević (deceased), Dr. Neda Bučan (retired), Dr. Eugenija Cividini-Stranić (retired) and Dr. Eduard Klain. It is needless to say that these analyses were carried out with great difficulties due to the transference contaminated by the external situation. Of some help was the fact that Professor Betlheim was much older than any of us, so some distance existed which reduced our real difficulties in analysis.

With the death of Professor Betlheim in 1970 a vacuum appeared in carrying out training analyses. Those of us who had finished analysis with him had no courage to continue this "incestuous" situation by doing training analyses in such a contaminated atmosphere, because we were all working in the same institution. Only professor Blažević, as the oldest among us, had two colleagues in analysis: Dr. Milica Vlatković (retired) and Dr. Staniša Nikolić, who continued his analysis in Paris. In the last decade Dr. Nikolić and I have remained as the only two analyzands from the first group. Dr. Nikolić was analyzed in Paris and returned to work in our institution. Then we decided, in spite of all the problems, to start with training analyses and constituted a small commission for psychoanalytic training. So, after four years, we got two more colleagues, analyzed by the two of us: Dr. Dragan Josić (now in private practice) and Dr. Marija Öiček, working with us in the same institution. On finishing their analyses we started supervision with them. At the present moment we have three more candidates in training analysis. Since 1992 the four of us – Dr. Nikolić, Dr. Öiček, Dr. Josić and I – have supervisions in Italy within the Italian Psychoanalytical Association, under the patronage of the IPA, which take place every second week. Thus we realize a long ago started collaboration with the IPA and probably acquire membership in that organization.

During the last two decades a cartain number of colleagues went abroad to psychoanalytic training, but regretfully no one has returned yet. However, we hope that with the independence of Croatia and the changed social situation in our country conditions will be created for the development of psychoanalysis in private practice, which might make our colleagues come back. The problem just mentioned certainly has influenced people's motivation for analytic training, which is long-lasting and hard. Not only were the conditions for psychoanalytic private practice non-existent, but the training in psychoanalysis offered an expert no status within his profession.

c) *The Application of Psychoanalysis in Psychotherapy*

Since the beginning of the work of the Psychotherapeutic Department Professor Betlheim and his closest collaborators have paid much attention to the psychotherapeutic treatment of their patients. All psychotherapeutic methods and techniques were inspired by psychoanalysis and all the efforts of the doctors were centered onto as effective as possible use of psychoanalytic principles in psychotherapy. Betlheim gave significant contributions to therapy of important patients by means of hypnosis and in the application of short term psychotherapy. For some period of time he practised group psychoanalytic therapy and produced quite a number of papers on that subject.

Over the decades of its work the small psychotherapeutic ward developed into a large Clinic for Psychological Medicine where various psychotherapeutic techniques were developed. Today the most important are group analysis (Foulkes' model), analytic psychodrama (Parisian model) and analytic family and marital psychotherapy. Besides these methods and techniques, individual analytic psychotherapy is permanently present.

d) *The Application of Psychoanalysis in Psychotherapeutic Training*

From the very beginning psychotherapeutic training in our institution has followed the principles of psychoanalytic education. It consisted of theoretical education, which was largely psychoanalysis, supervisions and group analytic training. Unable to do training analyzes, we offered group analytic training, which practically all the collaborators in the institution underwent, and which took about three years, or 200 hours. Basic education in our institution is analytical psychotherapy, which means three years of supervision with one supervisor and two years with another supervisor, one hour a week, and theoretical education. Collaborators decide themselves which of the above mentioned methods they will adopt. Group analysis developed most probably because of the connections with the Institute of Group Analysis in London, so we founded also the Zagreb Institute of Group Analysis.

An exceptional situation is that the Clinic for Psychological Medicine is a part of the Medical School and that we conduct the subject for medical students called medical psychology. We have also had opportunities to organize postgraduate studies for psychiatrists and other professionals, which all enabled us to introduce psychoanalysis to a large number of people. Third year medical students attend medical psychology courses, which are psychoanalytically oriented, and now they have several optional courses which are also psychoanalytically oriented. We organize two psychotherapeutic postgraduate courses: Psychotherapy and Child psychiatry. Attendants of several other postgraduate courses also attend courses in psychoanalytic psychotherapy.

e) Professional and Scientific Work in the Field of Psychoanalysis

After the war Professor Betlheim, because of his many duties and hard work on psychotherapy, wrote mostly about the use of psychoanalysis in psychotherapy. His associates also wrote much about psychoanalytic psychotherapy or the application of psychoanalytic knowledge in psychotherapy. On that basis the scientific research projects were also done. From time to time we described some problems from psychoanalytic therapies and published papers from seminars which were psychoanalytical. Recently most of the works from our institution deal with group analysis, analytic psychodrama, and family and marital analytically oriented therapies.

Development of the Psychoanalytic Idea in Croatia

a) The Impact of Different Schools in and out of Psychoanalysis

We also followed the development of the psychoanalytic idea and contributions of many outstanding psychoanalysts like Hartmann or Anna Freud or Melanie Klein or Kohut and Kernberg. But in our efforts to apply some of their knowledge in our analyses we remained with the principles of psychoanalysis, that is, the original theory of Freud. At the same time different psychotherapeutic orientations developed in Croatia that had not much in common with psychoanalysis, such as behavior therapy, gestalt therapy, transactional analysis, cognitive psychotherapies etc. People not basically trained in the psychoanalytic approach necessarily chose those other therapies and techniques, among other things also because of their shorter and easier training.

b) Psychoanalysis in Culture

Ever larger number of philosophers, sociologists and other humanistically educated experts in Croatia are interested in psychoanalysis. They write about psychoanalysis, talk about it, call foreign experts to give lectures, which all contributes to creating a favourable climate for psychoanalysis and facilitates penetration of psychoanalysis into cultural circles of Croatia.

c) The Popularization of Psychoanalysis

The first translations of Freud's works and some papers on psychoanalysis as well as lectures given by prof. Betlheim appeared before World War Two. After the war, and especially in the last decades, a large number of Freud's works and works of other psychoanalytic authors have been translated, provoking the interest of a wide reading public that exhibits hunger for psychoanalytic literature. Therefore an important initiative is the organizing of the Society for the promotion and popularization of psychoanalysis, founded in our clinic, which will surely give very good results in the development of the psychoanalytic idea.

When I write about the path we have followed I always ask myself: "Could we have done more for psychoanalysis in these last forty years?" Yes, certainly. But in the given circumstances and with the professionals who, with great enthusiasm and love, promoted psychoanalysis and analytical psychotherapy, I think we have done a lot. However, that remains for the future generation to judge, who will, I do believe, in free Croatia do more for psychoanalysis.

Appendix: Psychoanalysis at the Time of the War

The war is a direct obstacle to carrying out psychoanalysis and psychoanalytic therapy because of real, interpersonal and intrapsychic reasons. In our experiences some patients just stopped coming to psychotherapy because they were preoccupied with threats and fear because of the war events, i. e. shells and bombs. Some patients came regularly to thearapy in spite of air raids and snipers. Some therapists stopped doing psychotherapies during the war, others negated completely the real situation and tried to continue with psychotherapy in the same way as before the war. There were external reasons that prevented the patients from coming to psychotherapy (occupied regions, break of train or bus communication, mobilization to the army, displacement from their homes etc.). Some developed projections onto either the therapist or national groups, which also prevented them from coming to psychotherapy. There were patients who did not accept reality and came to therapy regularly. In therapy the patients, according to their personality, pathology and therapeutic phase, more or less introduced the war in the sessions.

Therapists were either passive, not doing psychotherapy nor anything else, or, negating and denying completely the real situation, continued to work as though nothing was happening. It can be said that a large number of therapists were oriented to helping the endangered groups of the population and offered to help with all their knowledge and experience. During the war we could observe psychoanalytically trained psychotherapists make corner stones of a network of mental health protection in war within the Mental Health Department of the Medical Corps Headquarters of the Republic of Croatia. Analytically oriented psychotherapists, and especially group psychotherapists, organized adequate protection of the endangered population (displaced persons, the wounded – invalids, released prisoners of war, family members of those killed or missing in the war etc.) offering their help as much as they could. They started immediately to educatc all interested experts, because the number of educated psychotherapists in relation to the number of people in trouble was extremely small. Analytically trained therapists have besides emphatic capacity, also the capacity to contain, the ability to endure frustration. In our war that meant that our psychotherapists tolerated underestimation and not being understood because the state thought that in the situation when there were no weapons, clothes, shoes, food, psychological help was not necessary. Our psychotherapists won their place and helped a lot of people who needed help during the war.

When the war destruction decreased and the situation began to calm down we continued and broadened the collaboration with the Societta Psicoanalitica Italiana and the Société Psychanalytique de Paris. We want our young experts to be lege artis trained abroad. That plan began to be realized in Italy, and soon, we hope, it will be realized in France,, too. French and Italian psychoanalysts come regularly to Zagreb, give lectures and conduct seminars and supervisions of analytic psychotherapies with our colleagues. That collaboration has proved to be very useful and stimulating and I am sure that it will continue and expand.

References

BETLHEIM, S. / H. HARTMANN (1924): On Parapraxes in the Korsakoff Psychosis. In: Rapaport, D. (ed.) (1951): Organization and Pathology of Thought. New York: Columbia Univ. Press.

BLAŽEVIĆ, D. (1971): Komemoracija profesoru doktoru Stjepanu Betheimo [To commemorate Stjepan Betlheim, M. D.]. *Psihoterapija* 1, 4.

KLAIN, E. (1976): The Analysis of Supervision Technique and Supervision process. Habilitation. Zagreb.

– (1977) Uspomene profesora doktora Huga Klajna na njegove prve kontakte sa psihoanalizom [Dr. Hugo Klajn's memories of his early contacts with psychoanalysis.] *Psihologija* 10, 217.

KLAIN E. / LJ. MORO (1987): The Application of Psychoanalytical Model in Training Psychiatrists (historical perspectives). In: A. M. Acerboni (ed.): La cultura psicoanalitica (Atti del convegno, Trieste). Pordenone: Studio Tesi.

OLVIDINI, E. / E. KLAIN (1970): Prof. Dr. Stjepan Betlheim. *Neuropsihijatrija* 18, 119.

Journals

Psihoterapija
since 1971; Ed.: Prof.Dr. M. Kulenovic
(summaries in English)
c/o Institute of Group Analysis

Institutions

Zagreb Institute of Group Analysis
c/o Klinika za psihološku medicinu
(Clinic for Psychological Medicine)
Kišpatičeva 12, 41000 Zagreb

Prof. Eduard Klain, M. D., Institute of Group Analysis, Kišpatičeva 12, 41000 Zagreb

France 1965–1994

by Michelle Moreau-Ricaud

I. The Situation of Psychoanalysis in France in 1965

Alain de Mijolla's account of the history of psychoanalysis in France, in Volume I of the present work, ended with the foundation of the "École Freudienne" (Freudian School) in 1964, although he layed down a ground plan as far forward as 1981, the year of Lacan's death. After 1981, adds Mijolla, "the process of establishing psychoanalysis in France enters a very different phase from that which preceded it".

It will be recalled that, at the time in question, three psychoanalytic societies shared responsibility for the analytic cures and also for training psychoanalysts: the "Société Psychanalytique de Paris" (1926), the "Association Psychanalytique de France" (1964) – both affiliated to the International Psychoanalytical Association – and the "École Freudienne" (1964). A fourth was soon to be created as the result of a schism within the Lacanian camp: the "Quatrième Groupe" (Fourth Group, 1969).

The psychoanalytic scene subsequently regained something of its old stability, but several internal modifications were to occur within each of the four groups. The analytic world was shaken by further upheavals in the wake of the events at the École Freudienne, namely Lacan's abolition of his own school on 6 January 1980, and the creation of the "École de la Cause Freudienne" (ECF). Lacan's death changed the situation still further. An implosion led to the formation of numerous small groups. About twenty were formed:

Le cercle Freudien (1982), Association Freudienne Internationale (1982), Centre de Formation et de Recherche Psychanalytiques (CFRP, 1982), Les Cartels Constituants de l'Analyse Freudienne (CCAF), Association des Ateliers de Psychanalyse, La Convention Psychanalytique (1983), Le Cout Freudienne (1983), École Lacanienne de Psychanalyse, Séminaires Psychanalytiques de Paris (1986), Groupe du trait du cas, Psychanalyse actuelle (1986), Fondation Européenne pour la Psychanalyse, L'Interprétation Psychanalytique, etc. Others are still forming. And we are witnessing another phenomenon: migration from one group to another. At the time of writing (1992), a new group has just been created under the impetus of Claude Conté and Claude Dumézil, both products of the Cartels Constituants.

During the 1980s, some of the main lines of development began to emerge:

- In 1981 an association, the "Inter-associatif" – cutting across institutional lines, and rejecting the legitimacy of the Lacanian transmission – was formed at the suggestion of Jacques Hassoun and others, to act as an umbrella organization for several Lacanian groups created at different times after the breakup of the École Freudienne;
- an "Association Internationale d'Histoire de la Psychanalyse", founded by A. de Mijolla in 1986, aimed to provide a haven, not just for analysts of every persuasion, but also for historians, men and women of letters, and others, in which they could work freely without debarment on the history of Freudian discoveries, and seek to infuse their corporate identity with a critical spirit towards Freudian theories and concepts, as well as towards the historical dimension of psychoanalysis, a dimension which many were unwilling even to consider;
- in 1989, initiated by Serge Leclaire, Lucien Israël and Jacques Sedat, the "Association pour une Instance des Psychanalystes" APUI, "Association for a psychoanalytic authority"), was formed, with the aim of establishing an interface between psychoanalytic institutions and individual analysts on the one hand, and the State on the other, in order to create the necessary forum for psychoanalytic debate, a field of discussion nowadays far too often contaminated by socio-medical ideals.

These organizations will need to prove their mettle by displaying both gravity and durability.

II. The Formation of the Quatrième Groupe. Organisation Psychanalytique de Langue Française

The Quatrième Groupe came into existence on 17 March 1969, two months after the École Freudienne's Annual Conference. Its founders, Piera Aulagnier, François Perrier and Jean-Paul Valabrega, resigned from the School to emphasize their radical opposition to Lacan on the subject of psychoanalytic training.

Lacan, in his Proposal of 9 October 1967 (published in the journal "Scilicet"), sought to impose a system of psychoanalytic training upon the École Freudienne which would control the right to use the title of "psychoanalyst". Ordinary analysts "need only authorize themselves, on their own initiative, to practise psychoanalysis" in order to acquire such a right. In contrast, the candidate who wished to be appointed an "Analyste Membre de l'École" (AME, Analyst Member of the School, roughly equivalent to a full member and training analyst in other organizations) had to furnish evidence of having progressed from being a mere analyser to being an analyst proper in front of two so-called "passeurs", who then provided an assessment of the candidate before an approval committee ("jury d'agrément"), which made the final decision. This was the procedure known as "la passe".

A year later, Lacan, taking no heed of the severe criticisms he had engendered (cf. "Documents Analytica Ornicar?", vol. 7, 1978), attempted a takeover by force, relying on the most ardent supporters among his pupils to secure the adoption of la passe at the Annual General Meeting of the École Freudienne, held at the Hôtel Lutétia, Paris, on 26 January 1969. Some of the School's analysts (though, admittedly, not very many of them) opposed the measure, denounced the procedures used, and handed in their resignations. Among the members to resign were Piera Aulagnier, François Perrier and Jean-Paul Valabrega, three analysts who had already jointly published (with J. Clavreul and G. Rosolato) "Le désir et la perversion" (Le Seuil, 1967), who were linked by bonds of mutual esteem and friendship, and who held similar convictions on the subject of psychoanalytic training, as well as identical critical opinions regarding the positions of the IPA and Lacan on "didactic" analysis. In the two months following their resignations, they held numerous working meetings. Several analysts undergoing training joined them. Faced with the impossibility of allying with any of the societies affiliated to the IPA – the standards of training of which they had, several years before, unsuccessfully criticized from within – they decided to create a new psychoanalytic organization. Their statutes were lodged on 17 March 1969 under the name "Quatrième Groupe. Organisation Psychanalytique de Langue Française" (Fourth Group. French-language Psychoanalytic Organization). The group's charter document (the so-called "Cahier Bleu"), written jointly, and published in the first issue of *Topique* (1969), explains their basic principles: separation of the analytical and institutional powers in the transmission of psychoanalysis, the abolition of the exercise of any power by the analyst over his candidates, the principle of "plurireferentiality" (see below), and the maintenance of a spirit of openness to other societies and internal criticism, etc.

Though a true "founders' charter", the "Cahier Bleu" was not seen as a final draft. Polished, amended, recast and voted on at some Annual General Meetings, it led to the publication of two much more recent documents, "Formation et habilitation" (1983) and "Principes et modalités de fonctionnement" (1985), published in *Topique* 32 and *Topique* 38 respectively.

The founders eliminated potential hierarchical differences between members by creating just one membership category, that of "Member of the Quatrième Groupe" (initially called "cotisant": subscriber), members of which would be co-opted in accordance with the accreditation procedure. An unaccredited analyst would merely have the status of "participant" (initially called "contribuant": contributor).

How exactly does one become a Member of the Quatrième Groupe? Some of them having belonged to the three older institutions, the founders of the Quatrième Groupe were well aware of the danger of institutionalization. To them, innovation was vital if psychoanalytic training was not to lose its special character.

Though they pointedly renounced the idea of a training institute, this did not prevent them from reaffirming the necessary preconditions for psychoanalytic training. The document "Formation et habilitation" (*Topique* 32, p. 135-6) emphasizes the need for "a broad and deep personal culture", for "specialized culture and experience, already acquired in one or several disciplines, both aesthetic and scientific", as well as clinical experience in psychopathology.

The idea of a course of study (cursus), which implied a standardized programme of training, was abolished and replaced by a "process". It is up to the trainee analysts themselves to assume responsibility for their own training, and to find, either within the Quatrième Groupe or elsewhere (the principle of "plurireferentiality"), the means of bringing it to a satisfactory conclusion.

If "the personal analytical experience is fundamental", the choice of his/her analyst remains "the subject's own private concern". The personal analysis is kept secret, and the analyst is "considered to stand apart from all the various deliberations which arise in the course of, or which help to conclude", the training ("Cahier Bleu"). This analysis may become "didactic" in the deferred action, but in no way must "the institution either anticipate or confirm the didactic nature of an analysis" (*Topique* 32, p. 137). In addition, it is "up to the subject, in his analysis, to examine the determinations and overdeterminations of his project of becoming analyst, and it is up to the analyst to work to give their accurate interpretation" ("Formation et Habilitation", *Topique* 32, p. 137).

All the group's scientific events (lectures, seminars, conferences, etc.) are open to analysts undergoing training. There they can deepen their knowledge of Freudian theory and technique, as well as the later ramifications of psychoanalysis. They may, however, also participate in the theoretic-technical study groups at whatever moment in their training they may find opportune. They may, on demand, ask to see one of the secretaries or even an analyst from the Group, to discuss the opportunities presented by one or other course of action, since, in the absence of the Training Commission, any analyst from the Quatrième Groupe, representing his own institution, has an individual responsibility regarding the decisions which he makes in respect of his patients and those of his young colleagues who are undergoing training.

Another innovation, relating to analytic supervision was "analyse quatrième" ("the fourth analysis"). The term "control", as well as its actual practice, was considered unsatisfactory. If, around 1920, the control which Eitingon had established in his Policlinic in Berlin had once helped many analysts by providing them with a "rapid and effective training" which enabled them to face the increased demand for treatment, it had also quickly become a form of indoctrination of the controlled by the controller. The power of the controller over the controlled was reducing the trainee analysts' responsibility towards their patients. The challenge was to invest this approach, which Valabrega denounced as more alienating than formative (Valabrega, 1979), with an analytical, formative dimension, while maintaining the continuity of the process.

It is a theory of supervision which Valabrega is proposing. "According to our understanding of the concept of control, there is but one aim, which is constantly to reinsert this dimension of Otherness into the circuit of the analytic process, from which it has a repeated tendency to escape" (Valabrega, 1979). In this "ternary" control situation, in which the challenge is to identify the nature of the analytic playing taking place between the patient (1), his analyst (2), and the controller analyst (3), what is lacking is what has traditionally served as the first (and neglected) point of reference – the analyst of the analyst (4). The control, conceived as some place where one can resume analytic work on oneself, and the attempt to capture the residue of the transference onto the first analyst, can both have a very formative influence. It becomes an experience of which the specific character is that it may provide an opportunity to act as "an intermediary, or a mediation between analysis of oneself and analysis of the Other" (Valabrega, 1979).

Additionally, the interpretations given to their patient can be discussed by the two analysts concerned, as colleagues, within the framework of an elaborative dialogue.

As for the "interanalytic sessions", we have seen that the supervision may rightly be considered a first session between analysts. As for the interanalytic session proper, this would be organized on the initiative of any analyst who wishes to "propose for elaborative dialogue certain points of difficulty – or even risky – to do with his practice, his technique, or his involvement in the transference or countertransference, as well as matters relating to the theoretical elaboration which he has worked out, or which may be causing him problems" ("Formation et habilitation", p. 146). But these sessions may be also requested with a view to accreditation. Several sessions with different analysts may be organized at the request and on the initiative of the accreditation candidate. The analysts concerned take the place of the "jury", but in this case the candidate chooses the analysts (two or three) with whom he is to work. We shall note that interanalytic sessions can also take place between full members/training analysts. In such circumstances, it constitutes a way of enabling the training process to be resumed: this is the analyst's "continuing education".

At least two "fourth analyses" are now required, including one with an analyst from the Quatrième Groupe, and several analytic sessions. The accreditation session is only the final stage of the process. It should not be seen as a "rite of passage", a ritual on the anthropological model, nor a "special admission ceremony" (cf. Freud to Pfister, 1909), but as a process which "aims to find out a) whether the candidate has acquired sufficient competence and experience in the practice of analysis, and b) whether he adheres to the fundamental principles of the Quatrième Groupe with respect to the professional code of ethics and moral standards which, in our opinion, the practice of analysis demands" ("Principes et modalités de fonctionnement", *Topique* 38).

An analyst's accreditation is thus based solely on analytic criteria.

At the institutional level, another innovation was incorporated into the institution's statutes to counteract the normal ageing processes undergone by any institution: this was the so-called "Assemblée Reinstituante" ("re-instituting assembly").

"[...] the Quatrième Groupe decided – from its foundation – to submit itself to a rigorous periodical critical examination of its own functioning – at one and the same time internally and in a wider field of application – with respect to the evolution of psychoanalysis as practice, theory and application, to its wider, external institutions, and to its 'vernacular' social powers.

This is – in a revised and redefined form – the aim of our Reinstituting Sessions.

Members and 'participants' are both invited to attend these sessions. At these meetings, criticisms and proposals are collated and examined by the Management Committee and the Assembly, who then decide which modifications and innovations are the best." ("Principes et modalités de fonctionnement", *Topique* 38, p. 165).

In 1992, the Quatrième Groupe numbered forty members and some 400 "participants".

The present Management Committee (le "Bureau") is composed of: P. Dubuisson (President), J. P. Moreigne (Vice-President), N. Zaltzman

(Analytical Secretary), J. Filloux and M. Moreau-Ricaud (Scientific Secretaries), D. Zaoui (Administrative Secretary) and J. Turbat (Treasurer), F. Segui (Permanent Secretary).

An internal Bulletin, available on subscription (Secretary of the Editorial Committee: Cathie Silvestre), appears twice a year, and contains reports of scientific activities (lectures, conferences, etc.), institutional meetings, meetings in the provinces and abroad, as well as various regular columns (e. g. "Psychoanalysis Abroad"), and the List of Members.

Since 1989, there have been formal scientific links with the APF: the presidents and the scientific secretaries of our two associations exchange invitations to meetings and conferences. Some links also exist with the SPP, but these are of an individual rather than an institutional nature.

Eminent persons from the Quatrième Groupe:

Piera Aulagnier (1924–1990)

Of Italian origin, Piera Aulagnier, née Spairani, studied medicine in Rome. After moving to France, she underwent analysis with Lacan during the 1950s. She became one of his pupils and followed him into the École Freudienne which he founded in 1964. Once she had become established as a psychoanalyst, she also maintained a consultancy in Dr. Daumézon's department at the Hôpital Saint-Anne, Paris, where she specialized in the clinical study of psychoses. Since 1966, she has chaired a seminar (first with Clavreul, then alone) on Monday evenings at the Magnan Amphithéâtre, where, over the years, she has worked out, in front of successive generations of psychiatrists and psychoanalysts, a theory which takes a fresh and questioning look at Freudian metapsychology by placing a greater emphasis on the clinical study of the psychoses.

In 1966, she founded, with C. Stein and L. Covello, who were its publishers from 1966 to 1968, the quarterly journal "L'Inconscient", followed by, in 1969, *Topique.* In these journals she has published articles both by her Quatrième Groupe colleagues, and by colleagues from other French or foreign societies.

François Perrier (1922–1990)

François Perrier was already an eminent figure in French neuropsychiatry when he first encountered psychoanalysis in 1949. He initially underwent analysis with Bouvet, then (in 1956) with Lacan. He became an active member of the Société Française de Psychanalyse (1953-64). With Wladimir Granoff and Serge Leclaire (who, with Perrier, were known as "the Troika") he occupied an important position in this society, which seceded from the SPP, but the three failed in their negotiations to secure recognition from the IPA.

Perrier then remained on the side of Lacan, who founded the École Freudienne. In 1966 he resigned from the School's Directorate, and in 1969 from the School itself. Involved in the creation of the Quatrième Groupe, he became its first President from 1969 to 1972. In 1981 he resigned from the Group for personal reasons.

An excellent clinician, he did original works on hypochondria, hysteria and phobia, and alcoholism. His interest in the history of French psychoanalytic institutions led him to write a caustic book. François Perrier was a complex and engaging individual who was also a talented musician on the piano and organ.

Jean-Paul Valabrega (b. 1922)

After studies in philosophy and biology and a period as a researcher at the CNRS, Valabrega trained as an analyst with George Parcheminey. During the schism of 1953 he sided, along with several other pupils, with Lacan. He became an analyst of the École Freudienne and a member of its first Directorate.

It was while working in Daniel Lagache's laboratory that Valabrega first discovered the works of Michael Balint, whom he helped to make known in France by his translation, begun in 1960, of Balint's best-known work, *The Doctor, His Patient and the Illness,* published in France by P. U. F., then by Payot as *Le médecin, son malade et la maladie.* He has been a member of the editorial board of *Topique* since its foundation.

His interests include psychosomatics and anthropology. For several years he has co-directed (with Nicole Belmont) a seminar at the EHESS on "Anthropology and Psychoanalysis". Questions of analytical training are as meaningful for him now as they were when he founded the Quatrième Groupe. He deserves credit for an original contribution to knowledge: his "fourth analysis" was (if we ignore the works of Vilma Kovacs, published in Hungary about 1935) the first theorization of the supervision.

Other eminent persons, from the CFRP:

Octave Mannoni (1899–1989)

After studying philosophy at Strasbourg, he taught in Tananarive, in Madagascar, where he lived for some twenty years, and where he also carried out amateur ethnological and botanical research.

He was a sufficiently keen champion of independence for Madagascar to be sent, in 1945, on a mission to Paris, where he compiled the work on the psychology of colonization. In 1947 he began analysis with Lacan, embarked upon the clinical study of mental illness (at the Hôpital d'Evreux), and then worked at the Bureau d'Aide Psychologique Universitaire. An associate analyst of the SPP, he became embroiled in that organization's institutional conflicts, but sided with the "Lacanians". He defended Lacan in front of the Commission of Enquiry dispatched by the IPA, and continued to support him during the two schisms (1953 and 1963). He became an "Analyst Member of the School" at the École Freudienne. Loyal to Lacan, he only left the École after Lacan's death, to found, with his wife Maud Mannoni, and a colleague, Patrick Guyomard, the "Centre de Formation et de Recherches Psychanalytiques" (CFRP).

A scholar and man of letters, with little interest in power for its own sake, he left important works on transference, clinical research and analytical theory. His biography of Freud earned him a place as a historian of psychoanalysis, one who was "careful not to end up embalming Freud in a hagiography, as though he were in a shrine," but who brought out Freud's radical originality: the production of a special form of knowledge derived from the transference relationship.

A born writer, he emerges as something of a rebel where institutions and theories are concerned, struggling against the dogmatism of his colleagues in an unceasing effort to lead them to the discovery of the real Freud.

References

AULAGNIER, P. (1975): La violence de l'interprétation. Du pictogramme à l'énoncé, Paris: P.U.F

– (1979): Les destins du plaisir, aliénation, amour, passion, Paris: P.U.F.

– (1984): L'apprenti historien et le maître sorcier. Du discours identifiant au discours délirant, Paris: P.U.F

– (1986): Un interprête en quête de sens, Paris: Ramsay.

Leclaire, S. / A.P.U.I. (1991): État des Lieux de la Psychanalyse, Paris: Albin Michel.
Levy, D. (1987): L'Agenda de la Psychanalyse 1, 1987–88, Paris: Similia.
Mannoni, O. (1950): Psychologie de la colonisation, Editions Universitaires 1956; English: Prospero and Caliban, London / New York: Frederick Praeger.
– (1968): Freud, Ecrivains de toujours, Paris: Seuil.
– (1969): Clefs pour l'imaginaire ou l'autre scène, Paris: Seuil.
– (1978): Fictions freudiennes, Paris: Seuil.
– (1980): Un commencement qui n'en finit pas, Paris: Seuil.
– (1982): Cà n'empêche pas d'exister, Paris: Seuil.
– (1988): Un si vif étonnement, Paris: Seuil.
Perrier, F. (1978/79): La chaussée d'Antin, Vols 1 and 2, Paris: 10–18, 2nd ed. by Albin Michel.
– (1980): Le désir au féminin, Paris, Aubier.
– (1982): L'alcool au singulier, Paris: Inter-Editions.
– (1984): Les corps malades du signifiant. Le corporel et l'analytique, Paris: Inter-Editions.
– (1985): Voyages extraordinaires en Translacanie, Paris: Lieu commun.
Roudinesco, E. (1983–1986): Histoire de la Psychanalyse en France, Paris: Seuil. 2 Vols.
Valabrega, J. P. (1954): Les théories psychosomatiques, Paris: Privat-P.U.F.
– (1962): La relation thérapeutique, Paris: Flammarion.
– (1979): La formation du psychanalyste, Paris: Belfond.
– (1980 & 1992): Phantasme, mythe corps et sens, Paris: Payot

Institutions (since 1969)

(mentioned only those giving psychoanalytical training with habilitation)

Quatrième Groupe
Organisation Psychanalytique de Langue Française
Siège social: 2, Villa Violet, 75015 Paris
Tel.: 45 75 59 25

Centre de Formation et de Recherches Psychanalytiques (CFRP)
16 Avenue du Général Leclerc, 75014 Paris
Tel.: 43 22 64 96

Ecole de la Cause Freudienne
1 rue Huysmans, 75006 Paris
Tel.: 45 49 02 68

Journals (since 1969; in addition to Vol. 1 of Psych. Int.)

Topique.
Revue freudienne
since 1969; Eds. Dunod, Paris
15 Rue Gossin, 92120 Montrouge

Le Coq-Héron
since 1969; Founders and Eds.: Judith Dupont and
Groupe du Centre Etienne Marcel
69 Rue Madame, 75006 Paris
Eds. diffusion

L'âne. Le magazine freudien
since 1979; Ed.: J. Miller
Eds. le Seuil

Littoral
since 1981; 11 Rue Alouettes, 31520 Ramonville
Eds. Eres, Toulouse

Apertura International
since 1987; Ed.: J. R. Freymann / A. M. Michels
Springer, Strasbourg

Esquisses Psychanalytiques
since 1983; Ed: J. Dor; CFRP Eds., Paris

Frénésie. Revue d'histoire de la psychiatrie et de la psychanalyse
since 1985; Ed.: M. Collée
15 rue de Lakanal, 75015 Paris

Che vuoi?
Revue du Cercle Freudien
since April 1992; Lharmattan Eds.
48 Rue Bernardins, 75005 Paris

Analyse freudienne
since 1992; Ed.: N. Milgram

L'inactuel
since 1994; Ed.: M. Moscovici
Ed. Calman Lévy, 3 rue Auber, 75009 Paris

Michelle Moreau-Ricaud, 31, quai de Bourbon, 75004 Paris

Greece

by Jannis Kontos, Sotiris Manolopoulos and Nikos Kouretas

The establishment of psychoanalysis in Greece was a particularly difficult and laborious undertaking. We shall try to show that the historic reality and the psychic structure of Greek people contributed to the exceptionally long delay as to the creation of a recognized group in Greece (the Hellenic Psychoanalytic Study Group being only founded in 1982).

a) Modern Greece is – due to historic and geographic reasons – a peripheral[1] country par excellence , "receiving the central product and distributing it" (Tzavaras / Pagagounos, 1990). When Freud visited the Acropolis in 1904, there was evidently no one to greet him. It took almost half a century before his daughter, Anna Freud, visited Athens and thus marked the beginning of the official psychoanalytic movement in Greece (Potamianou, 1988).

Greece had serious and grim priorities: the Balkan Wars (1912–1913), the involvement in the First World War, the national schism between royalists and republicans, followed by the Asia Minor disaster (1922) with well over a million refugees pouring into the mainland, and two military dictatorships (1926 and 1936) alternating with short-lived political governments. It was only in 1948, when Italy rendered the Dodecanese, that Greece acquired its final boundaries.

b) The characteristics of Greeks not favouring psychoanalysis are considered to be: their tendency to form close dependent relationships, with a lack of autonomy, and their projective mechanisms, which prevent "the encounter with themselves" (Potamianou, 1988). She also mentions the (oral) attitude of "I want it all as quick as possible", which creates a dif-

1 We borrow this expression from an unpublished article by A. Tzavaras (1989), in which he defines the "centre" in terms of producing knowledge, and the "periphery" as the one "receiving the product and distributing it" (see also Tsavaras / Papagounos, 1990). On the other hand, we believe there is a self flattering tendency of the Greeks to put themselves at the cross-roads between the West and the East, which conceals an ambivalence with which the new ideas coming from the western world are introduced while at the same time the framework from which these ideas derive is not taken into equal consideration.

ficulty in undertaking a psychoanalysis. She also talks about the "conservatism" in Greek society, in essence an agricultural one, with its strict moral codes which do not favour the acceptance of the psychoanalytic theory of sexuality (p. 249–250). We could add certain attitudes (jealousy, the demand for exceptional concessions, as well as the inhibiting idealization of the glorious past) that foster what can be called a "social resistance" to psychoanalysis.

Some of these factors played a part while the psychoanalytic movement was developing. In a Greek sense, we could compare them to forces in an ancient tragedy, where the strings seem to be moved by the Gods (i. e. the unconscious).

This comparison brings us back to the roots: Socrates, the supreme Athenian philosopher, was the first to profess what became for Freud the object of psychoanalysis: the Γνωθι σαυτον – Know Thyself.

Socrates, as Aristophanes' comedy, "The Clouds", depicts, made the first attempt towards a psychoanalytic cure. Strepsiades, a farmer whose name connotes "twisting", has amassed huge debts. He hears of the superior intellect and sagacity of Socrates and goes to him seeking advice about how to cheat his creditors. The philosopher-treater becomes aware that the cunning farmer has no use for his teachings and in a final attempt to help him asks him to lie on the couch and say everything that comes to his mind.[2]

1. The Groundwork (1915–1935)

It is no surprise, then, that in the country where the first reported analytic session took place psychoanalytic ideas were originally introduced by inspired people closer to the prototype of all teachers[3], Socrates, than to the prototype of all physicians, Hippocrates.

True to this tradition, a noted linguist, scholar and educator, Manolis Triandaphyllides, first published (in 1915) an original paper on the relationship between "The beginning of speech and Freudian psychology".

Twenty years later, it was again up to the poet and man of letters Andreas Embirikos, to launch the actual application of psychoanalysis as treatment.

During the same period the psychiatric establishment totally ignored the new ideas from Vienna. It was left up to paedagogues, trained in Germany,

2 This section is mostly based on information drawn from several articles included in A. Tzavaras (ed), "Psychoanalysis and Greece".

3 Still today, the persistence of the Greek people to give their children a good education is registered in their Ego-Ideal.

France or Switzerland (K. Sotiriou, G. Imbriotis, D. Moraitis), to see in psychoanalysis an intriguing new theory that met the educator's desire to influence and foster the sublimation of drives. Their papers contain lucid expositions of the importance of dreams and parapraxes, the unconscious, drives, repression, the Oedipus complex, transference, etc.

D. Moraitis published, in 1928, a book with the telling title *Psychoanalysis and its Application in Education.* Two years later he founded the Society of Analytic Psychology – and Journal – and organized the first Child Guidance Centre in Greece (1932).

Indeed, during the interwar years, teachers, educators, men and women of letters and progressive intellectuals were far more interested in psychodynamic aspects of behaviour than were psychiatrists. Their interest was drawn around the teaching of Alfred Adler. Individual Psychology, with its emphasis on conscious conflictual relationships within the family and its downplaying of the role of infantile sexuality and unconscious dynamics in character development, was much more palatable to educators eager to see change than the Freudian theory.

The first physician to lecture and write on psychoanalysis was a military psychiatrist, Dimitrios Kouretas (1901–1984), who had returned from medical and psychiatric training in Lyon and Paris. In 1927 he gave at the auditorium of the Lawyers' Association a lecture entitled "Psychoanalysis". A year later, an expanded version of the lecture was published in the prominent medical journal *Hellenic Medicine*. In the thirties he joined Moraitis in the activities of the Society and of the Child Guidance Centre.

In 1931, another psychiatrist, trained in Berlin, C. Constantinides, published a monograph on psychoanalysis.

Andreas Embirikos (1907–1975) was a poet and a writer, a cosmopolitan of broad interests, from Hegelian philosophy to aesthetics. He was among the first to join André Breton in the surrealistic movement of the late twenties in Paris, and the first Greek ever to be analyzed.[4]

A few years after his return to Athens in 1931, while he was writing avant-garde surrealistic poetry and prose, Emibirikos started the practice of psychoanalysis. Little is known about his practice during the years of fascist dictatorship in Greece, followed by German occupation (1940–1944) and the Civil War (1946–1949}. Two of his analyses come close to the character of training analysis: that of Kouretas, and of Frosso Carapanou.

The year 1940 marks the emergence of George Zavitzianos (b. 1909) in the newly-fledged Greek psychoanalytic literature. He was a neuropsychia-

4 By René Laforgue, in the period 1928–1931.

trist at the main general hospital in Athens, who was intrigued by Freud's writings; his paper, on the usefulness of the psychoanalytic method for the psychoneurotic manifestations of childhood, introduces basic concepts of child psychoanalysis, discusses the differences between children and adults and ends with the description of two clinical cases.

2. First Attempt at the Founding of a Psychoanalytic Group (1947–1950)

Embirikos was involved in the practice of psychoanalysis, and Kouretas and Zavitzianos were increasingly gripped by its explanatory power and therapeutic potential. What all three needed was a catalyst to bring a sense of group coherence. This came in the person of Marie Bonaparte, a Greek princess by marriage, analysand, student and protector of S. Freud and his family.

From 1946 on she spent the winter seasons in Athens. It was at her residence that the first "truly psychoanalytic" seminars, group and individual supervisions took place. For a while, a fourth member was considered, Nicos Dracoulides, but finally not included in the group.[5] A year later, in 1947, all three participated in the Congress of the IPA in Zürich.

The official launching of the Greek Psychoanalytic Study Group took place on January 13, 1949, with Anna Freud's visit and lectures at the Athenian Medical Society. G. Pamboukis, chairman of the Department of Neurology and Psychiatry, introduced her.

Meanwhile, with the supportive recommendations of M. Bonaparte (an influential factor in the IPA and already a founding member of the French Psychoanalytic Society) and the concurrence of A. Freud and E. Jones, Embirikos, Kouretas and Zavitzianos became associate members of the Paris Society and of the IPA. Their papers appeared in a prestigious international psychoanalytic journal (*Revue Française de Psychanalyse,* 1950).

Another achievement of the Study Group was the translation into Greek and the publication of Marie Bonaparte's *Three Introductory Lectures to Psychoanalysis.* For many years this was widely ciruclated among acade-

5 These meetings did not limit themselves to clinical psychoanalytic matters. At times, leading intellectuals (K. Tsatsos, P. Kanellopoulos, M. Triandaphyllides and others) were invited to discuss psychoanalysis from a broad theoretical and philosophical perspective.

mics, physicians, artists, educators and intellectuals and, with the exception of Freud's own writings, constituted the only authoritative psychoanalytic text that was available to the Greek audiences.

These events turned out to be but a brief shining moment. In 1950, Embirikos moved to Paris and Zavitzianos decided to emigrate to the United States. For Embirikos, the reasons were related to the fact that he was a lay analyst, a poet who cured patients. This had irked a number of influential neuropsychiatrists. The possibility of lawsuit made him feel threatened, embittered and unsure of how long he would be able to continue the practice of analysis (Tzavaras, 1985, 571).[6] Zavitzianos' decision appeared to be based on his poignant awareness that the Greek neuropsychiatric establishment was bound to restrain the development of psychoanalysis and, due to Embirikos' absence, that the potential to grow and mature as a psychoanalyst was limited.[7]

Marie Bonaparte had problems of her own: In March she fractured her femoral bone and her chronic diabetes became harder to manage; she decided to spend less time in Greece. Within a year the group dissolved quietly.

One could question whether the historical conditions were suitable for this attempt to prosper (Potamianou, 1988). She states that there was no basis for the success of that venture. The "unorthodox" and hasty activities did not take into consideration the inherent necessities of the process which would lead to a more formal organization. The personal destinies and especially the favourable conjuncture in Marie Bonaparte's stay in Athens, *her own desire* for the founding of a Study Group as well as being one of the most influential figures of the IPA,[8] determined the outcome of the attempt.[9] Looking back we should not let got of the fact that this was a

6 It appears that he had another worry in his mind. In a letter to his brother, he talks about the possibility of setting of in New Orleans, if another World War (connected to the Korean War) were to break out.

7 Zavitzianos went on to have a fruitful psychoanalytic career. He became associated with the Michigan and Washington D. C. Psychoanalytic Societies and was instrumental in the development of psychoanalysis in Canada. He wrote many articles on the relationship of fetishism, kleptomania, exhibitionism and transvestism and his long psychoanalysis of a patient with the above psychopathology has been frequently referred to in the literature.

8 This brings us back to the theory of the "centre" (which is represented here by the IPA through M. Bonaparte), and its role as regulator of the psychoanalytic movement (Tzavaras / Papagounos, 1990).

9 "Did this foreigner", asks Potamianou, "want to offer to the Greeks as a gift what can only be achieved through trial in time and through work?" (p. 252).

creative and pioneering effort and not comparable to what we nowadays understand as a psychoanalytic organization.

3. Interim Period

After the dissolution of the group, Kouretas was left practically isolated. He turned his interest to applied psychoanalysis and published voluminously on the interface of psychoanalysis and ancient Greek literature. He hosted in connection with the Centre of Mental Health and Research, some internationally famous psychoanalysts like: J. Lacan (1951), W. Niederland (1958), R. Spitz (1959), R. Sterba (1961), Margaret Mahler (1962) and M. Schur (1968). He also gave public lectures and radio talks, the latter with the encouragement of K. Meranaios, an erudite journalist and translator of many of Freud's works.[10]

With the dissolution of the first psychoanalytical group in 1950, every attempt to form an institutional setting seemed to cease. Embirikos devoted himself to literature,[11] Kouretas to the University[12] and psychoanalysis, but without taking any initiative towards future organization.

Later, A. Potamianou, a psychologist, and P. Sakellaropoulos, a psychiatrist trained in Paris, with special abilities in organization and great enthusiasm, succeeded in laying the foundations, not only in terms of individuals but in institutions as well. These were to become the source from where different persons would later be selected for training.

Potamianou founded the Centre of Mental Health and Research (CMHR) in 1956, mobilizing the Royal National Foundation.[13] At that

10 Meranaios had started translating Freud back in 1938, and continued in the fourties and fifties with his wife, Mina Zographou, regularly consulting with Kouretas, who wrote many of the prologues to these works.

11 Emibirikos, upon his return from Paris in 1953, refrained from speaking of psychoanalysis in public (*Hartis*, 17–18, 1985). Occasionally, when Zavitzianos visited Greece, the three would meet again and listen to Zavitzianos presenting the ongoing treatment of his famous case of Lilian.

12 In 1964 Kouretas was elected to the newly created Department of Psychiatry at the Athens University Medical School. His appointing to the departmental staff of P. Sakellaropoulos and of psychoadynamic psychiatrists trained in the USA or Canada, like E. Papathomopoulos and J. Babatzanis, brought about deep qualitative changes both in patient treatment and in graduate and postgraduate teaching of Psychiatry.

13 According to A. Potamianou's testimony, the Royal National Foundation having at that time undertaken the care of children who came back from communist countries, her suggestion for the creation of a Centre with the mental health of children as main objective was welcomed.

time, there were practically no services outside hospitals which had as an aim prevention, therapy and research concerning the mental health of not only children but of adults as well (Potamianou, 1976).

S. Lebovici and R. Diatkine had had regular meetings with the CMHR and undertook supervisions and seminars for the staff. Other psychoanalysts as well, such as the Americans M. Mahler, W. Niederland and others gave lectures and held seminars.

This positive development lasted a little longer than a decade. A year after the coup d'état of April 21, 1967, the continuation of its functioning had become problematic, as the junta had appointed, as it did in all scientific institutions, a state delegate. Potamianou resigned (addressing a letter dated 21. 2. 1969 to the "prime minister" Papadopoulos). But *every cloud has a silver lining,* as the regime of the junta gave the chance for some to complete (Sakellaropoulos, 1971, Potamianou, 1973) and for others to further (Carapanou) their psychoanalytic training.

4. Second Attempt (1967): The "Seminar" of Thassos

At the beginning of 1967, much preliminary work had been done to form a psychoanalytic group in Greece, the first effort being a Franco-Hellenic meeting in the summer (26–28 August), on the island of Thassos, to be repeated every year. P. Neubauer as well as W. Niederland from the American Association, and some others, had shown interest in the project.

From Greece, the ones to participate in this "seminar" were: Kouretas, Potamianou, Sakellaropoulos, G. Kostoulas (Geneva), D. Panayotopoulos (Lausanne), I. Kotsoni (École Freudienne de Paris), F. Carapanou, A. Kaloutsi and H. Leoussi. On the French side, the participants would be Serge Lebovici, Evelyne and Jean Kestemberg, Christian David and André Green. The topics suggested were "Narcissism" (to be introduced by David and Green), and "Acting Out".

The wish for these regular "seminars" was, to be recognized by the IPA as having a training value. This would facilitate the creation of a psychoanalytic group and, in due time, the creation of a Study Group. However, this "seminar" never took place as originally planned, because there were disagreements on the criteria of selection. Only a small number of participants met on Thassos and the idea of continuation was abandoned.

The problems involved in the founding of a psychoanalytic group on the "periphery" are raised in Potamianou's letter (17. 5. 1967) to Evelyn Kestemberg, then Secretary of the European Psychoanalytic Federation.

She states that if the IPA does not accept the special circumstances[14] existing in (and for) Greece and does not thereby facilitate the already existing plans, the prospect of creating a Greek Psychoanalytic Society will be lost. As a solution, the following possibilities were suggested:

a) Initially, a Society geographically close to Greece (e. g. Italy) would undertake the training of the members in the Greek group with ongoing travels from both sides. Or b) the IPA would support psychoanalysts from other countries to come and settle in Greece for a certain period of time. Or finally c) the recognition of a group consisting of Kouretas, Panayotopoulos, Sakellaropoulos, Kaloutsi, Carapanou, Kotsoni and Potamianou, all having had an analysis and working as psychotherapists. Potamianou leaves open the prospect of a future broadening of the group.

None of these suggestions were actually carried out. We notice once more how irreconcilable the three necessary elements were: the standards and requirements of the IPA, the limiting geographical and sociocultural conditions of Greece and the desires of psychoanalytically trained Greeks. The same applies to the third attempt in 1974, when the hasty efforts of the Greek analysts met with the inconsistent attitude of the IPA.

5. Third Attempt (1974)

With the fall of the junta, Potamianou returned once again as the scientific director of the CMHR. Sakellaroupoulos from his position as a senior registrar at the University Clinic of Eginiteion and in cooperation with the psychoanalyst Athina Alexandris (who had been trained in Canada and had settled in Athens), also developed parallel activities as to the recruiting and to the clinical and theoretical preparation of young professionals in psychoanalytically oriented psychotherapies.

As is stated at the beginning of the memorandum, the suggestion of Sakellaropoulos and Alexandris "contained an innovative and creative solution to the long existing problem in Greece".[15] As at least five members are required for the creation of a Study Group recognized by the IPA, the Greek plan was to establish such a Group in the future consisting of six members, two of whom would be the "training analysts" with two trainees each.

14 "Une solution orthodoxe du problème n'ayant pas abouti …"

15 It is probably a rather polite way of describing "unorthodox" suggestions.

Of great importance is the last paragraph in the text: "The above outline would serve the minimum needs for training in psychoanalysis in Greece".

Potamianou was in disagreement with this. In her letter of 3. 5. 1974 to A. Limentani, she expresses her objection as to the way the candidates will be selected – that is, for the analysts themselves to evaluate the candidates being already in therapy with them.[16] She states also her willingness to take part in the project (being herself now a member of the Societé de Paris) by accepting to analyse candidates selected by other psychoanalysts.

The visit of the committee (A. Limentani, L. Gairinger and M. Montessori) took place on 12.–14. 10. 1974. Alexandris and Sakellaropoulos presented cases of potential candidates to them. The meeting however could not have had a positive outcome, as a second memorandum by A. Limentani, followed on 14. 11. 1974 in which he in detail clarifies and defines the new terms for the functioning of the group and formulates new conditions as well. Thus, the concessions appearing in the former memorandum were abolished, while the requirement of the IPA, valid in similar cases, was brought back into force.[17]

From the archives of Hartocollis and Potamianou we have acquired information about the further outcome of this *project,* as the attempt is now called. We refer to certain points:

Alexandris and Sakellaropoulos in a letter to the Committee on 20. 2. 1975 referred to the changes in the spirit and the terms of the agreement.[18]

On 14. 10. 1975, a formal invitation from the Secretary of the IPA, D. Widlöcher, was formulated to Maurice Friend (NY) and P. Hartocollis (Topeca), asking them to become consulting members of the Committee.

P. Hartocollis was appointed consulting member of the Committee, and was thus able to convey information between the two parties. It seemed that because of discouragement there was no communication from Greece and the Executive Council intended "to discharge the committee because of the complete lack of progress".

16 Much later, during the preliminary agreement for the founding of the Study Group, Potamianou will express her wish "to discuss the conditions under which the candidates will be selected, as well as the role of the Greek analysts […] those having been the points of conflict in the past" (letter of 29. 1. 1981 to P. Hartocollis), implying that the standards of the IPA would apply to Greeks as well.

17 The memorandum referred to "serious misunderstandings" and made clear that the committee "is not empowered to grant training status to any person participating in the project".

18 Eight days later, Sakellaropoulos disappointedly wrote to Hartocollis that "with the new suggestions, [the project] seems to be a lost cause".

At the end, there was no development whatsoever in any direction, and the recognition by the IPA of the Greek Group as a Study Group slacked and was finally abandoned.[19]

The failure of this effort[20] led Alexandris and Sakellaropoulos, in co-operation with other psychoanalytically oriented psychotherapists, to the founding in 1977 of the Greek Society for Psychoanalytic Psychotherapy.[21]

A Personal Effort: The Case of Frosso Carapanou

It is worthwhile presenting here in detail the case of a Greek wanting to become a psychoanalyst, as it shows, in an exemplary way, the consequences of the geo-political, economic and cultural factors.

Born in 1909, F. Carapanou's interest in psychoanalysis leads her to a personal analysis with Andreas Embirikos in the years of 1943–1947. For the further training in psychoanalysis she leaves for Paris and starts a second analysis with René Laforgue. Simultaneously, she studies Psychology at the Sorbonne (1947–1949).[22]

With a scholarship from the Swiss Aid to Europe, she goes to Geneva (1950–1951) in order to obtain her diploma as a kindergarten teacher. She specializes in Child Psychopathology, with emphasis on the pre-schooling years, and soon publishes on the effects of the lack of maternal care (Carapanou, 1952–53). She returns to Athens for family reasons. In the years 1955–1958, she founded the first psychoanalytically oriented kindergarten in Greece.

From 1965, working in the CMHR, she is given the opportunity to have her psychotherapies supervised by different visiting psychoanalysts. One characteristic example of her pioneer attitude at the time is a five-year long

19 According to Hartocollis (personal communication), the matter fell through because of the previous promise that the Greek Group would promptly be recognized as a Study Group. When, however, the Committee of the IPA set new terms, some people in Greece regarded them as a breach of the agreement and found them rather derogatory.

20 Hartocollis had suggested to the Greek colleagues in the summer of 1975 to promote psychoanalysis without being concerned with the training aspect, and to confine themselves to the training of people suitable to undertake psychotherapies, so as to pave the way for future efforts.

21 This is affiliated non formally to the analogous British Society. As it seems, however, some trainers (and trainees) believe they train (are trained as) psychoanalysts.

22 F. Carapanou attends in Paris the seminars conducted by Françoise Dolto, and especially on drawings from children at the Trousseaux hospital.

supervision of each session in the psychotherapy of a psychotic child through a regular correspondence with S. Lebovici. Later, she shows a similar attitude when, in 1968, she grabs the opportunity to have supervision with André Green, for a short time, of the already completed psychotherapy of a patient who suffered from serious compulsive neurosis.

From 1951 to 1968, she often visits Paris and attends different training courses, including theoretical seminars and supervision of psychotherapies. Of major importance is her stay in Paris in the years 1965–1966 where, with a scholarship of the French government, she worked at the XIII Arrondissement directed by S. Lebovici, and attended the seminars of the Psychoanalytic Institute of Paris as well.

After the putsch of the junta in Greece, she leaves the CMHR in 1969 and returns to Paris. With a scholarship from the Ministry of Foreign Affairs in France, she starts a Ph. D.[23] with the famous ethnologist and psychoanalyst Georges Devereux. In the meantime, during the spring of 1968, she had applied to the Psychoanalytic Institute of Paris in order to be accepted as a trainee and thus finish her training. The Committee (consisting of Barande, Favreau and Marty) which was to examine her application accepted her, but asked her, though, to undergo a new analysis. Indeed, between 1969 and 1973, she continues her new analysis with Dr. Braunschweig, with many interruptions. Family reasons forced her to return in 1973 and settle permanently in Athens.

The already mentioned efforts to establish a Study Group in Athens in 1974, rekindles her hopes for the completion of her psychoanalytic training. She contacts two members from the Committee in Rome asking for supervision of psychoanalytic cases. This effort did not succeed either, since the Study Group was not created.

In 1983, (after the founding in 1982 of the Greek Study Group) and at the age of 74, her personal clinical and theoretical work as well as her contribution as an author finally recognized, Frosso Carapanou is elected as an associate member of the Greek Study Group.

6. Founding of the Greek Study Group (1982)

During the seventies and eighties, many changes occured in Greece aiming towards a democratization of political, social and academic institutions. Greece became a member of the European Community, which has offered

23 "Approche ethnopsychiatrique d'un cas d'obésité réactionelle."

generous help towards development and has put forth a major challenge for changes and adjustments in Greek people. A momentum towards openess and self-searching behavior was created. Alongside that came a loosening of the ties with the extended family and a more competitive and anxiety-producing life style.

These changes were reflected in the Mental Health area, too. Four university departments of Psychiatry have developed. Child Psychiatry was recognized as a distinct speciality on its own. The Mental Health Centres for Adults and Children have proliferated, and psychiatric units have started to function within General Hospitals. Many Mental Health professionals trained abroad returned to their native country.

Also there has been a recent proliferation of discussions, articles in magazines, publications, theatre productions, etc. which apply the principles of psychoanalysis in wider social-cultural issues as well as group, family and individual problems. At least the climate was favourable for another try.

This became possible when Peter Hartocollis, an internationally recognized contributor to psychoanalysis, was elected in 1980 Professor and chairman of the newly founded department of Psychiatry at the University of Patras. A little later, Stavroula Beratis, a member of the New York Institute and of the American Psychoanalytic Association as well, was elected to the same University. Consequently, at that time there were five psychoanalysts in Greece (Alexandris, Beratis, Hartocollis, Potamianou, Sakellaropoulos), all of whom were members of recognized psychoanalytic societies and of whom two were already training analysts (Potamianou and Hartocollis). Thus, for the first time in Greece, the (minimal) requirements needed to establish a Study Group recognized by the IPA were met.

Before the five participants managed to get together and reach agreement, a foreigner again made the first move. In September 1981, a Franco-Hellenic symposium on "Social Psychiatry in the Community" was organized. One of the participants was Lebovici, the main and tireless contributor to the development of psychoanalysis in Greece. Additionally, he took the initiative concerning the founding of a Study Group in Greece, and approached Hartocollis, writing on 15. 12. 1981 to Limentani about this matter. However, both Potamianou and Sakellaropoulos had their doubts as to the possibility of a successful cooperation.[24]

24 Lebovici mentions in his letter that "despite their conflicts [...] (they) are ready to cooperate". Hartocollis indirectly expresses this when writing to Potamianou: "Not much enthusiasm exists in our group as to a new beginning in the foreseable future."

On 10. 2. 1982, following the discussions between the Greek psychoanalysts, Hartocollis had a first sounding with Limentani – at the time President of the IPA – about the prospect of having the Greek group recognized as a Study Group. After his positive response, the Greek group applied to the IPA on 26. 2. 1982 for a formal Study Group Status. The Executive Council of the IPA asked Joseph Sandler (London), who at the time was Freud-Professor in Jerusalem, to arrange a fact-finding visit. Joseph Sandler came to Athens on 4. 6. 1982 and had preliminary contacts with the Greek group. The positive outcome was followed on 10. 12. 1982 by the visit of a committee composed of J. Sandler, J. de Saussure and S. Mentzos, who were to carry out further deliberations.

As a final result: on 11. 10. 1982, after 35 years (1947–1982) of efforts, the Greek group received at last the letter from Limentani which formally recognized it as a Study Group of the IPA.

A Sponsoring Committee was then set up, the president being J. Sandler, and Janine de Saussure (Geneva) and Stavros Mentzos (Frankfurt) being appointed as members. At the beginning of 1983, Sandler resigned, and Mme de Saussure took over the presidency, while Janine Chasseguet-Smirgel (Paris) became the second member. In 1991, Mme Chasseguet-Smirgel was replaced by Dr. Dinora Pines (London).

In June 1983, the Group started its training program, selecting candidates.

During the preliminary phases in the establishment of the Study Group, a conflict arose. The reason was that Alexandris and Sakellaropoulos felt that their general contribution toward the psychoanalytic movement in Greece should get recognition, and that they should be considered without further procedures as training analysts in the Study Group. This claim brought them in conflict with the standards of the IPA and, as a result thereof, a split in the Greek psychoanalytic group took place in 1987. Alexandris resigned form the Study Group and concentrated on the training of psychotherapists in the Society for Psychoanalytic Psychotherapy, while Sakellaropoulos chose to install a moratorium concerning his functions in the Group, continuing his training of psychotherapists and turning his attention towards Social (Dynamic) Psychiatry. Later, he was elected Professor of Psychiatry at the University of Thrace.[25]

25 Cremerius (1982) examines in detail the causes and effects of splits in the psychoanalytic movement. He writes: "The true reasons for the interruption of the scientific dialogue and the split are due to [...] very personal antipathies and to the sensitivities of personalities who have difficulty in compromising" (p. 490).

Gradually, however, the Hellenic Group became enriched with new members who had completed their training abroad: in 1983 Jannis Kontos returned from Germany (Frankfurt), in 1985 Sotiris Manolopoulos from Canada (Ottawa), in 1986 Nikos Kouretas from the USA (Boston) – he later returned to Boston, and in 1987 Nikos Tzavaras from Germany (Giessen).

At the present time (June 1993), the Study Group consists of ten members: seven full membes (Beratis, Hartocollis, Kontos, Manolopoulos, Potamianou, Sakellaropoulos and Tzavaras) and three associate (Carapanou, Gabriel and Zaharakopoulou). Beratis, Hartocollis and Potamianou have been recognized by the IPA as training and supervising analysts, making up the training committee. Corresponding members are: Nikos Kouretas (Boston), Nicos Nicolaides (Geneva), Thalia Vergopoulo (Geneva), Roy Callogeras and Toni Alston-Calogeras (Wiesbaden). Honorary members are: George Zavitzianos (Montreal), Harold Blum (NY), Charles Socarides (NY), and Serge Lebovici (Paris).[26]

7. The Present State of Affairs

There is no common history yet in Greece and, therefore, no "School of thought" which is specifically Greek. The "origin" of the Greek psychoanalysts, who up to now come from other countries and different "Schools", is on the one hand enriching, because it offers the possbility to immerse with various psychoanalytic currents abroad. It also gives the opportunity for a less dogmatic approach to the main theories, since "living" representatives of these theories practise them. On the other hand communication does not often seem as fruitful, because analysts in Greece speak and "think" in the different psychoanalytic languages with which they have been brought up. The same applies to the different psychoanalytic languages spoken by the Sponsoring Committee. There is not even a commonly accepted translation of the psychoanalytic terminology into

26 At the present, the number of trainees, at different stages of their development, has reached twenty-six. The training does not follow a class model as in some Societies, but several students from different levels may attend the same seminar. However, we have "inherited" from French and Swiss Societies certain procedures which make the training and qualification a long process. In November 1992, Ioanna Gabriel became the first analyst to be trained by the Hellenic Study Group where she was accepted as an associate member.

Greek and, more so, the theoretical base of this terminology is different for everyone.

The fact of being a psychoanalytic immigrant in one's own "mother" country may pose certain characteristic obstacles to one's path towards becoming a psychoanalyst.[27]

The scientific dialogue of the members in the Greek Group still takes place almost exclusively in (and with) their "country of origin". Furthermore, there is no publishing forum which would serve a dialogue and an exchange of ideas and would enhance the use of the mother tongue in the psychoanalytic Logos.

If one adds factors such as hostility and mistrust in the established groups, which feel the presence of psychoanalysts as a threat, and the general conditions which impede their work, then one can understand that the development of psychoanalysis in Greece was also delayed because many Greek psychoanalysts prefer to remain abroad (the "centre"), where conditions are more favourable (Hartocollis, 1983).[28]

8. Activities of the Hellenic Psychoanalytic Study Group

a) Because the number of Greek analysts was very small, it has been customary, inaugurated by Anna Freud in 1949, to invite well-known psychoanalysts from abroad to give lectures and hold seminars, which are often supported by the French and German Cultural Institutes.

With the founding of the Study Group, many more foreign psychoanalysts were invited, the number of Greek training analysts still being limited. In this way, they contribute to the training needs of the candidates. The list of speakers is indeed impressive, as is also the variety of the topics chosen: R. Diatkine, D. Widlöcher, A. Solnit, Piera Aulagnier, J. Chasseguet-Smirgel,

27 Tensions are anyhow inherent in every psychoanalytic group as they flow from its basic theme: the processes of internalization, which result in the transmission of the psychoanalytic thought. That is to say: what kind of psychoanalysis is to be transmitted? by whom? in what way? The spilt in the Greek Study Group in 1987 is a tangible example.

28 Greek intellectuals abroad contribute substantially to sciences and letters. In the field of psychoanalysis, taking into account the size of the country and its general culture level, one is surprised by the number of well-known Greek psychoanalysts working abroad, such as: C. Castoriades (Paris), S. Mentzos (Frankfurt), G. Moraitis (Chicago), N. Nicolaides and Th. Vergopoulo (Geneva), G. Zavitzianos and E. Papamatheaki-Lester (Montreal), Ch. Socarides (NY), and others.

André Green, A. Holder, G. Benedetti, Joyce McDougall, M. le Guen, H. Thomä, B. Cramer, and A. M. Sandler.

b) Very important for the promoting of psychoanalysis in Greece was the International Psychoanalytic Symposium of Delphi, which was the creative idea of two Greek-Canadians from Toronto: Georgia and Jannis Babatzanis (the first being a Child Psychotherapist and the second a Child Psychiatrist). The Symposium takes place every four years in Delphi and is organized in turn by the University of Toronto in cooperation with the Canadian Psychoanalytic Institute and the University of Patras together with the Greek Study Group. It is a psychoanalytic symposium with a set thematic, that is to say, relative to Ancient Greece.[29] Due to the fact that the conference space at Delphi is designed for a relatively limited number of participants, and to the rather long duration of the symposium, the formation of small groups gives the possibility to go deeper into theoretical discussions and to establish closer personal contacts.

The first Symposium at Delphi took place in 1984 (16–19 of August) with the following theme: "The Personal Myth: a Clinical Concept in the three Streams of Psychoanalytic Theory", with such illustrious participants as Jacob Arlow, André Green, Otto Kernberg, Robert Wallerstein, Ernest Wolf and others.[30]

In the second Symposium at Delphi (26.–31. 7. 1988), the theme was: "Maternal Configurations and Psychoanalysis: Clinical and Cultural Perspectives", and among the participants were again distinguished psychoanalysts such as James Anthony, Ilse Barande, Florence Begoin, Bernard Cramer, Alex Holder, Peter Neubauer and Albert Solnit. The result was another symposium of a high level.

At the third Symposium (19.–23. 8. 1992), the title of the theme was: "Tragedy: Cultural and Psychoanalytic Visions". Amongst many others, the participants were Robert Emde, André Green, Max Hernandez, Patrick Mahoney, Francis Pasche, Bennett Simon and Donald Spence.[31]

29 In his introduction letter of 10. 1. 1983 to P. Hartocollis, Ian Graham, the main initator of the project, suggests: "to use the historic relevance of the Delphi area and its links with the Oedipus and other classical Greek myths as an anchoring concept ...".

30 The high level of the contributors is documented in the book which was edited by P. Hartocollis and Ian Graham and published under the same title by the International Universities Press in 1991.

31 The fourth Symposium is planned to take place in the summer of 1996, most likely with a theme relating to the Oedipus myth.

c) The rather limited Greek reading public and the financial conditions do not especially favour publishing activities. There is no regular, periodical publication yet. The articles written by members of the Study Group have up till now been published in different journals concerning psychology, sociology or science in general. Earlier, the writing activities of the members were turned almost completely towards their "countries of origin". In the recent years though, the publishing effort is now turned towards their native country. For the occasion commemorating the 50 years from Freud's death (1989), two publications are worthwhile noticing: one volume which hosts articles by Greek psychoanalysts from all over the world, and one which hosts only French and French speaking Greek psychoanalysts.[32]

9. Personalities

Dimitrios Kouretas (1901–1984), born in Chryssovitsi, Peloponnese, studied Medicine in Lyon (France), and trained in Neurology and Psychiatry in Paris. In 1933 he was appointed associate Professor of Neurology and Psychiatry in Athens; in 1942 he was elected Professor of the newly established Medical School of Salonica, from which he resigned for health reasons in 1948. He formed with A. Embirikos, G. Zavitzianos and Princess Marie Bonaparte the first Greek Psychoanalytic Study Group (1947–1950). Became a Full Member of the Paris Psychoanalytic Association and the IPA (1950). In 1964 he was appointed Professor and Chairman of Psychiatry at Athens Medical School. He authored over 200 articles on internal medicine, neurology, psychiatry, psychoanalysis and literature and a book on *Abnormal Characters in the Ancient Greek Drama* (1928/1950).

Peter Hartocollis (M. D., Ph. D.), born in Athens, studied medicine at the Universities of Athens and Lausanne. He later went to the USA, where he studied Clinical Psychology at Clark and Michigan State Universities. He completed his psychiatric training at the Menninger School of Psychiatry, and his psychoanalytic training at the Topeka Institute of Psychoanalysis, where he remained as training and supervising psychoanalyst until 1981.

32 The increasing blossoming of the psychoanalytic Logos which has been noticed in the last years in Greece has definitely not left publishing houses indifferent. As a result, many texts are now being translated. As for earlier publications (including the works of Freud), we refer to the article of Ploumbides and Tzavaras in the volume "Psychoanalysis in Greece" (edited by Tzavaras, 1984, 379–388).

He was also the Director of the C. F. Menninger Hospital in Topeka. In 1980, he was appointed to the Chair of Psychiatry at the Medical School of the University of Patras and, since 1982, he has been the president of the Greek Study Group. Apart from a large number of publications in psychoanalytic journals, his main theoretical work is considered to be: "Time and Timelessness. The Varieties of Temporal Experience", Madison (Int. Univ. Press), 1983. He is also the editor of *Borderline Personality Disorders,* 1977 and, in collaboration with Ian D. Graham, *The Personality Myth in Psychoanalytic Theory*, 1991, both published by the Int. Univ. Press. In 1970 he published a volume of short stories and in 1993, a novel.

References

CREMERIUS, J. (1982): Die Bedeutung des Dissidenten für die Psychoanalyse. Psychoanalyse jenseits von Orthodoxie und Dissidenz. *Psyche* 36, 481–514.

Hartis, 17–18 (1985): Special edition dedicated to Andreas Embirikos (in Greek).

HARTOCOLLIS, P. (1984): Psychoanalysis abroad: A Report from Greece. *Psa. Quart.* 52, 250–254.

CARAPANOU, F. (1952–1953): "Early lack of maternal care". *Engephalos* 3, 68–80 (in Greek).

POTAMIANOU, A. (1976): "20 Years Life of the CMHR". Athens (in Greek).

– (1988): "Episkepsis". Pensées autour de la visite d'Anna Freud à Athènes. *Rev. Int. Hist. Psa.* 1, 247–254.

TZAVARAS, A. (ed) (1984): Psychoanalysis in Greece. Athens (The Society of Modern Greek Culture and Genreal Education Studies) (in Greek).

TZAVARAS, A. / G. PAPAGOUNOS (1990): "The Development of Freudian Theory: The Role of the "Centre" and "Excentric" in Theory Production and Diffusion, in: P. Nicolacopoulos (ed), Greek Studies in the Philosophy and History of Science, Dordrecht: Kluwer Academic Publishers.

Institutions

Hellenic Psychoanalytical Study Group
Arnis 3, 11528 Athens
Tel.: 01/7214662, Fax: 01/7214662

Dr. med. Jannis Kontos, 22 Socratous, 14561 Athens
Sotiris Manolopoulos, M. D., 4 Menandrou, 14561 Athens
Nikos Kouretas, M. D., 221 Dorset Road, Waban, MA 02168, USA

Norway

by Finn Hansen and Sverre Varvin

In an article on psychoanalysis and Norwegian literature published in the interwar period, Philip Houm, a Norwegian literary critic, states that the name of Freud was little known in Norway. He points to the 1909 edition of Aschehoug's Encyclopedia where Freud's name is not even mentioned and to the 1921 edition where Freud has only been accorded a few lines. According to Hoel the psychoanalytic movement first reached Norway in 1926/27. It may appear that the seed of the young science had either not been blown to our shores by favourable winds, or else that our cultural soil had been too poor for the seed to take root and grow into the viable plant it proved to be later.

Freud, however, writes in *The History of the Psychoanalytic Movement*, that the world's first psychiatry textbook introducing psychoanalysis was published in Norwegian by Ragnar Vogt. It was published in 1905 under the title *Psykiatriens grunntrekk (An Outline of Psychiatry).* Vogt, who was later appointed professor of psychiatry at the University of Oslo and medical director at the psychiatric clinic, published the book *Hysterisk sinnsykdom (Hysterical Mental Illness)* in 1911 in which he also referred to the writings of Breuer and Freud from 1893 to 1906. In 1923 this author also published the textbook *Medisinsk psykologi og psykiatri (Medical Psychology and Psychiatry)* which included a long chapter on psychoanalysis.

There was also another Norwegian scientist, John M. Vold, who was given a place in the history of psychoanalysis by Freud. Vold was professor of philosophy at the University of Oslo. He belonged to the Hegelian school of philosophy, but is primarily known for his experimental studies of the connection between dreams and different sensory stimulations. His book on dream research was published in two volumes under the title *Über den Traum* (1910–12) *(On Dreams).* Freud greatly valued his research and especially his methodology.

Even though psychoanalysis was not practised in Norway before the twenties, it was not unknown. And also the other way around as is illustrated by Freud's keen interest in the works of Henrik Ibsen.

It should be mentioned that a "wild analyst", J. I. Strømme, practised in Oslo from 1916, gaining a reputation as psychoanalyst in the public and even gathering pupils during the years.

Scandinavian Psychoanalysts Break out of their Isolation[1]

In 1931 there was a meeting with Scandinavian psychoanalysts in the home of the Swedish psychoanalyst Alfhild Lamm in Stockholm.[2]

They agreed on establishing a psychoanalytic study-circle and wanted to establish an affiliation with the IPA. The letter from this meeting was discussed at the congress in Lucerne in 1934. After a heated debate and an important appeal from Kristian Schjelderup, warning against the practice of wild analysts in Scandinavia, it was agreed that a Finnish-Swedish society and a Danish-Norwegian society were to be established. This was an important step for the Scandinavians, breaking the relative isolation from the international debate.

The Social and Political Situation in the 1920s and 1930s

Similar to other parts of the Western world after World War I, our country too plunged into an economical and social crisis in the 1920s and far into the 1930s.

Our banking system collapsed, industrial concerns went bankrupt, farmers had to leave their land, the rate of unemployment rose to alarming heights.

In those days we lacked the social security-system that would have helped all those who had become losers in modern society. The international Labour movement had failed to prevent the war. A wave of nationalism was soon to spread throughout all the countries at war and international solidarity was sacrificed on the altar of nationalism. And yet the Bolshevists' seizure of power in Russia did hold a certain promise for a number of people. As could be expected, the Norwegian Labour party became in-

1 For biographical notes on some of the pioneers of Freudian psychoanalysis see chapter "Pioneers of Freudian Psychoanalysis".

2 The participants at this meeting were: Dr. S. Naesgård, Denmark, Y. Kulovesi, Finland, O. Raknes, Prof. H. Schjelderup. Dr. J. I. Strømme (with two assistants; F. Svendsen and G. Ivarson), Norway, B. Anderberg, I. Bratt, N. Nilsen, E. B. Nordlund, T. Sandstrøm and A. Lamm, Sweden.

creasingly radical after World War I. In 1918 a majority in the Norwegian Labour Party endorsed a statement declaring the Party a revolutionary party. The history of Conservatism holds forth that even though much of what was said by the Labour party at that time may be looked upon as mere rhetorical phrases, the middle classes were frightened. The Government decided, if necessary, to use police and military force to protect strikebreakers in labour disputes. On the initiative of banks, industrial organisations and others, permission was given in 1921 to organize a civil corps which was supplied with arms. This corps was also to protect strikebreakers, and be sent into action wherever the established order was threatened. Even certain employers were supplied with automatic pistols, ammunition and bandoleers in order, if necessary, to keep their employees under control. These measures intensified the growing bitterness within the working class. But it was not only among the working people that the mood turned revolutionary; many sons and even some daughters of the established middle class joined those who had dreams of a communist society.

The Norwegian Students' Association, founded in 1813 in Oslo, to which not only students but also senior academics belonged, had at times played a significant part in the political and cultural life of Norway. In 1921 a political group was formed which was given the name "Mot Dag" (Dawn).

"Mot Dag" was actually the name of a journal which was to be published but it also became the name of this group which was to leave its decisive mark on the political and cultural scene in years to come. Its undisputed leader and organizer was Erling Falck (b. 1887). After living in the United States for eleven years he returned to Norway at the age of 31.

According to the historian Trygve Bull, Falck had been in contact for some years with the powerful revolutionary syndicalistic trade union movement "Industrial Workers of the World". It is also likely that Falck frequented the circle of the leaders of that organization in Chicago. However, he was not only engaged in politics – he was also greatly preoccupied with Freud and psychoanalysis. Freud thus occupied a central position in this academic political organisation, and some even regarded him as one of the great prophets of the movement. Bull (Bull, 1968) thought that "Mot Dag" had a communist dream of revolution, but that, psychologically, it was made of the same stuff as the ancient Christian dream of the millennium. In this particular dream an attempt was made to create a synthesis of Freud and Marx. It might even strike one that in the minds of these radicals of the 20s and 30s, Freud was about to displace Marx.

The "Mot Dag" adherents made a distinction between a bourgeois psychoanalysis which one thought would adjust the analysand to the environment, and Marxist psychoanalysis which would liberate the analysand's potential which would then be transformed into active and critical social commitment. Wilhelm Reich was regarded as a representative of the latter type of psychoanalysis. The Norwegian "Mot Dag" adherents considered sexual information for young people as their primary objective.

One of the "Mot Dag" adherents, the physician Karl Evang, who was later to become Surgeon General in Norway, published the journal *Sexual Information.* This journal was greatly conducive to a healthier attitude towards sexuality, thus improving public health in our country.

Wilhelm Reich, Otto Fenichel and Norwegian Psychoanalysis in the Thirties

After arriving in Norway as a refugee in l934, Reich soon stirred up a heated conflict. Inspite of the fact that he was never accepted as a member of the Norwegian Society, those belonging to the Society were greatly influenced by him. He gave lectures and held seminars on character analysis. Some of the members of the Society were also in analysis with him, Havrevold, Raknes and Waal, among others.

For the radical leftwing intellectuals he became a front figure. While in Norway he developed a new form of therapy which was called vegeto-therapy. While character analysis referred to the psychic defence mechanisms, vegeto-therapy focuses on the muscular and visceral mechanisms. Character analytic vegeto-therapy therefore aims at both these defence mechanisms. As long as Reich kept within the framework of character analytic vegeto-therapy, he enjoyed the recognition of the professional community. It is true that opinions were divided about vegeto-therapy, but he was still considered *salonfähig* (presentable). However, when he slowly began to set up his biological-physical experiments and theories and developed his orgon-therapy, his activities stirred up considerable scepticism. Reich imagined himself to have discovered a new cosmic form of energy inherent in all forms of life, and he believed he could charge a so-called orgon-accumulator with orgon to be used in the treatment of a number of diseases. He even claimed to be able to create life from anorganic matter.

Reich founded an Institute for Sexual Economy. There were nine members, six from Oslo, two from Denmark and one from England. The Institute closed down in l940. Raknes, who had been Reich's faithful supporter, acquired an orgon-cabinet which he used in the treatment of his patients.

Reich's biological-physical experiments were considered unscientific and Reich himself was looked upon as a charlatan.

Reich gradually met with a great deal of criticism. A very well-known Medical Director, Johann Scharfenberg, wrote a few articles in the *Arbeiderbladet"(Labour newspaper)* in 1938 criticizing Reich, as well as expressing doubts as to his medical qualifications. In a letter to the Ministry of Health he expressed his opinion about Reich, suggesting that he should be deported from Norway. In spite of protests from Harald Schjelderup and others he was ordered to leave the country.

When describing Norwegian psychoanalysis during the 1930s, it has often been emphasized that we had Reich and Fenichel here at the same time and that this proved to be a complicated situation. Both of them were – or had been – members of Communist parties, and both had been on a study tour in the Soviet Union at the invitation of the Soviet government. They both belonged to a Marxist opposition group within the IPA. Fenichel had established a Communist cell in connection with the Berlin Institute and had possibly similar plans when presenting himself with a lecture at the Psychological Institute of the University of Oslo entitled "Psychoanalysis and Marxism". In other words, on the political level both men had much in common. However, professionally, they did not see eye to eye. Fenichel defended the Freudian positions, while Reich's ambition was to develop them further. He was deeply unhappy after his last meeting with Freud to whom he had submitted his own theories only to be met by Freud's frosty attitude and total rejection. Later he drew comfort from the thought that Freud had become an old man enfeebled by sickness. On the personal level, too, Fenichel and Reich greatly differed. Fenichel is described in the *Biografisches Lexikon der Psychoanalyse (Biographical Encyclopedia of Psychoanalysis),* as a pedant with a photographic memory and a remarkable working capacity. Reich is described by those who knew him as a charismatic personality with the ability to inspire others, while other sources often point to his capriciousness and unreliability.

Norwegian Psychoanalysis during the War

The Norwegians dissolved the Society for the duration of the war. This was partly motivated by the knowledge of the fate of the German Society after the National-Socialists came to power.

Among the members, Landmark was killed while fighting in northern Norway, Harald and Kristian Schjelderup were sent to the Norwegian concentration camp Grini, Paul Bernstein died in a concentration camp in

Germany, and several had to flee to Sweden due to illegal activity (among others Havrevold and Nic Waal).

Norwegian Psychoanalysis after the War and in the 1950s

The Danish-Norwegian Society was reinstated in 1947 and functioned until 1953 when the Danes formed their Society. The Danish Society was accepted as a study-group by the IPA.

The Norwegians re-christened their Society; "The Norwegian Psychoanalytic Society", and this was the start of a long fight for international recognition.

An application in 1952 was turned down on the grounds that some of the Society's members were not practising psychoanalysts. As it turned out, the IPA was considering the Reichian influence on the technique of some members.

At the Edinburgh congress in 1961 the Norwegian Society was recognized as an independent Study Group directly under the Central Committee of the IPA. The application was signed by members who were members of other societies accepted by the IPA.[3] A committe of three was assigned by the central committee to assist the Norwegian Thorkil Vangaard, Copenhagen, visited Norway to "familiarize himself with the local conditions". He had separate interviews and a meeting with the whole group. A debate on the frequency of sessions for training analysis ensued, mostly between Schjelderup and Vangaard. Schjelderup had for practical reasons practised down to two sessions per week and claimed good results. No agreement was established and the result was that the Central Committee withdrew its recognition of the Norwegian Society as a study-group.

The work to let the standard of training meet the requirements of the IPA was given priority and foreign training analysts were invited to give seminars and lectures. (Among others; Else Frenkel Brunswik, Erik Bjerk Hansen, Børje Løfgran, J. J. Sandler and Alberta Szalita). Szalita continued visiting our Society and had an important influence not only in the psychoanalytic Society but also in psychiatry through her supervision and educational activities.

3 Harald Schjelderup, Hjørdis Simonsen, members of the Finnish-Swedish society, Olav Brodwall, ass. member of the Finnish-Swedish society and Finn Hansen, ass. member of the German society.

At the beginning of the sixties there were only two training analysts. This situation was greatly improved in the following ten years, making it possible for a new generation of psychoanalysts to have their training in Norway.

The Norwegian Psychoanalytic Institute

The necessity of establishing a training institute had long been felt. Preparation was made already in the mid-fifties and in 1967 it could be realised with the support from the Institute of Social Research (a non-governmental research-institute).

Peter Andreas Holter was the first head of the institute which now (1994) has 58 candidates. In the last years, the activities of the institute have proliferated (besides the regular psychoanalytic training), including, among others, training in child-analysis and child-psychotherapy, psychoanalytic courses for psychiatric health-workers and the establishment of the largest psychoanalytic library in Norway.

Research activity has been given a priority and it is now possible for members to apply for research grants.

The institute now receives about 1 million Nkr 100 000 £) a year from the government.

Recognition by the IPA – at last

In 1969, the IPA was approached anew, and after a couple of years' work, the Norwegian society was given the status of a study group at the congress in Vienna in 1971.

A new Sponsoring Committee was appointed,[4] which resulted in the achievement of temporary membership status of the IPA at the congress in Paris in 1973, and in 1975 the Society was finally given formal recognition as a society affiliated to the IPA.

Now a new period could begin where the main tasks were to educate new analysts and the establishment of psychoanalysis as clinical practice on a broader scale in Norway.

4 The comittee consisted of the following: Kjell Örberg, Stockholm, chairman, Stig Bjørk, Helsingfors, Mario Montesorri, Amsterdam, Louis Munro, London, Alberta Szalita, New York and Helmuth Thomä, Ulm

The Society has now (March 1994), 36 full members and 16 associate members. There are 19 training analysts.

Some of the Pioneers of Freudian Psychoanalysis in Norway

Harald Krabbe Schjelderup (1895–1974) was the most outstanding representative of psychoanalysis in Norway in the 1920s and subsequent years. He had a solid background in philosophy and the natural sciences when he was appointed professor at the University of Oslo in 1922. He had studied science with physics as the main subject and had worked for three years as research assistant at the "Institute of physics" in Oslo under Lars Vegard who later was to become widely known for his research of northern lights.

He also studied philosophy. In 1916 he was awarded Monrad's golden medal for his dissertation *Main lines in the history of philosophy from the middle of the 19th century to the present day (1920).* While holding a scholarship in philosophy, he concentrated on the study of experimental psychology. He worked with Alfred Lehmann in Copenhagen and with Georg Elias Müller in Göttingen, two distinguished names in the history of experimental psychology. Schjelderup's interest had obviously swerved from the natural sciences and philosophy towards psychology.

As a result, the Chair he held was changed from philosophy to psychology.

In order to gain personal experience of psychoanalytic treatment, Schjelderup set out to Vienna in 1925 to start personal analysis with Edward Hitschmann, who was then Head of the Vienna Psychoanalytic Institute. At the same time he studied psychiatry at the University Clinic under Julius Wagner Ritter von Jauregg and hypnosis with Paul Schilder. Later he had analysis with Oskar Pfister in Zürich. On March 31st 1928 he became a member of the Swiss Society. He also went into analysis with Schultz-Hencke in Berlin. When Wilhelm Reich came to Norway in the 1930s he went into analysis with him in order to acquire his character analytic technique.

In his books *Psykologi (Psychology)* from 1927 and *Innføring i psykologien (Introduction to Psychology)* from 1957, he attempts to bridge the gap between academic psychology and psychoanalysis. The former is considered to be the very first book in the world with that objective. It was also translated into German. The book was given special mention in the International Journal of 1932. In 1937 the book *Nevrose og oppdragelse* (Neurosis and Education) was published. An enlarged edition of this book was published in 1948 with the title *Nevrose eller sunnhet – hvordan oppdra våre barn? (Neurosis or health – how to bring up our children?).* By means of such books as well as a number of articles in journals and newspapers, Schjelderup contributed to a greater understanding of what children need in order to develop a healthy personality. In 1940 his book *Nevrosene og den nevrotiske karakter (Neuroses and the Neurotic Character)* was published. Here he dismisses the Freudian monotheism and in its place he creates a trinity based on Freud, Reich and Schultz-Hencke. Freud is here represented by his amputated Libido Theory, Reich by his views on character formation and its physical correlates, and Schultz-Hencke by his emphasis on the mechanisms of inhibition. Where Schjelderup speaks of banal conflicts, Schultz-Hencke speaks of inhibitions and inhibitory mechanisms.

In 1955 Schjelderup published an article "Lasting Effects of Psychoanalytic Treatments" in the journal *Psychiatry* where he presented a follow-up study of patients who had undergone psychoanalytic treatment. The article attracted international attention.

During the German occupation of Norway, Schjelderup became the leader of the underground movement at the University of Oslo and in order to prevent Nazi infiltration he ordered the University to be closed down. He was arrested in 1943 and spent the years until 1945 in prison and concentration camp.

Kristian Schjelderup (1894–1980), Harald's younger brother, a very liberal theologian, called attention to himself by advocating an extremely liberal theology. Together with his brother Harald he wrote the dissertation *Three main types of religious forms of experience.* His doctoral thesis from 1923 was entitled: *Religionens sannhet i lys av den relativitetsorienterte virkelighetsoppfatning. (Truth in religion in the light of relativity-oriented realism).* His liberal theological outlook stood for a long time in the way of an ecclesiastic career. Yet he ended up as bishop of the Norwegian Church in Hamar. Kristian Schjelderup translated Freud's Five Lectures into Norwegian. He had analysis with Pfister in Zürich and was accepted as a member of the Swiss Society in 1928.

He spent the war years of 1942-45 in a concentration camp where he acted as priest for his fellow prisoners.

Trygve Braatøy (1904-53) was the central figure in our psychoanalytic community. He was a Dr. med. from 1936, Medical Director at the Ullevål psychiatric department in Oslo, and from 1949-1951 he worked at the Menninger Foundation in Topeca, USA. He had his psychoanalytic training in Berlin.

Braatøy was an experienced debater in journals and newspapers and he was one of those who inaugurated the use of psychoanalysis as an auxiliary discipline for the understanding of literature. He also wrote a book about the poet Knut Hamsun in which he attempted to draw a portrait of the poet by combining the theories of Freud and Adler (*Livets sirkel – The Circle of Life,* published in 1929). Braatøy advocated psychodynamically oriented psychotherapy for the treatment of neurosis, and he went strongly in for humanizing the therapist in his relationship to the patient in the therapeutic situation. Influenced by Reich's vegeto-therapy and in cooperation with the physiotherapist Aadel Bülow-Hansen, Braatøy developed a method of muscular treatment which focused on the hypertonic musculature and was originally intended to be used in psychotherapy.

We can find Braatøy's views on neuroses and the treatment of neuroses in his main work from 1947 entitled *De nervøse sinn (The Nervous Minds).* His book *Foundations of Psychoanalytic Technique* was first published after his death in 1954.

Odd Wåge Havrevold (1900–1992), cand. med. in 1926, was a specialist in neurology from 1934. He had his psychoanalytic training in Vienna in 1933. His training analyst was Dr. Eduard Hitschmann. He also attended clinical seminars during that year. In Norway he was supervised by Harald Schjelderup.

Johannes Landmark (1897–1940) was a physician. He had his psychoanalytic training in Berlin and was accepted as an associate member of the German Psychoanalytic Society on June 21, 1932. After the congress in Lucerne his membership was transferred to the Danish-Norwegian Society. He was an officer in the Army Medical Corps during the war and died during a skirmish in northern Norway in 1940.

Ola Raknes (1887-1975). Norwegian philologist, Dr. phil. in 1927 with his thesis *Møtet med det heilage, en religionspsykologisk avhandling (Meeting with the Sacred. A Dissertation on the Psychology of Religion).* He taught Norwegian at the Sorbonne in Paris. He received his psychoanalytic training in Berlin. On June 25, 1929 he gave a paper in Berlin with the title "Aspects of the psychology of religion". He was subsequently accepted as a member of the German Psychoanalytic Society on October 15, 1929. For many years Raknes was an advocate of Freudian psychoanalysis, but after Reich came to Norway he became his faithful disciple, accompanying him on his road from character analysis via vegeto-therapy to orgon therapy. When the Danish-Norwegian psychoanalytic Society was formed in Lucerne in 1934, Raknes' membership was transferred to Norway. Gradually his form of therapy began to deviate greatly from the form predominantly practised within the Society with the result that he withdrew his membership in 1945.

Hjørdis Simonsen (formerly Christensen; 1899-1980) philologist, cand. mag. She completed her psychoanalytic training in Berlin and was accepted as an associate member of the German Society on July, 11, 1933. After the congress in Lucerne her membership was transferred to the Danish-Norwegian Society. For many years she was one of the central figures in the Society.

Nic Waal (formerly Hoel), born in 1905, died in 1960. She was a specialist in psychiatry in 1951 and in child psychiatry in 1953. She received her psychoanalytic training in Berlin, and was accepted as an associate member of the German Society on July 11, 1933. Her membership, too, was transferred to the Danish-Norwegian Society after the congress in Lucerne in 1934. She went subsequently into analysis with Wilhelm Reich and became one of his supporters. Nic Waal visited Child Guidance Clinics while staying in the United States and her experiences at these clinics with their interdisciplinary approach inspired her to establish the Nic Waals Institute in Oslo. The Institute has now developed into one of Norway's most prestigious centres for treatment and training in child-psychotherapy, based on depth-psychological theory.

Conclusion

Psychoanalysis is now established as an important clinical discipline in Norway. Leading psychoanalysts have for many years had leading positions in academic psychiatry, academic psychology and in clinical psychiatry/psychology. When training for psychiatry, it is obligatory to have at least two years of supervision on psychoanalytically oriented psychotherapy with the purpose of learning the dynamics of the doctor-patient relationship. There are also a fair number of analysts in private practice and an educational activity at the Psychoanalytical institute will secure a steady growth of the discipline.

In the recent years important papers by analysts on literary criticism and other areas of applied psychoanalysis have been published.

Although Freud seemed to be sceptical towards the possibility of an acceptance of psychoanalysis in the Nordic countries, and even though there have been great controversies, psychoanalysis in Norway seems now to have a solid base. There are a steady recruitment and a growing interest in developing the scientific status of the discipline.

References

ALNÆS, RANDOLPH (1980): The Development of Psychoanalysis in Norway. A historical overview, *Scand.Psychoanal.Rev.* 3, 55–101.

– (1994): Psykoanalysen: Norge, Historie – utdannelse – behandling – forskning. *Nordic Journal of Psychiatry,* Suppl. 32, Vol. 48, 1–103.

BRAATØY, TRYGVE (1965): De nervøse sinn, Oslo: J.W. Cappelens forlag.

BULL, TRYGVE (1968): Mot Dag og Erling Falk, Trondheim: J. W. Cappelens forlag.

DANIELSEN, ROLF (1984): Høyres historie, bind 2, Oslo: J.W. Cappelens forlag.

FENICHEL, OTTO (1945): The psychoanlytic theory of neurosis, New York: W. W. Norton & Company.

JOHNSEN, LILLEMOR (1990): Det frigjørende åndedrett, Aventura forlag.

MAURSETH, PER (1987): Arbeiderbevegelsens historie i Norge, bind 3, Oslo: Tiden Norsk Forlag.

MÜHLLEITNER, ELKE (1992): Biographisches Lexikon der Psychoanalyse, Tübingen: Edition Diskord.

NORDBY, TROND (1989): Karl Evang. En biografi, Oslo: Aschehoug.

SCHJELDERUP, HARALD (1988): Nevrosene og den nevrotiske karakter, Oslo: Universitetsforlaget,.

– (1968): Nevrose eller sunnhet? Hvordaa skal vi oppdra våre barn? Trondheim: J. W. Cappelens forlag.

SCHULTZ-HENCKE, HARALD (1980): Einführung in die Psychoanalyse, Göttingen: Vandenhoeck & Ruprecht.

– (1988):Lehrbuch der analytischen Psychotherapie, Stuttgart / New York: Thieme.

WALL, HELGE (1991): Nic Waal, Det urolige hjerte, Oslo: Pax Forlag.

ÅS, ARVID et. al. (1965): Forskerferd i sinnets dybder. Festskrift til Harald Schjelderup på 70-årsdagen. Oslo: Gyldendal Norsk Forlag.

Journals

The Scandinavian Psychoanalytical Review (in English)
since 1978; Ed.: Psycho-Analytical Societies in Denmark, Finland, Norway and Sweden
Munksgaard International Publishers Ltd., P.O.Box 2148, Copenhagen, Denmark

Nordic Journal of Psychiatry
(with many articles on psychoanalysis)
since 1946; Ed.: Lars von Knorring
Scandinavian University Press, P.O. Box 2959 Tøyan, 0608 Oslo

Institutions

Norsk Psykoanalytisk Forening
Norwegian Psychoanalytic Society
Industrigaten 46, 0357 Oslo
Tel.: 47-22-60 5820; Fax: 47-22-46 8422

Nic Waals Institutt
Spångbergvei 25, 0853 Oslo

Norsk Psykoanalytisk Institutt
Industrigaten 46, 0357 Oslo 3

Finn Hansen, P.B. 910 Bergersborg, 1517 Moss
Sverre Varvin, Gustav Vigelandsv. 40, 0274 Oslo

Portugal

by Carlos Amaral Dias

1. Brief History

Looking back at the history of the psychoanalytic movement in Portugal it seems that, at least from an official point of view, it is relatively recent. Portugal only starts to have formal relations with the International Psychoanalytical Association as a Study Group in 1966.

However, a reading, albeit brief, of the period preceding the official installation of psychoanalysis in our country, would indicate a different situation. Dating from the beginning of the century, manifestations of psychoanalytical thought could be found in the scientifical-medical *milieu.* Egas Moniz, Medicine Nobel Prize winner, published several articles about the theories and methods of psychoanalysis (Valle, 1977; Moniz, 1915, 1921, 1924, 1928). In fact he appears to have treated some cases of neurosis through the analytical method (Moniz, 1921). Although with a different approach, probably a less deeper one, Sobral Cid (1924), Psychiatry Professor at Lisbon University, used psychoanalytical conceptual constructions, mainly in the approach to schizophrenia. At another level, Abel de Castro, a graduate in History and Philosophy, a journalist and a writer, seems to have taken an interest in psychoanalysis, having exchanged correspondence with Freud between 1924 and 1929 (Valle, 1979).

It is nevertheless in the fifties, under the strong influence of Diogo Furtado, a university professor of the highest importance to Portuguese neurology and psychiatry, that a few doctors opted for psychoanalytical training and education.

Consequently two of his assistants, Francisco Alvim and Pedro Luzes, go to Genebra. There, in association with two Spanish psychoanalysts, they eventually form the Luso-Spanish Society of Psychoanalysis, accepted by the IPA, at the Paris Congress, in 1957. These two analysts were subsequently joined by a third, João dos Santos, who had meanwhile completed his studies in Paris, and later still joined by Eduardo Luís Cortesão, from the British Psychoanalytical Society.

Unfortunately of all the pioneers only one is still alive, Pedro Luzes, currently exercising the presidency of the Portuguese Pychoanalytical Society. The latter was accepted as a full member Society at the New York

Congress in the seventies, which enabled all its founders to witness the integral recognition of the Portuguese Psychoanalytical Society by the IPA.

2. Internal Development and Growth

Despite the relatively scarce number of analysts practising in Portugal in the sixties and seventies, the importance of psychoanalysis not only remained significant but grew. Concurring with this fact was the enrolment of prominent figures from Portuguese psychiatry, with responsibilities in directing mental health facilities in Portugal, and also its installation in the universities, both in the medical schools and in the psychology faculties. As an example, from the five medical faculties existing in our country, three of them have a psychoanalyst in charge of psychiatry; the teaching of clinical psychology and psychotherapy is to a great extent under the direction of psychoanalysts. The present situation at this level is a consequence of the rigour put in training and of the resulting prestige that the pioneers succeeded in applying to the development of psychoanalysis in Portugal. In this sense, despite the present contradictions inherent to the developments in the neurosciences, no matter how grave those may be, and despite being criticised by medical and psychiatry sectors, the fact is that the psychoanalytical practice is undoubtedly the most prestigious in our country.

Perhaps due to these implications in health and university, a corresponding adherence on the part of intellectuals has not been as great as in other countries.

Nowadays this picture seems nevertheless to be undergoing a change, helped by the organization of annual colloquia promoted by the Portuguese Psychoanalytical Society, which interest a wide public, because of the undeniable importance of the themes debated. This colloquium is complementary to another one, also public, dedicated to the more specific problems of psychopathology and psychotherapy, and where the psychoanalysts see fit to intervene. In this way, the Portuguese psychoanalytical movement is not enclosed in itself, which naturally enables it to conduct a dialogue with other sciences and subjects and allows the cooptation of professionals interested in psychoanalytical practice.

Structurally the society is organized around the Psychoanalytical Institute's board of directors and the Teaching Committee. The Psychoanalytical Institute is the place where conferences, seminars and other educational activities are held, and where the candidates can look for and find their first patients. Founded in 1977, the Psychoanalytical Institute has played a central role in analytical education. The Training Committee, composed of five training analysts, is responsible for the training structure and the admission of new members. Having the most recognized elements in the Portuguese psychoanalytical field, it has accomplished its functions with the utmost rigour and seriousness, thus being a support for the identification and transformation of the new members.

Some of the Portuguese psychoanalysts are internationally known for their work. That is the case with Pedro Luzes, who already in 1968 was responsible for the report presented to the French-Language Psychoanalysts Congress, as well as others, some of whom currently teach in Europe and Latin America on a regular basis.

At this point we cannot but emphasize the role played by Pierre Luquet, from the Paris Psychoanalytical Society, who guaranteed a regular training and discussion seminar for many years – undoubtedly an important contribution back then. Although his teachings were characterized by a strict adherence to Freud's thought, consequently involving the exclusion of Melanie Klein, Pierre Luquet most certainly catalized many of the analytical anguishes in our country.

Now (1992) the Portuguese Psychoanalytical Society has more than 100 members, of which 10 are full members, and 20 associate members. Though preferentially placed in the capital, Lisbon, it is also installed in Oporto (the second biggest Portuguese city), where it has three full members and one associate member, among more than ten analysts; and in Coimbra (one of the oldest university cities in the world), where the Portuguese Psychoanalytical Society has 8 members, one of them being a full member and the others associate members. Presently there are candidates exercising their practice in other cities, namely in Faro, Braga and Aveiro. All this development testifies to the interest and establishment of psychoanalysis in Portugal.

3. Portuguese Psychoanalysis in the face of Post-Freudian Developments

The most relevant factor, at the level of the scientific models with better acceptance in the Portuguese Psychoanalytical Society, is undoubtedly a certain capacity for cohabitation, demonstrative of a sense of tolerance, most probably inherent to the Portuguese people.

This factor (we say factor because its undeniable cohesive ability makes it a known one), allows that from the training *curriculum* until the individual or collective investigations a great sense of openness is felt with the society. That sense, together with the relatively small number of its members, enables it to have enough solidity which in turn makes the semantic variety in our speeches and practices easier. In other words, without letting the disintegrative and dissociative processes become dominant.

We can properly state that both Francisco Alvim and Pedro Luzes led from the early days of the society two fundamental currents of analytical thought: The one was of rather more Freudian roots, "marked" by the importance of the pulsion language, and where the hysteria model was central (we are referring to Francisco Alvim). The other was led by Pedro Luzes, where Melanie Klein and the equation of the schizo-paranoid and depressive positions, the destination of projection, introjection and the integrative processes represent indispensable references.

The scientific blending of these two paradigmatic benchmarks gave way in Portugal, as it did in the rest of Europe, to the appearance of intermediate positions, as well as to the development of parallel, yet convergent scientific interests. To some extent Eduardo Luís Cortesão and João dos Santos represented these standpoints. From there, a renewed interest in infantile psychotherapy (Santos) and in psychosomatic medicine (Cortesão) arose. More recently Coimbra de Matos has developed some works following a model of the same nature.

Since the eighties we have seen a growing interest in the works of Bion, justly considered as the initiator of a significant epistemological concern in psychoanalysis. To this concern, which has gradually been spread in the *Portuguese Psychoanalytical Revue,* has corresponded a change in the ways of considering psychoanalysis as the activity of the analyst; but then again it was only the way a previous intuition was expressed. Already in 1968 Luzes presented a study, back then a pioneer one, about thought disturbances and psychoanalytical practice, and where the works of W. R. Bion were the fundamental reference. We ourselves published several works reflecting the importance of that author (Dias, 1988, 1992).

But as a reference, Bion appears like Socrates: "The school is over, when the class is over." Therefore it certainly shall not be from that idea that the Portuguese Psychoanalytical Society will encounter any ideological dissensions ...

References

DIAS, C. A. (1988): Para uma Psicanálise da relação. Porto: Editora Afrontamento.
– (1992): Aventuras de Ali-Babá no túmulo de UR. Lisboa: Editora Fenda.
MONIZ, E. (1915): As bases da psico-análise. Lição do Curso de Neurologia, *A Medicina Contemporânea* 33, 337.

– (1921): O conflicto sexual. Conferência plenária do Congresso Luso-Espanhol das Associações para o Progresso das Ciências, *Portugal Médico* 6, 385.
– (1924): Júlio Diniz e a psico-análise, *A Medicina Contemporânea* 42, 185.
– (1928): A Vida Sexual (Filosofia e Patologia), 7ª ed., Lisboa: Casa Ventura Abrantes (v. principalmente: "Prólogo").
Sobral Cid (1924): A Vida psíquica dos esquizofrénicos, *Journal da Sociedade das Ciências Médicas* 88, 180.
Valle, M. et al. (1977): Quatro Cartas Inéditas de Freud, *Análise Psicológia* 1,1, 7–13.
– (1979): Four recently discovered letters by Freud to a Portuguese correspondent. *Int. Rev. Psycho-Anal.* 6, 437.

Journals

Revista Portuguesa de Psicanálise
since 1985; Ed.: Edições Afrontamento
Rua de Costa Cabral, 859, 4200 Porto

Anuário Ibérico de Psicoanálisis
since 1989; Ed.: The Portuguese and Spanish Psychoanalytical Societies,
The Madrid Psychoanalytical Association

Institutions

Sociedade Portuguesa de Psicanálise
Portuguese Psychoanalytical Society
Av. da Republica, 97 5° , 1000 Lisboa
Tel.: 351-797 2108; Fax: 351-793 6224

Prof. Dr. Carlos Amaral Dias, Av. Elisa de Moura 445–5°B, 3000 Coimbra

Romania

by Vera Şandor

Has it been possible for psychoanalysis to survive in the Communist countries? If so, what is the specific character of psychoanalysis in those countries? What are the problems faced by psychoanalysts in Eastern Europe with respect to training, transmission and practice? What is the current position of psychoanalysis in Romania? So many questions relating to psychoanalysis in the former Communist countries have arisen in the wake of the fall of the Iron Curtain, and the consequent opening up of a new arena of development and research to the European psychoanalytic movement. The following is an attempt to supply skeleton answers to these questions from a specifically Romanian perspective.

The history of the Romanian psychoanalytic movement is a disjointed one, due largely to the impact of major historical events: the Second World War, the establishment of the Communist regime, and its subsequent collapse in 1989. These events had an impact upon the Romanian psychoanalytic movement precisely because of their ideological implications, which disrupted its continuity. Later, continuity was further disturbed by the impact of cultural and ideological isolation and/or increased cultural and ideological openness upon attempts to solve the problems presented by analytic training, transmission and practice.

It will be obvious from this that Romanian psychoanalysis has passed through three stages, each differing from the preceding one by virtue of the manner in which the demands of analytic practice and training were met. These three periods were:

1. The period before the Second World War;
2. the period of „clandestine“ analysis under the Communist regime;
3. psychoanalysis in Romania after 1989.

If psychoanalysis has had a chance to survive in Romania, it is because it has been able to maintain, throughout these three periods, a fragile thread of transmission, the origins of which are either presently unknown or even, as some would argue, open to question.

I. Psychoanalysis before World War Two

Before the First World War and, even more so, in the inter-war period, the development of the Romanian psychoanalytic movement suffered from the same hesitations, setbacks and antagonism as was experienced by psychoanalysis everywhere at the time of Sigmund Freud's discovery.

The discovery of the unconscious found an echo in Romanian intellectual and medical circles. Several publications on this theme, both articles and books, appeared at this time. A list of some of them will be given at the end of this chapter. The results of the extremely painstaking archival researches into the major psychoanalytic publishing events of this period will be found in G. Bratescu's book *Copilaria psihanalizei românesti (Early Romanian Psychoanalysis)* 1912–1940.

I intend to dwell only on certain key factors, such as first publications, transmissions, the conflict and resistance within different sections of the intelligentsia, and the (still significant) repercussions of such factors in philosophical circles.

First Publications

In Nicolae Vaschide's book *Le sommeil et les rêves (Sleep and dreams)*, published in Paris in 1911, the author adopts an intellectual position favourable to the Freudian theory of dreams. A. Hesnard stated that Vaschide was one of the first writers to make known to the French public certain aspects of Sigmund Freud's doctrine. In Romania, the first articles and doctoral theses on psychoanalysis began to appear in 1912–13, including G. Preda's *Consideratii asupra psihoterapiei metodice (Considerations on methodic psychotherapy)*, M. Ilian's *Starea actuala a psihanalizei lui Freud (Current state of Freud's psychoanalysis)*, and others.

Transmission

The Romanian analytic transmission began, in rather obscure circumstances, sometime during the First World War. Our researches are continuing. C. Vlad has testified that, while serving on the Eastern Front, he was introduced to psychoanalysis by a Czech officer, Otto Pick. We know next to nothing about how this introduction was effected – whether it was simply a matter of theoretical discussions in the officer's mess, or whether it was a so-called "wild analysis", of the kind which Freud himself carried out in the early years, and which formed the basis of the transmissions current today, i.e. dream and content analyses without analysis of the transference, and undertaken outside the analytic situation. Nor do we currently have any information regarding the nature of the transmission to Otto Pick. What we do know is that, once he had returned to Bucharest, Vlad became the first Romanian psychoanalyst, who held fast to both analytic practice and his psychoanalytic "faith" right up to the time of his death in 1971, despite the extremely unfavourable political circumstances.

The small number of analysts practising in Romania today are all products of the C. Vlad – I. P. Sibiu – E. Papadima transmission. It was during this period that the first correspondence with Freud began. We have evidence that a correspondence took place between Freud and I. P. Sibiu, but we have, as yet, no actual examples of it, although I. Westfreid has published, by way of a preface to his book *Instinctul sexual (Sexual instinct),* a letter from Freud warning Westfreid about the resistance to psychoanalysis, and encouraging him not to give up.

Conflict and Resistance

At this period, Romanian intellectuals did have access to a certain amount of information about psychoanalysis, even if it was only acquired through reading. The prevailing attitude towards psychoanalysis was ambivalent. It was against such a background that there appeared Vlad's book *Mihai Eminescu din punct de vedere psihanalitic (Mihai Eminescu – a psychoanalytic view).* This book belongs to the notably problematic genre of "applied" psychoanalysis. Vlad tried to "debunk" Romania's national poet in a way which was not welcomed by anyone. For this purpose, the author used a book by G. Clinescu, a literary critic and one of the leaders of the Romanian intelligentsia. Clinescu's riposte was severe but well informed: not only did he assume responsibility for defending Eminescu, and challenging the kind of debunking that, according to him, no one really wanted, he also ensured that psychoanalysis itself was defended against the ravages of excessive popularization and, for that matter, the whole "wild psychoanalysis" tendency. Clinescu's book is therefore a milestone in the history of the resistance to psychoanalysis in Romania. Its repercussions are still being felt there today.

The Philosophers and Jung

Among the Romanian philosophers active between the two World Wars, two are of particular significance for the history of psychoanalysis: Lucian Blaga and Mircea Eliade.

Lucian Blaga studied in Vienna from 1917 onwards. The influence of psychoanalysis is readily apparent from his dramatic works and from his writings on the philosophy of culture. In an article published in 1930 entitled "On the track of psychoanalysis", he defended psychoanalysis against the charge of pansexualism, while analysing Freud's philosophical precursors, Plato and Goethe. His writings on the philosophy of culture reveal a slight Jungian influence.

Mircea Eliade, the well-known historian of religions, was also quite close to Jung. He left Romania to serve as a cultural attaché in London and never returned. He describes his meeting with Jung in his journal. The influence that this great exile has had on Romanian philosophy may explain a penchant for Jung which is still discernible today.

In 1952, the Academy of the then People's Republic of Romania condemned psychoanalysis in open session. This event ended the first period of our history and initiated the second.

II. Psychoanalysis Goes Underground

The years immediately following were characterized by efforts, undertaken in varying degrees of secrecy, to "save" psychoanalysis. These efforts were concentrated most notably upon the application of psychoanalysis to education. The activities of this period were in some ways reminiscent of the "psychoanalytic nursery schools" for the children of Soviet apparatchiks.

It was not only the years immediately following the Academy's condemnation but the entire post-war period up to 1989 which was to be characterized by an effort to keep psychoanalytic ideas alive, even at the expense of "going underground" and/or adopting a "critical" attitude, the latter being the price one had to pay, and the compromise one had to make, to enable the publication of the small number of books and articles which appeared during this period. We were quite happy to pay this price to help safeguard both the body of Freudian thought and (at the very least) freedom of speech and publication.

"Underground" Practice

Until 1970, only C. Vlad, I. P. Sibiu and I. Vianu maintained analytic practices, all of them "underground".

In 1971, E. Papadima began a psychoanalytic training with I. P. Sibiu: this year marked the start of the training of a new generation of analysts. Psychoanalysis was enjoying something of a revival, although conditions in

Romania were both precarious and dangerous – precarious from the point of view of analytic training, and dangerous in that "idealistic therapies" and unrestricted practice were strictly forbidden.

The decision to practise psychoanalysis was a personal one, made in the light both of the personal history of each individual, and of the repressive political system, with its "triumphant materialism", and "chemical", "organicist" and "Pavlovian" psychiatry. The internationally agreed training requirements were not met. While this is not the place to discuss whether psychoanalysis needs to be institutionalized, we can say that, in the absence of the IPA's "seal of approval", psychoanalytic practice developed through a process of self-invention and self-reinvention. It worked just like the wooden bicycle invented by a Russian peasant in some remote corner of the globe (a bitter comparison made by E. Papadima during a lecture in Paris in February 1992): the bicycle may not have conformed to the "official specifications", but it worked nevertheless. In this case, it falls to us to analyse, post festum, the consequences of having to work in secret. The effects upon the transference and countertransference of having to work clandestinely should provide food for thought for every analyst in those former Communist countries in which, throughout this period, psychoanalysis was practised "underground". When we first met with Western analysts, the questions we were asked were essential:

- Is it possible to reinvent psychoanalysis on the basis of Freud's texts?
- What were the effects upon analytic treatment of having to work clandestinely?
- Why did we opt for psychoanalysis?
- What chance is there of us becoming a part of the international network of psychoanalytic institutions?

The Publications

At the cultural level, psychoanalysis had no opportunities for self-expression until 1965–70, when, for a brief period, there was a relative thaw.

The late fruits of this short period of relative cultural freedom were two books devoted to psychoanalysis: I. P. Sibiu and V. Sahleanu's *Critical introduction to psychoanalysis,* published by Dacia-Cluj, and *Ethics and psychoanalysis* by V. Zamfirescu, published by Éditions scientifiques of Bucharest.

By a happy chance, 1980 also saw the publication of two of the earliest translations of Freud into Romanian. One, published by Éditions didactiques et pédagogiques, was a collection comprising *Introductory lectures on psychoanalysis, Five lectures on psychoanalysis and The psychopathology of everyday life*, in a translation by L. Gavrillu. The other was a translation into Romanian by V. Zamfirescu of Freud's essays on literature and art, published by Éditions Univers.[1]

The translations in question thus addressed themselves to some of Freud's earliest writings, texts that had never been translated into Romanian before. Subsequently, our ideological masters barred the way to any further attempts to translate Freud into Romanian. In spite of this ban, which was aimed specifically at psychoanalysis, 1985 was marked by the publication of V. Zamfirescu's "Between the logic of the heart and the logic of the mind".[2]

Material on psychoanalysis also began to appear in certain psychiatric publications for the first time in many years. In 1975, I. Vianu's *Introduction to psychotherapy* was published, which described certain aspects of analytic therapy. Although Romanian psychiatry was denied access to psychoanalysis, some young psychologists and psychiatrists displayed a theoretical interest. It was against such a background that the *Encyclopaedic dictionary of psychiatry* appeared, containing definitions of the most important psychoanalytic concepts and terms, most of it written by two psychologists who were also practising psychoanalysts, I. Andrucovici and V. Andor. All these publications were characterized, to a greater or lesser extent, by a phoney "critical attitude", an essential requirement if one was to be able to talk freely about psychoanalysis (an ironic destiny for the resistance to – and the counter-resistance by – psychoanalysis).

III. The Present-Day

The Romanian Psychoanalytic Society (RPS) was founded in February 1990. It was first suggested as a way of underlining the need for an institu-

1 We can also mention a publishing of a selection of Freud's writings in 1977. Author of the selection of the texts, of the notes, and of the introductory study ("Freud and Psychoanalysis") was Sondor Simo, at the time working as a psychologist in Cluj. The presentation of Simo, by far the most important study on psychoanalysis, written by a Transsylvanian author after the Second World War, attempts to offer an objective view on psychoanalytical theory and practice and on the merits of its founder" (Vargha, 1993).

2 The S. Freud Romanian Translation and Publication Center, New York, tries to achieve funds to support the renovation of psychoanalysis in Romania (personal communication from Andrei Codrescu and Florin V. Vladescu to the editor).

tional framework, affirming and supporting the need for training in psychoanalysis, and opposing a scientific, professional and ethical attitude to the phenomena of charlatanism and/or magical investment with which psychoanalysis in Romania was already confronted.

Most foreign analysts have detected, in our efforts to found a psychoanalytic school, some of the characteristics of the earliest days of psychoanalysis – the days of the pioneers, when the need for a personal analysis was not unequivocally asserted, when theory and practice were developed during each analytic session, and when resistance to psychoanalysis was both violent and undisguised. The RPS's theoretical seminars are duplicated by a parallel underground movement and development, in which training and controlled analyses are left to individual discretion, and invested with all the anxiety and responsibility that such a decision inevitably involves.

At an institutional level, in 1990 the RPS voted in favour of adherence to the principles of the IPA.

"[...] the RPS has now about 40 members, 8 of whom are part of the Constanta Subsidiary, represented by Mrs. Iona Georgescu. Another subsidiary is going to be created at Cluj, by Mr. Eugen Vargha. The activities and organisation of the subsidiaries are independent from the Bucharest group, whose experience is broader" (Clit, 1993).

References

Bratescu, G. (1993): Copilaria psihanalizei romanesti (1912–1940) [The Early Romanian Psychoanalysis (1912–1940)], Bucharest: Editura Humanitas.

Clit, Radu O. (1993): Some Informations Concerning the Romanian Psychoanalytic Society. Psychoanalytical Bulletin/Buletin de psihanaliza 1, p. 6–8.

Ionescu, Aurora (1993): Constantin Vlad. Psychoanalytical Bulletin/Buletin de psihanaliza 1, p. 4–5.

Şandor, Vera (1993): An Overview on Psychoanalysis in Romania. Psychoanalytical Bulletin/Buletin de psihanaliza 1, p. 2–4.

Vargha, Jeno-Laszlo (1993): Contributions to the History of Psychoanalysis in Romania. Psychoanalytical Bulletin/Buletin de psihanaliza 1, p. 5–6.

Journals

Buletin de psihanaliza
(with summaries in English and French)
Ed.: Alfred Dumitrescu
Intr. Aurora 17D, apt. 3
70.754 Bucuresti, Romania

Institutions

Societatea Psihanalitica Româna
Romanian Psychoanalytical Society
Intr. Aurora 17D
754 Bucuresti, Romania

The S. Freud Romanian Translation and Publication Center
1 Marine Midland Plaza, East Tower
Binghampton, New York 13901, USA

Vera Şandor, Calea Vacaresti 201, Buchuresti

Russia

by Alexander M. Etkind

The Reception of Psychoanalysis in Russia until the Perestroika

Russian psychoanalysis has an interesting and highly documented history. Jack Marti (1976) was the first who tried to describe it; the value of his evidence is still highly due to his unique emigrant sources. H. Lobner and V. Levitin (1978), J.-M. Palmier (1982), E. Roudinesco (1986), I. Maximov (1983), A. Mikhalevitch (1989), M. Ljunggren (1989), M. Miller (1985, 1990), A. u. B. Pružinini (1991) described the general sequence of events. A. Carotenuto (1982) discovered extremely important archive data on the life and love of the distinguished Russian psychoanalyst S. Spielrein. J. L. Rice (1982) presented an analysis of the Russian stereotypes that were held by the founders of psychoanalysis. I. Manson (1991) described the Russian translations of Freud. In my recent book (1993) the history of Russian psychoanalysis is shown against the background of Russian intellectual life from the beginning of the 20th century to the Stalin era. Nevertheless this piece of history is far from being understood completely. Senior historians of Russian psychology both inside and outside the country still ignore Russian psychoanalysis.

Indeed, crucial problems of its history are still unclear. Among them are the biographies of leading figures and even the dates of the organization of Russian psychoanalytic institutions; the fate of S. Spielrein after her return to Russia; the nature of the Bolshevik support of psychoanalysis with visible easiness and profound distortions. The sources of archive and interview data becoming recently available both in the East and West might help to give new answers to these questions (Etkind, 1991).

The early history of psychoanalysis is full of Russian connections. Several major figures in the international history of psychoanalysis were of Russian origin. Lou Andreas-Salome, Sabina Spielrein and Max Eitingon were among them. Russian politics and culture were an important subject to everybody in this circle. For example, according to Jones, the psychoanalytical concept of censorship was imported by Freud from Russian political life (Jones, vol. 1, 403). "Even those Russians who are not neurotics are deeply ambivalent", wrote Freud to A. Zweig.[1] The intensive and rather

1 S. Freud / A. Zweig, Correspondence. New York 1988, 55.

ambivalent attitude can be seen in Freud's own reactions to those Russians who interested him – "The Wolf Man" Sergei Pankeev (Gardiner, 1989), Sabina Spielrein, Dostoyevsky. In the same letter to Zweig Freud said that Russians seem closer to the Unconscious than Western people. If it is so it explains the relatively quick reception of psychoanalysis in pre-revolutionary Russia.

The early recognition of psychoanalysis in Russia was fully recognized by Freud. In 1912 he wrote to Jung with some irony: "In Russia (Odessa) there seems to be a local epidemic of psychoanalysis". In his "History of the Psychoanalytical Movement" he gave the following account of the Russian events: "In Russia, psychoanalysis has become generally known and has spread widely." Freud added that a "really penetrating comprehension" has not yet been achieved there; Russia in 1914 was the European country with the highest popularity of psychoanalysis as esteemed by Freud.

There are many indications of the natural affinity between Freud's circle and Russian intellectuals. Even in Paris Freud found the Russian milieu. His best friend at the time of his fellowship with Charcot was the Russian psychiatrist Darkshevich, the future doctor of Lenin.[2] Charcot himself was concerned with his patients from the Tsar family. Freud dreamed of curing Nicholas II. of his obsessional neuroses and of financing the psychoanalytical congresses with the Tsar's fees[3] – a plan that reminds us of Charcot's successes, the Odessa venture of Jacob Freud and also the profitable years of the Wolf Man's treatment. According to Jones (vol. 2, 14), a major part of Freud's patients in the first decades of his practice were from Russia and other East European countries.

Freud and his early followers lived in an environment full of Russian political and economic influences. In fact, many of the Russian acquaintances of Freud were of Jewish origin. Only one generation separated both Russian and Austrian Jews from their common Yiddish-speaking ancestors. Their cultural space covered all Eastern Europe. Two empires, the Russian and Austro-Hungarian, divided this space by military borders. Freud's mother spent several years in Odessa; Freud's father began his business there and failed (Jones, vol. 1, 3). Freud's sons fought against Russia in the battles of the war. Freud's disciples went there to spread his teachings.

Around 1910 he received several Russian visitors. In 1909 Nicolai Bazhenov (leader of the psychiatric reforms in Russia and founder of the influential free-masonic lodge in Moscow sent him a patient. In the same

2 Letters of S. Freud. Ed. E. L. Freud. New York 1960, 177.
3 Ibid, 338.

year, Eitingon organized the first Russian translations of Freud's books. Freud's fame in Russia came very fast. His fame could be compared, as some authors say, only with the Russian popularity of Nietzsche in the previous decade.

Nicolai Ossipov remembered that he read Freud from 1907 and "then was the first to popularize Freud in Russia". His correspondence with Freud began in 1910. Ossipov worked in the clinic of V. P. Serbski, a respected psychiatrist with a mild professional approach and leftist political beliefs. With several members of this clinic Ossipov founded a seminar which was psychoanalytically oriented. In 1910 Ossipov and N. Virubov founded a special journal *Psychotherapy* which published original psychoanalytical articles and translations and was published from 1910 to 1914 in Moscow. Ossipov emigrated in 1921 and started psychoanalytical practice and teaching in Prague.

Tatiana Rosenthal, another pioneer of Russian psychoanalysis, began as an activist in political strikes of 1905. She graduated in Zurich and came back to Petersburg. There she worked under V. Bechterev with children and wrote on psychoanalysis. She committed suicide in the same year, when Ossipov emigrated.[4]

Freud had the highest opinion of another Russian psychoanalyst, Moishe Wulff, whom he specially mentioned in his *History* as the "only trained psychoanalyst" in Russia. A Psychiatrist with German education, Wulff was analytically trained by K. Abraham. In 1909 he was expelled from the Berlin clinic for his analytical approach. Wulff deciced to go back to Russia. When Jones later described this story he commented that in those years Russia was more liberal in these questions than Germany (vol. 2, 166). Wulff was instrumental in introducing psychoanalysis in Russia. He published several translations and must be credited for developing Russian psychoanalytical terminology. From 1924 to his emigration in 1927 he was the President of the Russian Psychoanalytical Society. Then he worked in Germany and, after his second political emigration, in Palestine.

Leonid Droznes from Odessa called Freud in 1911 to inform him that Ossipov, Virubov and other Western historians took it as the date of the foundation of the Russian Psychoanalytical Society (Jones, vol. 2, 286). I found no confirmation of this fact in the Russian press or archives. History was more complicated. In September, 1911, the First Congress of the Russian Union of Psychiatrists and Neurologists was held. Bazhenov was elected to be the President of the Union, Virubov became the Union's Secretary,

4 Psychoanalysis in Russia. *Int. J. of Psychoanal.* 3 (1922), 513–520.

Ossipov was his deputy. The last two perceived themselves as professional psychoanalysts, the first was sympathetic to analysis. Instead of organizing the closed psychoanalytical "sect" like in other European countries after the Nurnberg Congress, Russian psychoanalysts become dominant among professionals in mental health.

Institutional psychiatry was not the major enemy of psychoanalysis in the Russian pre-revolutionary field. Psychiatry was in a deep crisis and looking for new ways itself (Brown, 1990). The major enemy was hypnosis. It was traditionally known in Russia and had there many influential adherents. Even Rasputin, according to police accounts, took formal lessons from one of the Petersburg "magnetizers". Hypnosis was the only method of psychotherapy that survived in the Soviet realm. It is clear that the problems of power, submission and freedom had dominant significance for Russian psychoanalysts. Those who belonged to the Moscow circle of Ossipov (M. Asatiani, N. Dobvnia) had personal contacts with Jung. His teaching was close to emigré Russian philosophers and philologists with mystical orientations, like Viacheslav Ivanov. But in medical circles Adlerian ideas become far more popular. It was especially clear in the influential journal *Psychotherapy*, edited by Virubov. Adler's wife, Raisa Epstein-Adler, a Russian Jew with radical-socialist views, systematically wrote in Russian on the Viennese events in Moscow *Psychotherapy.* Several authors of this journal, like Aron Zalkind, explicitly took Adlerian positions and terminology. In one of his articles of 1913, Zalkind wrote that psychoanalysis had much better positions in Russia than in the West.

Early popularity of psychoanalysis can be illustrated by the performance that one of the famous Russian producers, Nicolai Evreinov, put on the stage in Petersburg in 1912. Three actors played three "Is" of the same person – rational, emotional and unconscious. They woke the unconscious "I" up in the final scene of the suicide of the hero. The prologue contained the direct reference to Freud. In the last pre-War years the psychoanalytical sanatorium in Krucovo near Moscow was established and became known. Partly it was financed from the money of the late Russian writer Anton Chekov. Known people from the cultural elite were treated there.

The activity of the early Russian psychoanalysts was stopped by the War. The journal *Psychotherapy,* the sanatorium in Kurcovo, the seminar of Serbski were closed for ever. The post-revolutionary history of Russian psychoanalysis was made in a very different style, though often by the same people. In May/June 1922 the Russian Ministry of Education officially established the Russian Psychoanalytical Society. Application documents were signed by 14 founders: four top functionaries from the Ministry of Education, four medical doctors, two professors of art, two professors of physics and two writers. As fas as we know, only three of the 14 founders had analytical practice. Ermakov was elected to be the President. The real leader of events was Otto Schmidt, astronomer, publisher and politician who was a member of several influential bodies of Bolshevik power. He was also the chief of the State Publishing House that translated many of Freud's books into Russian. His wife, Vera Schmidt, became the head of the Psychoanalytical Kindergarten, which was opened in Moscow in August, 1921.

There was another independent initiative which competed for recognition: The Kazan Psychoanalytical Circle with Alexander Luria. The young people from Kazan (Luria was 19 years old at the time) managed to outrun Moscow professors. Officially, the Russian Psychoanalytical Society applied for membership in the International Psychoanalytical Association at the 8th Congress in Berlin in 1922. Discussion at the Congress was difficult: The President Ernest Jones and another Englishman, Dougles Brian, braked the recognition of the Russian Society; Freud and Spielrein supported it.[5] The obstacle was the existence of the Kazan local group that seems to be specially supported by Jones for unknown reasons. A formal decision was postponed until the next Congress at Salzburg. Otto and Vera Schmidt travelled to Europe and explained to Freud and Abraham the difference between Kazan and Moscow. Finally, influential organizers of Soviet psychoanalysis solved the problem simply: they invited Luria with two other Kazan people to Moscow. Luria became the scientific secretary of the Russian Society. By the way, even in his 1957 volume Jones still considered the Kazan Society to be among the autonomous divisions of the IPA (Jones, vol. 3, Index).

In 1923 the same group (Schmidt, Ermakov, Luria) founded the State Psychoanalytical Institute. As a state body, it was financed directly by the Ministry of Education. The Psychoanalytic Kindergarten became a part of the Institute. Other activities were out-patient department, lectures, workshops and publications. Spielrein and Wulff were respected members of the staff and surely aspired to keep the professional level. But young enthusiasts in the Institute and Association were more concerned with other problems. Luria and his friend Leo Vigotski, a member of the Russian Psychoanalytical Society, wrote in 1925: "Psychoanalysis attracts exceptional attention in Russia […] new original direction in psychoanalysis is coming into being before our eyes in Russia. It carries out the synthesis of Freudism and Marxism on the base of Pavlovian theory of conditional reflexes". Compa-

5 *Int. J. of Psychoanal.* 4 (1923), 240 f.

risons between Freud and Marx were the main subject of the discussions. Heavy political involvement was continued by the new elections in the Russian Psychoanalytical Society in 1924. It gave the office of president to M. Wulff; the vice-presidents were Ermakov and Victor Kopp, Bolshevik ambassadors in Berlin and Tokyo close to Trotsky.

The Psychoanalytical Kindergarten was financed partly by the State, partly by the share in profits from Freud's publications in Russian, partly by international support from a German Trade Union. In 1923, 18 educators were busy with 12 children from 2 to 4 years old. According to the unpublished Charter of the Kindergarten written by Ermakov, "the major part of the children are children of the Party executives who give all their time to their work and are not able to rear their children (Ermakov-Archive). In fact, it was an elite institution supported by the officials to keep their children in hard times. Luria recalled orally that among these children was the son of Stalin (Vasilii, born in 1921). For parents of this kind psychoanalysis could be just an acceptable decoration.

The Kindergarten provoked rumors of sexual experimentation with children and complaints about their "non-proletarian composition". The unusual elite institution in the heart of Bolshevik Moscow was doomed. Numerous ministerial inspections checked its ideological and financial purity. The last inspection claimed that children in the Kindergarten practised masturbation which they didn't know when living with their parents.

But all the time up to 1925 a very strong hand from the top saved the State Psychoanalytical Institute with its kindergarten. The most powerful figure who supported early Soviet psychoanalysis was Lev Trotsky. He had personal experience with psychoanalysts in his Viennese emigration in 1908. He was friendly with Adler and his wife, visited psychoanalytical meetings and left curious memoirs on this subject. In 1931 Trotsky sent his own daughter to Berlin psychoanalysts. His disciple, friend and life-long collaborator Adolph Ioffe was a patient of Adler. Once Ioffe even published in the journal *Psychotherapy* (1913, No. 4) a clinical case which he had analytically treated himself while doing slave labour in Siberia. Trotsky believed that "the Revolution cured Ioffe better than psychoanalysis". After 1917 Ioffe occupied the leading positions in Bolshevik's diplomacy.

In Spetember, 1923 Trotsky, the Minister of Defence, wrote a personal letter to Ivan Pavlov, the Nobel prize winner. Trotsky recommended him to synthesize Pavlovian physiology with Freudian psychoanalysis. According to Trotsky, Pavlov and Freud looked in the same well of the human spirit: Freud looked from above, Pavlov from below, and both visions should be combined. The aim of the letter was to reinforce the ideological attempts of Moscow psychoanalysts with Pavlov's authority. Pavlov didn't respond to this appeal.

The immediate reason for the crash of the psychoanalytical movement in Bolshevik Russia was the political defeat of Trotsky. He was gradually removed from his chief positions in the Party in 1924–1927. Time limits of Soviet psychoanalysis coincide exactly with the ups and downs of Trotsky's power. When the Russian psychoanalytical institutions were founded in 1922, he was at his peak. The State Psychoanalytical Institute was closed by a governmental decision in August, 1925. The year of Trotsky's final defeat, 1927, was the year of the collapse of the Russian Psychoanalytical Society. President Wulff emigrated; secretary Luria retired; the ex-patient Ioffe committted suicide.

Trotsky's writings of this period contain obvious reminiscences of his Viennese interests formulated in Bolshevik terms. Human nature should be reconstructed to let Bolsheviks pursue their goals. The problem was hardly foreseen by Marx, though it reminds us of the Nieztschean idea of constructing the super-man. Trotsky's project was to mobilize the best achievements of modern science for this most ambitious goal. Like others of Trotsky's projects, this one was rejected, then simplified and put into action by Stalin. The fall of Soviet psychoanalysis led to the development of paedology – the new, genuinely Bolshevik science of the "Construction of the New Mass Man". In 1926, the Psychoanalytic Society held meetings on the problems of paedology. Aron Zalkind became its official leader. An ex-psychoanalyst, he became the author of the unbelievably restrictive "The new sexual commandment of the proletariat" and infinite accusations against "bourgeois psychoanalysis" (Zalkind, 1930). Paedology had its boom around 1930; many psychoanalysts and psychologists, among them Sabina Spielrein in Rostov and Lev Vigotski in Moscow, found refuge in its immense material.

To the Bolshevik mind psychoanalysis was identical with the new, most "progressive" development of radical social thought. Rational knowledge was perceived to be able to change history, society and human nature. Everything should be conscious, planned, calculated, intellectually controlled; nothing should be spontaneous, random, unconscious. Psychoanalysis was taken for the scientific tool to achieve this aim in the application to the individual personality, like Marxism in its application to the whole society. To be sure, this interpretation of psychoanalysis distorts its basic truth. But it wasn't very unusual. W. Reich, for example, shared the same beliefs. He visited Moscow in 1928 to find them dominating (Wulff, 1930). It was too late. In fact, totalitarian power was built on the direct violence that didn't need all these psychological subtleties.

Evidence of the political involvement of Max Eitingon is important for the understanding of Soviet psychoanalysis. Evidence published in the West on his participation in the General Miller kidnapping is controversial. Russian sources confirm that Dr. Max Eitingon was the brother (or "brother-in-law") of General Nahum Eitingon, chief of the counter-intelligence of the Stalin Government until 1952. He was personally responsible for several terrorist acts in Europe in the thirties and for the Trotsky assassination in Mexico. Sandor Radó, Eitingon's assistant in the Berlin Psychoanalytical Clinic, told in his oral memoirs: "(Max) Eitingon's personal income didn't come from medical practice, which he didn't have; but came from this fur establishment they (the Eitingons) had in five counries. The Eitingons were one of the biggest fur traders. They had an establishment in Russia, one in Poland, one in England, two in Germany, one here (in the USA). The old man died and the brother-in-law of Max Eitingon ran the whole establishment [...] For a while, even under the Communist regime, they had the biggest contract with the Russians for furs".[6] Soviet foreign trade was under strict Bolshevik control. In the mid-twenties it was supervised personally by Trotsky. Radó also said that "(Max) Eitingon paid every nickel that was spent in the (Berlin Psychoanalytical) Institue". Taking all this into account, I can say that collaboration between Russian Bolsheviks and German psychoanalysts had some aspects that are still unkown. To leave aside the moral evaluation of the Eitingon brothers' actions, the intellectual reason that Max Eitingon had for the collaboration with the Bolsheviks was the same that was important for the Russian psychoanalysts. To be sure, Eitingon wouldn't take money from the Nazi Government.

The most symbolic figure in Russian psychoanalsis, who combined great achievements with tragic failures, was Sabina Spielrein. Her outstanding role in the early history of the psychoanalytical movement was well-known after the publication of her diaries and correspondence (Carotenuto, 1984). Treated for psychosis, she later became the lover of C. G. Jung and was an important cause of his conflict with Freud. She was the first patient to become an analyst; she originated the concept of the death instinct. She came back to Russia in 1923, and up to now any valid information on the long Soviet period of her life was absent. I collected the interviews with Spielrein's relatives, her nieces and her stepdaughter and found her personal file in the archive of the Bolshevik Ministery of Education. She decided to go back to Russia because of financial, professional and personal reasons. Her

6 Reminescences of S. Radó, kept in the Office of Oral History of Columbia University, p. 84.

husband left her with her daughter long before, just before the War, and went to Russia. Her practice in Geneva didn't give her enough money. She wasn't content with her Swiss colleagues. Though at least one of her patients, Jean Piaget, had a high opinion of her (Rice, 1982).

From September, 1923 Sabina Spielrein became a staff member of the new State Psychoanalytical Institute in Moscow. She worked also in two other positions, mainly with children. Her brother, Isaac Spielrein, was an important figure in Soviet applied psychology. Her file contains her unusual response to the formal question on her satisfaction with her job: "I work with enjoyment; I consider myself to be called for my job, born to do it". She wrote also that she was going to finish two new texts on symbolic thinking. Nothing was published in Russian under her name. Her Western publications of that time were directed towards psychological understanding of a child's speech and thinking (Spielrein, 1920). Her ideas were close to the later contribution of Piaget,[7] whom she left in Geneva; and the same approach was accepted then by Alexander Luria and Lev Vigotski, who collaborated with the Institute. I hypothesize that Spielrein was the common source for both these important developments in child psychology, Swiss and Russian.

Despite her enthusiasm, she didn't stay in the State Psychoanalytical Institute for long. In 1924 she left Moscow for Rostov-on-Don. We don't know the reasons for this decision. Probably the atmosphere in Moscow scientific circles was too distant from the accustomed European one. There could be equally important personal reasons. In Rostov her husband returned to her. They had a daughter born in Europe; now, in 1926, another daughter was born. In Rostov Spielrein worked partly in the psychiatric hospital, partly in the school. There are some memories that she continued her private practice. Despite all moving she kept her intensive library in German and French. In her forties she made the impression of an old, very strange, unpractical and old-fashioned woman. Her last publication in the West was dated 1933. That means that she was able to keep some communication despite all the terrors of Russian provincial life. In 1935 her brother was executed as a Trotskyist. Her father was tortured and deprived of all his property. S. Spielrein was expelled from the hospital and had part-time employment as a school doctor. At any rate, she wasn't persecuted by the Bolsheviks.

7 J. Piaget, La psychanalyse sur rapports avec la psychologie de l'infant. *Bulletin de la Société A. Binet* 20 (1920), 18–34; 41–58.

In 1941 Nazi troops advanced on Rostov. There were chances to evacuate. The Russian ex-wife of her husband did it and saved her daughter. Spielrein made the free-will decision to stay in Rostov. We can compare her decision with Freud's hesitant behavior in occupied Vienna. Probably she didn't believe in a word of the Bolsheviks and thought that all information on Nazi massacres was just one more piece of propaganda. Soon after the occupation she was executed with both her daughters in the crowd of Rostov Jews.

There is no information on psychoanalytical activity in Russia in the thirties. Private practice continued by the secret efforts of several personalities; but it is doubtful that this practice could do more than diagnosis. Soviet psychoanalysts were not persecuted by law. As far as I know, only Ermakov died in prison, but he was arrested much later, in 1940, and for a different reason. The possible explanation is the presence in Moscow in 1933–1936 of William C. Bullit, the first ambassador of the USA in the USSR, the ex-patient and co-author of Freud. It is known that Bullit tried so save some Russians from the repressions. It is known also that during his service in Moscow he kept contacts with Freud. In 1934 the *Journal of the IPA* published the new list of the members of the Russian Psychoanalytical Society.[8] The list was a fiction; it named people who had betrayed psychoanalysis long ago, and many others who were not happy to be announced as psychoanalysts. It may be that this publication was designed by Bullit and Western psychoanalysts in an attempt to save Russian colleagues by giving them international recognition.

Perception of psychoanalysis as a kind of psychic power over the individual evoked resistance of an unusual nature. It was a kind of resistance that Russian liberal intellectuals have traditionally demonstrated. Vladimir Nabokov called psychoanalysis "the totalitarian state of the sexual myth". Anna Achmatova just said to a friend that she hated Freud. Michail Bachtin claimed that any psychologist was a spy. In fact, they resisted "Freudism" along with their resistance to Communist political power which would be genuinely omnipotent if it managed to master psychoanalysis. Despite all this, psychoanalysis survived in the minds of several creative individuals. The satirical writer Michael Zoschenko explicitly wrote on its influence and allegedly cured himself through a unique self-analysis. Sergei Eisenstein, the world-famous Russian film-maker, was analyzed in California and kept a life-long interest in psychoanalysis.

8 *Int. Z. f. Psychoanal.* 20 (1934), 147.

As a result, psychoanalysis in Russia was well known but often misunderstood. It was heavily politicized, maybe more politicized than anywhere. Professional psychoanalysts in some cases supported this perception by unrealistic promises. The Bolshevik political elite misrepresented it as an instrument to remake human nature. When direct violence was proved to be the only efficient way to keep totalitarian power, the Bolshevik flirtation with psychoanalysis was finished.

Paedology was prohibited in 1936 by a special Party decision. It was replaced by the "collectivistic pedagogy" that stressed identification with the leader, obedience to the group and aggression towards outsiders. New Stalinist theories neglected any kind of traditional psychology. But in practice, the process of communist society-building was highly psychological. The construction of a new society was designed as a social-psychological process of changing human perceptions, motivations and behaviors. The usual self-description of it was the concept of ideology. Ideology was perceived as a powerful instrument that can change human behavior, influence the effectiveness of labour and even increase military efficiency. To be sure, this ideological "psychology" was quite distant from the science which the West knows by this name. It exploited such psychological phenomena as conformity, emotional leadership, persuasion, suggestion and role playing, interpersonal manipulations, group cohesiveness, deception and self-deception. It used plenty of criminal techniques less known to scientific psychology because it is impossible to reproduce them in the laboratory. Sophisticated methods of practical psychology were invented and professionally realized by semi-literate politicians, officials and investigators as the most important part of their day-to-day activities. Primitivization of power techniques under Socialism gives way to the simplest methods of psychological (and biological) domination. If politics and economics conform to the networks of personal relationships, then the laws of these relationships rule everything in social life.

Psychoanalysis was impossible under these conditions. Indeed, in the decades before and after the World War Two psychoanalysis was practically absent from the Soviet scene. The local tradition of Russian psychoanalysis was broken for ever. The only branch that kept this genuine analytical continuity survived in Czechoslovakia. The senior Russian analyst Nicolaj Ossipov with his disciple, Fedor Dosužkov, established in Prague a psychoanalytical school. Their Czech followers transmitted the unique experience of surviving under Socialist conditions.

In Russia the official position of the established state structures towards psychoanalysis was highly negative until the late eighties. A rude and ignorant critique of "Freudism" was written by Marxist philosophers specialized in the "critique of Bourgeois ideology". Universities, academic institutions and psychiatric clinics ignored psychoanalysis both as a science and a clinical method. Among methods of clinical psychotherapy, only hypnosis survived under the decades of Communist rule. The failure of psychoanalysis and the success of hypnosis under conditions that were full of genuine magic go in parallel with similar events in Nazi Germany; both cases are important examples of the congruence of the clinical milieu with the general cultural and political atmosphere.

References see at the end of the following article, pp. 348 f.

Russia

by René and Eugenia Fischer

After the ending of dictatorship

After the ending of dictatorship in the Soviet Union, perestroika and the removal of ideological barriers, interest in psychoanalysis has become very keen in Russia, particularly among Russian intellectuals. Etkind (1992) reports that in 1989, for example, at least three parallel editions of Freud's great theoretical writings appeared in Moscow with a total edition of more than 500,000 copies. Freud's writings have also been published in Petersburg, Minsk, Tiflis and Eriwan. An edition of selected writings in ten volumes is being printed.

Psychoanalytical thought has become an integral part of public and political discussion; psychoanalysis enjoys great popularity.

The gradual return of psychoanalysis to Russia began in the seventies, although as early as in the late sixties Russian doctors proclaimed their interest in psychoanalysis to Theodor Dosužkov (1899–1982, a training analyst in Prague, a pupil of Ossipov, Russian-born), asking him to return to Russia. A. Piatigorski, an emigrant, reported in 1977 that there were eight analysts in Moscow. They had no training and treated in accordance with their understanding of Freud. Even then one of these self-appointed analysts was Boris Kravtsov, who is described as a charismatic psychologist. He read Freud's writings and continued treating even when private practice at that time was totally prohibited and punishable. In the late seventies he had an influence on psychological groups in Moscow. He developed his concept of treatment on psychotic patients, also using various body and breathing techniques. A group of pupils gathered around him who are treating patients today in the third generation.

Two of Freud's major writings were not available until 1980 when they appeared in a reader on the history of psychology. The writings concerned are *The Ego and the Id* and *Five Introductory Lectures to Psycho-Analysis.* Until 1988 the reader was the only available major publication of psychoanalytical texts. Only then did new editions of Freud's works start to appear. For the most part they were new editions of old translations from the early years.

On 31 May 1985 the profession of medical doctor/psychotherapist was officially approved by the Health Ministry of the USSR. Before then many psychologists were already applying psychotherapeutic methods in psychiatric clinics and other institutions. In 1988 they founded the "Association of Practising Psychologists". In 1989 the Section of Psychoanalytical Therapy was formed within the framework of this association, under the directorship of Dr. Pavel Sneschnevski. Originally there were fifteen analytical psychologists and psychiatrists altogether, now there are approx. thirty members, including artists, mathematicians and engineers. The section organizes case discussions and visits by foreign psychoanalysts. Kravtsov's group was one of the founders of the psychoanalytical section. Seminars are also organized in other parts of the former Soviet Union, in Estonia or in Vladivostok. The section also maintains contacts to psychoanalytical societies in Europe and the USA (Agrachev, 1993; Obuchov, 1993).

In 1989 the Psychoanalytical Association of the USSR was formed, renamed the Russian Psychoanalytical Association in 1990. The majority of its members are psychiatrists. Its director is Professor Aron Belkin.

On 2 October 1989 a joint conference of the Societies of Psychologists and Philosophers took place on the occasion of the fiftieth anniversary of Sigmund Freud's death. In 1991, after eighty years, a psychoanalytical periodical was created again: *Russian Psychoanalytical Bulletin.*

In 1990 the Leningrad Psychoanalytical Society was formed in Leningrad (St Petersburg), whose first president is the psychiatrist Professor W. Gilbo. The society's members are for the most part people interested in psychoanalysis from other professions. In 1992 the Psychoanalytical Institute was opened in St Petersburg, the former one had been closed in 1925.

The vast majority of practising psychotherapists in St Petersburg formed the "Association for Training and Psychotherapy" in 1989. The founders included the Scientific Centre for Clinical Psychology and Psychotherapy at the Bechterev Psychoneurological Institute, and the Training Centre of the State Technical University. The approx. 200 members are divided into seven sections, including the Section for Psychoanalytical Psychotherapy. The condition for admission is two years of practising as a psychotherapist; the association offers seminars and further training for its members, foreign visitors of various psychotherapeutic directions are invited. The president is Dr. Alexander J. Palay, a psychologist.[1]

1 In 1991 the "Rostov Psychoanalytical Association" was founded. Its president is Victor Nikolajev, its vice-president Sergej Ulyanitski. At the time the Association has 10 members. It organized a Sabine Spielrein memorial conference in May 1994.

The societies mentioned often fulfil two functions: some are only scientific societies, but most of them are also institutes of training and further training. The groups mentioned are but a few examples from Russia. Apart from these, there is an uncertain number of practising "psychotherapists", as well as psychoanalytical "training centres" which train "psychoanalysts", even completing their training with an "international diploma". Training may even last a few months. It is therefore evident that chaos is prevalent in the present psychomarket in Russia, as there is no control on the part of state agencies, there are no criteria regarding qualifications.

There is at present no psychoanalytical training in the western sense in Russia. Besides psychoanalysis, there are of course all the other psychotherapeutic directions. Representatives of many directions are sent to Russia to give lectures and offer seminars. So far, however, no psychotherapeutic school has been able to organize a well-ordered training system in Russia. So people seriously interested in psychoanalysis are forced to seek their training abroad, above all in the USA, where the American association provides generous help and where a number of candidates from Russia are trained to western standards. They are said to include former followers of Kravtsov (Agrachev, 1993).

Other psychoanalytical societies, too, are trying to get regular contacts. The European Psychoanalytical Federation supports Russian colleagues attending congresses in the west, as does the International Psychoanalytical Association, and both of them have installed special commissions for eastern contacts. Analysts from the west are encouraged to visit Russia and receive support to do so. The International Association for Analytical Psychology is supporting the publication of the complete works of C. G. Jung in Russian. Members of the Lacanian École Freudienne in Paris travel regularly to Moscow and St Petersburg for lectures and seminars.

Despite this enormous interest on the part of Russian psychologists and psychotherapists, the future of organized psychoanalysis in Russia appears unsure and dependent on the frail political and economic situation. As Freud's idea , psychoanalysis has proved that it has not allowed extreme terror and dictatorship in Russia to suppress or drive it out of the people's consciousness.

Concluding Remarks

The history of psychoanalysis (of Freudism) in Russia has not been fully recorded and made transparent to this day. The time to work through the extensive material of several decades has been too short. Therefore many questions remain open, above all questions concerning the fate of individual analysts, the pressure and reprisals they were subjected to during Stalin's time, questions regarding the censoring of specialist publications up to the possible forging of essays. All these things are imaginable and known in other fields. Questions also remain open regarding links between Max Eitingon, for example, and General Eitingon, W.C. Bullitt in Moscow and Russian psychoanalysis. The increasing opening of archives in Russia will hopefully help to clarify the situation soon.

On balance two conclusions can be drawn from the history of psychoanalysis in Russia. The one conclusion is drawn from the positive experience that psychoanalytical thought cannot be suppressed by decades of terror and prohibitions.

The second conclusion concerns the dangers and distortions that threaten psychoanalysis if it tolerates the influence of the state and politics with all their short-term party-political objectives. Finally, we should like to repeat Freud's warning from 1927: "You are aware of the truth that our science will not under any circumstances allow itself to be placed at the service of a political party, but rather requires for its development a certain liberty."

References

AGRACHEV, S. G. (1993): The division of psychoanalytical therapy of the Association of Practising Psychologists. (unpublished paper).

BASSIN, PH. V. (1968): Problema bessoznatelnovo [The problem of the unconscious]. Moskow: Medicina.

BROWN, J. V. (1990): Social influences on psychiatric theory and practice in late imperial Russia. In: Health and society in revolutionary Russia, eds. S. G.Solomon / J. F Hutchinson. Indiana Univ. Press.

CAROTENUTO, A (1984): A secret symphony. London: Routledge.

ELROD, N. (1989): Freud und Luria und Wygotski. Psychoanalytiker und Kritiker der Psychoanalyse in der Sowjetunion. In: Freud und die akademische Psychologie, ed. B. Nitzschke. München: Psychologie Verlags Union.

ETKIND, A. (1991): Histoire de la psychanalyse en URSS. *Series de la Decouverte Freudienne* 9, 95-110.

– (1993): Eros nevosmoshnogo. Historia psychoanalisa w Rossii. St. Petersburg: Meduza [Russian]. French: Eros de la Impossible. Paris: PUF 1994 (in print).

FISCHER, E. (1991): Nikolaj Jegrafowitsch Ossipov – sein Leben und Werk. Referat in der Sigmund-Freud-Gesellschaft Wien, Sept. 1991.

– (1992): Czechoslovakia. In: Psychoanalysis International, ed. P. Kutter, Vol. 1. Stuttgart-Bad Cannstatt: frommann-holzboog.

FISCHER, E. and R. (1977): Psychoanalyse in Rußland. In: Psychologie des 20. Jahrhunderts, Vol. 3, 122–124. Zürich: Kindler.

FREUD, S. (1914d): On the history of the psychoanalytical movement. SE 14, 7–66.

GARDINER, M (ed.) (1989): The Wolf-man and Sigmund Freud. London: Karnac Books.

LJUNGGREN, M. (1989): The psychoanalytic breakthrough in Russia on the eve of the First World war. In: Russian literature and psychoanalysis, ed. D. Rancour-Laferrière. Amsterdam/Philadelphia: Benjamin, 174-191.

LOBNER, H. / V. LEVITIN (1978): A short account of Freudism: Notes on the history of psychoanalysis in the USSR. *Sigm. Freud House Bulletin* 2, 5–30.

JONES, E. (1953-57): The life and work of Sigmund Freud. 3 Vols. New York: Basic Books.

MANSON, I. (1991): Comment dit-on "psychanalyse" en Russe?. In: *Revue internationale de histoire de psychanalyse* 4, 407–422.

MARTI, J. (1976): La psychanalyse en Russie et en Union Sovietique de 1909 à 1930. *Critique* 346, 199–236.

MAXIMOV, I. (1983): Histoire de la psychanalyse. La psychanalyse russe. *L'Ane* 10, 3–5

MIKHALEVITCH, A (1992a): Premier implantation et rejet (1904–1930) *Frenesie* 2, No. 7, 125–146.

– (1992b): Discontinuities and contradictions in the Russo-Soviet cultural integration of psychoanalysis (1900-1945). Paper on the Congress of the A.I.H.P., Brussels 1992.

MILLER, M. (1985): Freudian theory under Bolshevic rule. *Slavic review* (winter), 625-646

– (1990): The reception of psychoanalysis and the problem of the unconscious in Russia. *Social Research* 57, No. 4, 876–888.

OBERHOLZER, K. (1980): The Wolf-man sixty years later. London: Routledge.

OBUCHOV, J. (1993): Psychoanalysis in Moscow. (unpublished paper).

PALMIER, J.-M. (1982): La psychanalyse en Union Sovietique. In: Historie de la psychanalyse, ed. R. Jaccard, Vol. 2. Paris: Hachette, 213–270.

PIATIGORSKI, A. (1977): O psichoanalise is sovremennoi Rossii. [On psychoanalysis in Russia of today]. *Russia* 3, 29–50.

RICE, J. L. (1982): Russian stereotypes in the Freud-Jung-correspondence. *Slavic review* 41, No. 1, 19–35.

ROUDINESCO, E. (1986): Histoire de la psychanalyse en France, Vol. 2 (Chapter 1.2: Marxisme, psychanalyse, psychologie). Paris: Seuil.

SPIELREIN, S. (1920): On the origin and development of the speech. *Int. J. of Psychoanal.* 1, 359.

WULFF, M. (1930): Zur Stellung der Psychoanalyse in der Sowjetunion. *Die psychoanalytische Bewegung* 1, 75.

ZALKIND, A. B. (1930): Psichonevrologišeskie nauki i sozialistišeskoe stroitelstwo. *Pedologia* 3, 309–322. [Russian]

Journals

Russian Psychoanalytic Bulletin
since 1991; Ed.: Aron I. Belkin; Prospect Vernadskogo 89,
Corpus 1, Apt. 68, 117526 Moscow
25 Arbat, 121002 Moscow

Nevskoye Vremya
since 1989; Ed.:Association of Training and Psychotherapy
State Technical University
29 Politechnicheskaya, 195251 St. Petersburg

Institutions

Russian Psychoanalytical Association
25 Arbat, 121002 Moscow
Tel.: 7-095-291 6028
Fax: 7-095-200 2216

East European Institute of Psychoanalysis St. Petersburg
18, Bolskey prospect, Petrogradskaia
storana, St. Petersburg

Association of Training and Psychotherapy
Management Training Center of St. Petersburg
State Technical University
29 Politechnicheskaya, 195251 St. Petersburg

This association is open to all directions of psychotherapy, not only psychoanalysis, set up in 1989, in connection with the Scientific Center for Clinical Psychology and Psychotherapy at the Bechterev Psychoneurological Institute.

Rostov Psychoanalytical Association
c/o Viktor Nikolajev, Krasnoarmeiskaya 54, 344082 Rostov-on-Don
Tel.: 7-8632-64 3338
Fax: 7-8632-64 0930

Drs. med. Eugenia and René Fischer, Fasanenweg 16, D-65835 Liederbach, Germany.
Dr. Alexander Etkind, Kuibishev 22, apt.20, Box 488, 197046 St. Petersburg

Serbia

by Peter Klein

The development of psychoanalysis in Serbia began in the 1920s, when the first psychoanalysts began to practise (Nikola Šugar in Subotica and Hugo Klajn in Belgrade). Further important steps followed in the 1930s, when some works of the classics of psychoanalysis were translated and published (Freud, Adler). In his book *Psihologija,* 1926, Borislav Lorenc, professor at Belgrade University, gave a short review of the psychoanalytic method, concisely presenting some of the basic psychoanalytic concepts (Lorenc later introduced to the Yugoslav public the first work by S. Freud, *Introductory Lectures on Psychoanalysis,* in 1933). In the journal *Nova Literatura* H. Klajn published the article "Thoughts on Psychoanalysis" (1929), in which he, in a popular way, wrote on some of the ideas of psychoanalysis. Those were some of the first written traces of psychoanalysis in Serbia.

In 1932 the Yugoslav Psychiatric Association was founded and in the same year some psychologically oriented psychiatrists established the Yugoslav Society for Mental Hygiene, which was influenced by Freud's theory. The Psychoanalytic Society in Belgrade was founded in 1938. The prime mover and leader of the group was N. Šugar, while the other members of the first psychoanalytic society in Yugoslavia were the physicians Ljubomir Dumić, Hugo Klajn, Vladislav Klajn (no relation to Hugo), Vojin Matić and Ljubomir Živković and the philosophers Vladimir Dvorniković, Miloš Durić and Nikola Popović. The Society organized scientific discussions, lectures and translations of professional works, popularized the basic principles of psychoanalysis and engaged in the training of future analysts. However, the Society was not tied to any scientific or professional institution, had few members and did not have its own premises and journal. Of the members of the group only some remained active in the field of psychoanalysis. The Belgrade Psychoanalytic Society existed for less than four years (until the German invasion of Yugoslavia in April of 1941), but it paved the way for the future affirmation of psychoanalysis in Serbia. The Society helped the beginning of the application of psychoanalysis in therapy and introduced psychoanalytic concepts into the interpretation of psychological, psychiatric and cultural phenomena. Only two members of the Society engaged in psychotherapy prior to World War II (H. Klajn and N. Šugar) and only Šugar worked as a training analyst.

The five most influential members of the first psychoanalytic group in Serbia were N. Popović, N. Šugar, H. Klajn, V. Matić and V. Klajn. Nikola Popović (1883–1970) was head of the Department of Philosophy at the University of Belgrade. A scholarly author and translator, Popović was a precursor of psychoanalysis in Serbia. He published the first works in the Serbo-Croatian language in which the theories of Freud, Jung and Adler were systematically presented (Popović, 1934; Popović, 1935). Popović placed his office of the Dean of the Faculty of Philosophy at the disposal of the Psychoanalytic Society, which held its meetings there. So, from the first days, psychoanalysis in Serbia was linked not only to physicians, who formed the nucleus of the first group, but to the Faculty of Philosophy; as well. N. Popović coined some of the Serbo-Croatian translations of psychoanalytic terms.

Nikola Šugar (1897–1945) was one of the three Yugoslav psychoanalysts (beside H. Klajn and Stjepan Betlheim, who worked in Zagreb, Croatia) who practised psychoanalytic psychotherapy before World War II. Born in Subotica, a town on the Yugoslav-Hungarian border, Šugar studied medicine at the German University in Prague, graduating in 1923. He spent his residency in neuropsychiatry in Berlin-Charlottenburg, where he was also for two years in training analysis with Felix Boehm. In 1925 Šugar went to Vienna and became an associate member of the Vienna Psychoanalytic Society (from 1933-38 he was a full member of that Society and from 1938 of the Budapest Psychoanalytic Society). In the 1920s Šugar collaborated in Vienna with Paul Schilder and they published an article on the disturbances of speech in schizophrenia (Schilder & Šugár 1926). From 1927–37 Šugar lived in Subotica and practised as the only psychoanalyst in his home town and in the whole province of Vojvodina (which is part of Serbia). He was one of the first in Subotica to recognize alcoholism as a specific psychic disturbance and many of his patients were alcoholics. Beside his private practice Šugar was propagating the ideas of psychoanalysis in articles published in the local press (Šugar 1932, 1933a, 1938a, 1939, 1940).

Šugar often travelled to Belgrade and in 1937 moved there. In 1938 he brought together and formed the Psychoanalytic Society, becoming its leader. He worked in private practice, but also as a training analyst (V. Klajn and V. Matić were in training analysis with him). When in 1940 the meetings of the Society in the Dean's office at the Faculty of Philosophy were made impossible, the meetings continued in Šugar's apartment, where members of the group could use Šugar's rich psychoanalytic library. After the German bombardment of Belgrade (1941) Šugar fled to Subotica (which came under Hungarian occupation) and continued to work in private practice until 1944. During that time he was also engaged in training analysis. When mass deportations of Hungarian Jews and Jews living under Hungarian occupation began (1944), Šugar was first interned in a labor camp in Austria and later was taken to Bergen-Belsen concentration camp. He died in the Theresienstadt concentration camp.

Šugar published several articles in the *Internationale Zeitschrift für Psychoanalyse.* They are signed by the German or Serbian version of his first name (Nikolaus, Nikola); the articles Šugar wrote in the Hungarian language (in the local press in Subotica) carry the by-line "Sugár Miklós". Some of his articles are book reviews (Šugar, 1938b, 1941c), obituaries (Šugar, 1934) or communications about events in the psychoanalytic community (Šugar, 1933b). But he also wrote papers on the role of tooth stimulation in the psychoses (Šugar, 1925), on the question of mimical affirmation and negation (Šugar, 1941a) and on the question of "contagious" parapraxis (Šugar, 1941b). These papers affirm Šugar as a perceptive psychologist, a psychoanalytic interpreter of customs (he was the first to give a psychoanalytic interpretation of the fact that in Southern Europe the mimical affirmation and negation are opposite to those in other parts of Europe) and a therapist who relatively early applied psychoanalytic concepts to the explanation of psychoses. Had he survived, Šugar would have surely played a prominent role in re-establishing psychoanalysis in Yugoslavia.

Hugo Klajn (1894–1981) was for many years the "trade mark" of psychoanalysis in Serbia. He studied medicine in Vienna and during those years attended the lectures of Viktor Tausk and Freud. Klajn was in residency for psychiatry with Julius Wagner-Jauregg (Vienna) and with Emil Kraepelin (Munich) and in training analysis with Paul Schilder (Vienna). Beside Šugar, Klajn was the only psychoanalyst in Serbia who at the time practised psychotherapy. He worked at a psychiatric clinic and in private practice. Jewish and a prominent left-wing theatre critic, Klajn spent the German occuption hiding under a false identity. After World War II he became professor of stage direction at the Academy of Theatre and Film and was himself an eminent director and theoretician of the theatre. Except for Šugar, H. Klajn was the only psychoanalyst from Serbia who published an article in the *Internationale Zeitschrift für Psychoanalyse* (H. Klajn, 1939a). He was the editor of the *Selected Works of Sigmund Freud* (I–VIII, 1969) in the Serbo-Croatian language. Though Klajn did not practise psychoanalysis after the war, he published articles on psychoanalysis (H. Klajn, 1958), Freud (H. Klajn, 1969) and other subjects. He also wrote several books, some of them of importance for psychoanalysis (H. Klajn, 1936, 1939b, 1955).

In addition to H. Klajn, the most original creative mind of the first psychoanalytic group in Serbia is Vojin Matić (b. 1911). He studied medicine in Vienna and Belgrade. In Vienna he began to read psychoanalytic literature and having returned to Belgrade, he took up his residence in neuropsychiatry. When Šugar came to Belgrade, Matić became one of the members of his group and was in training analysis with Šugar. During World War II Matić worked as a doctor in a POW camp in Berlin (being a prisoner himself). After the war he specialized in child psychiatry in Paris (with Georges Heuyer). For six years Matić was a teaching assistant at the University of Belgrade School of Medicine and in 1953 he organized (in Belgrade) the Medico-pedagogical Guidance Centre. The Centre was a pioneer institution of its own kind (not only in Serbia, but in the whole of Yugoslavia). In it a multiprofessional team of specialists engaged in the psychotherapy of children and adolescents in psychodynamic principles. The staff of the Centre consisted of psychiatrists, psychologists and of an educator and a social worker. Patients from all over the country came to the institution. Alongside psychotherapy, the Centre also performed training analysis, supervision of cases (by Matić) and group discussions. By the end of the 1950s the Centre had developed into a significant psychoanalytically oriented institution, engaged in individual and group therapy, play-therapy and guidance, while training analysis made the Centre the first "psychoanalytic intstitute" in Serbia. V. Matić was the director of the Centre (1953–63), but also its moving spirit. Unfortunately, it was administratively abolished in 1963 and its team of specialists dissolved and dispersed. Matić continued his career at the Faculty of Philosophy Department of Psychology, where he became professor of child psychopathology, general psychopathology and of mental hygiene. In his courses Matić presented the theory and practice of psychoanalysis, from Freud to ego-psychology, and educated generations of psychologists.

V. Matić, who beside Šugar is the most significant training analyst in Serbia, continued his training and supervision even after the abolishment of the Guidance Centre – at the Institute for Psychiatry of Children and Adolescents. He published numerous articles on psychoanalytic and mental hygienic problems (Matić, 1970a, 1970b et al.) and original books in the field of cultural anthropology, psychodynamically interpreting myths, primarily of the Yugoslav peoples (Matić, 1976, 1979, 1984).

Psychiatric and psychologists who were in training analysis with V. Matić are among the most respected therapists in Serbia (and Yugoslavia) today.

Vladislav Klajn (1909–84), who has no relation to Hugo Klajn, studied medicine in Belgrade. After graduation he was in training analysis with Šugar, but his education was interrupted by war. He was taken prisoner and until the capitulation of Italy (1943) was interned in a POW-camp in northern Italy. Klajn then came back to Yugoslavia and fought with the partisans. After the war he was a medical officer in the State Security Service and organized the psychiatric ward in "Dr. Dragiša Mišović" Medical Centre in Belgrade. Klajn spent his residency in psychiatry in Belgrade and Zagreb. One of the key personalities in the field of psychodynamic therapy in Serbia, Klajn became, beginning from the 1950s one of those psychiatrists whose name was associated with psychoanalysis. As head of the department of neuropsychiatry at the hospital mentioned above, Klajn organized seminars on psychotherapy (which were initially opposed) during which he introduced the basic theories of Freud, Jung, Stekel, Fromm and others to young psychiatrists. Klajn's ward was the first psychotherapeutic hospital department in Yugoslavia and he developed a specific therapy – clinical in-patient therapy, which includes analytically oriented psychotherapy, group therapy, work therapy, autogenic training and biological therapy, in the course of which the patient is hospitalized in a special ward. Klajn brought together an important group of specialists; members of the group are held today in high esteem. His book *Neuroses* (1964) was at the time the most comprehensive presentation of psychodynamic theories. Klajn also published numerous articles (Klajn, V., 1961, 1966, 1968, 1971, 1973 et al.).

As told before, the Psychoanalytic Society ended its activities in 1941. A new era of the development of psychoanalysis in Serbia began after World War II. Development was halted for a time, because, due to dogmatic conceptions about the unscientific and "bourgeois" character of psychoanalysis, but also an account of the influence of antipsychologically inclined physicians, the opinion about the incompatibility of Freud's and Marx's theories prevailed for a while. The status of psychoanalysis was further complicated by the relative undeveloped state of psychiatry in Serbia, so the enthusiams of individuals and of their gifted followers had to wait for more convenient circumstances. With the advance of the democratic process in the country the necessity of the application of psychological theories became obvious. As Yugoslavia chose its own course of social, political and econimic development, psychoanalysis was reborn in the scientific centres. The affirmation of psychoanalysis was also influenced by the growth of the number of neurotic patients and the psychoanalytic school was the most experienced in the treatment of neuroses.

The founding of the Medico-pedagogical Guidance Centre and of the department of psychotherapy in "Dr. Dragiša Mišović" hospital were mentioned already. The Institute for Mental Health was established in Belgrade in 1963. V. Matić supervised the psychoanalytic therapy of some of the institute's psychiatrists and psychologists, who till today remain the ranking names of psychoanalysis in Serbia. A further impetus for psychodynamic psychotherapy was given by the setting up of the Division of Psychotherapy of the Serbian Medical Association (1965). That made possible the gathering of specialists and the presentation of papers. A great recognition of psychoanalysis was when its theory began to be taught at universites, particularly at the Department of Psychology of the Faculty of Philosophy in Belgrade.

Publishing in the field of psychoanalysis began in Serbia in the 1920s. Before World War II some works of Freud and Jung were translated. After the war scores of works of Serbian analysts were published and the books of foreign authors translated (Freud, Fromm, Fenichel, M. Klein, Federn, Kris et al.). While in the beginning the theoretical attention was directed primarily to the study of neurotic processes and practice to the therapy of neurotics, from the 60s there has been a marked interest in the psychogenesis and psychodynamics of other phenomena (psychology of personality, psychoses, psychosomatic disorders, toxicomania etc.). Nevertheless, the number of original psychoanalytic works is limited. At the time when psychoanalytic theory was in its beginnings, when its followers had at their disposal the whole field of psychopathology and different areas of human creativity of interpretion in the light of psychodynamics, psychoanalysis in Yugoslavia did not formally even exist. So, entirely original works by authors from Serbia concern applied psychoanalysis. Of special significance are studies by H. Klajn (*Shakespeare and Humanity,* 1964), V. Matić (already mentioned) and Vladeta Jerotić (*Psychoanalysis and Culture,* 1974; *Illness and Creativity,* 1976). V. Jerotić (who worked at the Dr. Dragiša Mišović hospital) also wrote, with Milan Popović, professor at the Department of Psychology (but a psychiatrist) an important book on neuroses (*The Psychodynamics and Psychotherapy of Neuroses,* 1984).

Some of the characteristics of psychoanalysis in our midst stem from the history of psychoanalysis in Serbia and from the nature of the social and political organization of Yugoslavia. We have already emphasized that some members of the Belgrade Psychoanalytic Society were philosophers and the tendency towards the prominent role of non-medical psychoanalysts became more evident after World War II, when the Department of Psychology at Belgrade university emerged as one of the centres of psychoanalytic theory and education. So, beside psychiatrists, psychologists played an equal part in promoting psychoanalytic thought in Serbia. We have no exact statistical data on this issue, but we can assume that with regard to this phenomenon our milieu (at least for a long time) belonged to those in which, so called, "lay" analysis affirmed itself most.

As in Yugoslavia until recently there was no private practice of psychotherapy, practically all forms of therapy were linked to institutions – general or psychiatric hospitals. That can render more difficult the establishment of the first contact with the therapist (the client needs a formal reference from a general practitioner). The fact that the analyst usually worked on the psychiatric ward could mobilize the resistances of neurotics concerning the commencement of therapy and a number of neurotics were thus left without expert help. As treatment used to take place primarily in institutions, therapy was free of charge, i. e. the client was (and is) entitled to psychotherapy on the basis of his/her social insurance. So, psychoanalysis without a fee was for years a specific feature of our society (although therapy is sometimes, partially or completely, paid by insurance agencies in the US, too). The private practice of psychologists was legalized in Serbia in 1990 and some psychoanalytical therapists work that way.

Psychoanalysis in Serbia is not organized well enough even today. However, even though there is no formal psychoanalytic society, associated to the IPA, nor a psychoanalytic institute with its journal, there is a Belgrade psychoanalytic group with almost 20 members. They had formal analytic training (training analysis) or are in training analysis, discussion seminars and case presentations with group supervision are held, members of the group have taken part in psychoanalytic conferences held in Budapest (1989), London (1990) and Stockholm (1991). The Belgrade psychoanalytic group organized in November 1990 the Second East European Seminar (attended also by representatives of the IPA and EPF). Several members of the group will be soon supervised under IPA terms and all these activities justify optimism for the future of psychoanalysis in Serbia.

References

Jerotić, V. (1974): Psihoanaliza i kultura [Psychoanalysis and Culture], Beograd: BIGZ.

– (1976): Bolest i stvaranje [Illness and Creativity], Beograd: BIGZ.

Jerotić, V. / M. Popović (1984): The Psychodynamics and Psychotherapy of Neuroses. Belgrad: Nolit.

Klajn, H. (1929): Misli o psihoanalizi [Thoughts on Psychoanalysis], *Nova Literatura* I/5–6, Beograd.

– (1936): Abnormalnosti normalnih [Abnormalities of the Normal Ones], Beograd: Knjižarnica "Svetlost".

– (1939a): Fehlleistung infolge unbewußter Todeswünsche gegen das einzige Kind, *Int. Zeitschrift für PA. Imago*, XXIV.
– (1939b): Vaspitanje sa gledišata medicinske i socijalne psihologije [Education from the Aspect of Medical and Social Psychology], Beograd: Izdavačko i knjižarsko preduzeće Gece Kona.
– (1955): Ratna neuroza Jugoslovena [The War Neurosis of Yugoslavs], Beograd: Sanitetska uprava.
– (1958): Razvoj psihoanalize u poslednjim decenijama [The Development of Psychoanalysis in the Last Decades]; in: S. Frojd: Uvod u psihoanalizu, Beograd: Kosmos.
– (1964): Šekspir i čoveštvo [Shakespeare and Humanity], Beograd: Prosveta.
– (1969): Frojd i smrt [Freud and Death], *NIN* 977, Beograd.
KLAJN, V. (1961): Osvrt na mesto i značaj psihoanalitičke teorije neuroza u savremenoj nauci o neurozama [The Place and Significance of the Psychoanalytic Theory of Neuroses in the Contemporary Science of Neuroses]; in: O. Fenichel: Psihoanalitička teorija neuroza, Beograd / Zagreb: Medicinska knjiga.
– (1964): Neuroze – teorija i klinička praksa [The Neuroses – Theory and Clinical Practice], Beograd: Naučna knjiga.
– (1966): Savremeni medicinski i socijalni aspekti impotencije [The Contemporary Medical and Social Aspects of Impotence], *Medicinski glasnik* 10.
– et al (1968): Savremeni medicinski i socijalni aspekti homoseksualnosti [The contemporary Medical and Social Aspects of Homosexuality], *Medicinski glasnik* 12.
– (1973): Supervizija kao metod edukacije u individualnoj psihoterapiji [Supervision as an educational method in individual psychotherapy], *Psihoterapija* 3.
KLAJN, V. / V. JEROTIĆ (1971): O metodama kratke psihoterapije kod nas [On the methods of short psychotherapy in our country], *Anali Zavoda za mentalno zdravlje* III(2–3).
LORENC, B. (1926): Psihologija, Rajković i Ćukovic, Beograd.
MATIĆ, V. (1970a): Uloga razvoja hvatanja u prevazilaženju anaklitičkog straha [The Role of the Development of Grasping in Overcoming Anaclitic Fear], *Anali Zavoda za mentalno zdravlje* II/2.
– (1970b): Dinamika nastajanja i razvoja psihičhih poremećaja [The Dynamics of the Origin and Development of Psychic Disturbances], *Neurophsihijatrija* 18, no. 11.
– (1976) Psihoanaliza mitske prošlosti [Psychoanalysis of Mythical Past], Beograd: Prosveta.
– (1979): Psihoanaliza mitske prošlosti II, Beograd: Prosveta.
– (1984): Psihoanaliza mitske prošlosti III, Beograd: Prosveta.
POPOVIĆ, N. (1934): Predavanja iz psihoanalize [Lectures on Psychoanalysis], Beograd: Gece Kona.
– (1935): Psihoanaliza – osmove učenja Sigmunda Freuda [Psychoanalysis – The Basic Theories of S. Freud], Beograd: Gece Kona.
SCHILDER, P. / SUGAR, N. (1926): Zur Lehre von den Schizophrenen Sprachstörungen, *Zentralblatt für die gesammelte Neurologie u. Psychiatrie.*

ŠUGAR, N. (1925): Zur Genese und Therapie der Homosexualität, *Jahrbücher für Psychiatrie u. Neurologie* XLIV, 2–3.
– (1932): Sigmund Freud magyarul, *Napló* July 24.
– (1933a): A pszichoanalizis mestere, *Jugoszláviai Magyar Ujsák* 242.
– (1933b): Mitglieder der Ungarischen Psychoanalitischen Vereinigung: Psychoanalytische Studien, *Int. Z. für PA.*
– (1934): Milly Vosviniek, *Int. Z. für PA.*
– (1938a): A pszichoanalizis és az orvostudomany, *Napló* Dec. 25.
– (1938b): Lectures on Psychoanalysis by N. Popović, *Int. Journal of Psychoanal.*
– (1939): Freud és jelentösége, *Napló*, Dec. 25.
– (1940): Pillantás a pszichoanalizis jövöjébe, *Napló* Dec. 25.
– (1941a): Zur Frage der mimischen Bejahung u. Verneinung, *Int. Z. für PA* a. *Imago.*
– (1941b): Zur Frage der unbewußten Verständigung der "ansteckenden" Fehlhandlung, *Int. Z. für PA* a. *Imago.*
– (1941c): Vaspitanje sa gledišta medicinske i socijalne psihologije von Hugo Klajn, *Int. Z. für PA* a. *Imago.*

Peter Klein, D. Petrovića 4/I, 24000 Subotica

Editor's Note referring to Bosnia-Hercegovina

Dr. Alexandar Marković from Sarajevo has spent some time in analytic training in Germany and provided analytically oriented theoretical education and additionally individual and group supervisions to psychiatrists in Sarajevo for many years but, unfortunately, died in 1986. There exists a Centre of Mental Health in Sarajevo which works as good as possible to care for war victims and survivors. Any applications of psychoanalysis under the unfavorable conditions of war are, of course, tragically restricted. It is known that the leader of the Bosnian Serbs, Radovan Karadžić is originally a psychiatrist, who worked at the Psychiatric Clinic in Sarajevo. He joined the Diploma course in group analysis which was organized by IGA London and IGA Zagreb and left the course before the beginning of the war. He was, as all other candidates, an associate member of the London Group Analytic Society. When his activities became known, he was dismissed from the Society.*

* Courtesy of Dr. Eduard Klain

Slovenia

by Matjaž Lunaček

Coming to the Psychoanalytic Congress in Budapest in 1918 Freud gave an interview to the Hungarian journalist Denes, who he knew from Vienna as a person seeking his consultation when she was in trouble. Asked about the future of psychoanalysis he was quite optimistic about Anglo-Saxon and Romanic countries and much less about Slavic ones. On another occassion he expressed his doubt of Slavs being at all analysable. His judgement proved to be justified in the case of Slovenia and up to now Slovenians haven't had a single trained analyst. The interest in psychoanalysis had rather a strange destiny which was the result of unhappy circumstances which I intend to describe below. Above all this is a negative history.

For those who know little or nothing about Slovenia, I have to say at least that it is a small country, twenty thousand square km large (around one half of Switzerland), the capital of which, Ljubljana, is 400 km from Vienna and less then 100 km from Trieste, two places important for early psychoanalysis. Vienna, where Freud worked nearly his whole life, was also the town where Slovenian people studied at the time when Slovenia was a part of the Austro-Hungarian Empire. Among them there were many medical students and psychiatrists. An outstanding figure was Alfred Šerko, born in 1879, who attended, as a student of logic and psychology, Freud's lectures in 1902–1903. Later on he gained a double doctorate in psychology and medicine and became assistant to a famous professor of psychiatry, Wagner-Jauregg, who himself had made a brilliant academic career and was the Nobel prize winner for medicine in 1926. He was Freud's school fellow and one of the few persons to whom Freud was on first-name terms. Wagner-Jauregg later strongly opposed Freud's theories and his discontentment was transmitted to his collaborators and pupils.

Alfred Šerko was a man of large interests and great erudition. He became world famous for his experiments with Mescalin and for his contribution to research into Paraphrenia. He published his results in leading European psychiatry journals. After World War II he came back to Slovenia where he became the greatest authority on the field of psychiatry and a prominent university professor.

When psychoanalysis spread greatly after World War Two, its influence also reached Slovenia. Especially the generation of young artists, born around 1900, showed great interest in the new science. I have to mention at least two of them: Vladimir Bartol and Slavko Grum. Both of them had a strong collision with Professor Šerko who tried to stop their influence and to suppress them.

Slavko Grum was an artist of great ability and around 1930 he had an enormous success with one of his expressionist plays. This drama was proclaimed the best play in the theatre in Yugoslavia in the season 1928–1929. His works are full of psychoanalytic allusions. He was a medical doctor as well, studying medicine at Vienna University and being a pupil of Wagner-Jauregg. That's why he opposed psychoanalysis at the beginning of his career, which can be seen from his early plays. Later on he changed his opinion and started to be interested in psychoanalysis in a positive sense. After the year 1927 he gave some lectures about the essential premises of psychoanalysis to a broader audience. In the public was also Professor Šerko, who furiously attacked him, but after the lecture he came to Slavko Grum and discussed the issue at length, showing in this way his ambivalence in this field.

A short time before, in 1924, a young Slovene from Trieste, Vladimir Bartol, showed great interest in psychoanalysis. He was an extremely educated man who gained a double doctorate in philsophy and biology only at the age of 25. In comparison with Grum his interest in the field was much more profound and constant. Whereas Grum only knew of very few of Freud's works, Vladimir Bartol carefully studied all Freud's published works and followed also other contemporary psychoanalytic writers with a special interest in applicative psychoanalysis. He was also the first who actually tried psychoanalytic practice. I had in my hands the manuscripts of some of his analytic sessions. At the same time he tried two other ways: first to popularize psychoanalysis through his articles in different magazines and through radio, second to use psychoanalysis as a subject of his literary works. Among rarities in the history of psychoanalysis of the period is, in my opinion, his novel *A miracle in the village* in which a hero is a young student of psychology who solves the neurotic problems of a peasant girl using psychoanalytic methods.

Alfred Šerko responded to such a spread and popularization of psychoanalytic thought with a pamphlet *On Psychoanalysis.* It was the first book in Slovenian dealing with psychoanalysis. Its first eight chapters deal quite precisely with the main theoretical issues of Freud's theory, but the ninth chapter is a sarcastic and brutal critique of it. With his negativism Šerko for sure suppressed Grum, but not Bartol. He answered Šerko with a long and calm critique of his inconsistencies. However, after 1934 interest in psychoanalysis was diminished also for other reasons and no psychoanalytic circle was formed. We can only guess about the causes of such a situation. One of them could be the too individualistic approach. It is known that Bartol and Grum had little contact in spite of the fact they both belonged to the same generation. They also had no contact to a small circle of Marxist oriented students who found interest in Freud in the early thirties. These young people soon gave up their interest under the directive of the communist party in which they were members. However, they were more interested in certain uncommon psychological ideas like Weininger's. It is strange enough that we had in Slovenian the translation of Weininger's book forty years before the first book of Freud was translated.

After World War Two the situation in Slovenia was approximately the same as in other socialist countries, that is not in favour of psychoanalysis, which was considered a great danger for socialist ethics. However, in the sixties the psychologist Leopold Bregant went to Göttingen to be educated in Harald Schulz-Hencke's neo-analytic school, which he found suitable for transplanting to Slovenia. He taught the entire generation of future psychotherapists in its theory and technique. In this way quite a strong psychoanalytically orientied psychotherapy developed but no proper psychoanalysis. The teaching of psychotherapy soon became very systematized and there have been courses in psychotherapy at the Medical Faculty of Ljubljana for the last twenty years. In the field of psychoanalytically oriented child psychotherapy there was Professor Bazilija Pregelj, who offered teaching after being in London and seeing Anna Freud work in the early fifties.

Theoretical knowledge was growing constantly all those years, but there was no personal psychoanalytic training and practice. In the late eighties there was a growing interest in psychoanalysis proper which led to the formation of a small psychoanalytic circle in 1991. Since then its members have tried to establish international contacts, first with the IPA and later with the EPF and some national Societies. At the same time we were looking for the possibilities of psychoanalytic training and the efforts are now becoming reality with the help of the Italian Psychoanalytical Society and especially with its members of Slovenian origin. In the autumn of '93, a training started in Trieste. Through the EPS's East European Committee the door has opened widely for our participation in important psychoanalytic events (Pultusk, Venice, Paris, Vienna, Bologna, Amsterdam). It is a pity that the East European Psychoanalytic Seminar which was to held in Slovenia in 1992 was cancelled for political reasons.

I must mention the important role played in Slovenia by the École Freudienne, a group of Lacanian oriented theoreticians which is popularizing psychoanalytic concepts through intensive translation work and through original papers mainly in applicative psychoanalysis.

Although the development of interest in psychoanalysis in Slovenia had so many above mentioned obstacles it goes on now with great speed and I hope that in some time we also will be able to say that psychoanalysis has found soil to grow on in our country.

References

Sigmund Freud – Conversation avec le Pr. Freud (Interview donnée a Budapest le 4 Aout 1918 à Mme Z. Denes, *Revue Française de psychanalyse* 52, No. 4, 1988.

Institutions

Psychoanalytic Society of Slovenia
Zaloška 29, 61001 Ljubljana

Matjaž Lunaček, Zaloška 29, 61000 Ljubljana

Index of Names

Pychoanalysis International

A Guide to Psychoanalysis throughout the World

Edited by Peter Kutter

Volume I: Europe. *1992. XV, 327 pp. Cloth.*

It is well known that the cradle of psychoanalysis was in Vienna, the scene of Sigmund Freud's activities at the beginning of the century. But how and when did psychoanalysis reach the other countries of Europe? What developments did it undergo there? How did the different mentalities, political and cultural backgrounds as well as the personal particularities of its respective advocates affect psychoanalysis? What was its position in the past and what is its position today? - These and other questions on the varied development and the present situation of psychoanalysis in the countries of eastern and western Europe are investigated by renowned psychoanalysts drawing on the experience and knowledge acquired in their own work. The result is a *new compendium on psychoanalysis in Europe* containing all up-to-date information; informative and instructive, at times as exciting as a detective story, possibly of interest even to non-analysts.

CONTENTS: Preface by *R. Horacio Etchegoyen* - Foreword and Introduction by *Peter Kutter*. Austria: The Viennese Psychoanalytical Society from 1918 to 1945 by *Harald Leupold-Löwenthal*. Austria: The Viennese Psychoanalytical Society after 1945 by *Wolfgang Berner*. Further Institutions in Austria Not Connected with the IPA, Additional Note *by Annemarie Laimböck* - Belgium by *Maurice Haber* - Czechoslovakia by *Eugenie Fischer* - Denmark by *Henning Paikin* - Finland by *Elsa Roos* - France 1893-1965 by *Alain de Mijolla* - Germany by *Peter Kutter* - East Germany by *Michael Geyer* - Great Britain by *Pearl King* and *Alex Holder* - Hungary by *János Harmatta* and *Gábor Szönyi* - Israel by *Uri Lowental* and *Yechezkiel Cohen* - Italy by *Arnaldo Novelletto* - Lithuania by *Rimvydas Augis* and *Virginijus Pocius* - The Netherlands by *Han Groen-Prakken* and *Leo de Nobel* - Poland by *Krzyszof Pawlak* and *Zbigniew Sokolik*, with additions by *Andrzej Kokoszka* and *Jerzy Pawlik* - Spain by *Maria Luisa Muñoz* and *Rebeca Grinberg* - Sweden by *Johan Norman* - Switzerland by *Alexander Moser*. - INDEX OF NAMES